Garden and Landscape History

CHARLES BRIDGEMAN (c.1685–1738)

Garden and Landscape History
ISSN 1758-518X

General Editor
Tom Williamson

This exciting series offers a forum for the study of all aspects of the subject. It takes a deliberately inclusive approach, aiming to cover both the 'designed' landscape and the working, 'vernacular' countryside; topics embrace, but are not limited to, the history of gardens and related subjects, biographies of major designers, in-depth studies of key sites, and regional surveys.

Proposals or enquiries may be sent directly to the editor or the publisher at the addresses given below; all submissions will receive prompt and informed consideration.

Professor Tom Williamson, School of History, University of East Anglia, Norwich, Norfolk NR4 7TJ, UK.

Boydell & Brewer, PO Box 9, Woodbridge, Suffolk, England, IP12 3DF, UK.

Previous publications are listed at the back of this volume.

CHARLES BRIDGEMAN
(c.1685–1738)

A LANDSCAPE ARCHITECT OF THE EIGHTEENTH CENTURY

SUSAN HAYNES

THE BOYDELL PRESS

© Susan Haynes 2023

All rights reserved. Except as permitted under current legislation
no part of this work may be photocopied, stored in a retrieval system,
published, performed in public, adapted, broadcast,
transmitted, recorded or reproduced in any form or by any means,
without the prior permission of the copyright owner

The right of Susan Haynes to be identified
as the author of this work has been asserted in accordance with
sections 77 and 78 of the Copyright, Designs and Patents Act 1988

First published 2023
The Boydell Press, Woodbridge
Paperback edition 2025

ISBN 978-1-83765-117-7 hardback
ISBN 978-1-83765-133-7 paperback

The Boydell Press is an imprint of Boydell & Brewer Ltd
and of Boydell & Brewer Inc.
website: www.boydellandbrewer.com

Our Authorised Representative for product safety in the EU is
Easy Access System Europe - Mustamäe tee 50, 10621 Tallinn, Estonia,
gpsr.requests@easproject.com

A CIP catalogue record for this book is available
from the British Library

The publisher has no responsibility for the continued existence or accuracy
of URLs for external or third-party internet websites referred to in this book,
and does not guarantee that any content on such websites is, or will remain,
accurate or appropriate

For Angus

Bridgeman sites in England.

CONTENTS

List of Illustrations		ix
Acknowledgements		xi
List of Abbreviations		xiii
	INTRODUCTION	1
Chapter 1	WHO WAS CHARLES BRIDGEMAN?	9
Chapter 2	TOWARDS A RELIABLE CORPUS	25
Chapter 3	A REVISED CATALOGUE	45
Chapter 4	READING THE PLANS	61
Chapter 5	THE ART-HISTORICAL CONTEXT REVISITED	79
Chapter 6	THE 'INGENIOUS MR BRIDGEMAN'	95
Chapter 7	BUILDING A LANDSCAPE	113
Chapter 8	A COMMERCIAL ENTERPRISE	137
	CONCLUSION	167
Appendix I: A summary of Willis's catalogue from Charles Bridgeman and the English Landscape Garden		171
Appendix II: A revised catalogue		175
Appendix III: Bridgeman's projects by year		179
Appendix IV: Bridgeman's income		183

Gazetteer of Bridgeman sites	189
Glossary	233
Bibliography	235
Index	247

ILLUSTRATIONS

MAPS

	Frontispiece: Bridgeman sites in England	vi
1	Ordnance Survey, Essex, 1st Edition/Revised XLI.4 1897 (detail). Reproduced with the permission of the National Library of Scotland	54

FIGURES

1	Windsor Forest. Credit: National Archives MR 1/279	38
2	Blenheim Palace. Reproduced by kind permission of Blenheim Palace	39
3	Hampton Court. SM 36/3/1 © Sir John Soane's Museum, London. Photograph by Ardon Bar-Hama	40
4	Amesbury Abbey. MSGD a3* fo.32. The Bodleian Libraries, University of Oxford	41
5	Part of a Map of the Parish of Rousham 1721. OHC PAR 226/17/MI/1. Courtesy of the Oxfordshire History Centre	49
6	Rousham House. BoL MSGD a4 fo.63. The Bodleian Libraries, University of Oxford	50
7	Sketch map of the relict landscape at Down Hall, annotated by Adrian Drift. MSGD a4 fo.29. The Bodleian Libraries, University of Oxford	53
8	A survey of Great Saxham Hall in Suffolk, overdrawn with a pencil sketch of his proposal for the landscape by Bridgeman. MSGD a3 fo.41. The Bodleian Libraries, University of Oxford	57
9	Lodge Park. MSGD a4 fo.68. The Bodleian Libraries, University of Oxford	69
10	Wolterton Hall. MSGD a4 fo.20. The Bodleian Libraries, University of Oxford	76
11	Gay's Cave and the Diamond in 1915. WRO 798/2. Reproduced by kind permission of Wiltshire and Swindon Record Office	105

12	Location of the principal garden features at Gobions based on the Bodleian Map. Reproduced by kind permission of Dr Anne Rowe and Professor Tom Williamson	107
13	An unidentified plan for a theatre. MSGD a4 fo.25. The Bodleian Libraries, University of Oxford	119
14	The amphitheatre at Claremont. Photograph: Susan Haynes, 2013	122
15	Bridgeman's plan for the drainage of the fens to the south and east of King's Lynn. NRO EA 386.32. Item from the collections of Norfolk County Council Library and Information Service	129
16	Receipt for £25 signed by Charles Bridgeman. BH BM17. Reproduced by kind permission of the Buccleugh Archives, Boughton House	153

The author and publisher are grateful to all the institutions and individuals listed for permission to reproduce the materials in which they hold copyright. Every effort has been made to trace the copyright holders; apologies are offered for any omission, and the publisher will be pleased to add any necessary acknowledgement in subsequent editions.

ACKNOWLEDGEMENTS

I WOULD LIKE to thank all those who have helped me in the preparation of this book. My greatest thanks must go to Tom Williamson for his help and encouragement. His own scholarship in designed landscapes has been highly significant in determining the direction of my research, and his humour, kindness and enthusiasm have been material factors in getting to publication. Other members of the Landscape History Department at the University of East Anglia – Sarah Spooner, Jon Gregory and Rob Liddiard – have all also provided invaluable help, much of it with the technical aspects of landscape study. I am indebted to the scholarship of Peter Willis, whose initial research and comprehensive catalogue laid the foundations for this work. I would also like to thank David Jacques, who first directed my interest in landscape history at Amesbury. My particular thanks go to members of the Hertfordshire Gardens Trust, in particular to Anne Rowe, and also Jenny Milledge, Alison Cassidy and Andrew Skelton, who have all provided significant help with Bridgeman landscapes in Hertfordshire and beyond. This book draws heavily on material held in archives, both public and private, libraries and record offices. I would like to thank the staff of the National Archives, the British Library, the Bodleian Library (especially Colin Harris) and the Sir John Soane Museum (especially Stephen Astley) for their help. I would like to thank the Duke of Buccleugh, the Earl of Scarborough, Lord and Lady Walpole, Sir Edward and Lady Antrobus, Mike and Gilly Clarke, David Cornelius-Reid, Swee Lan Miller and Hazel Howson, for allowing me access to the landscapes in their care. My thanks also go to Sir William Worsley, Elizabeth Routledge, Axel Klausmeier and, in particular, Crispin Powell, for their help with archive material. I am indebted to staff at county records offices who continue to offer an exemplary service in spite of severe cuts: the staff at Essex County Record Office, Northamptonshire Archives, Warwickshire County Record Office, the Wiltshire and Swindon History Centre, the Norfolk Archives, the Oxfordshire History Centre, the Millennium Library in Norwich and Hertfordshire Archive and Local Studies have all been of enormous help. Finally, I would like to express my gratitude to my family and friends who have encouraged me in the writing of this book: to my children Daniel, Alice, Kate, Joseph, and their partners, Samantha,

Mattias, and, in particular Nick, who helped me with the pictures; to Angus's daughter Amelia and her partner Jon; to my sister and brother-in-law, Gilly and Andy; and to my friends Diana, Adrian, Tricia, Bill, Mim, Rob, Dave and Sue. They have all offered me practical and psychological help, and an unquestioning and unwavering faith in my ability to write this. My thanks go, finally and most importantly, to Angus, for his love, for being a patient and constructive sounding board, and for maintaining a genuine fascination with Charles Bridgeman.

ABBREVIATIONS

BoL	Bodleian Library
BH	Boughton House
BL	British Library
BP	Blenheim Palace
CA	Cambridgeshire Archives
CL	Caird Library
ERO	Essex Record Office
GA	Gloucestershire Archives
HALS	Hertfordshire Archives and Local Studies
HEH	Henry E. Huntington Library
HFH	Hatfield Hall
HH	Hovingham Hall
IHR	Institute of Historical Research
KH	Kedleston Hall Archive
LL	Longleat House
MLN	Millenium Library Norwich
NA	National Archives
NLS	National Library of Scotland
NRO	Norfolk Record Office
NS	Nationalmuseum, Stockholm
NT	National Trust
NTS	Northamptonshire Archives
OHC	Oxfordshire History Centre
OT	Otterden Place
RC	Royal Collection
SC	Scarsdale Collection
SP	Sandbeck Park
SM	Sir John Soane Museum
SRO	Suffolk Archives
V&A	Victoria and Albert Museum

WH	Wolterton Hall
WO	Warwickshire County Record Office
WRO	Wiltshire and Swindon History Centre

INTRODUCTION

CHARLES BRIDGEMAN WAS a landscape architect and gardener of seminal importance. His work for the landed elite of the early eighteenth century, and his role as Royal Gardener, should have ensured him a prominent place in the canon of English landscape gardeners. Yet his name is not well known and only one monograph has been devoted to him and his work. He is regularly reduced to a footnote in garden history discourse. In fact, giving his work the close scrutiny it deserves might change the way we understand the development of garden design in England.

Early in the eighteenth century, Charles Bridgeman began designing vast, austere landscapes. He stripped away all the elaborate ornamentation and formal intricacies of the late seventeenth century and replaced them with simple grass plats, trees in long spare avenues, or in groves sparsely cut through with straight and serpentine walks, water in simple geometric shapes, and, most strikingly, sculpted earth in terraces and amphitheatres of audacious proportions. They changed the shape of the land on a monumental scale in estates from the Home Counties to Yorkshire. Admittedly, most of his landscapes have not survived; a combination of a change in fashion towards the more 'natural' landscapes of the later eighteenth century, typified by the work of Lancelot 'Capability' Brown, and the ingress of the modern built environment, the housing estates and the golf courses of the twentieth and the twenty-first centuries, has wiped out much of his work. Some landscapes have survived in a degraded form, the bones of the designs visible in crop marks in dry weather, or in digital laser surface mapping (LIDAR[1]). A few have survived intact, and where they have, they are extraordinary in both their imaginative conception and their execution. At Claremont in Surrey,

---

[1] LIDAR is an acronym for laser imaging, detection and ranging. It targets the surface of the earth with a laser beam and measures the time taken for the light to be reflected back to the receiver. By this means it builds up a three-dimensional picture of the ground targeted called a Digital Terrain Model or DTM. Because it measures tiny variations in the surface of the ground, it provides a good picture of features where the gradation of the surface is too small to be observed with the naked eye, or is hidden beneath vegetation. It is invaluable for finding traces of lost landscape features.

the amphitheatre, cleared of rhododendrons by the National Trust, dominates the landscape. At Lodge Park in Gloucestershire, a vast sweep of sculpted woodland and grass draws the eye to the estate boundary, one kilometre away.

In addition to the ghostly imprints and the few surviving earthworks, we also have other evidence of Bridgeman's works. The most comprehensive is a significant number of plans, the majority of which are held in the Bodleian Library in Oxford, the National Archives in London and the British Library. Some are held in regional Record Offices, and a few remain in the hands of the families for whom they were originally created. The plans vary in size and scope; the most striking are in pen and watercolour, beautifully and meticulously painted, while others are in pencil and brown ink, or are simple pencil drawings. They are striking not simply for their artistic skill, but also for their accuracy of surveying. They act as a mirror for the landscapes that do survive, and a vision of those that have not.

The landscapes were created for the monied elite of early eighteenth-century England: the Royal Family, the landed nobility and those whose wealth from other sources allowed them to buy substantial landed estates. From 1714, and so from the early stages of Bridgeman's career, following the death of Anne, the last Stuart queen, the Royal Family were members of the house of Hanover, brought from Germany by the Whig administration to ensure the Protestant succession. Bridgeman served the first two Hanoverian kings, George I and George II, as Royal Gardener. He was appointed to the post jointly with Henry Wise in 1726, and then, following the retirement of Wise, was sole Royal Gardener to George II from 1727 until his death in 1738. With Wise, he designed gardens at Kensington Palace for George I, then redesigned them for George II on his accession in 1727; the Round Pond and the geometric walks we see today in Kensington Gardens are his. He also worked at Richmond Palace for George II and his wife, Caroline of Anhalt, in 1725, when they were Prince and Princess of Wales. Caroline, both as Princess of Wales and as Queen, seems to have taken a close interest in Bridgeman and his work.

Many of Bridgeman's noble clients were Whigs, the powerful clique and predominant political force in English politics in the first half of the eighteenth century, also roughly for the period of Bridgeman's career. In broad terms, it was the Whigs who had supported the Glorious Revolution of 1688 and the accession of the Hanoverian monarchs in 1714. They took full control of the government from 1715 onwards, largely under Sir Robert Walpole, First Lord of the Treasury from 1722 and *de facto* First Minister.[2] The Tories, their political opponents in parliament, were – again broadly – supporters of the deposed Stuart monarchy, the landed interest and high-church Anglicanism, and of more conservative values. The complications of factionalism within a broadly Whig persuasion mean that not all Whigs were in power at the time, and, of course,

---

[2] See online at https://doi.org/10.1093/ref:odnb/28601

many who identified themselves as Whigs were not actively involved in politics at all (Langford 1989; Hill in Dickinson (ed.) 2002). It was also a period of shifting political allegiances not always determined by a deeply held ideology, especially as Walpole's power weakened (Langford 1989; Williamson 1998). Indeed, even the political labels of Whig and Tory might not be very helpful, especially when considering the beliefs of the ruling oligarchy.

Bridgeman has gained a reputation as gardener to the Whigs because he worked for so many high-profile members of Walpole's government, for opposition Whigs, and for many with close ties to the Whigs. His clients included Sir Robert Walpole himself, who employed Bridgeman at Houghton, his then newly built house in Norfolk, and his brother, Horatio Walpole, Walpole's envoy in The Hague and Paris, for whom Bridgeman designed the landscape at Wolterton. He also worked for prominent members of Walpole's administration, including Thomas Pelham-Holles, Duke of Newcastle and Secretary of State under Walpole, at Claremont, and probably for his younger brother, Henry Pelham, Secretary at War, at Esher Place, for George Bubb Dodington, a Lord of the Treasury, at Eastbury, and for Thomas Winnington, Lord of the Admiralty and also a Lord of the Treasury, at Brocket Park. He was employed by other members of the House of Commons and of the House of Lords who were supporters either of Walpole's administration, or at least of Whig ideas; for example, he worked for Sir William St Quintin at Scampston, Sir William Harbord at Gunton in Norfolk, and Charles Powlett, third Duke of Bolton, at Hackwood. Other clients with Whig sympathies included Matthew Prior, at Down Hall, and Henrietta Howard, mistress of George II, at Marble Hill. He also worked for opposition Whigs, such as the Duke of Queensberry, who served as Gentleman of the Bedchamber to Prince Frederick, at Amesbury. Although much has been made of the idea of Bridgeman's connection with the Whig elite (Willis 2002; Eburne 2003), he was certainly not exclusively employed by the ruling Whig faction; he also worked for a number of Tories, some with strong Jacobite sympathies, including the Duke of Beaufort, Lady Betty Hastings and Lord Cobham.

A sizeable minority of Bridgeman's clients were from what might loosely be termed 'new money', in that their wealth, which was often considerable, did not originally come from inherited land but had been acquired from commercial enterprises usually spanning one or two generations. They were, to all other intents and purposes, members of the establishment, 'directors in the larger monied companies', often Members of Parliament by virtue of the land they had bought, and often married to members of the aristocracy (Rogers in Dickenson (ed.) 2002, 173). Sir William Gore, who owned Tring Park in Hertfordshire, and was Bridgeman's client in the 1720s, was typical. He was a director of the South Sea Company (a joint stock company which notoriously crashed in 1721, in what was termed the South Sea Bubble, ruining many investors) until 1715, and of the Bank of England (then a private company which had secured the monopoly of lending to the government). He was also a Tory politician, and married to

Lady Mary Compton, daughter of the Earl of Northampton. He had inherited Tring Park in Hertfordshire from his father, a successful merchant and a founding director of the Bank of England. Benjamin Styles of Moor Park was similar. He was the son of a successful Amsterdam merchant and inherited a fortune from both his father and his younger brother. He was also a Member of Parliament, for Devizes from 1721 to 1734. Sir Jeremy Sambrooke, of Gobions, was the son and grandson of officials in the East India Company, formed in the seventeenth century to monopolise the trade with South-east Asia and India. Both his title and his fortune were inherited from his father. Edward Rolt was a Tory MP from 1713 onwards. His fortune, and Sacombe Park, were inherited from his father, who was a merchant in the service of the East India Company of which he rose to be chief in Persia and president of Surat. Bridgeman also designed landscapes for three other directors of the South Sea Company before the crash in 1721. He certainly designed the landscape at Purley in Berkshire for Francis Hawes, and probably designed for Sir John Fellowes, at Carshalton in Surrey, and for Robert Chester, at Briggens in Hertfordshire. Thomas Hall, at Goldings, which Hall inherited on the death of his brother in 1725, was still actively involved in trade; he was a shipowner and a merchant when he commissioned Bridgeman in around 1735.

A designed landscape must always be understood in the context of the house with which it is associated. At the centre of the landscapes Bridgeman designed for his wealthy elite clients were some of the most prestigious houses in the country. A significant number of these were newly built Palladian mansions or villas for the Whig elite. Indeed, as Williamson suggests, Palladianism became the 'distinctive badge of Whig ideology' (Williamson 1995, 63). There was a resurgence of interest in Palladianism, a style of architecture based on formal classical principles, in the early part of the eighteenth century, influenced by the publication of *Vitruvius Britannicus*, Volume 1, by Colen Campbell in 1715, and of Leoni's translation of Palladio's *I Quattro libri dell'architettura* also in 1715. Houses of particular note were Marble Hill in Surrey, designed by Lord Pembroke, and Wolterton Hall in Norfolk, designed by Thomas Ripley. Other houses were comprehensively remodelled to appear Palladian; Moor Park was a house built in 1680 for the Duke of Monmouth, refurbished, extended and encased in Portland stone by Benjamin Styles at the cost of £130,000 (Williamson 2000, 28). Many of the garden buildings in the landscapes Bridgeman designed were Palladian too, as, for example, the Water House at Houghton, designed by Lord Pembroke, or the summerhouse in Tring Park, designed by Gibbs in 1722 (Fletcher 2007, 46).

Although Palladianism was the most significant architectural style of the age, and a large proportion of new houses built in the early eighteenth century were in the Palladian style, what emerges from a close study of the houses at the centre of Bridgeman's designs is, however, a much more complex picture. Equally significantly, a number of these houses and garden buildings architecturally predate the eighteenth century's renewed interest in Palladianism. Some, such as Amesbury Abbey designed by Webb in 1660 in the style of Inigo Jones, belong to the first wave of neo-Classical buildings. Some, such as Blenheim, built by Vanburgh (1705–1720), are Baroque, a highly ornate and exuberant style of architecture. Some, such as Ledston Hall and Moor Park, were houses with medieval, sixteenth- or seventeenth-century origins, remodelled several times, including at the time of Bridgeman's involvement. What seems clear is that Bridgeman's landscapes were largely designed to accompany some kind of updating, sometimes involving a complete rebuilding of the house, sometimes a remodelling of existing features, usually in the Palladian style. It could be that Bridgeman's work represented a reworking to match the Palladianism of the house, as Williamson suggests: 'It is probable that the development of this vast yet geometric style was closely associated with the emergence of Palladian architecture' (Williamson 1998, 55). It is equally possible, though, that a Bridgeman garden might have presented a less expensive option than rebuilding the house. It must also be noted that there are significant Palladian houses with which it appears Bridgeman had no involvement – for example, Holkham Hall.[3]

Yet, in spite of what seems to have been a glittering portfolio of clients and work, Bridgeman remains largely unknown, except within the discourse of garden history, and even there he is usually reduced to a peripheral reference in modern academic works on eighteenth-century garden history (Green 1956; Dixon Hunt and Willis 1975; Stroud 1975a; Harris 1985; Dixon Hunt 1986; Jacques 1990; Fretwell 1995; Mowl 2006; Dalton 2012). There is, in fact, as mentioned above, only one substantial text of any kind devoted to Bridgeman: *Charles Bridgeman and the English Landscape Garden* (Willis 2002). Although it includes a comprehensive overview and evaluation of Bridgeman's work, together with an exhaustive catalogue of plans attributed to him and the few extant letters in Bridgeman's hand, Willis devotes a significant proportion of his text to the clients for whom Bridgeman worked, and the architects, artists and gardeners with whom he was professionally connected, and about whom considerably more is known. Bridgeman and his work often appear as an adjunct to the lives and work of these literary, artistic and aristocratic figures. Charles Bridgeman himself remains an opaque figure throughout the book. A significant part of the reason for this seems to be that it is simply not easy to find out much about him or about how he worked. While he may have left behind the extensive corpus of plans and drawings mentioned above, and his tenure as Royal Gardener is well documented in the minutes and accounts of the Office of Works, there are few surviving written sources of any other kind and none which explain his artistic vision. There have subsequently been a number of detailed and rigorous studies of individual landscapes, notably Tom Williamson's comprehensive studies of Houghton, Wolterton and Gunton in Norfolk (Williamson 1998), his

---

[3] Biographies of all Bridgeman's major clients and a brief history of the estates he worked on are included in the Gazetteer of Bridgeman Sites which follows on page XX.

work with Anne Rowe on Gobions in Hertfordshire (Rowe and Williamson 2012), significant studies on sites in Hertfordshire by Anne Rowe, Jenny Milledge and Andrew Skelton (Skelton 1994/6; Milledge 2009;) and Nicky Smith's work at Lodge Park in Gloucestershire (Smith 2006), but, taken together, Willis's book and these separate studies represent only an outline of his career and snapshots of moments within it.

However, neither the paucity of information about him, nor the absence of a comprehensive evaluation of his work, have prevented a narrative so often rehearsed as an explanation of Bridgeman's work that it has become the received orthodoxy about him. His designs are considered as an important stage on the trajectory from seventeenth-century geometric gardening to the English landscape garden of Lancelot Brown and his contemporaries. The discourse that places him as a convenient bridge between the formal gardening style of the seventeenth century and the 'natural' gardening style of the middle to late eighteenth century is summed up in the introduction of *The Genius of the Place* by John Dixon Hunt and Peter Willis (1975). They set out in detail the teleological narrative in which the end point is the 'natural' garden. Their contention is that the 'typical English landscape of undulating grass that leads somewhere down to an irregularly shaped piece of water over which a bridge arches, of trees grouped casually' and of 'houses ... glimpsed in the middle or far distance' was the result of 'much exploration and experiment over at least one hundred and fifty years' and 'the outcome of a long process whereby the stiff and geometric gardens of Tudor and Stuart England were transformed into an art that the rest of Europe imitated' (Dixon Hunt and Willis 1975, 1). This is a curious argument; it seems to suggest a planned two-century-long development towards a style that cannot possibly have been envisaged when it began. It has to be said that many modern garden historians and writers have begun to challenge this narrative. In fact, as Williamson has shown, the development of fashion in landscape design in the eighteenth century is far more complicated. The late geometric garden continued to be popular into the 1730s and 1740s, and writers such as Lord Shaftesbury and Stephen Switzer were producing geometric gardens in apparent contradiction of their pronouncements in print (Williamson 1995, 49).

The source of this narrative is writing on garden history from the later eighteenth century, and in particular Horace Walpole's *The History of the Modern Taste in Gardening* published in 1780. Walpole's argument, which will be well known to anyone interested in the history of garden design, is that the gardens of the ancient world, for example the Greek garden of Alcinous, the ancient Roman garden of Pliny, or even the hanging gardens of Babylon, were all too uniform, too full of evergreen sculpture, or too small. He ranges through the regrettable regularity and 'impotent displays of false taste' in the Dutch and French gardens of the seventeenth century, and English gardens of the late seventeenth and early eighteenth centuries such as those designed by George London, garden designer and joint proprietor of Brompton Park Nursery, and Henry Wise. He finds the embryonic beginnings of the ultimate 'natural' style in Milton's poetic work *Paradise Lost* and in Sir William Temple's seventeenth-century description of Moor Park in Hertfordshire, but it is not until he reaches the work of William Kent that he finds the apotheosis of the English landscape garden; Kent, he claims, was 'painter enough to taste the charms of the landscape, bold and opinionative enough to dare and to dictate, and born with a genius to strike out a great system from the twilight of imperfect essays' (Walpole 1995, 43). In the (now) famous words, Kent 'leapt the fence and saw all nature was a garden'. Walpole's essay was not alone in presenting the English landscape garden as a wholly superior, and entirely English, creation. His near contemporaries, William Falconer whose 'Thoughts on the Style and Taste of Gardening among the Ancients' appeared in 1789, and William Mason writing in 1772, present a similar notion, albeit with slightly different reasoning, as Bending has shown (Bending 1994). Bending has argued that 'eighteenth-century narrative history was largely responsible for creating the very *tradition* of the English Landscape Garden' (Bending 1994, 213).

It is Walpole who establishes Bridgeman's place in this narrative. He writes dismissively of all aspects of the formal style and casts Bridgeman as the first to move away from it. Bridgeman is, in a much-quoted passage, the gardener who allowed 'absurdity' to go 'no further' and who 'turned the tide'. He was 'far more chaste', and 'banished verdant sculpture'. He 'enlarged his plans, disdained to make every division tally with its opposite, and though he still adhered much to straight walks with high clipped hedges, they were only his great lines; the rest he diversified by wilderness, and with loose groves of oak, though still within surrounding hedges'. In Bridgeman's work at Gobions, in Hertfordshire, Walpole 'discerned many detached thoughts, that strongly indicate the dawn of modern taste' (Walpole 1995, 42). Bridgeman is also credited by Walpole with the invention of the haha; 'But the capital stroke, the leading step to all that followed, was [I believe the first thought was Bridgman's] the destruction of walls for boundaries, and the invention of fossés ...' (Walpole 1995, 43).

The assimilation of Walpole's narrative into garden history has included a tacit acceptance of Bridgeman's place within it and it remains stubbornly potent in any description of Bridgeman's work. Willis begins his brief analysis of Bridgeman's style by citing Walpole: 'Horace Walpole, whose analysis of the Royal Gardener's style, though brief, is the most comprehensive we have and [is] worth restating' (Willis 2002, 130). As a result, many modern writers on garden history have followed Walpole's lead in seeing Bridgeman as a bridge between the formality of the sixteenth and seventeenth centuries and the natural garden of the mid-to-late eighteenth century (Walpole 1995, 43) (Dixon Hunt 1986; Jacques 1990; Mowl 2006). It is easy to see how Bridgeman's work slots neatly into this narrative. His long straight avenues and geometric tree planting are seen as the heirs of the late seventeenth-century gardens, while his relative austerity, apparently demonstrable interest in the 'genius of the place', and construction of vistas into the wider landscape, perhaps created by a haha, are seen as the precursors of the work of William Kent and, ultimately, of Lancelot Brown. Willis's attempt at defining Bridgeman's style, which divided his work into three separate, largely chronological, categories, also reflects this view. He suggests three categories for Bridgeman's work: formal, which includes parterres, straight avenues and lakes; transitional, which Willis suggests is 'combining established motifs in a new way', for example in the construction of amphitheatres, and his use of statues and garden buildings; and progressive, suggested by his use of cultivated fields and 'morsels of forest' (Willis 2002, 132).

So strong is the perception that Bridgeman has a place in the rise of the English landscape garden that the possibility that he might have been influenced by his immediate contemporaries and those gardening in the generation before him is rarely considered. No rigorous attempt has been made to trace any stylistic links between his work and that of Henry Wise, with whom he was joint Royal Gardener in 1726 and 1727, or that of George London, who was so prolific in gardening that, in Switzer's words, he 'gave Directions once or twice a Year in most of the Noblemens and Gentlemens Gardens in *England*' (Switzer, cited in Willis 2002, 15), or to link him with garden design in Europe. There has also been little scholarly interrogation of the term 'Nature' as applied to gardening in the early part of the eighteenth century. There has been a general consensus that the meaning Walpole attaches to the term in 1760 can stand for the whole century.

Bridgeman was not as peripheral a figure as popular gardening discourse presents him, but even so, both he and his work descended rapidly into obscurity after his death and have largely remained there. A gardener so popular in his period and so prolific in his output deserves better than the tangential references he is reduced to in much of the writing about garden history. It is time to dismantle the limited number of frames which have, up to this point, been used to define Bridgeman's work and to re-examine and re-evaluate whatever evidence of his work still survives. This book seeks to fill in, as far as possible, the gaps in our knowledge about Bridgeman and his work, and to restore him to his rightful place in the history of gardening in England.

CHAPTER 1

WHO WAS CHARLES BRIDGEMAN?

IN 1714 CHARLES BRIDGEMAN designed a garden for Sir Edward Rolt at his mansion at Sacombe in Hertfordshire. The plan for the landscape, held in the Bodleian Library in Oxford as part of the Gough Collection (BoL MSGD a4 fo.64), is in vibrant watercolour. Beyond the house and formal garden, it shows an axial walk leading to a rectangular canal which stretches out to the southeast of the house. At right angles, another walk stretches through woodland. There is a *patte d'oie*, one branch of which leads to a small theatre with an oval pond at its base, fed by a conduit from a triangular basin on slightly higher ground. The whole covers 42 acres (0.17km^2) and much of it is still visible today, including the outline of the canal and basin in a ploughed field to the south east of the house; to a very large degree it correlates exactly with the plan (https://earth.google.com/web/search/Sacombe). Sir Thomas Rolt, Sir Edward's father, a former Governor of the East India Company, had bought the house and park in 1688. Sir Edward had inherited Sacombe in 1710 (Milledge 2009, 40). It is impossible to say how Bridgeman got the commission. Perhaps it was through a connection with Henry Wise, Royal Gardener between 1704 and 1727, and proprietor of the most prestigious plant nursery in England, Brompton Park Nurseries, for whom Bridgeman probably worked; Wise was clearly known to Rolt and had been paid £8.14s.6d by Rolt in 1714, perhaps for advice, perhaps for plants (Milledge 2009, 40). Possibly it was through Sir John Vanbrugh, the playwright and architect with whom Bridgeman had probably worked at Blenheim Palace and would subsequently work at Lumley Castle and Hackwood. Vanbrugh had designed a walled kitchen garden at Sacombe in the military style. Bridgeman's involvement in the project appears to have been long term, and highly lucrative. Between 13 June 1715 and 1720, the Sacombe estate accounts show that Bridgeman was paid substantial sums, in total amounting to £160,000, the greatest being the final payment of £534. He was still working at Sacombe in summer 1722, when the canal was being dug (Milledge 2009, 42), and was Rolt's principal creditor when his estate was taken into administration on his death from smallpox in the same year.

We have three reliable references to Charles Bridgeman before his triumph at Sacombe. He was already working at Stowe, Viscount Cobham's masterpiece of a garden in Buckinghamshire, in 1714. An undated entry from the '1714' packet of the Stowe Accounts 1710–1720 records that 'Mr bridgmans man' was paid £1.2s.6d (HEH Box L9F6, cited in Willis 2002, 109 n. 14). In 1711 his name also appears alongside that of James Fish the younger, one of a family of surveyors from Warwick, on a survey of Warwick Town and Priory, done, probably for Henry Wise, on his acquisition of Warwick Priory. The inscription reads: 'By/ Mr Fish, being assisted &/ Completed by Cha:Bridgman' (WO CR 26.2.2). In 1709 his name is found on a plan for the landscape at Blenheim Palace which now hangs in the entrance hall at Blenheim Palace; in the cartouche of the beautifully finished plan are the words 'Bridgman descript.'. However, Bridgeman's life before 1709 is almost entirely obscure, although this has not stopped speculation, both wild and well-founded. Willis offers a summary of the theories in *Charles Bridgeman and the English Landscape Garden* (Willis 2002, 149). There was clearly a need for earlier garden historians to give Bridgeman elite connections. In 1824 J.W Croker suggested that Charles Bridgeman was the second son of Orlando Bridgeman, a relative by marriage of the Earl of Bradford. In fact, as Willis points out, this suggestion, although generally accepted in the nineteenth century, is impossible because Sir Henry's younger brother was called George and was not born until 1727. Another suggestion is that he was in some way connected with Thomas Bridgeman, a nineteenth-century American horticulturist, which also seems extremely unlikely (Willis 2002, 149).

Parish records have only relatively recently become available as databases that can be searched. Even so, there are limitations to the information they can provide, particularly when the records are from the end of the seventeenth and beginning of the eighteenth centuries; they are reliant on the transcription of often semi-legible and sometimes unhelpfully incomplete handwritten records. Nevertheless, they are able to provide some flesh for the bones of the speculative enquiries about Bridgeman's origins. Searches of the databases available reveal that there was a concentration of Bridgmans, with or without an 'e', in the west country around Wiltshire, Gloucestershire and Somerset, although the family history databases there contain no record of the baptism of a Charles Bridgeman. There is one record of a Charles Bridgeman marrying a Sarah Robinson at Beverston to the west of Tetbury in Gloucestershire in 1720, but this clearly has no relevance; Bridgeman's wife was called Sarah Mist.

There were also concentrations of Bridgemans in the east of England, around Hertfordshire, Essex and Suffolk. In Suffolk, in the parish of Exning, there are four Charles Bridgemans recorded in the parish records; the references span the late seventeenth and early eighteenth centuries. The first, son of an Oliver Bridgeman, was baptised in 1690, and a second, probably his son, was baptised in 1720. A third Charles Bridgeman from Exning married Anne Wheeler in 1729 and a fourth married in 1737. It seems unlikely that any of these is Charles Bridgeman the Royal Gardener. Although the first, baptised in 1690, has a plausible baptismal date, the baptism of his son in Exning makes it unlikely because Bridgeman's own son Charles was baptised in the parish of St Ann's Soho.

The borders of Hertfordshire and Essex are altogether more promising. Willis makes two suggestions about Bridgeman's father, both of which link him to the area. The first is that he might have been the son of the gardener mentioned in an account book for the Archer family in 1691, at Coopersale in Essex,[1] but this also seems unlikely since there is no record of the baptism of a Charles Bridgeman in any of the registers of the parishes within a ten-mile radius of Coopersale between 1650 and 1700. The other is that Bridgeman's father might also have been a gardener and that he was employed by Edward Harley, Earl of Oxford, at Wimpole (although presumably after 1713, when Harley came into the possession of Wimpole through his marriage to Lady Henrietta Cavendish Holles), and that he died at Wimpole in 1726. Willis does not cite any evidence for this, and admits that the death is not recorded in the parish records for Wimpole (Willis 2002, 26), but some connection with the Earl of Oxford is more plausible (see below). There is also a reliable connection between Bridgeman and Hertfordshire. Bridgeman had a cousin, also Charles, who was Mayor of Hertford, and it is possible that this family were nurserymen (pers. comm. Sheila White). Willis reproduces a letter from Bridgeman to his cousin of the same name, who was Alderman and Mayor in Hertford (HMC 19: Townshend, 352, cited in Willis 2002, 156) and Bridgeman is named as one of the executors of his will (NA PROB.3/37/95). He may even have had a mini Bridgeman garden. A garden with some Bridgemanic characteristics is shown on a 1766 map of Hertford (pers. comm. Anne Rowe). At the very least there were strong familial connections between Bridgeman and the area.

Interestingly, there also appear to have been several Bridgemans working as gardeners in this area in the late seventeenth and early eighteenth centuries. Richard Bridgeman of Writtle, described as a gardener in his will, left his son Charles £30 on his death in 1676. Another Richard Bridgeman was described as 'gardener' in the Manor Court Book from 1683 of Brickendonbury, immediately to the south of Hertford (Jean Ridell pers. comm. 2017). The Bridgeman at Coopersale was a gardener (pers. comm. Lewis Wyman, Library of Congress, Washington DC). In the early eighteenth century, a Stephen Bridgeman worked at Down Hall, Essex, a Bridgeman landscape. On 10 April 1729 he wrote to Edward Harley, by then Earl of Oxford, that 'Pursuant to Yr Lordships Command' he had 'Accomplished' work on 'ye Bastion att ye head of ye Bowling Green to

---

[1] In fact Willis speculates that the reference might be to Coopersale in Essex, or to Welford in Berkshire; the Archer family owned both properties. The account book, now held in Library of Congress in Washington DC, is in fact for Coopersale in Essex (pers. comm. Lewis Wyman, Library of Congress, Washington DC).

make it fit for Planting ye Ellms which have been planted about 3 weeks' (BL Add MS 70370/160).

The name Charles recurs in the parish records of the area in the late seventeenth and early eighteenth centuries. One of them, son of Benjamin and Elizabeth, was baptised in Terling to the north-east of Chelmsford in 1713; another, son of Edward and Sarah, was baptised in Standon to the north east of Hertford, on the border with Essex; yet another married an Elizabeth Williams in Great Baddow in 1736. The most promising Charles, in a search through rather muddy waters for Charles Bridgeman the Royal Gardener, is Charles Bridgeman, son of Richard Bridgeman, who was baptised at Writtle just to the west of Chelmsford in 1664; he is likely to be the son of Richard Bridgeman the gardener mentioned above, and therefore the recipient of £30 from his father's will. It is possible that this, though not Bridgeman himself, was his father. A 'Mr Bridgeman Senior' is twice mentioned in relation to the affairs of Down Hall in Essex. Account books for the estate note that on 10 March 1721/2 'Mr Bridgeman Senior' paid 'Mr Carpenter ['s] Bill for seeds for the Gardens at Down Hall', and on 13 March of the same year the account book records that 'Mr Bridgeman Senior gone to Down Hall to clear all debts due' (Add MS 70362). While we cannot be sure that 'Mr Bridgeman Senior' was actually Bridgeman's father, it seems likely that he was. In the list of those given mourning rings to commemorate the death in 1721 of Matthew Prior, the diplomat and poet for whom Bridgeman designed the garden at Down Hall, Bridgeman is denoted as 'Charles Bridgeman Junior'. It is hard to imagine why this would be, unless father and son shared the same name and were both well known to those suggesting the distribution of mourning rings. If Bridgeman's father was also called Charles, it is quite plausible that he was the child baptised in 1664 in Terling. It also makes sense of Willis's suggestion that he was a gardener at Wimpole. Perhaps he worked for Lord Harley at Down Hall, owned by Harley after Prior's death. He seems to have had some connection with Down Hall, and it may be that he was buried at St Mary's, Matching, in 1726, the parish to which Down Hall belongs. The parish records there show the burial of a Carolus Bridgeman. The National Burial Index of England and Wales records the name as Caroles. Carolus is the Latinised form of Charles, but the replacement of 'u' with 'e' in the National Index may indicate that a semi-legible 'Charles' has been wrongly transcribed, given the fluidity of spelling, handwriting and nomenclature in the early eighteenth century.

But if Charles Bridgeman had his family origins in Hertfordshire, there is one flaw: simply, there is no record of the birth of a Charles Bridgeman in Hertfordshire or Essex at anything like the right date. If we assume that Bridgeman must have been at least, say, 15 at the time of his drawing of the plan of Blenheim in 1709, and probably older, he must have been born before 1695. This rules out all except the Charles Bridgeman born in 1664 in Writtle. Theoretically, this could be him, and not his father, but it would make him 53 on his marriage to Sarah

Mist in 1717 and 74 when he died in 1738, neither of which are impossible, but seem unlikely.

There is another possibility. The family history databases show another Charles Bridgeman, this one born at a much more plausible date, but in London. The parish records of St Margaret, Westminster record the baptism of Charles Bridgeman, son of Charles and Mary, in 1685 (Ancestry.co.uk FHL Film 924 B4HA V.89). This birth date would make Bridgeman 24 when he worked on the plan for Blenheim in 1709, 41 on his appointment as Royal Gardener in 1726, and 53 on his death of dropsy in 1738. The surname Bridgeman occurs with such frequency within five miles of Westminster at the beginning of the eighteenth century that it is possible that this Charles Bridgeman, son of Charles and Mary Bridgeman, baptised on 31 May 1685, may not be the man who became Royal Gardener, but, looking at the evidence of the parish records available on family history databases, he remains the most likely.

Bridgeman does appear to have had strong personal and familial connections to London. The first reliable date in his biography is 2 May 1717, when he married Sarah Mist of the parish of St Anne's Holborn, at Gray's Inn Chapel. Bridgeman was resident in Kensington at the time. Sarah was the sister of John Mist, who worked extensively as a pavior for the Office of Works in the early eighteenth century, and the sister-in-law, through the marriage of her sister Elizabeth, to George Devall, master plumber with the Office of Works. Their marriage at Gray's Inn Chapel was perhaps a little unusual. Gray's Inn Chapel was a non-parochial chapel which offered marriages by licence rather than by banns, and weddings there were available with speed and discretion. It was, however, respectable, unlike some other London private chapels (pers. comm. Andrew Mussell, Archivist at Gray's Inn Chapel). It is not clear why Bridgeman married there. It seems unlikely that Sarah was pregnant at the time, since the Bridgeman's eldest child, Charles was baptised on 12 March 1718 at St Anne's Soho. All the children of the marriage appear to have been baptised in London, [2] although again the bewildering number of families with the surname Bridgeman resident in the parishes in and around Westminster and Kensington makes it difficult to

---

[2] A daughter, Sarah, was born on 3 February 1720 and baptised on 18 February, and a son, John (?), was born 4 January 1721 and baptised on 25 January 1721. Another daughter, Elizabeth, was baptised on 26 November 1724. She married Philip Price in 1745. Charlotte, born 25 October 1725, baptised 21 November 1725; Charlotte, born 18 December 1727, baptised 14 January 1728; Carolina, baptised 9 June 1729, St James's Piccadilly; Ann, baptised 13 November 1731. Of these children only his son Charles, and his daughters Sarah, Elizabeth and Ann, were still alive when he made his will on 6 July 1738, and by the time Sarah Bridgeman made her will in 1743, only the three daughters are mentioned. Bridgeman's son, Charles, entered Westminster School in 1728, where he was a contemporary of the sons of Sir John Vanbrugh and Stephen Switzer, and went to Christchurch, Oxford, as a contemporary of Henry Wise's son (Willis 2002, 28).

distinguish the children of Charles and Sarah Bridgeman from other Bridgeman children born at the same time. This may have led to some confusion in the family tree which Willis produces.[3] Until 1723, the children appear to have been baptised at St Anne's Soho, and after that date at St James's Piccadilly, which is consistent with a move between Dean Street in Soho to Broad Street (see below). The Westminster Rate Books record that Bridgeman was paying rates on a house in Dean Street, Soho, in 1718, and on a house in Broad Street from 1729 to 1737 (https://www.findmypast.co.uk). His will records that he owned both the property in Broad Street and a house in Henrietta Street, also in Soho (NA PROB.3/37/95). This shows that he was living in London and a man of substance well before he was appointed Royal Gardener in 1726. All of this perhaps points to a significant history in London, rather than Hertfordshire, possibly beginning with his birth there. It does not, of course, explain what Bridgeman's putative father, Charles Bridgeman a gardener from Writtle in Essex, was doing in London when his son Charles was born.

Although Sacombe probably marks the beginning of Charles Bridgeman's solo career, the size and complexity of the project, and the expertise in surveying and the hydraulics required to execute it, make it unlikely to be the work of a novice. So by 1709 Bridgeman had probably already learnt the skills which enabled him to pursue his illustrious career as a garden designer: gardening, surveying, draughtsmanship and hydraulics. It is plausible that Bridgeman's skills as a gardener came about because he was descended from gardeners and nurserymen, or because he worked at Brompton Park Nursery, or possibly both. It is not clear from this whether he was involved with the growing and supply of the plants at Brompton Park Nursery, but it would, in any case, have been a helpful environment for an aspiring garden designer. Bridgeman's appointment as Royal Gardener in 1726, jointly with Henry Wise, suggests that by then he had acquired the skills of a gardener, and a significant reputation as one. His duties, specified in the contract drawn up when he became sole Royal Gardener in 1728 after Wise's retirement, are precise in their references to daily gardening practices. The contract stipulates that Bridgeman's responsibilities include, for example, 'the several hardy Ever Greens & other plants to be stak'd Tyed up Pruned and Clipped', 'the several Collections of Housed Greens & Flower roots to be well managed & kept in good Order' and 'the Borders Earthed Dunged, digged, Hoed, raked and weeded' (NA Work 6/114 fos. 12v–15v). Bridgeman must have been familiar with, and had expertise in, flower gardening. Although there is no direct evidence of this from his designs, a responsibility for the flowers in the royal gardens is implicit in his role as Royal Gardener. Certainly the minutes of the Board of Works from 1724, when Wise and Carpenter had this role, allude to

---

[3] The John Bridgeman who Willis includes on his family tree as born 3 November 1723 and baptised 28 November 1723 is, in fact, the son of Orlando and Anne Bridgeman (www.findmypast.co.uk).

their responsibility for flowers in the Royal Gardens when 'new stand for blowing July flowers' is ordered for Hampton Court (NA Work 4/1), and Jan Woudstra has shown that, in the Glass Case Garden at Hampton Court, originally laid out by Wise in 1701–2, the beds were planted with bulbs in spring which were then lifted and replaced by exotic plants, some in pots, which had been housed in the adjacent greenhouses during the winter; he shows that this practice was in operation in 1732 when Bridgeman was Royal Gardener (Woudstra 2009, 81, 87).

It is important to recognise Bridgeman's very superior skill as a surveyor and a draughtsman; these are quite often overlooked in any examination of his career. It is only necessary to compare his plans with those of his contemporaries to realise that he was both an accomplished artist and a very accurate surveyor within the limitations of his period. It is hard to know whether these skills were learnt in the pursuit of a career in gardening, or whether they came first. There would almost certainly, in any case, have been a blurring of the lines between related professions in the early eighteenth century, so that it is probably inappropriate to demarcate Bridgeman's roles in a modern way. Eden makes the point that surveying was often one of several occupations in different but related trades in the early eighteenth century: 'Throughout the kingdom, [at the beginning of the eighteenth century] the [surveying] profession was still relatively undeveloped and surveyors had to have a variety of alternative occupations as a cushion against variations in demand' (Eden 1975, 474).

Bridgeman's competence in surveying points to some training in mathematics and in the professional skills needed to successfully execute projects. By the close of the seventeenth century, the period in which Bridgeman was presumably educated, both mathematics and geometry had reached a modern state of development and the focus of mathematical education had shifted from universities to secondary schools (Richeson 1966, 143). It is possible that Bridgeman received his mathematical education at school, although, as Pannett suggests, in relation to the mathematical training of the Warwickshire surveyors James Fish, and Robert and Thomas Hewitt, some financial means was necessary to obtain it (Pannett 1985, 70). It would, therefore, have been possible for Bridgeman's mathematical expertise to have been self-taught. There was a great boom in the publication of mathematical works following the Civil War (Bendall 2009, 120).

Formal training in surveying, however, appears to have been harder to come by than mathematical education. As Richeson suggests, 'Although great strides had been made in mathematics and its teaching, there was still little instruction given in surveying, and instruction in mathematics with particular reference to its use in surveying was frequently hard to obtain' (Richeson 1966, 143). Land surveying was taught in some grammar schools, and in private academies, in the latter half of the eighteenth century and the nineteenth century, but it seems likely that, while Bridgeman might have learnt mathematics at school, he is unlikely to have studied surveying there (Bendall 2009, 127–128). It is quite possible that, as with many surveyors, Bridgeman learnt through an apprenticeship, possibly through familial connections (Bendall 2009, 125). Pannett makes the point that, of 127 surveyors working in Warwickshire between 1710 and 1840, at least ten were father-and-son teams (Pannett 1985, 80). This must include James Fish, with whom Bridgeman worked on the survey of Warwick Town and Priory (CR 26.2.2), raising the interesting possibility that Bridgeman served an apprenticeship with Fish and his father.

Bridgeman was also, demonstrably, a competent hydraulics engineer. Much of his work involved some manipulation of water around a site or the construction of sizeable ponds and canals. His only publication, in 1724, entitled *'A Report of the present State of the Great Level of the Fens, called* the Bedford-Level, *and of the Port of* Lynn, *and of the Rivers Ouse* and *Nean*, the two great Sewers of the Country With Considerations on the Scheme propos'd by the Corporation of Lynn for Draining the said Fens, and Reinstating that Harbour' is also an indication of his level of ability in this field. It has been largely ignored by garden historians, although its existence, and the expertise it displays, suggest both a competence in levels and water management, and a reputation for it beyond the confines of garden construction. It was prepared for the Earl of Lincoln, to whom it is also addressed, which presumably means Lincoln understood Bridgeman's expertise in this area, especially as a rival plan for the Corporation of King's Lynn was being prepared by Thomas Badeslade, a topographical draughtsman, and John Armstrong, the Chief Engineer of England.

Whenever his career as a landscape architect actually began, Bridgeman was probably working, at some point before 1709, as a draughtsman and a surveyor for Henry Wise. Wise was an important figure in gardening in the last part of the seventeenth century and the early part of the eighteenth. He became a partner with George London in Brompton Park Nursery, when Moses Cook sold his share in it to him in 1689, eight years after it was founded. Brompton Park Nursery was highly successful in the design and construction of gardens and the provision of plants for them (Harvey 1974b, 56). Harvey suggests that its continued success was due to the partnership of George London and Henry Wise; while London visited the gardens, Wise administered the Nursery (Jacques and van der Horst 1988, 29). Jacques and van der Horst suggest that the purpose of the nursery was 'threefold: to provide plants of all descriptions; to regularise the use of correct names, particularly of fruit trees; and to undertake the design and construction of gardens' (Jacques and van der Horst 1988, 28). Harvey shows how successful it was; in 1685, only four years after its establishment, the business had the organisational capacity to send an order for 200 apple trees, 50 pears, 100 gooseberries and peaches, nectarines and mulberries to Woburn (Harvey 1974b, 56). Green, Henry Wise's biographer, suggests that London and Wise were joined at Brompton Park Nursery by 'foreman and apprentices', and that Bridgeman was one of these. He shows that a number of Bridgeman's contemporaries also worked there: Stephen Switzer replaced Leonard Meager as foreman, and Joseph

Carpenter was 'among the lesser recruits' (Green 1956, 31). Green's suggestion is that Bridgeman joined them at a later date (Green 1956, 31). Green assumes that Bridgeman worked extensively as Wise's draughtsman: 'Wise, it is true, was no accomplished draughtsman; but what did that matter with Bridgman to draw for him as Hawksmoor often drew for Vanbrugh?' (Green 1956, 185). Bridgeman may have been the surveyor referred to in a quotation from Wise's 'State of the Royal Gardens and Plantations at Ladyday 1713': 'For making Severall Surveys and Draughts of Her Majesty's Palaces, Gardens, Parks and Plantations Mr. Wise never had or Craved any thing, tho' he has kept one Man constantly in pay and sometimes more for that purpose ...' (Green 1956, 105). If it is the case, it may well be that the collaboration between Wise and Bridgeman predates 1709. It is possible that an unfinished plan of Hampton Court in Gough Drawings (a4 fo.62), which shows the Lower Wilderness Garden as a blank rectangle yet to be planted, may be the earliest of Bridgeman's drawings. It may have been done for Wise in 1701/1702 when Bridgeman was around 16. He was certainly working for Wise again in 1711, as his collaboration with James Fish the younger on the survey of Wise's new property, Warwick Priory, in 1711 shows.

There is scant evidence of what, other than Sacombe, Bridgeman was doing between 1714 and 1716. As noted above, he was certainly working at Stowe. There are two notes from 1716: one from 11 August 'in which Bridgeman acknowledges payment of £188.16s.0d from William Jacob (then steward at Stowe), and the other from 16 August, in which Bridgeman asks Jacob for a further £20.0s.0d' (Willis 2002, 109 n. 14). Whether he was working anywhere else is not clear, but once we reach 1720 there is far more reliable, specific evidence of his projects, although not all of it can be fitted reliably into any kind of chronology. Even the partial picture the evidence paints suggests that the 1720s and much of the 1730s were highly successful and filled with breathless activity. Perhaps through some familial connections he was employed at Wimpole Hall in Cambridgeshire and at Down Hall in Essex. They are linked by the involvement of Edward Harley, Earl of Oxford, who employed Bridgeman to remodel the gardens at Wimpole Hall, and who had bought Down Hall for his friend, the diplomat and poet Matthew Prior, and to whom it reverted on the death of Prior in 1721. He was probably working at Rousham House in Oxfordshire, the seat of Colonel Robert Dormer-Cottrell, at a similar time. In the early 1720s there were also commissions from three men connected with the South Sea Company, Francis Hawes, Sir John Fellowes and Robert Chester, and for four others whose money came from commerce: Benjamin Styles at Moor Park, Jeremy Sambrooke at Gobions, Sir William Gore at Tring in Hertfordshire, and Samuel Tufnell at Langleys in Essex. He may also have been engaged in the reshaping of Westbury in Sussex for Admiral Philip Cavendish, who had bought the estate in 1722, and he was almost certainly working at Eastbury in Dorset for 'Bubb' Doddington. He also began work at Hackwood in Hampshire, owned by the 2nd Duke of Bolton. In 1723 Bridgeman was working on a major design for the Earl of Orkney at Cliveden. There were also projects at Houghton for Sir Robert Walpole, at Wolterton for Walpole's brother Horatio, at King's College, Cambridge, at Kedleston, at Marble Hill, at Richmond Palace, probably at Pope's garden at Twickenham, together with the aforementioned 1724 study of the drainage of the fens, 'A Report of the present State of the Great Level of the Fens ...', all before 1726, when he was appointed Royal Gardener.

Bridgeman was appointed joint Royal Gardener with Henry Wise following the death of Joseph Carpenter (NA Work 6/114), and became sole Royal Gardener from Lady Day 1728, following Wise's retirement (NA Work 6/114 fo.12v–15v and 16/39/1). It is not clear what led to Bridgeman's appointment as, although his close working relationship with Henry Wise, his connection with Sir Robert Walpole, with the Prince and Princess of Wales through his work at Richmond, and his familial associations with other master craftsmen already working for the Office of Works, must all have contributed, directly or indirectly, to it. Practically, this was probably also an important moment in Bridgeman's career; the total remuneration per annum, stipulated in his contract, was £2220, paid in quarterly instalments of £555. This money, equivalent to around £500,000 today, even when outgoings for labourers and materials were taken out, must have provided a level of background income which made Bridgeman's career secure and underpinned whatever private work he chose to take on. His appointment as Royal Gardener suggests that he was also held in high esteem by the ruling elite and by other craftsmen and artists. Presumably not coincidentally, he was also elected in the same year to the Virtuosi of St Luke, a small but prestigious society of artists whose members at the time included Gibbs, Thornhill, Wootton (all elected in 1716), and Vertue (elected with Bridgeman).

Bridgeman's appointment as Royal Gardener did not curtail his private activities. There were two very lucrative contracts for the construction and landscaping of two London Squares. For one, the construction of St James's Square in 1726, undertaken with his brother-in-law John Mist, the Minutes of the Trustees of St James's Square record he was paid £5630. It is possible that Bridgeman was involved in at least two other landscapes in 1726, both probably in collaboration with Nicholas Dubois, Master Mason in the Office of Works: Audley End and Stanmer. It is also likely that Bridgeman was the draughtsman of the plan for a remodeled landscape at Warwick Priory (WO CR. 56); and of the landscape at Bower House near Havering-atte-Bower, c. 1729, although the only evidence for this is a plaque over the door which reads 'H.FLITCROFT. ARCHITECTUS. C.BRIDGEMAN. DESIDNAVIT'. Between 1729 and 1730 he worked at Lodge Park in Gloucestershire, and in 1731 he certainly worked at Ledston Hall in Yorkshire for Lady Betty Hastings. He began working for the Duchess of Marlborough at some point after 1732, when she began to build a house in Wimbledon Park. Although there are apparently no surviving plans, Bridgeman was clearly employed at Badminton House in 1733 for the 3rd Duke of Beaufort, and by 1734 at Brocket Park in Hertfordshire, the home of Sir Thomas Winnington, a close political ally of Sir Robert Walpole. He may also have done some work at Esher Place for Henry Pelham. After 1735 it appears that there were only three new commissions, at Goldings in Hertfordshire for Thomas Hall in 1735, at Longford Castle in Wiltshire between 1736 and 1737, and – what seems to have been his last commission – at Amesbury Abbey in 1738.

There were also contracts which involved maintenance of established gardens, which Bridgeman seems to have run alongside the new commissions he undertook. Some of these contracts involved the maintenance of projects he was completing. The contract for work on Kensington Gardens makes provision for this (NA Work 6/114). In other cases it is not clear whether Bridgeman had any part in the design, but the regularity of the payments to him from 1724 onwards suggests that he was responsible for the upkeep on a routine basis of the gardens of Montagu House in London for the Duke of Montagu. A receipt for £25, held at Boughton House in the Buccleugh Archives and dated 4 August 1731, reads 'Rec[ceive]d then of his Grace the Duke of Montague by the Hands of Mr Andrew Marchant, the Sum of Twenty five pounds in full for one In[s] keeping the Gardens at Montague House to Mic[haelmas] last' and is signed 'Charles Bridgeman' (BH BM17) (see Figure 16). Again, as his work as Royal Gardener clearly shows, being contractually responsible for the ongoing maintenance of his design after construction was part of a design brief. There is also a possibility that a similar arrangement was in place at Compton Place in Sussex, where Bridgeman was paid £120 annually between 1729 and 1738. The same arrangement seems to have existed at Richmond; Sarah Bridgeman made a request to the Treasury, after Bridgeman's death, for payment of debts 'for keeping the Royall Gardens at Richmond, by Contract, and Extra Bills there, ye Sum of £1847.8s.5d' (NA CCXCIX (T.1:299) 10, fos.23–24). The correspondence of the Duchess of Marlborough to Sarah Bridgeman after Bridgeman's death shows that she had a similar arrangement with him.

There does seem to have been a slowing of activity in the three years before his death, perhaps because he was succumbing to ill health, probably to the dropsy from which he eventually died. (Dropsy is a term used to denote oedema, caused by heart failure or kidney failure (Peitzman 2007)). Sufferers would find movement difficult, since fluid accumulates in the lower limbs, but would also struggle with breathing, especially when lying down. It seems probable that this condition would have limited his movements and his ability to work. There are several other pointers to this. In 1736, Bridgeman purchased The Bell Inn at Stilton. Plans for this inn are held in Gough Drawings (BoL MSGD a3 fos. 40r and 40v, a4 fo.3 and a4 fo.51) but an annotation on the back of MSGD a4 fo.51 suggests that they were done by Mr Ransom. It is probable that 'Mr Ransom' worked for Bridgeman as a draughtsman (see Chapter 3), but it may also be significant that a survey which required some travel was done by someone else. There is also evidence that his performance as Royal Gardener was suffering. Minutes of the Board of Works for the period after his death record that when George Lowe took over as gardener at Hampton Court after Bridgeman's death he reported to the Board that the 'state & Condition of His Majestys Orangery, Exoticks & other Plants, as likewise the Melon Frames doth find that greatest part of the Tubs (in which the Trees are planted) and likewise the frames in Mellon Ground are in so Ruinous a condition, that there is necessity of making a great part new and thoroughly repairing the other; that His Majesty's Plants and Fruit may be preserved' (NA Work 1/1), suggesting that Bridgeman had not been attending closely to the day-to-day running of the garden. He may also have struggled to reach Amesbury and, again, it is perhaps significant that the survey of the hill fort known locally as Vespasian's Camp, which comprises part of Bridgeman's design here, for BoL MSGD a3* fo.32, is inaccurate, unprecedented in Bridgeman's corpus. It may also be the reason why Jacob Bouverie, at Standlynch, was 'at a loss for Bridgeman's company'; and why Bridgeman's excuse for his absence from Goldings in c.1735 is 'I have for this fortnight been laid up with a terrible broken shin & under the surgeons hands', an ailment which may have been connected with oedema.

Bridgeman died on 19 July 1738, as reported by Boyer in his *Political State of Great Britain*, at 'his House in Kensington' (Willis 2002, 41). His death was also reported in a number of other publications (Willis 2002, 41 n. 84). The inventory taken, on behalf of Sarah Bridgeman, after his death suggests that he died a man of substance. He left the house in Broad Street, although the inventory suggests that this was 'of Little or no Value' because the lease had only 15 years to run, the house in Henrietta Street with a lease of 99 years, of which only seven had run, and the plates for the 'Views of Lord Cobham's Seat and Gardens'. The inventory also states that Bridgeman was owed 'divers Sumes of Money ... from the Crown and several of the Nobility and Gentry', although it was not possible 'till the Accounts thereof can be made up and adjusted' to say quite how much was owed. His will, dated 6 July 1738, apparently left a considerable estate (NA PROB.II.692). He left his wife, Sarah, £300 and the interest of £600 'now in the hands of Thomas Rea Esquire and Mr George Devall Plumber'. She was also to have £80 a year from The Bell Inn in Stilton and a house in Henrietta Street, to be paid in half yearly instalments. He left his son Charles the Bell Inn and its lands, and the copyhold of the house in Henrietta Street, and each of his daughters £2000 on their reaching 21. Bridgeman certainly believed that, even after the funeral expenses and these legacies had been paid, there would be a residue: '... and if my personall Estate should be more than sufficient (as I apprehend it will) for the payment of my Debts Funeral Charges and Legacies aforesaid Then the residue or surplus I give to my beloved Wife during her natural life and at her death to such of her Children as she shall think fit ...' (NA PROB.II.692).

In fact, this appears not to have been the case. There are a number of indications that Bridgeman left his wife, Sarah, in straitened circumstances. Bridgeman was clearly owed money at his death, and some of those debts seem to have proved hard to collect. Sarah Bridgeman attempted to recover £5541.12s.8½d from the Treasury, including £600 owed from the time of George I (NA CCXCIX (T.1:299)

10, fos.23–24). She also wrote several letters to Sarah, Duchess of Marlborough, asking for payment of debts, although only the Duchess of Marlborough's replies survive (BP MSS F1–35, and Letter Book No.2 fos.24r––25v). Debts of £880.17s.0d were eventually paid to Elizabeth Price, Bridgeman's second daughter, in 1748, by the Duchess of Marlborough's executors. Sarah Bridgeman also offered plans for the Royal Gardens to the Treasury and to the Office of Works, and made a number of attempts through booksellers to sell Rigaud's engravings of Stowe. It seems likely that Bridgeman's estate did not amount to 'the sum of some twenty thousand pounds or some such large sum …' that Bridgeman's eldest daughter, Sarah, estimated in her deposition supporting her claim for the £2000 left her by her father in his will (NA C11/1596/8).

What emerges from this overview of Bridgeman's career and probable origins is a picture of a successful artist and practitioner, talented, and highly regarded in his field. He certainly is Matthew Prior's 'virtuoso grand jardinier' (virtuoso great gardener) and 'operator hortorum et sylvarum' (maker of gardens and of woods) (LL HMC 58:Bath III, 483). However, all of this gives us very little sense of who he was, of his personality and of his relationships. There are a few extant letters written by Bridgeman to others, in which we might hope to hear his voice, but they are largely functional and transactional, and, as we might expect, to do with the business of landscape design or with oiling the wheels of his dealings with his social superiors. The purpose of his letter to the poet Alexander Pope on 28 September 1724 is the delivery of the plan for Marble Hill: '[O]n Saturday morning I begun on the plan & and have not [lef]t off from that time to this so long as I could see nor shall I leave it till 'tis finished which I hope will be about tomorrow Noon …' (BL Add MS 4809, fo.141V). His long letter to Horatio Walpole, brother of Robert Walpole, dated 22 August 1736 is a rehearsal of the work done and an exposition of the work to be done at Wolterton in Walpole's absence: 'wee have orderd to be cleard of trees to the above width of the Terrace & the end of the house; & to be levelld & sewd wth grass seeds : the trees so taken up to go towards planting up the walks in that ground as you had agreed to'(8/12 Box 3LX). Two letters are not about gardening but are formulaic letters to social superiors. The letter from Bridgeman to the Earl of Oxford on 26 June 1734, which congratulates him on the marriage of his daughter, is the letter of an artist to his patron: 'I hope Your Lord[shi]ps goodness will permit me in this manner, tho' late, to congratulate Your Lord[shi]p, and my Lady Oxford, on the marriage of Lady Margaret with his Grace the Duke of Portland …' (BL Loan 29/90 Portland Papers). Lady Margaret was married on 11 July 1734. The letter to Viscount Townsend (29 September 1733) concerning the voting intention of his cousin in Hertford is in a similar register: '… my good Friend & Patron orderd me to desire my Cosin Bridgeman not to engage his vote' (Willis 2002, 156). The letters Bridgeman wrote to Thomas Hall, perhaps more of a social equal, at Goldings in 1735 are also largely about the practicalities of landscape design, but convey some sense of the personal. As well as the reference to the injury to his shin quoted above, there are thanks for presents: 'I return many thanks for your kind presents of arrack. I will endeavour to deserve them'. There is even some humour: 'I am at last returned off my journey & and will if alive and able attend you at Goldings before you come safe with your family to Town ......' (NA C103/133).

For more of a sense of Bridgeman, we fall back on reading between the lines of references to him by others. He seems to have been on comfortable terms with Adrian Drift, Matthew Prior's private secretary, who refers to him a number of times in correspondence with Lord Harley after Prior's death. He clearly visited Drift. Drift writes to Lord Harley: 'Mr Bridgman to whom I am much oblig'd, called on me this Morning, and told me that Mr Hartshorn had settled his Affairs by a Will, (which is found) wherein he has left his Wife executrix, so that when the Widow again sends to me I am ready if your Lordship pleases to pay her'. Drift is also assiduous in making sure that Bridgeman receives the Bust of Flora, the Roman goddess of flowers and the spring, which Prior apparently intended for him.

> Mr Prior having in his life-time bespoke of Mr Dickenson at high-park Corner (at which time I was with him) Two copies of the Buste of Flora for Messieurs Bridgman and Gibbs; which he recommended to Dickenson to do in perfection, as being designed a Present to two of his Brother Virtuosi. I beg, My Lord, You will on this head honour me with Your Commands for this I take to be a debt due to Two worthy Men whom he much Esteemed ... (BL Add MS 70362)

Drift's insistence suggests that Bridgeman and Prior may have been friends. He certainly visited Down Hall in Prior's company, and, although it was not unusual for Bridgeman to accompany his clients to the site, Drift's correspondence with Harley about the funeral does suggest something more than a business arrangement. Bridgeman was issued with a mourning ring after Prior's death and was apparently one of the first to be invited to his funeral:

> I do not know what other friends Mr Prior had except those you mention, except Mr Howard and Mr Southern and Mr Gay, and since I see Mr Bridgeman and Mr Gibbs named, I think Sir James Thornhill, Mr Wootton, Mr Dhael and Mr Richardson should be sent to, to come to the Funeral. (BL Add MS 70362)

The correspondence between Lord Harley, Prior and, after his death, Drift may tangentially confirm a link between Bridgeman and his father, and Lord Harley's estates at Wimpole and Down Hall. It is also clear that Bridgeman was on visiting terms with Alexander Pope. The same letter quoted above also reads:

> I have been continually abroad on business I knew not of; but of great moment, &of which You shall know more when I have the Honr. to see You ... the affair

> I mention to You above will not let me move from Home this fortnight, so shall be glad if Your affairs call you to Towne on Tuesday or any other day this week that I may explain it to you ... (BL Add MS 4809, fo.141V)

It is hard to tell whether this contact was transactional or an indication of habitual social contact.

In a search for Bridgeman, it is easy to be seduced by these glancing intimations of his personality and personal relationships. They may simply be how the conventions of eighteenth-century written communication were used to negotiate the strictly stratified society in which Bridgeman operated. In fact, they may not give away anything more about him than Hogarth's benign-faced portrait of him that hangs in Vancouver Art Gallery, and which Willis uses as the first plate in *Charles Bridgeman and the English Landscape Garden* (2002). It is, to a great degree, conjecture. He is, in fact, far more visible in the plans that make up the corpus of his work.

CHAPTER 2

TOWARDS A RELIABLE CORPUS

IN *CHARLES BRIDGEMAN and the English Landscape Garden* (originally published in 1977 and revised in 2002), Peter Willis draws together a collection of plans which he attributes to Bridgeman. They are published as black and white photographs. This form gives us a sense of the size of the body of work, but unrolling the real artefacts in the archives of the institutions where they are held is a much more exciting business. They come in a variety of sizes, colours, media and preservation. Some are bright, pristine watercolours, carefully conserved. Others are barely more than scraps of paper in which ink, pencil and wash jostle with each other. They would be significant even if written texts in which Bridgeman explained his artistic vision and working practices had survived, but in the absence of such documents, they become of crucial importance.

It is perhaps odd that the significance of these drawings has been overlooked. Art-historical scholarship, the discipline that is most closely associated with research in garden design, seems to regard them simply as evidence that Bridgeman worked at a site and of the style of his design. In fact, we can read the plans almost as well as we could if they were written texts. They can be interrogated and their meaning revealed through deconstruction. 'To deconstruct … is, so to speak, to reverse the imposing tapestry in order to expose to all its unglamorously dishevelled tangle of the threads constituting the well-heeled image it presents to the world' (Eagleton 1986 cited in Harley 2001, 159). By metaphorically turning over Bridgeman's plans, we can unpick the threads that compose their meaning. The plans are also artefacts; they have a materiality, composed of the paper or parchment of which they were made and the medium used to make the marks on them. As artefacts, they have a provenance, an origin and a subsequent story and a purpose, both one for which they were originally designed and one which might, at any stage, have been renegotiated (Johnson 1996, 187). They also have a language which can be read, composed of the marks made on the paper. Some marks are actually words and numbers, but most are a language of symbols and of decorative features which can nevertheless be read, since they are designed to convey meaning, both overt and implicit.

Willis's task of bringing together plans from a number of disparate sources to form his corpus was especially complicated, since only five plans can be reliably linked to Bridgeman: Windsor Forest (NA MR 1/279) (Figure 1), Blenheim

Palace (held at Blenheim Palace) (Figure 2), Hampton Court (SM 36/3/1) (Figure 3), Amesbury Abbey (MSGD a3* fo.32) (Figure 4) and the plan accompanying the survey of Warwick Priory (WO CR 26.2.2) which is identified as being partly by Bridgeman on the title page of an accompanying survey (WO CR 26.2.1). Willis categorises the first four as 'A: Signed drawings' (Willis 2002, 175), although none of these is actually signed in Bridgeman's hand with the signature that appears on his letter to Horatio Walpole about work at Wolterton, or on a receipt for £25 for work done at Montagu House in London (see Figure 16). However it is not unreasonable to categorise them as 'signed drawings' on the assumption that the presence of his name marks them as his work. There are 97 plans in the catalogue of the 1977 edition of Willis's book. His 2002 revision of the book amends this list, with additions and some subtractions, but the corpus remains roughly the same size. The final tally is 101, including two bird's-eye views, one of Boughton House in Northamptonshire, and one of Stowe (MSGD a4 fo.46), and four plans and surveys of parts of the Bell Inn in Stilton.[1]

Willis's method in creating his corpus uses these first four of the signed plans as a model to establish Bridgeman's draughtsmanship and design. From the style of these drawings, Willis identifies unsigned drawings as being 'probably' (his category 'B') or 'possibly' (his category 'C') by Bridgeman (Willis 2002, 175). This method seems to have produced a body of work which has been largely, though not completely, accepted by academics and by garden historians, although this may well be for lack of investigation rather than for sound academic reasons. However, by failing to distinguish between draughtsmanship and design, Willis's corpus conflates these two essentially separate areas of Bridgeman's expertise. This results in the mixing of three separate kinds of drawing: those which are simply in Bridgeman's hand and show no evidence of his designs, those that are his designs and probably in his hand, and those which look like his designs but appear not to have been drawn by him. Because the contents of his corpus are also informed by 'documentary evidence or published material' (Willis 2002, 175), Willis also adds a number of plans for landscapes where documentary evidence shows Bridgeman worked, even though the drawings themselves are apparently linked neither to Bridgeman's graphic techniques, nor to his style as a designer. Obviously for a re-evaluation of Bridgeman's work and his legacy in garden history, it is important to know, as far as it is possible, whether a plan is by Bridgeman, or whether it shows a Bridgeman landscape but is, for some reason, by someone else; or whether, in fact, it simply shows a landscape where Bridgeman probably worked, but otherwise is not connected with him at all. As a result, Willis's corpus probably needs some revision. We need a plan to fit into three separate investigative frameworks if we are to be able to place it reliably in a corpus of Bridgeman's work. We need to know the provenance of a plan, where and when it was created, where it has been since its creation, and why. We

---

[1] A full list of Willis's attributions and suggestions appears in Appendix I.

need to be able to evaluate whether the graphic style of the plan matches those four plans which we know were drawn by Bridgeman. We also need to know whether or not there is any documentary evidence which points to Bridgeman's involvement in a site.

The plans are material artefacts, with a history of ownership, which make up their provenance. Attribution would be far simpler if all Bridgeman's plans had remained in the archives of the houses and families for which the landscapes were designed, but, in fact, surprisingly few have. A plan of cascades and a canal is in the Scarsdale Collection at Kedleston Hall (SC Object 109274); two plans and a bird's-eye view are held at Boughton House; two plans for Lumley Castle, originally executed for the 2nd Earl of Scarborough, are currently held at Sandbeck House in the collection of the current Earl of Scarborough; a plan for Ledston is held at Otterden Place in Kent, the property of a distant relative of Bridgeman's client Lady Betty Hastings; and four plans of Wimpole Hall are held in the Bambridge Collection curated by the National Trust, at Wimpole Hall. We might also add to these a plan for Wimpole (BL Add MS 36278, MI) currently held in the British Library, which appears to have been part of the papers of the Earl of Hardwicke to whom Wimpole was sold in 1740 (BL Add MS 35349-36278). Presumably these were originally in the possession of Bridgeman's clients and have remained with the estate. This is certainly the supposition of Crispin Powell, archivist at Boughton House (pers. comm. 2015) and the Earl of Scarborough (pers. comm. 2019).

Sometimes it is possible to trace a direct line back to one of Bridgeman's clients, even though the plans are now held in another archive. For example, one of the two plans for Down Hall is part of the Harley Papers in the British Library (BL Loan 29/357) (see below), even though annotation on it reads 'Copy of the first Plan/for Down Hall' and it is inscribed on the back 'for Mr Prior 1720'. Although it is not immediately clear why a plan which appears to have been specifically designed for Prior should have been part of the Harley archive, it is probably because the Earl of Oxford was funding the development of Down Hall and owned half the freehold, so that, on Prior's death in 1721, the house and documents pertaining to it reverted to him.

A small number of plans can be traced to the estate of Henry Wise, Royal Gardener to Queen Anne from 1702 to her death in 1714, and then subsequently to George I and, briefly, George II, and joint proprietor of Brompton Park Nurseries. As we have seen, he was closely connected with Bridgeman on both counts. Most of these plans relate either to Wise's personal property or to his work jointly with Bridgeman. They all come from the Waller Collection, some parts of which were passed to the Warwickshire County Record Office by the Waller family, direct descendants of Wise, on the death of Sir Wathen Arthur Waller. This bequest is the source of the 'Survey of Warwick Priory and its attendant Manors' (WO CR 26.2.1), which identifies Bridgeman as one of its authors, and its accompanying map (WO CR 26.2.2). Willis assumes that it is the bird's-eye view at the bottom of the document for which Bridgeman is responsible, linking it to his bird's-eye view of Stowe. He suggests that 'it is too accomplished for his collaborator James Fish, the Younger ...' (Willis 2002, 184), a view endorsed by Dr Christine Hodgetts (pers. comm. 2016). A second version of this plan, without the bird's-eye view, is catalogued as CR 217. It is not clear whether this is also in part by Bridgeman, but it seems likely. The other plan is for Lillington Manor, part of Wise's newly acquired property (WO CR 556/197). Willis also plausibly attributes this to Bridgeman, too, since it is referred to in CR 26.2.1. (Another version of this plan was formerly at Lillington Vicarage, but has since been lost (Willis 2002, 181).)

However, the Warwickshire County Record Office was not the final destination for all the plans in the Waller Collection. Some were sold in a single sale of documents on 12 December 1947 at Christie's (Jeffrey Pilkington pers. comm. 2016). The sale catalogue identifies the contents of lots 126–131 as by Henry Wise, but it is clear that some plans are actually by Bridgeman. Contained within these lots is, in Lot 130, a watercolour plan of 'The Priory'. It was bought by a Mr Reinard. It has been returned to Warwickshire County Record Office where it is also catalogued as by Wise (WO CR 56), but its graphic style, and its design of a small amphitheatre of trees and avenues stretching down to a geometric lake which takes advantage of a damp valley of springs, strongly suggests it is by Bridgeman. There is a possibility that the plan of Blenheim, dated 1709, which now hangs on the wall at Blenheim Palace, was part of Lot 129 from the Christie's sale, which lists 'A Plan of Blenheim', together with 'two smaller versions of the same' and 'a preliminary draft of the same'. Unfortunately, the provenance of the drawing hanging at Blenheim is not recorded and so it is impossible to verify (John Forster and Karen Wiseman pers. comm. 2016). A preliminary sketch, shown in *Gardener to Queen Anne*, Green's monograph on Henry Wise, shows an almost identical, though less finished, version of the Blenheim Palace plan (Green 1956, plate 32). His reference for this plan is 'From a manuscript book in the possession of Mrs Disbrowe-Wise', which presumably means it was originally part of the Wise family archive. Green certainly suggests that he was responsible for diverting a plan of Blenheim to the Palace, sometime after 1947, although he is unspecific about the details. Writing in 1987, he says: 'Some thirty years ago Providence saw to it that I was able to divert this noble plan to the Great Hall at Blenheim, where it customarily hangs and surely belongs (Green in Bond and Tiller 1987, 76). Perhaps this is the plan that now hangs in the entrance hall there.

The plan for Greenwich Park, although now held in the Caird Library at the National Maritime Museum at Greenwich, also appears to have originally come from the sale of parts of the Waller Collection in 1947. It comes from Lot 128, and is recognisable by the wording in the catalogue, 'An Exact Plan of Greenwich Park', as CL CMP/30 now held in the Caird Library. Evidence suggests that this plan of Greenwich (CL CMP/30) was probably drawn by Bridgeman for Wise, executed for a private sale of land belonging to Wise. As well as this plan of

Greenwich, Lot 128 in the Christie's sale also included 'A small plan of Greenwich Hospital' which is reproduced by Green as Plate 17 (Green 1956). This plan, which is, as Green very plausibly suggests, through comparison to a bill for Melbourne, annotated in Wise's hand, shows only the Royal Hospital and its environs. To the west of the King William building, it shows a three-acre plot of land marked as 'Mr Wise's Ground'. This land was sold in 1714 to the Directors of Greenwich Hospital by a Mr Wise for £1800 for the erection of an Infirmary, because 'the original grant of land to the Hospital had been insufficient for any but the principal buildings and therefore any infirmary schemes were dependent on the acquisition of further ground', although this infirmary was not built on it until the 1760s (Bold 2000, 207–208). Both Bold and Green suggest that the seller of this land was Henry Wise, who Bold states was 'a big landowner around Deptford' (Bold 2000, 263 n. 25). The likelihood that both the plan CMP/30 and the smaller drawing relate to this sale is strengthened by the identical depiction in both of the, as yet unbuilt, hospital buildings. They are presented in a design put forward for these buildings by Hawksmoor in 1701, rather than the design to which they were finally built. Hawksmoor's proposal is reproduced by Bold as illustration 146 (Bold 2000, 107). Since Hawksmoor advised the Directors on the purchase of the land for the Infirmary (Bold 2000, 208), it is plausible to suggest that Bridgeman had access to that plan, through Wise, who had employed him in c.1714, to produce a presentation drawing of Greenwich Park, to show the land Wise was selling in the context of the rest of the park.

A significant number of the plans Willis attributes to Bridgeman are in the National Archives at Kew. They are all for Royal landscapes and have arrived there from the archives of a variety of government departments: some are from the Office of Works, subsequently the Ministry of Public Buildings and Works, but some are from the Treasury, the Office of Land Revenue and Enrolments, and, most surprisingly, one is from the War Office. It is hard to explain their complicated path to the National Archives via these government departments, but it is likely that Bridgeman originally produced most of them for the Office of Works, which was in charge of all construction work for the monarchy from the early medieval period until it became a government ministry in 1851 (Kerry Downes, http://www.oxfordartonline.com); it was effectively Bridgeman's client during the period he was Royal Gardener from 1726 to 1738. During this period the Office was run by a Board consisting of four members: the Surveyor General, the Comptroller, the Master Mason and the Master Carpenter. From 1719 onwards, the roles of Master Mason and Master Carpenter were held by architects rather than artisans, to stop them acting as contracting workmen (Colvin 1976, 48). In what Colvin refers to as its 'lower reaches' (Colvin 1976, 105), the Office of Works employed master artisans, one of whom, George Devall, Master Plumber, was Bridgeman's relation by marriage. The Board met once a week, with a General Meeting once a month attended by all the officers (Colvin 1976, 67–68).

Although we cannot rule out the possibility that some plans were retained by the Office of Works from the moment of their creation, many seem to have been in Bridgeman's possession when he died on 19 July 1738, and, as suggested in the previous chapter, were sold to the Board in two separate sales made by Sarah Bridgeman to alleviate what she refers to in her petition of the same year to the Lords of the Treasury as the 'very narrow Circumstances' (NA T 1/299; Willis 2002, 168). In 1738 Sarah Bridgeman offered the Lords of the Treasury '... Plans Curiously done by the Deceas'd, of all the Royall Gardens, which may be of Great Service to the Crown, and for which your Memorialist hopes may be worth £200.00'. Willis reproduces this document in his Appendix VI (Willis 2002, 168). It is not clear whether Sarah Bridgeman was paid for these plans. On a separate occasion, recorded in the minute book for 15 March 1743 for the Board of Works, Sarah Bridgeman sold plans of specified Royal gardens to the Board of Works:

> The Widow Bridgman having laid before the Board several fair drawings of His Majesty's Palaces & Royal Gardens of Hampton Court; Windsor Castle, Richmond and Kensington, the Board upon Examining them found them to be Correct and they being of great Use to this Office, Agreed to allow the Widow Bridgman the sum of Sixty pounds in full satisfaction to her for the said Drawings. (NA Work 4/8 cited in Willis 2002, 92)

Because these are the only documented sales of Bridgeman's plans, they may be the source of all his plans of the Royal Gardens in the National Archives. Most are finished plans that presumably would have had monetary value. It is hard to imagine that Sarah Bridgeman would have been able to sell unfinished or roughly annotated drawings to the Treasury or the Office of Works, but it is possible. Perhaps the second transaction with the Board of Works refers to the same drawings as those in Sarah Bridgeman's original petition, referred on from the Treasury and finally bought by the Office of Works, but it seems unlikely since the two sales are nearly five years apart.

The two sales are probably, then, the source of the seven plans held in the National Archives. Their cataloguing may well reflect which of the two sales they come from because National Archives prefixes denote where a document originated before the catalogue was rationalised. Plans from the Treasury have the prefix MPD. This makes it likely that Sarah Bridgeman's sale of plans to the Treasury is the source of the plan for Hampton Court (NA MPD 1/23) and the sketch of Lamp Row (now known as Rotten Row) (NA MPD 1/164). It seems unlikely that these plans alone would have been valued at £200 so it is possible that the sale also included other plans loosely connected with land revenue, and that these passed through the Treasury and on to other, perhaps more relevant, departments. They may have included the plan for Richmond Gardens (NA MR 1/696 or LRRO 1/399). The prefix MR denotes a document that was moved to rolled storage from another department (http://discovery.nationalarchives.

gov.uk). Its alternative catalogue number beginning with LRRO shows that it originated in the Office of Land Revenue and Enrolments. It has a key showing acreages, which suggests that its purpose was the measurement of land after the purchase of Richmond Park by the Prince of Wales and Princess Caroline in 1719. (All of this is conjecture. It is also equally plausible that, since they relate to the enrolments of grants and leases of crown lands, these surveys were originally done by Bridgeman for the Office of the Auditors of Land Revenue, and retained by them as an assessment of the value of crown lands). The plans from Willis's corpus with the prefix 'Work' may well have come from Sarah Bridgeman's second sale, this time to the Office of Works. The minutes are specific about the gardens these plans depict: 'Royal Gardens of Hampton Court; Windsor Castle, Richmond and Kensington Hampton Court'. This sale might then be the source of two plans of Richmond Gardens (NA Work 32/96 and 32/282), and possibly the plan of St James's Park (NA Work 32/70). The plan showing the bank of the Thames in Richmond Park (NA MR 1/528) is more of a puzzle and could have come from either sale. It apparently originated from the War Office (WO 78/1232). It is not clear why a survey by Bridgeman of the bank of the Thames in Richmond Park should be found in the War Office, which in the eighteenth century was the Office of the Secretary for War.

The Office of Works was probably the source of three other plans for Royal landscapes currently held in other archives. Two plans are held by Sir John Soane's Museum; one is for Hampton Court (SM 36/3/1), and the other for St James's Park (SM 62/1/1). While it is not certain how they arrived there, Stephen Astley speculates that they may have originally come from the Office of Works where Soane was one of the attached architects from 1813 to 1832. He believes that this was the case for other drawings (Stephen Astley pers. comm. 2013). Hovingham Hall holds a plan of the Lower Wilderness at Hampton Court. Sir William Worsley believes that the Office of Works was the source of the plan he holds. His ancestor Sir Thomas Worsley was Surveyor-General at the Office of Works under George III (Sir William Worsley pers. comm. 2014).[2]

There are other, more speculative links between the Office of Works and plans held in repositories both in England and abroad. There are plans for Royal landscapes, attributed to Bridgeman, held in the British Library, the Henry E. Huntington Library in San Marino, California, and the Nationalmuseum, Stockholm. The British Library plan is entitled 'Two different designs of Viewing the Thames & Country, from Great Elms, between Hampton Court Green and Hampton Town end' (BL Maps K. Top.XXIX 14.u). It is part of the King's Collection, a library of books and drawings established by George III after 1763 and donated to the British Museum in the nineteenth century (http://www.bl.uk/reshelp). It is therefore possible that this plan originated from Sarah Bridgeman's sale of material to the Office of Works, although it might originally have been held by

---

[2] See online at https://doi.org/10.1093/ref:odnb/63121

the Crown. The provenance of the two, almost identical plans of Kensington Gardens which are held in the Henry E. Huntington Library (HEH ST Map 147), and in the Cronstedt Collection in the Nationalmuseum in Stockholm (NS CC.2753), respectively, is more of a puzzle. The plan in the Nationalmuseum is part of the Cronstedt Collection, collected in the second half of the eighteenth century by Carl-Johan Cronstedt and his son F.A.U. Cronstedt. Although neither is known to have visited England, F.A.U. Cronstedt visited France and Italy on his Grand Tour in 1770–1773 (Magnus Olausson pers. comm. 2016). The provenance of the plan bought by Henry E. Huntington (1850–1927), a railway magnate and collector of antiquarian books, is also unknown. It may be of relevance that the provenance of the plans held in the British Library and the Cronstedt Collection can be traced back to the latter part of the eighteenth century, as, in fact, can those held in Sir John Soane's Museum and at Hovingham Hall. It is possible that, while they might all have left the Office of Works in separate ways, they might also have been part of a sale of manuscripts in the late eighteenth century.

However, by far the greatest number of plans, roughly one third of Willis's corpus, are in the Gough Collection, documents bequeathed to the Bodleian Library by Richard Gough (1735–1809), an antiquary, on his death in 1809.[3] Gough's father died in 1751 and, when his mother died in 1774, he inherited great wealth. He was interested almost exclusively in British topography and antiquities, and collected a large library of books, maps and engravings, chiefly to do with topography, including many volumes from the libraries of antiquarians such as Reverend Francis Blomefield, author of a county history of Norfolk, and Peter Le Neve, the first president of the Society of Antiquaries. He published *British Topography* in 1768 and 1780, *The Sepulchral Monuments of Great Britain* in 1786, and an augmented version of *Camden's Britannia* in 1806. The Bodleian Library has no record of how Bridgeman's drawings were collected by Gough (pers. comm. Colin Harris). Nearly 40 years separate Bridgeman's death and Gough's inheritance of his fortune. Willis suggests two possible routes by which the plans might have come into the Gough Collection, neither of which is particularly convincing. One is that Gough inherited the drawings from his father, Harry Gough, who was a confidante of Sir Robert Walpole (Willis 2002, 174). He does not suggest how Harry Gough came to have them or why they would have been of interest to him. The second is that Gough bought them at the sale of the possessions of the politician and antiquary, James West, in 1773. A page in one of West's manuscripts notes that he bought 'books, medals and prints' at 'Mrs: Bridgeman's Sale'. Although undated, this entry falls between 21 February 1742 and 15 June 1743. It is possible that the sale referred to in West's notes is of Sarah Bridgeman's possessions. Sarah Bridgeman's Will was proved on 21 January 1744, suggesting that she did not die until the end of 1743 (PROB 31/244/57). However, Willis points out that the note could refer to a sale

---

[3] See online at https://doi.org/10.1093/ref:odnb/11141

in February 1743 of the library of a Mrs Katherine Bridgeman (Willis 2002, 174 n. 4). This does seem more plausible. The sale of Mrs Katherine Bridgeman's library, and subsequently of the contents of her house, was advertised in the *Daily Advertiser* from January to March 1743, and amongst the items advertised are 'Coins and Medalions' (Burney Collection). If the sale is of Mrs Katherine Bridgeman's library, then it is unlikely that this is the route by which Gough came by Bridgeman's drawings.

The plans in Gough Drawings probably need to be considered as a cohesive whole, because they do not appear to have been collected piecemeal. They were certainly catalogued together in 1809 when the Collection was bequeathed to the Bodleian Library. The *Summary Catalogue* of 1809 lists those drawings for which a location has been identified, on pages 167 and 168, under numbers 17593 and 17594. A handwritten note which is undated but clearly written after the publication of Willis's book in 1977, on the page facing p. 168, draws the reader's attention to Willis's catalogue. The plans were classified under their size and placed in a3 or a4, by the librarian John Nichols (Colin Harris pers. comm. 2013). There is a partial typed list of those in MSGD a4 and a handwritten list of the contents of MSGD a3 (Colin Harris pers. comm. 2013). Other than these, there appears to be no full catalogue description of Gough Drawings a3 or a4 in the Bodleian Library (Colin Harris pers. comm. 2013). Fifteen plans are held in Gough Drawings a3, and 45 in a4. Those catalogued in a4 are all presented as separate documents, grouped in folders, making it easy to examine the reverse sides. All but three of those catalogued as a3 are stuck into a single bound volume, sometimes making it difficult to examine the manuscript. The remaining three, of Kensington Gardens (MSGD a3* fo.7), of Eastbury (MSGD a3* fo.9) and of Amesbury (MSGD a3* fo.32), are presented individually in a single folder. Both a3 and a4 contain drawings which Willis does not identify as by Bridgeman, and are probably not by him. Some, such as a survey of Great Eltham from 1750 (MSGD a3 fo.2), clearly postdate Bridgeman. In the original 1809 catalogue there was a drawing of Boughton House, which is now no longer there. It is possible that this is one of the two plans now held at Boughton.

This evidence suggests that the drawings entered the Gough Collection together, and, as far as it is possible to establish, the history of the drawings immediately after Bridgeman's death seems to corroborate this. It appears that after Sarah Bridgeman's death, the plans in Gough Drawings a3 and a4 passed into the hands of Clement Lemprière (1683–1746), an artist and cartographer born in Jersey, who was appointed Draughtsman to the Civil Branch of the Ordnance Survey in 1727 (The Biographical Dictionary of Jersey by George Balleine cited at http://www.theislandwiki.org/index) and who had an office in the Tower of London where military draughtsmen were housed (Sponberg Pedley 2005, 24). At the time of her death, Sarah Bridgeman was also living in the Tower of London, although it is not clear why (NA PROB 31/244/57). Sarah Bridgeman's will appointed Lemprière as her executor, and one of two guardians of her daughter Anne (NA PROB 31/244/57). One set of drawings in Gough Drawings a3, 'Diagrams and descriptions of fortifications and different terrains' (MSGD a3 fos. 82-86), dated 1715, is catalogued by the Bodleian as by Lemprière. It is possible that some of the other drawings in a3, for example a plan of the town of Nassau in New Providence (MSGD a3 fo.20), architectural drawings of a temple in Sicily (MSGD a3 fos. 21, 22, and 23), Vigo in Portugal (MSGD a3 fo.34), and 'A Draught of Great and Little Exuma' and 'a Draught of Stocking Island Harbour', both in the Bahamas (MSGD a3 fo.35), may also have been drawn by him, since he is known to have visited and sketched in those locations (The Biographical Dictionary of Jersey by George Balleine cited at http://www.theislandwiki.org/index). A further drawing, originally catalogued as by Bridgeman (MSGD a4 fo.47), may well also be by Lemprière. It appears to be a map of the mouth of a river.

Legal documents held at the National Archives suggest that Bridgeman's drawings passed to Lemprière probably as a result of his executorship of Sarah Bridgeman's will, and possibly his friendship with her. The legal documents pertain to the suit of Sarah Bridgeman, the eldest daughter of Charles and Sarah, who sued first her mother and then, after her mother's death, Lemprière, to recover the £2000, left to her in her father's will to be inherited when she reached the age of 21, which she did sometime early in 1741 (C11/1596/8) (Willis 2002, 148). It appears from her deposition that she believed that her mother had deliberately defrauded her of her inheritance by a variety of obfuscating tactics, including 'pretending that your Ora[tri]x father never made any such Will or gave any such Legacy to your Ora[tri]x as herein before set forth' and insisting 'very untruly that the said Charles Bridgeman your Ora[tri]x said father died greatly indebted to several persons in divers Large sums of money amounting in the whole to much more of his personal estate' (C11/1596/8).

Whatever the truth about Bridgeman's wealth, after her mother's death and at some point before 21 January 1744, the date on which her mother's will was proved by Clement Lemprière, Sarah Bridgeman the daughter began proceedings against Clement Lemprière. His 'Answer' of 2 April 1744, exonerating himself from having appropriated any of the estate after Sarah Bridgeman's death, contains a reference to what appears to be the drawings:

> And he further says that no part of the Estate or Effects of the Plaintiff's said late Father or Brother have at any time before or since the death of his said Testatrix come to his hands custody possession or knowledge except the Copperplates of the several views of Stow Gardens & about two hundred setts of prints of the same views & a *parcel of other odd prints* and Drawings of Plans of various kinds & twenty pictures of various sorts part of the Estate & Effects of the Plaintiff's said late Father remaining unsold in the custody of his said Testatrix at the time of her death & are now in the Defendant's custody ready to be disposed of as the Hono[ur]able Court shall think fit … [my italics]. (C11/1842/23)

It seems likely that the 'parcel' referred to was, in fact, the drawings now in Gough Drawings a3 and a4.

There are two possibilities which might explain how these drawings came into Gough Drawings. Lemprière died in 1746. A note in the margin of Sarah Bridgeman's will states that:

> On the Sixteenth day of October in the Year of our Lord 1746 Admcon (with the Will annexed) of the Goods, Chattels and Credits of Sarah Bridgeman late of the Tower of London Widow dece'd left unadminstered by Clement Lemprière one of the Ex[ecu]tors named in the said Will now also dece'd was granted to Elizabeth Price (Wife of Philip Price) the Daughter and one of the residual Legatees named in the said Will ... (PROB 11/731)

Elizabeth Price was Bridgeman's second daughter. Either the drawings had already been sold privately by the time Lemprière died, or, much more likely, Bridgeman's and Lemprière's drawings passed together to Elizabeth Price after Lemprière's death in 1746. It is possible that their fate was tied to that of the etched copper plates of the views of Stowe, and two hundred prints from those plates, which Lemprière states were in his possession in 1744. These views of Stowe, commissioned by Bridgeman from the French artist Rigaud at a cost, variously estimated by the classified sections of the newspapers, of £1400 and £2400, had been advertised for sale in 1739 through London booksellers and print makers, immediately after his death, by Sarah Bridgeman 'at the Proposer's House in Broad-Street' for 'four guineas'. It is not clear whether any were sold, but certainly a large residue of the prints, and the plates themselves which remained in Sarah Bridgeman's possession at the time of her death, passed to Lemprière, as his deposition suggests, and may have passed to Elizabeth Price in 1746 on Lemprière's death. It seems likely that this is the case because the views were offered for sale by the London booksellers T. and J. Bowles, C. Hitch and W. M. Toms, in the Classified sections of a variety of newspapers in London and Dublin, between 22 February 1746 and 1 May 1752. After 1752, the advertisement disappears from the Classified sections (Burney Collection). It is also interesting, in this regard, that Toms sold engravings of Lemprière's sketches, made by Boydell, between 1738 and 1754 (www.cichw1.net/pmlempri.html). It is plausible that the drawings had passed to one of these booksellers with the views of Stowe, but were not perceived to have any saleable value. They are not listed with the views of Stowe in any advertisements (Burney Collection). It is possible that they remained in the possession of one of the booksellers and were eventually sold, once an interest in Bridgeman's work had been rekindled, perhaps by Horace Walpole's *History of Modern Gardening*, possibly to Gough himself. It is more likely that their connection with Bridgeman was lost when they became separated by one of the booksellers from the plates of Stowe, and identifying his authorship would have been difficult as his name only appears on the plan for Amesbury Abbey. Annotations on the reverse of a number of drawings suggest that attempts have been made to identify the client for whom the plan was intended. These are in two distinctly different hands. One is polished, and may be a designation written by Bridgeman or his draughtsman, or part of the cataloguing process after the plans were bought by Gough. For example, we find 'Mr Stiles' on the plan for Moor Park (MSGD a4 fo.58), and 'Esq Walpole' on the reverse of the plan for Houghton (MSGD a4 fo.57). However, there are also some annotations on the reverse in a much untidier hand, always on the very edge of the plan, which may be notes written about it by a bookseller. Perhaps notes on the very edge would have been easier to read when the plans were in a pile. For example, on the edge of the plan for Mereworth (a4 fo.52) there is an annotation which reads 'a small plan without a name', heavily scored out, and then 'Lord Northumberland but of no use now'. This may indicate that at first a bookseller was unable to identify the plan at all, and then, that having identified it, realised that in its unfinished state it had no saleable value. Interestingly, in this regard, on the plan for Hackwood (a4 fo.24), in the same handwriting, and in a similar place, a note reads 'to be sold'. Probably, then, a provenance from the Gough Drawings makes it more likely than not that a plan is by Bridgeman, although obviously not all the plans in Gough Drawings are by him.

Of course, we cannot easily trace the provenance of all the plans that Willis suggests are by Bridgeman. The plan for Claremont (SM 62/1/2), for example, held at Sir John Soane's Museum, was probably collected by Sir John Soane, but where he collected it from is less clear. The second plan, for Down Hall, is in the topographical section of the Gough Collection, in Gough Maps, in a bound volume (BoL Gough Maps 46, fo.262). It is not clear how it was collected by Gough. However, the provenance of the vast majority of Bridgeman's plans can be traced and this is very helpful in establishing a reliable corpus.

Another way of establishing whether a drawing is Bridgeman's is to analyse its graphic style. Unfortunately, the process of using mark making to establish authorship is complicated by the possibility that a number of draughtsmen were involved in the preparation of Bridgeman's plans. In fact, it is possible to see more than one hand in a number of the drawings; for example, on the plans for Boughton and for Rousham (BoL MSGD a4 fo.63) (see Figure 6), very much more crudely drawn trees have been added in pencil. The name of another draughtsman and surveyor, Mr Ransom, actually appears on the plans for the Bell Inn at Stilton.

It appears to have been common practice that the drawing of estate maps, commercial maps and garden designs was a collaborative process. As Harley suggests, 'Most maps are the product of a division of labour' (Harley 2001, 38). It is likely that this was also true for the creation of plans for landscape designs, and it is partly what makes the attribution of a design so difficult. Henry Wise, Bridgeman's predecessor in the role of Royal Gardener, employed draughtsmen, one of whom was Bridgeman (see above), and Stephen Switzer, Bridgeman's contemporary in garden design, appears to have employed his son, certainly in the production of the plan for Beaumanor: 'T. Switzer, junr.' appears on the cartouche credited with ornamenting the plan (Brogden 1973). In the work of André Le Nôtre, landscape architect and principal gardener to Louis XIV, the collaborative nature of the drawing process is well documented. Bouchenot-Déchin suggests that the enormous amount of work required to produce a drawing must have precluded it being only the work of one hand. 'It is in no way surprising that at the final design stage of a project by Le Nôtre, its material representation – the presentation drawing – should be the work of his colleagues, considering the dozens of hours required by its realisation' (Bouchenot-Déchin and Farhat 2013).

It is clear from Bridgeman's letter to Alexander Pope about plans for Henrietta Howard, the mistress of King George II, probably for the landscape at Marble Hill, that he drew plans himself: 'I begun on the plann & have not [lef]t from that time to this so long as I could see nor shall [I] leave it till 'tis finished which I hope will be about tomorrow Noon' (Willis 2002, 156). It is interesting that Bridgeman deliberately chose to mark out his draughtsmanship in the four signed plans. Perhaps it was how, in a working environment where a number of draughtsmen were involved, he identified his own part in a work. The survey for Windsor Forest (NA MR 1/279) (Figure 1) is signed 'Bridgman Pinxit' on the cartouche, a term used from the late Renaissance onwards to denote the painter of a work of art. 'Pinxit' is commonly used when a drawing has been copied or engraved, to denote its original artist. It is difficult to date, but the National Archive online catalogue places it between 1702 and 1714, during the reign of Queen Anne (http://discovery.nationalarchives.gov.uk).

The plan of Blenheim, dated 1709 (Figure 2) is signed 'Bridgman discript.' which, as has been pointed out by Dalton, is much more likely to indicate that Bridgeman was the draughtsman rather than the designer (Dalton 2012, 86). The third, of Hampton Court (SM 36/3/1) (Figure 3), held in the Soane Museum, is signed 'Bridgman Fect.', the convention used since the medieval period by sculptors and painters to denote authorship of their work. The Soane Museum online catalogue states that it is 'datable after the completion of the new canal within the Fountain Garden and to the early stages of the laying out of the Lower Wilderness, both in 1711' (collections.soane.org/OBJECT466), both of which were laid out by Wise in his capacity as Royal Gardener. The fourth signed plan, that of Amesbury Abbey (BoL MSGD a3* fo.32) (Figure 4), is marked 'by Ch. Bridgeman' on the cartouche.

There is a remarkable quality of clarity about the depiction of the design in each plan, and a number of common graphic motifs. All use ink and watercolour. Trees, presumably deciduous, whether in grey or brown ink or in bright green watercolour, are depicted in a triangular shape, with foliage shadows to the right. Close examination shows a remarkable conformity in shape and detail. They are particularly impressive when presented in geometric plantations or

Figure 1. Windsor Forest. Credit: National Archives MR 1/279.

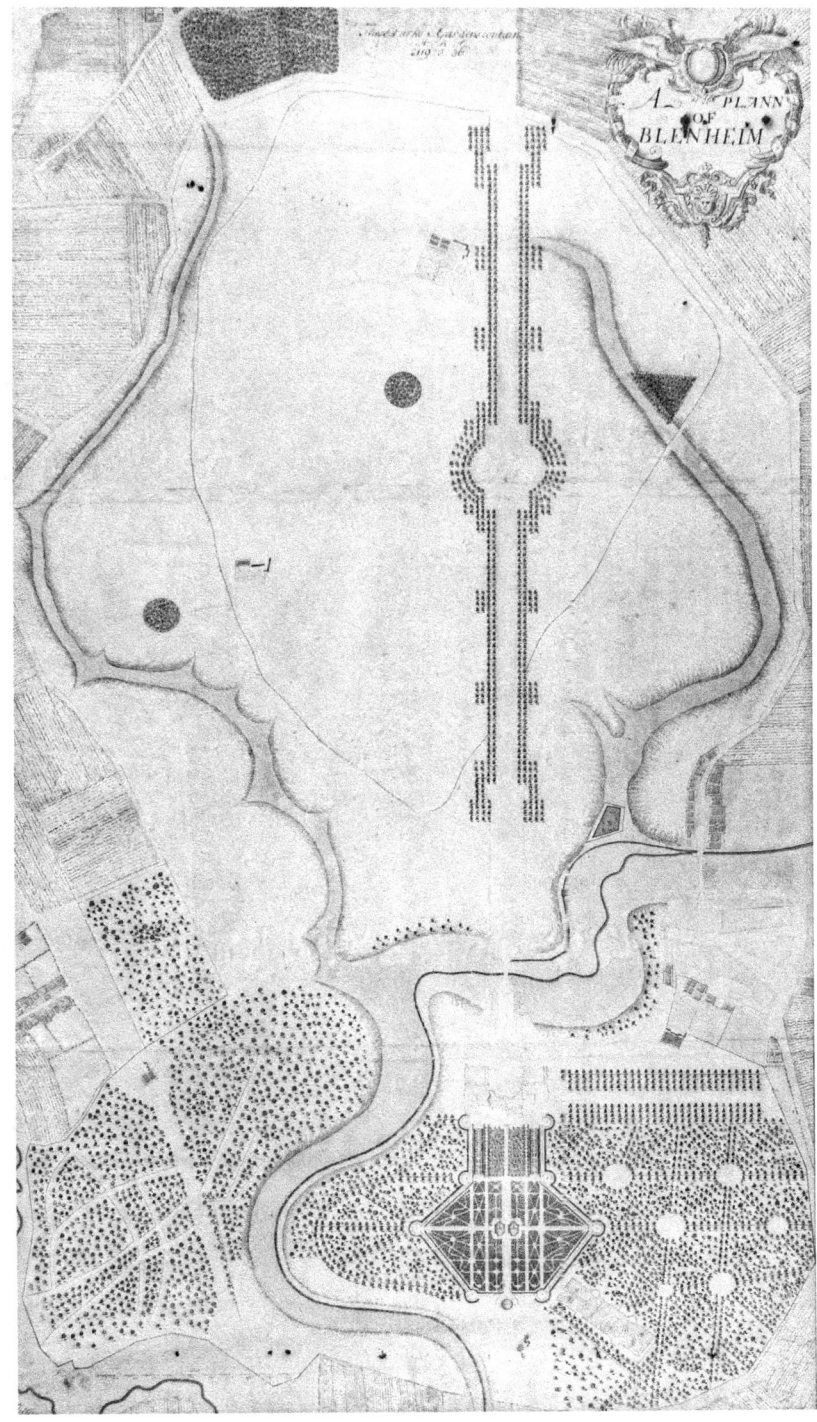

Figure 2. Blenheim Palace. Reproduced by kind permission of Blenheim Palace.

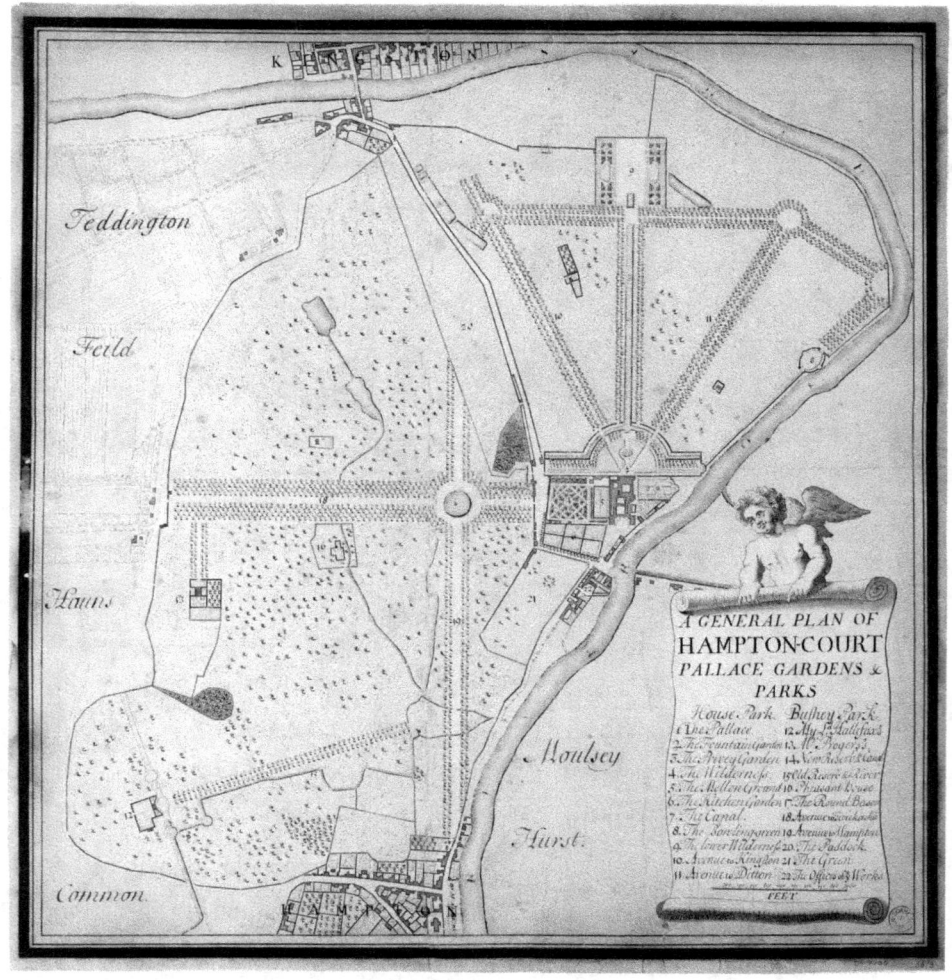

Figure 3. Hampton Court. SM 36/3/1 © Sir John Soane's Museum, London. Photograph by Ardon Bar-Hama.

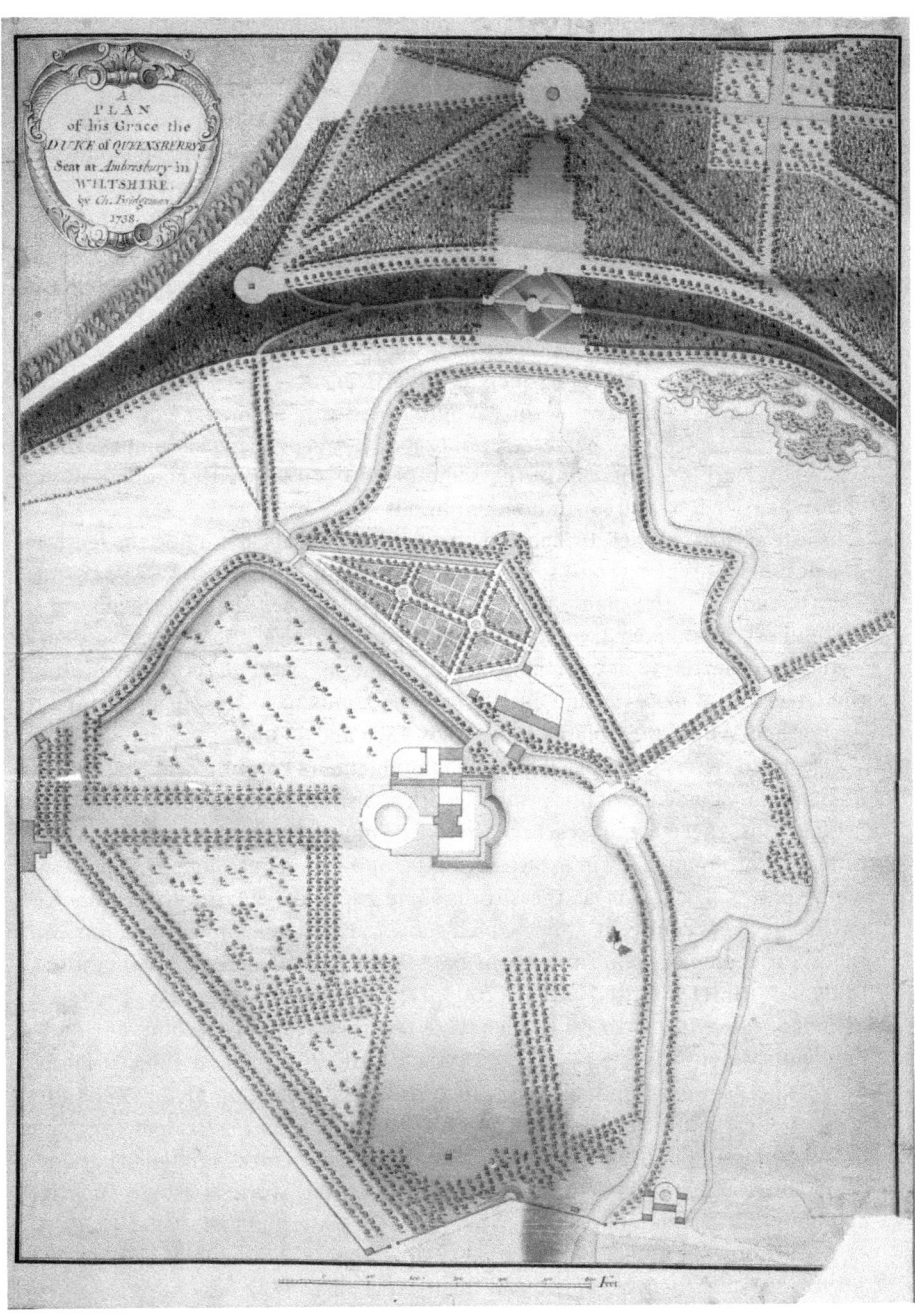

Figure 4. Amesbury Abbey. MSGD a3* fo.32. The Bodleian Libraries, University of Oxford.

avenues, where their careful, regular placing and uniform depiction suggests considerable precision. Arable fields, usually on the margins of the landscape, are depicted with straight furrows, and, where fields abut, these furrows are made to run at right-angles to each other. In the plan for Hampton Court (Figure 3), hedgerows are also sketched in. Buildings are shaded in pink and shown in plan. Water is shaded in blue, darker at its outer edges, and parterres are shown with meticulous, and often minute, detail. Shading is used in all but the plans of Hampton Court, which is a largely flat site, to denote the topography. At its simplest, in the plan of Blenheim (Figure 2), this takes the form of hatching to show how deeply incised the valley of the river Glynne is. In the plan for Windsor Forest (Figure 1), a single thick line delineates an area of higher ground. On the plan for Amesbury (Figure 4), deep shading is used to show the steepness of the slope down to the river Avon. Sophisticated three-dimensional effects are used for the depiction of parterres, pools and landscaped lawns. Compass roses, where they are present, are in the same pattern: circles with compass points shown as triangles, and north denoted by a fleur-de-lys.

These stylistic tropes, Bridgeman's way of symbolically depicting the features of a design, are replicated to some degree in most of the plans in Willis's corpus. Their meaning in the plan and the way Bridgeman uses them are explored in more depth in Chapter 3, but they are probably more reliably indicative than a signature or lettering of work in his hand, although, as Willis shows, by printing the lettering on plates facing each other, the hands have strong similarities to each other (Willis 2002, plates 162a, 162b, 163a and 163b).

The third criterion for placing a plan in Bridgeman's corpus is whether there is documentary evidence of Bridgeman's work at a site. Although there is relatively little of this, there are sites where there is firm written evidence, either in the form of a letter, an entry in estate accounts, or a payment from a bank account, which places Bridgeman at the site in some capacity. There are a number of entries in the accounts at Stowe which show that Bridgeman was paid for work there: for example, 'John Gurnet was paid 9s 4d for having a trench dug for Mr Bridgman' (HEH L9F9 cited in Willis 2002, 111 n. 19). At Sacombe, as we have seen, a number of payments to Bridgeman were recorded from his account at Hoare's Bank (Customer Ledgers: 17 fo.339, 18 fo.266, and 20 fos.6 and 436). At Purley, in West Berkshire, an undated entry records Bridgeman being paid £122.11s 'for laying out the Gardens at Purley' (South Sea Company *Particulars and Inventories* II, 71 cited in Willis 2002, 61 n. 89). There is extensive correspondence between Prior and Harley, documenting the progress of the work at Down Hall and alluding to Bridgeman's presence at Wimpole (LL HMC III 483/490/492/498/504). At Kedleston Hall in Derbyshire, on 14 September 1722, Sir John Curzon paid 'Mr: Bridgeman's man a guinea' and on 10 November 1722 he was paid £51.11s (Hoare's Bank, Ledger G fo.157). Bridgeman's presence at Wolterton Hall in Norfolk is extensively referred to in letters in the Wolterton archive between 1724 and 1738 (WH Boxes 8 and 29L). The letter from Bridgeman to Pope dated

28 September 1724 (see above) suggests that he was preparing plans for 'Mrs Howard' and, although there is no mention of Marble Hill, it seems likely that this is the site on which he was working (BL Add MS 4809, fo.141V). Sir John Dutton's estate accounts record expenses paid to Bridgeman in 1725 and 1729 for visits to Lodge Park in Gloucestershire (Smith 2006, 237). There are letters between Diston Stanley, land steward at Boughton House, Northamptonshire, and his employer the Duke of Montagu, and entries in the accounts at Boughton House, to suggest Bridgeman's involvement between 1728 and 1730 (BH Vol. 16 NTS X881 B, Montagu Archive Box 54). Three letters in 1731 between the Duchess of Queensbury and Henrietta Howard complain of Bridgeman's absence from Amesbury Abbey in Wiltshire, with the implication that he had been expected there (Murray 1824, Vol. 2, 20–21). Also in 1731, Sir Thomas Robinson wrote that 'Sir Robert [Walpole] and Bridgeman showed me the large design for the plantations in the country, which is the present undertaking ...' (Willis 2002, 85), implicitly suggesting that Bridgeman was in some way involved at Houghton in Norfolk. There are records of payments from Lady Betty Hastings, owner of Ledston Hall in West Yorkshire, to Bridgeman in 1731 for work at Ledston (Hoare's Bank Ledgers K and L). In 1732 the Duchess of Marlborough wrote, presumably about her new house at Wimbledon, that 'Mr Bridgeman may finish the ground and gardens in the manner I agreed upon with him' (Willis 2002, 58 n. 78). A letter from Lord Hervey to Stephen Fox dated 10 August 1734 suggests some involvement at Brocket Park, owned by their mutual friend Thomas Winnington; the reference is to 'the execution of my friend Winnington's commissions' from the estate to Bridgeman's widow after his death, on June 14 1739 (Hoare's Bank Ledger O). There are also extensive records in the Office of Works archive which explicitly record Bridgeman's work as Royal Gardener (NA Work 4). Those which pertain to the gardens at Richmond are held separately in the Royal Archives (Julie Crocker pers. comm. 2017). There are also references to Bridgeman's involvement in projects in contemporary published writing of the period. Switzer credits Bridgeman with the design of the amphitheatre and pond at Claremont in his *Introduction to a General System of Hydrostaticks and Hydraulicks* of 1729. Colen Campbell credits Bridgeman with the plan of Eastbury published in *Vitruvius Britannicus III*.

By tracing the paths of these drawings through time to the archives where they are held today, by subjecting to close examination the way they have been drawn, and by finding out whether there is good evidence that Bridgeman worked at a site, we can measure whether an unsigned plan which shows a Bridgemanesque design is actually a plan of a Bridgeman landscape drawn by Bridgeman. What emerges when the plans are viewed through these lenses is clearly not going to be unequivocal proof of Bridgeman authorship, and will, to some extent, still be conjectural. However, the process may well provide a better basis for further discussion and, ultimately, a more secure corpus of Bridgeman's work.

CHAPTER 3

A REVISED CATALOGUE

THE BUSINESS OF creating a more reliable corpus of Bridgeman's work begins with the 101 plans in Peter Willis's catalogue (shown in Appendix I). His carefully curated list provides a very useful, if not totally secure, base line. Investigating the provenance of the plans Willis lists, examining their graphic style closely and finding out whether we can say with any certainty that Bridgeman worked at the site, allows us to cast a critical eye over the contents of the catalogue. What this immediately shows up is that there are some plans, although not many, which have found their way into Willis's corpus erroneously. There is also a group of drawings which Willis has omitted from his catalogue, but which should be included. Using the same criteria of provenance, style and presence, close study of a number of plans, some perhaps not seen by Willis, some identified by academic sources, suggests they are probably by Bridgeman. Of course, as pointed out in Chapter 2, their inclusion or rejection will always be a matter of judgement rather than fact, and so the resulting revised corpus (Appendix 2) may well be contentious.

We might deal first with the removals. Some plans in Willis's catalogue are unequivocally by another author. Work 32/96, in the National Archives, which depicts Richmond Gardens, is actually in Willis's category 'B' – 'probably'; he suggests it 'reveals how the Royal Gardener proposed to loosen the outline of fields and replace clumps by wavy belts of trees'. It is, in fact, identified as being by Lancelot Brown in Dorothy Stroud's 1984 biography of him (Stroud 1984a, 128 n. 12), although Brown is not identified as its author in the National Archives catalogue (http://discovery.nationalarchives.gov.uk). The plan of Kensington Gardens, K. Top XXVIII 10 d.1, in the British Library, is in a bound volume, and is followed, on the next page, by K. Top XXVIII 10 d.2, 'A Survey and particular Admeasurement of the Royal Gardens at Kensington', two pages detailing the acreages of parcels of land in Kensington Gardens. Although it is painted in colours characteristic of Bridgeman, it is, as suggested by the contemporary title page which immediately precedes it in the bound volume (catalogued as K Top XXVIII 1.c), a survey by Joshua Rhodes dated 1762, and engraved in 1764 by George Bickham; 'Plan of the Palace Gardens & of Kensington by Joshua Rhodes 1762: engraved by G. Bickham, 1764 8 sheets A Roll 2 Tables (BL K Top XXVIII 1 c). The description here clearly fits the plan and survey. It also seems likely that the plan of Greenwich contained in a bound volume (CL MSS ART/2 II) is by Hawksmoor. It is in the second volume of three containing prints and plans compiled by Robert Mylne, Clerk of Works at Greenwich Hospital between 1776 and 1782. The library catalogue attributes this plan to Hawksmoor; it reads 'These plans were originally drawn by Nicholas Hawksmoor, Architect, 1728'. The architectural plans for the Bell Inn, at Stilton in Cambridgeshire (BoL MSGD a3 fo.40v and r, MSGD a4 fo.3 and MSGD a4 fo.51), are included in Willis's corpus. They are of Bridgeman's property, The Bell Inn at Stilton, acquired in 1736. They are clearly not in Bridgeman's hand and, in fact, are annotated 'Mr Ransom's Plan for the Bell-Inn at Stilton' and dated 29 July 1736.

We can also remove those where there is academic debate which is seriously at variance with Willis's attributions. Sir John Soane's Museum, for example, attributes the plans for Buckingham House (SM 111/42) (c.1702) to Henry Wise; their catalogue suggests that 'the drawing is strikingly similar in its conventions to those for the gardens of Hampton Court c.1710–11 (SM 111/39 and 40)' which it also identifies as being by Wise (www.soane.org). The online catalogue also attributes the plan of the Maestricht Garden at Windsor Castle, c.1708 (SM 111/45), to Wise because of its stylistic similarities to his final design for the garden in the Royal Collection. Both of these objections seem reasonable, although Jacques joins Willis in attributing the drawing for the Maestricht Garden to Bridgeman (Jacques 2014, figure 9). Willis attributes two sketches for Blenheim held in the Bodleian Library to Bridgeman (Top. Oxon a37 and a37*). However, these are identified by Green as being by Henry Wise or Sir John Vanbrugh (Green 1956, 98). It seems likely that they are by Vanbrugh. The draughtsmanship bears a close resemblance to that in 'Plan and elevation of a garden pavilion' by Vanbrugh, held in the Victoria and Albert Museum (D107-1891). Dalton suggests that they are part of Vanbrugh's design for the park and dates them to c.1705 (Dalton 2012, 105–107). She does not attribute them to Vanbrugh, although this is the implication of what she writes. It is possible that they were drawn by Bridgeman for Vanbrugh, but the draughtsmanship is stylistically unrelated to any of his other work. It is also possible that they are by Henry Joynes, clerk of works for Wise at Blenheim from 1704, who the Duchess of Marlborough said was 'a sort of a Foot-man to [Wise]' and 'an Ingenious person and skilled in drawing Draughts of buildings' (Green 1956, 97).

Close scrutiny casts doubt over some of Willis's other attributions. Brampton Bryan (SM Misc. drawings), for example, is not a landscape on which Bridgeman is known to have worked. The drawing is held in Sir John Soane's Museum, and the online catalogue offers no attribution. Willis bases his putative attribution on the style of the plan, which he suggests is Bridgemanic, although this is questionable, and a letter from Alexander Pope to Bridgeman, dated 1725, which refers to a journey they were both to have made to 'My Lord Oxford's', which he suggests might be a visit to the first Earl of Oxford at Brampton Castle. Unfortunately, although the plan is for the first Earl of Oxford and dated 1722, the journey referred to, on which Willis bases his attribution, postdates the death of the first Earl by a year. It is much more likely, as Willis himself conjectures, that the visit referred to is to Wimpole Hall, which came to Edward Harley, 2nd Earl of Oxford, through his marriage to Lady Henrietta Cavendish-Holles in 1713.

Several other plans appear to be existing surveys which Bridgeman might have been given before beginning work on a landscape. One is the plan for Wolterton Hall (BoL MSGD a3 fo.33), an ink and pencil survey entitled 'A Survey of Woolterton Hall &c. belonging to Horatio Walpole Esq.'. It is undated but shows the landscape with a small canal in the eventual location of Bridgeman's lake. This canal appears to have been part of a design by Joseph Carpenter, George London's successor at Brompton Park Nurseries. Carpenter's design, and the difficulties of constructing it, are mentioned in a letter from Britiffe, the clerk of works, to Horatio Walpole in 1724: 'I Have been at Wolterton And found your worke about the House as forward as needful Harvest being begun your Canal works is at a Stop for the present indeed the wett Season wee had some time befor prevented the workmen getting on so well as otherwise the w[ou]ld ...' (WH Box73L 8/5A). It is mentioned again, later in the year, in a further letter from Britiffe in which he states that work on the canal has stopped '... [b]y an order from Mr Carpenter ...' and it is clear from the same letter that Britiffe considers Carpenter to be in charge: '... I durst not pretend to advise in this case what will be proper to be done where you have so great a Master as he is ...' (WH Box 73L 8/5A). Previous research has dated this letter to 2 November 1726 (Peters 1991; Klausmeier, 1999). In fact, closer examination shows that it is actually dated 2 November 1724, which seems more likely since Carpenter died in 1726. The canal was unfinished at the time of the fire which destroyed the house in 1724 (WH Box 8/5A Box 73L). It seems likely, then, that this is a survey that preceded Bridgeman's work; possibly it was part of Joseph Carpenter's proposal. A plan for Ledston (BoL MSGD a3 fo.19) probably falls into the same category. It does not appear to show any of the graphic techniques characteristic of Bridgeman's draughtsmanship and may well also be a survey that preceded Bridgeman's involvement. The survey of Greenwich Park (BoL MSGD a4 fo.49) is also unlikely to be by Bridgeman. Graphically it does not suggest his hand, and although it is possible that it is a survey for Bridgeman's plan CMP/30, its provenance, in Gough Drawings, suggests it is not; it is unlikely that Bridgeman's rough preliminary sketch for a survey for Wise in 1711 would have found its way to the workshop from which he conducted his business later in his career. Perhaps the rudimentary sketch plan of Lamp Row (now Rotten Row) (NA MPD 1/164), which Willis also includes, falls into the category of existing survey. It may have been annotated by Bridgeman, but is certainly not principally in his hand.

Five of the plans which Willis catalogues as 'unidentified' also seem unlikely to be by Bridgeman. One of these, catalogued as MSGD a4 fo.81, is assigned by Willis to Claremont in the 2002 edition of the book, on the basis of a suggestion by John Harris (Willis 2002, 427). It shows the landscape at Claremont before Bridgeman's amphitheatre and pond. On the reverse is a rough sketch, probably by Vanbrugh, of part of the garden at Eastbury. Dalton also suggests that this plan is of Claremont, but in Vanbrugh's hand (Dalton 2012, 132). Two of the 'unidentified' plans – identical except that one, MSGD a4 fo.43, is in pencil and the other, MSGD a4 fo.33, is in ink and watercolour – have been correctly identified by Camilla Beresford in 2016 as being of Donington Park (www.treeandwoodland.co.uk/unidentified-map-discovery-donington-park). She does not, however, suggest any links with Bridgeman, other than the presence of these two plans in Willis's corpus. The two plans show a landscape that might loosely be described as Bridgemanic, but neither the graphic style of the plans nor any written evidence available to date link them to Bridgeman. In fact, the compass arrow on both identifies north in French, 'Nord', which suggests that the draughtsman was not Bridgeman. They may be maps of an unrecorded Bridgeman landscape at Donington Park, but the link is too tenuous for inclusion in a reliable corpus. The remaining two plans, MSGD a4 fo.22 and MSGD a4 fo.36, have some tangential similarity to Bridgeman's style as a designer, but there is nothing to suggest his graphic style, and no evidence of which sites they are for.

There are also sufficient problems with the plans for Marble Hill, both held at the Norfolk Record Office, to suggest that Bridgeman is not the author. Marble Hill was a gift from George II to his mistress Henrietta Howard. In 1724, work was begun on a house designed by Lord Pembroke and Roger Morris. It is clear that a garden was intended early on in the construction. Morris was paid for the building of some garden features, and a plan, held by Norfolk Record Office (NRO MC 184/10/3) and dated c.1724, has been attributed to Alexander Pope (https://historicengland.org.uk/). At some level, Bridgeman appears also to have been involved. His letter to Pope from 28 September 1724 (see above) shows that Bridgeman had probably visited the Marble Hill site with Pope and Henrietta Howard in the days before (although the letter refers only to Twickenham), and that he was preparing a plan (BL Add MS4809. Fo.141V). From this evidence, Willis and others have attributed to Bridgeman two other plans for Marble Hill held by Norfolk Record Office and catalogued MC 184/10/1 and 2. However, this attribution seems unlikely. They are stylistically different from Bridgeman's work and they must postdate 1724 by a number of years, since the cartouche refers to Henrietta Howard as the 'Countess of Suffolk', a title she did not accede to until 1731. Their provenance, from the Hobart archive at Blickling, also casts doubt on an attribution to Bridgeman. In fact it has been suggested, with good evidence, that the plans date from 1752, and were done by James Dorret, cartographer to the third Duke of Argyll (pers. comms Norfolk Archives).

This completes the list of plans that probably need to be dropped from Willis's original list. It seems plausible to attribute the remainder to Bridgeman, although some do require a little qualification. One is a plan which Willis identifies as for Tring Park (BoL MSGD a4 fo.25). In fact, this is unlikely to be its location, in

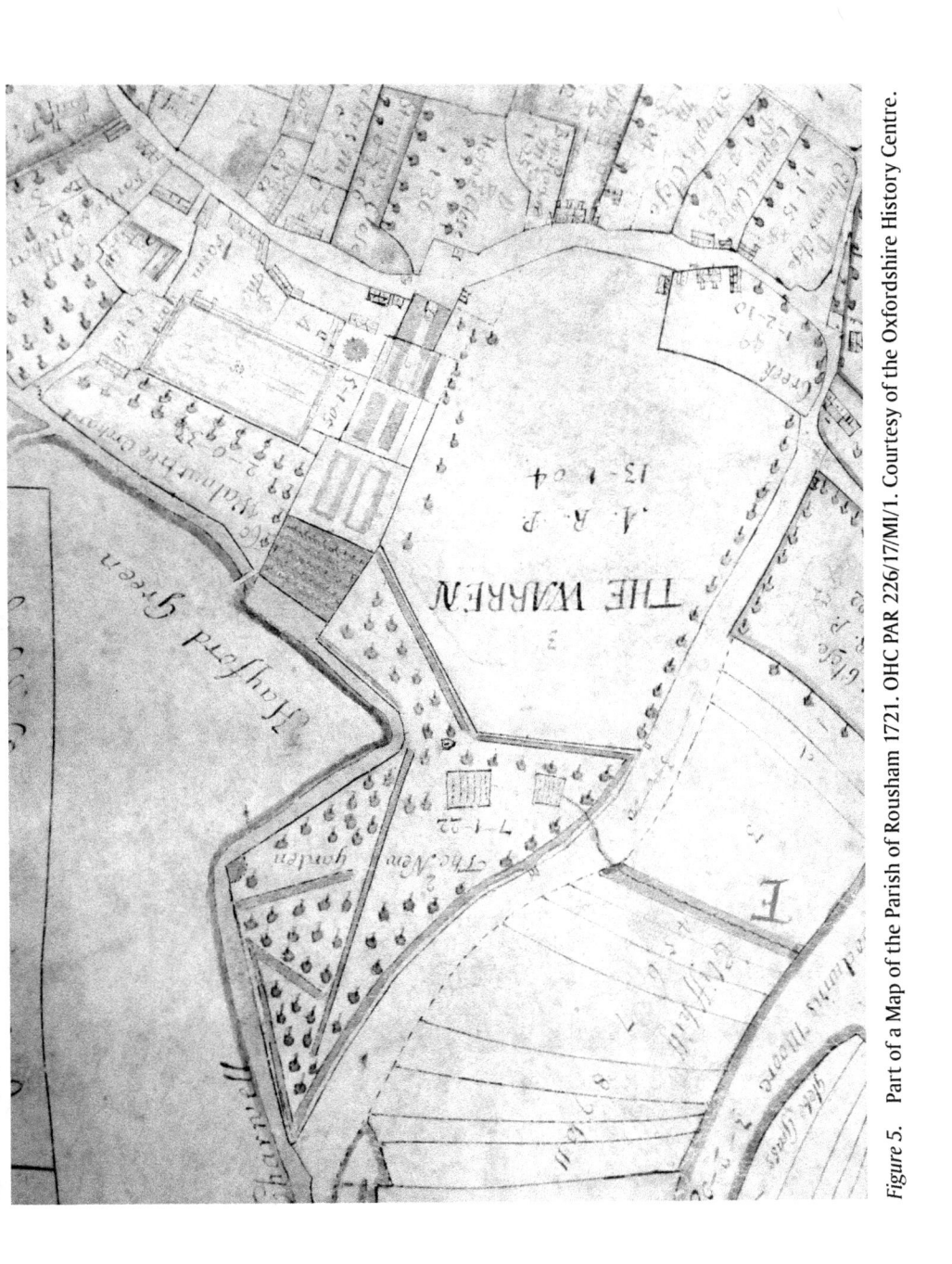

Figure 5. Part of a Map of the Parish of Rousham 1721. OHC PAR 226/17/MI/1. Courtesy of the Oxfordshire History Centre.

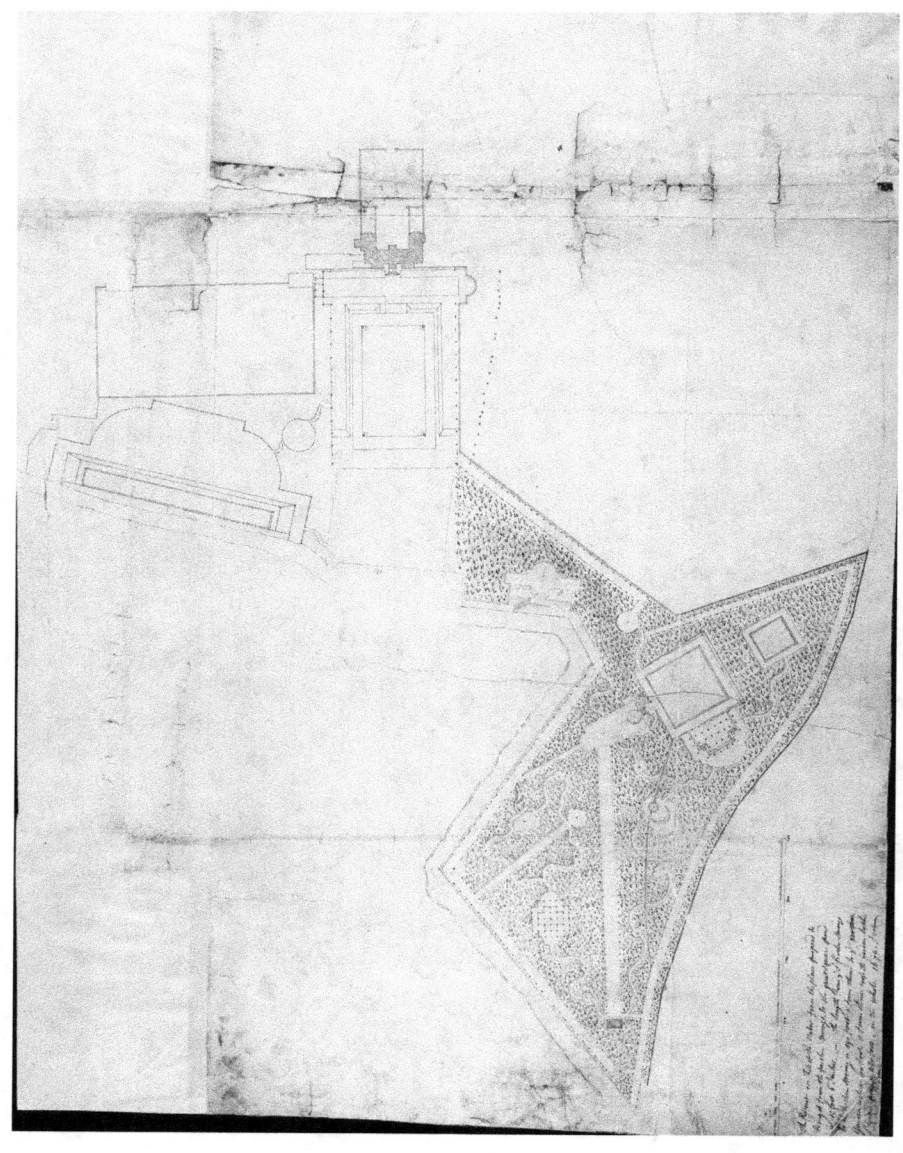

Figure 6. Rousham House. BoL MSGD a4 fo.63. The Bodleian Libraries, University of Oxford.

particular because the walk which runs diagonally across the top of the plan is annotated 'To Cowley Wood'. There is no Cowley Wood in the vicinity of Tring and so the likelihood is that the plan is for some other, as yet undiscovered, location (see Figure 13). Another plan, of Rousham in Oxfordshire (MSGD a4 fo.63), may well be much earlier than the date Willis gives for it. Willis dates the plan to between 1725 and 1737, but a parish survey dated 1719 (OHC PAR 226/17/M1/1) (Figure 5) shows the 'The New Garden' with the same two square ponds, the Elm Walk and two other walks, one of which is shown on Bridgeman's plan (BoL MSGD a4 fo.63) (Figure 6). It is possible that this was the existing garden at Rousham, and that Bridgeman adapted it, but it is much more likely that this is a proposal by Bridgeman, included in a survey taken when Sir Robert Dormer Cottrell inherited the estate in 1719. The annotations on MSGD a4 fo.63 then become instructions for constructing this proposal. They read 'The Current or Fall of the Water from the place propos'd to bring it from further springs to the great square pond is 15 foot 6 inches – The length from ... further springs to the Nether Spring is 890 foot & from thence to ye Garden water is 100 foot & from thence cross the Garden to the sd Square pond is 480 foot – in the whole 1670. foot'. This would probably place the date of both the drawing and the garden earlier than 1725.

Both these plans are clearly by Bridgeman, but there are several where, although there is documentary evidence that Bridgeman designed the landscape, the plans are almost certainly not in his hand. Two such are the plans for Down Hall. This is one of the few landscapes where documentary evidence is extensive and unequivocal. Bridgeman worked at Down Hall in Hertfordshire for Matthew Prior, a writer and diplomat, on a project funded by Prior's patron, Edward Harley, the Earl of Oxford. Prior wrote regularly to Harley, and charted the progress of the landscape with frequent references to Bridgeman (Portland Papers). The plans also clearly show a landscape of Bridgeman's design and one which, as LIDAR shows, survives under the dense woodland that now surrounds Down Hall. It is odd, then, that the two plans for Down Hall, Gough Maps 46 fo.262 and BL Loan 29/357, are both clearly in the same hand, although very obviously not that of Bridgeman. Gough Maps 46 fo.262 has 'From Wimpole' inscribed on the back, while BL Loan 29/357 is entitled 'Copy of the first Plan/ for Down Hall'. Neither, interestingly, are in Gough Drawings. Comparison with Prior's correspondence, however, reveals that they are almost certainly in the hand of Adrian Drift, private secretary to Matthew Prior. It is not clear why this would be, but Drift copied all of Prior's correspondence to Lord Harley (partly presumably because Prior's handwriting was almost illegible). At least one of the two plans was intended for Lord Harley, so perhaps this was simply part of Prior and Drift's *modus operandi*.

There is a third drawing, albeit of a very rudimentary nature, which may also be by Drift because it is annotated in his handwriting. Willis catalogues the drawing, MSGD a4 fo.29, as a sketch map of Sacombe, not unreasonably because it is annotated with 'Mr Rolt Sacomb' on the reverse. In fact, closer examination of it, coupled with the key in Drift's handwriting, suggests it also might well be of Down Hall. Comparison between it and the Ordnance Survey 1st edition (revised in 1897) (Map 1) reveals a number of similarities (Figure 7). The boundary hedges in the north of the sketch appear to be roughly in the shape of the northern boundary of Down Hall. The sketch map also shows the small triangular parcel of land, to the north-east of the estate, which also appears on the 1st Edition OS map. Both have a road running around the south-eastern corner of the estate, joining with the drive to the house. On the OS map, this is Matching Road. None of this precludes the sketch map from being by Bridgeman, but the balance of probability suggests that it is not; it seems more likely that it might be a preliminary sketch map annotated by Adrian Drift for Bridgeman's use in his planning. The question is, should these three be included in the corpus? Since they represent an unequivocal Bridgeman landscape and are clearly contemporary with the work done, the answer is yes, so long as we acknowledge they are not in his hand.

The two plans for Brocket Park, MSGD a4 fo.40 and MSGD a4 fo.7, present even more of a problem. Here is a landscape with some evidence of Bridgeman's involvement. Brocket Park in Hertfordshire was the home of Sir Thomas Winnington, close friend of Stephen Fox, a Whig politician. A letter from Lord Hervey to Stephen Fox, dated 10 August 1734, refers to 'the execution of my friend Winnington's commissions' including 'giving the plan to Bridgeman' (BL Add MS 51345). Forty guineas were also paid to Bridgeman's widow on 14 June 1739 (Hoare's Bank Ledger O). The two plans are based on an identical survey. One (BoL MSGD a4 fo.40) appears to show the landscape before work has begun, while the other (BoL MSGD a4 fo.7) shows a watercolour design superimposed on this template, including the original course of the river Lea beneath a suggested lake. The draughtsmanship bears some resemblance to Bridgeman's, but the design is less obviously his. Although there are typical vistas and rond-points to make the most of the steeply rising ground to the north of the site, there is something about their curvilinear nature, particularly in the east of the site, that is less characteristic. It looks as though a geometric design by Bridgeman has been allowed to degrade, but this cannot be the case, since one drawing (MSGD a4 fo.40) represents a landscape which is a *tabula rasa*. It predates a later design made for the landscape in 1752 by Richard Woods for James Paine, and a survey of 1752 (HALS D/P/P9), which shows the landscape largely unchanged; indeed, it is still visible in palimpsest today. Although both drawings are rather uncharacteristic, their presence in Gough Drawings and the documentary evidence make for a plausible attribution to Bridgeman as both designer and draughtsman. The payment of £40 made in 1739 to Sarah Bridgeman may have been for a plan and survey. It is a similar amount to that paid at Lodge Park (see Chapter 5). It may be that subsequent research will uncover Bridgeman's role in the gardens at Brocket and so they probably deserve a place in Bridgeman's corpus. The same is true of

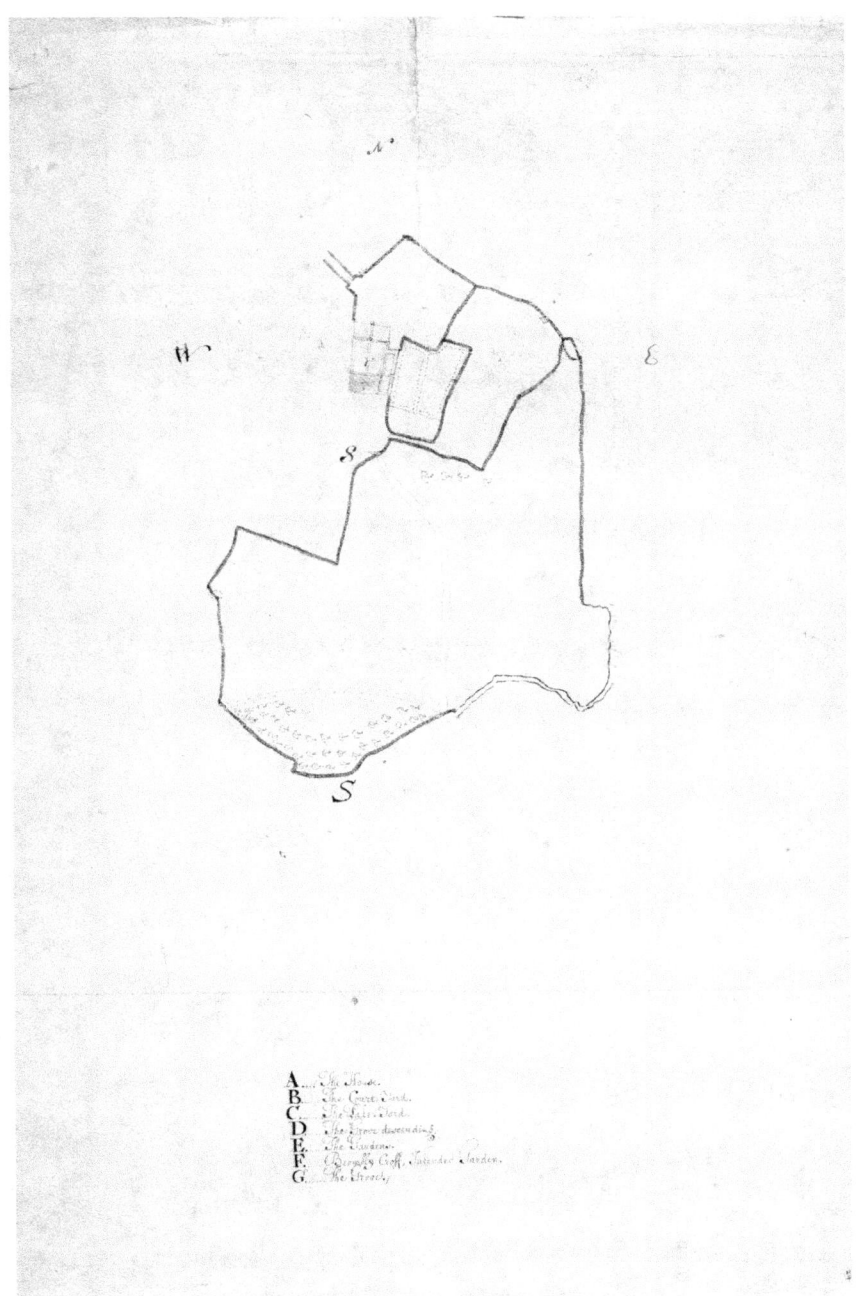

Figure 7. Sketch map of the relict landscape at Down Hall, annotated by Adrian Drift. MSGD a4 fo.29. The Bodleian Libraries, University of Oxford.

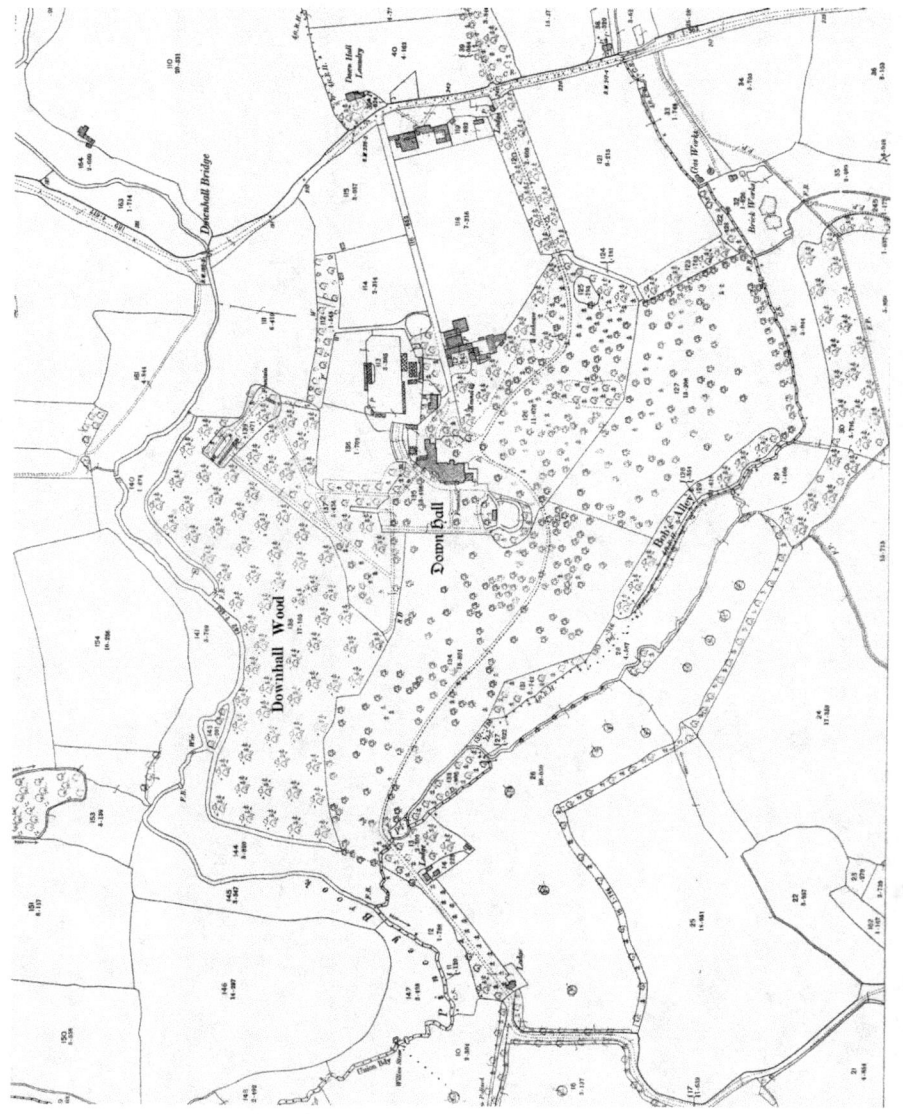

Map 1. Ordnance Survey, Essex, 1st Edition/Revised XLI.4 1897 (detail). Reproduced with the permission of the National Library of Scotland.

the plan for Mereworth (BoL MSGD a4 fo.52). The plan is so embryonic that its presence in the corpus is negligible. However, it may be by Bridgeman, and more evidence of his involvement at Mereworth may emerge.

Willis includes a plan for Hackwood Park in Hampshire in his corpus. Catalogued as MSGD a3 fo.4, it is in fact rather obviously an estate survey of the park, gardens and house taken before Bridgeman's work to transform it began, and is in a very different and much less accomplished hand. However, superimposed on it are extensive pencil marks, very probably in Bridgeman's hand, outlining his design for the site which appears on a finished drawing (MSGD a4 fo.34). It is likely that the manuscript, although originally by an estate surveyor, probably represents both a resurveying of the wood and an embryonic design by Bridgeman. It is difficult to know whether to include it in a corpus of his work, but, on balance, the detailed drawing and measurements suggest that it represents part of the design process.

The deletions suggested earlier in the chapter result in a somewhat depleted corpus, but there are a number of additions. The first is a plan which Tom Williamson and Anne Rowe have identified as Bridgeman's work (BoL MSS Map Herts a.1). In the 2002 edition of *Charles Bridgeman and the English Landscape Garden,* Willis adds Gobions in Hertfordshire to his corpus, based on the survey by Thomas Holmes (undated but c.1735) in the Gloucestershire Record Office (Willis 2002, 428). A map of the estate of Gobions, apparently unfinished and in a rather degraded state, wrongly catalogued as 'North Mimms' but using what certainly appears to be Bridgeman's graphic style, was found by Dr Anne Rowe in the Bodleian Library in 2011 (Rowe and Williamson 2012). There are references to Bridgeman's landscape at Gobions in Horace Walpole's *The History of the Modern Taste in Gardening.* The map, although in the Bodleian Library, has no links with the Gough Collection, being part of a miscellaneous bequest to the Library in the nineteenth century, and catalogued by the Library then as 30629 (Colin Harris pers. comm. 2013). It is possible that it entered the Library after 1835 when the house at Gobions was demolished, but there is no direct evidence of this (Tom Williamson pers. comm. 2016). The plan is shown schematically in Figure 12.

Another is a plan catalogued in Gough Drawings as MSGD a3 fo.41 (Figure 8). It is bound in the a3 volume of Gough Drawings, but the possibility that it might be attributable to Bridgeman has been overlooked. It seems to show the garden in the immediate vicinity of Great Saxham Hall in Suffolk, recognisable by its distinctive moat and square-sided pond from an estate map which is part of a survey from 1729 held in Suffolk Record Office (SRO t4/33/1.24); a house owned by Sir John Eldred. The location of the plan in Gough Drawings is confirmed by the annotation on the reverse, 'John Eldred Esq.'. John Eldred, a Levant merchant, bought Great Saxham Hall in 1597. Bridgeman's client was Eldred's grandson. The Hall shown on the plan is presumably the seventeenth-century house which was demolished in 1774. The plan shows the garden enclosed by the geometric canal, with straight avenues and an apsidal-ended bowling green, delineated by solid and dotted lines in ink, and annotated with 'Gravell' and 'Grass', also in ink. Within this structure, roughly sketched in, there are pencil marks showing serpentine paths, cabinets and trees, and annotations, faint, also in pencil, with the words 'Gravell' and 'Wilderness'. It appears to be a rough sketch map of alterations that might be made to an existing garden. The placement of cabinets and the serpentine paths that connect them are reminiscent of a number of other plans, including those for Down Hall and Moor Park. A pencil note at the bottom of the plan appears to read 'For John Eldred Esq. to be left at The Ram / at Newmarket 22 fruit trees to be sent next week as concluded by particulars / Bury Carrier at ye Bull Inn Bishopsgate'.[1] The message appears to be initialled 'B'. The features of the plan are picked out in pin pricks which suggests that either it was used to create a copy, or was itself a copy. There is little cartographic evidence to suggest that this garden was ever constructed. Neither the tithe map of 1840 (SRO MR 11B.P15 Ts1/1), nor the map in the sale catalogue for the estate from 1924 (SRO HD 1750/117), show any trace of it. However, this might be because the garden was redesigned in the later eighteenth century for Hutchinson Mure, who bought the estate in 1754. William Mills recorded in his diary that he had spent 'considerable sums in embellishing the grounds under the great "Capability" Brown', and, although there appears to be no evidence that Brown was involved, some remodelling of the landscape clearly occurred.

There are nine plans, all the subject of extensive scholarly debate about their links to Bridgeman, which may well be by him. Importantly, all nine derive from one lot at the sale of the Waller Collection at Christie's in 1947. The plans of Hampton Court (Work 32/313 A&B), held in the National Archives, are attributed to Henry Wise (no doubt because they come from the Waller Collection) (http://discovery.nationalarchives.gov.uk), but are actually copies of Bridgeman's survey of Hampton Court held by the Soane Museum (SM 36/3/1). Simon Thurley attributes them to Bridgeman, but suggests that 'It is likely that Work 32/313 A&B were part of the collection of drawings sold to the Office of Works in March 1742/3 by Bridgeman's widow' (Thurley 2003, 421 n. 56). In fact, their provenance shows that they came to the National Archives (or the Public Record Office as it was) via a dealer from the sale at Christie's. The plans of the Fountain Garden at Hampton Court (NA Work 32/311) and of Kensington Gardens (NA Work 32/312), both also held in the National Archives, come from the same sale, as do the following plans, all held in the Royal Collection: 'A General Plan of Windsor Great Park' (RCIN 929578), 'An Accurate Plan of Windsor 2 Parks and Forest' RCIN 929579, 'A Preliminary Sketch of the same' (RCIN 929579), and a plan for the Octagon Basin, Windsor (RCIN 929581). It is highly likely that they are all by Bridgeman, when he was working as a draughtsman for Wise. A fifth drawing, of St James's Park (RCIN 929582), is part of the same numerical catalogue sequence and was part of the Christie's sale. It is unavailable to view on line, so it is not

---

[1] I am indebted to Alison Cassidy for deciphering this for me

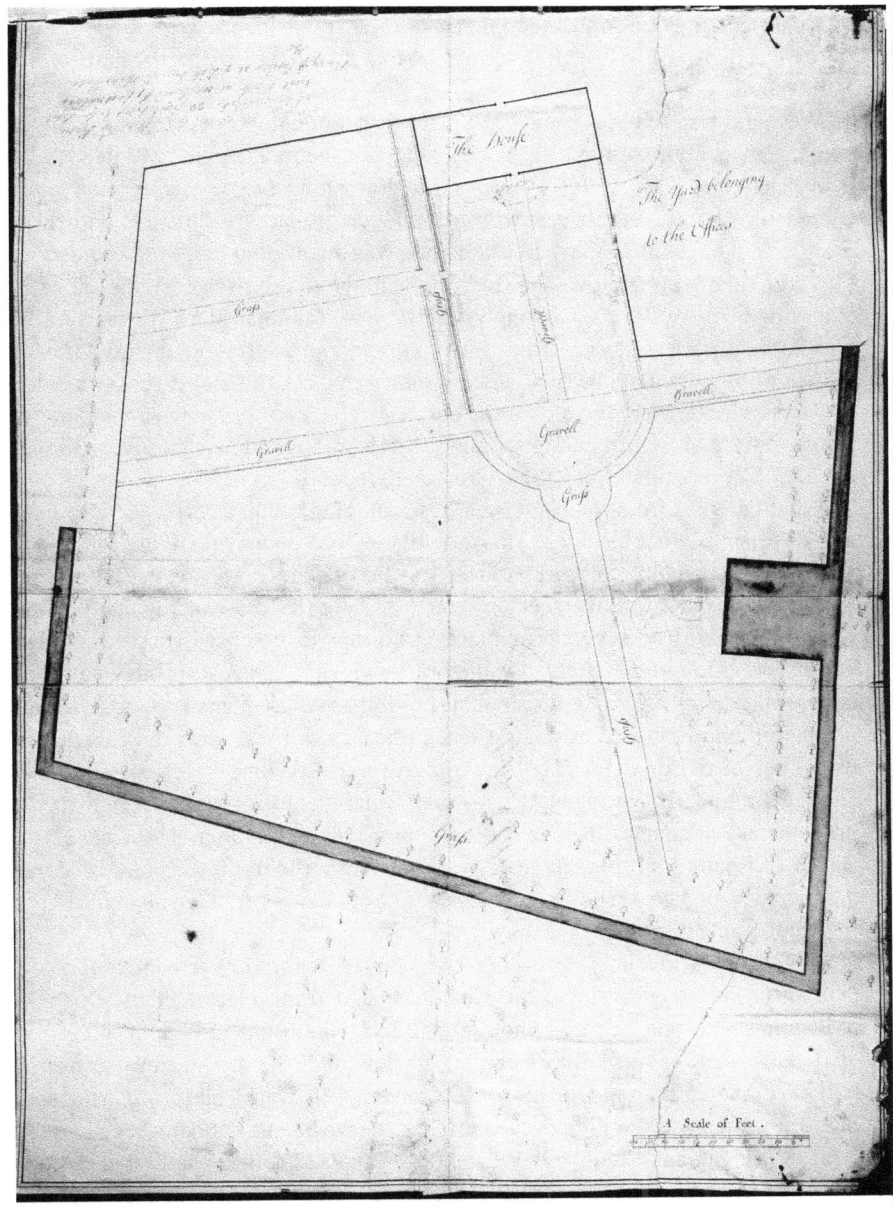

Figure 8. A survey of Great Saxham Hall in Suffolk, overdrawn with a pencil sketch of his proposal for the landscape by Bridgeman. MSGD a3 fo.41. The Bodleian Libraries, University of Oxford.

possible to see whether it is stylistically linked to the others, but it may well be. The plan of the Fountain Garden (NA Work 32/311) is identical to the Fountain Garden as depicted in Gough Drawings a4 fo.62, which suggests they are by the same hand.

We might also reinstate one of the plans for Standlynch (now Trafalgar House), which Willis's 2002 catalogue excludes. In fact, it seems likely that MSGD a3 fo.25 is by Bridgeman. The plan is a pencil sketch for a putative landscape lying along the eastern bank of the river Avon at Trafalgar House in Wiltshire, known as Standlynch, made in 1733 when Bridgeman was involved in creating a landscape for Peter Vandeput. It shows the steep slope down to the river embellished with, from north to south, a small amphitheatre, a rectangular platform reached by two straight paths rising up from the river, and a grove threaded through with a serpentine path linking two viewing platforms. On the slope above, a small wilderness is shown in the old formal parterre. The features shown are echoes of similar ones at Amesbury and Rousham, and the draughtsmanship is very similar to that of a preliminary plan for Wolterton (BoL MSGD a4 fo.56).

What emerges from the exercise of re-examining Willis's corpus is that there are surprisingly few changes. The majority of the plans that Willis originally identified remain in the corpus. The full list of the new corpus appears in Appendix II, and the Gazetteer on page 189 lists the drawings which pertain to each site. For the sake of completeness, it has to be noted that there are a number of other sites where documentary evidence suggests Bridgeman may have worked, for example, Cassiobury, but for which no plans survive. Without plans, it is impossible to evaluate the significance of these sites in Bridgeman's work, but plans for them may yet be discovered. In some cases we are lucky enough to find that Bridgeman's layout probably survives in a later map. At Briggens, a Bridgemanic layout is shown on a 1781 estate map (HALS acc2216), and at Carshalton a Bridgemanic layout is shown on John Roque's *Map of Surrey* dating from the late 1750s or early 1760s. In both cases there are also payments to Bridgeman (Skelton 2017, 33).

Sometimes Bridgeman's presence rests on references in correspondence. At Badminton, although no plan survives, it is clear from a letter of the Duchess of Beaufort that one existed: 'The draught Bridgeman sent to Badminton is one of the Grandest things I have seen ...' (Willis 2002, 425), and at Longford in Wiltshire, the correspondence of Jacob Bouverie, Viscount Folkestone, suggests that Bridgeman was working for him in 1737: 'I have been a good deal at a loss for want of Bridgeman's Company' (Willis 2002, 58). At Cliveden, the Earl of Orkney writes of the amphitheatre that Bridgeman is planning (Willis 2002, 427). The minutes of the Board of King's College, Cambridge, record Bridgeman's contract.

Sometimes Bridgeman's involvement is signalled only by payments from a client's bank account. Bridgeman was paid by Sir Joseph Jekyll, in both 1721 and 1735, for unspecified work at either possibly the Rolls House in London or, more likely, at Dallington in Northamptonshire (Willis 2002, 428). Henry Pelham paid Bridgeman £52.10s from his bank account at Hoare's Bank in March 1734/5, presumably for work at Esher Place, and Sir Samuel Tufnell paid him £156.7s.2d in 1722 for 'Works and plants in ye Gardens' at Langleys in Essex (CRO D/DTu276). Montagu Garrad Drake paid Bridgeman £50 in 1725/6 for work at Shardeloes. At Bower House, the evidence is only the tantalising inscription over the door: 'C.BRIDGMAN. DESIGNAVIT'.

Even though there are sites for which no plans survive the modified corpus does represent a surprisingly large survival of attributed plans, especially in comparison with the number surviving from Bridgeman's immediate predecessors in England. It is only possible to find 24 examples surviving of the work of Henry Wise, 15 of which relate to royal landscapes (Green 1956). Even fewer by George London appear to have survived, although Switzer describes his tireless pursuit of business (*The Nobleman, Gentleman, and Gardener's Recreation* 52–53 in Green 1956, 7). It is difficult, without a gazetteer of London's work, to quantify the number of plans that might have been produced, although some examples have survived: a parterre at Herriard in Hampshire for Thomas Jervoise (Jeffrey 1985, Pl. 14 No. 61), and a design for Castle Howard (V&A E433.1951 and E434.1951). It would also appear that Vanbrugh represented few of his projects cartographically. Much of the evidence for his work rests on entries in *Vitruvius Britannicus*, and on contemporary drawings and engravings by artists such as Kip and Knyff (for example Kings Weston (Special Collections University of Bristol)), Stukeley (for example of Grimsthorpe 1736 (BoL MS Top. Gen D.14 fo.36v)), and Rocque (for example of Claremont 1738 (BL Maps K.Top.40 19a)).

Fewer examples of the work of Bridgeman's close contemporaries seem to have survived. Perhaps the closest comparison available is the work of Stephen Switzer, Bridgeman's exact contemporary. William Brogden's PhD thesis (Brogden 1973) gives a comprehensive list of Switzer's commissions. Of the 23 projects listed, it appears that plans survive for only four: Exton Park in Rutland (MSGD a4 fo.7), Nostell Priory (plan held at Nostell Priory), Beaumanor in Leicestershire (Leicestershire Record Office DG 9/2738), and Audley End (MSGD a4 fos. 60 and 67), although these last two plans for Audley End are attributed by Willis to Bridgeman (Willis 2002). Of the remaining 19 landscapes with which Switzer is associated, five appear in *Ichnographia Rustica*, two in *Vitruvius Britannicus*, one was drawn by Kip and Knyff, three rest on accounts or contracts in estate records, and it appears that no evidence exists for the remaining eight. William Kent, also Bridgeman's contemporary, appears to have presented his designs for landscapes in the form of sketches and paintings only, perhaps because his background was in painting rather than in surveying (Dixon Hunt 1986; Mowl 2006). This is true, for example, of Rousham (Dixon Hunt 1986, figure 111), at Chatsworth (Mowl 2006) and Twickenham (Mowl 2006). A significant number of Kent's designs survive in the form of pen and ink sketches of the finished landscape, executed in elevation. Half of Kent's corpus is in the Devonshire Collection at Chatsworth House, deposited there by Lord Burlington, while at least half of the remainder are in the places for which they were designed (Dixon Hunt 1986, 41). Even after the middle of the eighteenth century, survival of plans was not guaranteed. Fiona Cowell's Gazetteer lists Richard Woods's 45 commissions dated between 1758 and 1783 (Cowell 2009, 176–242). Of these, 24 plans still survive in repositories, or are known to have existed, mentioned in estate accounts or letters, but subsequently lost.

The survival of so many of the drawings attributed to Bridgeman seems to be an anomaly when placed in the context of his contemporaries. It is largely, perhaps, because of the happy accident of the survival of the material in Gough Drawings. The only comparable survival of this sort of material in the late seventeenth and early eighteenth centuries, on such a large scale, seems to be material from the workshops of André Le Nôtre in France. Here there seems to be a wealth of drawings, showing various stages of the process of design, held in the Bibliothèque de l'Institut de France in Paris and the Nationalmuseum, Stockholm (Bouchenot-Déchin and Farhat 2013). In England, the survival of plans in these numbers in the eighteenth century only seems to occur in the case of Lancelot Brown. We are fortunate, then, to have so much cartographic material to work with. The task now is to find out what it has to tell us about Bridgeman and his work.

CHAPTER 4

READING THE PLANS

THE PLANS IN the revised corpus of Bridgeman's work create a baffling sense of heterogeneity. There are plans which are in ink and watercolour, some with cartouches, some with compass wheels. There are plans in pencil and brown ink with detailed annotations. There are plans in pencil overdrawn with corrections. They are almost all on paper, but of a variety of thickness and quality. They range considerably in size. The biggest, the plan for Gobions in Hertfordshire (MS Herts Map a.1), is very large indeed, covering an entire table top when unfolded. The smallest, for example the plan for Wolterton (MSGD a4 fo.56), are roughly the same size as a sheet of a3 paper. It is hard to make sense of such a multiplicity of media and presentation. However, if we see them as part of a process of physically building on the land a design which originated in Bridgeman's imagination, they begin to make more sense. If we assume that the presence of a design indicates that the new garden had already been commissioned, then one purpose of a drawing must have been to help a client to visualise an entirely new landscape, or, at the very least, new features in an existing landscape. However, this cannot have been the only purpose of a plan. At some point in the construction process there must also have been documents with detailed measurements which would have allowed a foreman and labourers to accurately create Bridgeman's design on the land. There had to be clarity, and presumably instructions, framed in such a way that it was not even always necessary for Bridgeman to be present; in other words, there had to be working drawings as well as those designed for presentation.

Bridgeman's clients and those who facilitated the building of his designs must have shared with him a mutual understanding of the coding, the signs and symbols he used on his plans. So it follows that the decisions Bridgeman made, consciously or unconsciously, with regard to the way a plan was created were based on custom and practice, and presumably informed by the graphic conventions with which he and his clients were most familiar. It is helpful to place Bridgeman's plans within the context of other types of map which were, in form, purpose and coding, most like the plans he presented to his clients, and with which they would have been most familiar.

In the late seventeenth and early eighteenth centuries both Bridgeman and his clients would have been familiar with the coding used on estate maps and surveys, usually the work of a surveyor employed by the estate. Many estate stewards were also accomplished surveyors and map makers, as was, for example, John Booth (d.1737), chief land steward to the Duke of Montagu at Boughton House, whose surveys, framed, line the walls of its corridors (Crispin Powell pers. comm. 2015). Harley has called the period between 1700 and 1850 'the golden age of the local land surveyor' (Bendall 2009, 25). In the late seventeenth and the early eighteenth centuries there was a sharp rise in the number of surveyors, and a corresponding increase in the number of surveys or estate maps produced. Although there was considerable variety in both the appearance of estate maps and the technical competence with which they were surveyed and drawn, in form and purpose they were multifunctional. Their primary function was 'to show an individual's landed property' (Bendall 2009, 160); many estate maps were often also intended for display, and were decorated as a result. As Andrews and Harley point out, decoration 'is not a marginal exercise' but 'both decorative and geographical images on a map are unified parts of a total image' (Andrews in Harley 2001, 110). A displayed estate map was also a means for the surveyor to advertise his skills and for the landowner to demonstrate his ability to employ the most competent practitioner, and this probably affected the degree of ornamentation (Bendall 2009, 49). There is also a tradition in estate mapping, whether intended for display or not, of recording subsequent developments to the land of the estate on working documents. Sometimes they were extensively annotated, as happened, for example, with the Hatfield map of Gobions on which successive sales and purchases of land were recorded (Hatfield House Archives). It would appear that maps were not sacrosanct even when intended for display, and the distinction we make today between working drawings and those for display was probably not so relevant in the late seventeenth and early eighteenth centuries.

Probably because of the fundamentally utilitarian nature of the estate map, the coding used in them in the late seventeenth and early eighteenth centuries was remarkably uniform across a wide geographical area. Maps and surveys concentrated on what was economically productive or useful, of geographical significance, or prestigious. Estate maps were often accompanied by some kind of table, either as an explanation or a key, as a description of tenurial arrangements, or as a list of acreages of agriculturally productive parcels of land. Woodland, consisting either of pre-existing standard trees felled for timber with a coppiced understorey, or plantations planted deliberately without a coppiced understorey, partly for profit and partly as cover for game birds, was productive, and so was drawn on an estate map, its value often quantified in the estate survey (Barnes and Williamson 2011, 91). Its depiction was largely homogenous across a number of geographically diverse regions. Individual trees were drawn as 'stylised lollipops' (Pannett 1985, 70), usually in straight lines, in elevation, and not to scale, in estate maps from as geographically disparate locations as Great Saxham in Suffolk, 1729 (SRO t4/33/1.24), Gobions in Hertfordshire, c.1718 (Hatfield Archive), Arbury in Warwickshire, dated 1700 (WO CR 136/m/11), Amesbury Abbey in Wiltshire 1726 (WRO 944/1), and Boughton House in Northamptonshire (Boughton House). The tree symbols rarely attempted to differentiate between species, although Bendall suggests that they were often shown in their correct positions, especially when they occurred in hedgerows (Bendall 2009, 66). Coppicing and the understorey, when they were shown on estate maps, were represented as a mottled green backdrop, as in the Holmes map of Gobions, or sometimes simply as green, as in the Booth survey (1715) of Boughton House. The boundaries of water courses or ponds were shown, although the water was not always coloured. Distances were shown using a scale, either in words or using a scale bar. Compass roses were the most common way to show orientation (Bendall 2009, 40). Buildings on estate maps could be shown in plan or in elevation, often in sufficient detail for architectural features to be discerned (Bendall 2009, 67). However, both Pannett and Bendall show that the conventions for the presentation of buildings were in the process of change in the early eighteenth century. Pannet shows that, between 1597 and 1710, while buildings were 'shown in "bird's eye view" either conventionally or faithfully drawn according to their importance' (Pannett 70), their replacement with buildings in plan form was a general trend throughout the early eighteenth century. Buildings in plan appeared in Cumberland in 1694, in Norfolk in 1708, in Essex in 1721 and in Worcestershire in 1731 (Bendall 2009, 49; Pannett 70).

Bridgeman was clearly familiar with the coded symbolism used in estate maps and surveys. There was substantial cross-fertilisation of both technique and personnel between the making of estate maps and landscape design. Indeed, it is possible that a rise in the number of surveyors, and their increased competence, had a direct impact on the greater size and complexity of landscape garden design. As discussed above, some of the plans in Bridgeman's corpus are, in fact, surveys rather than designs: his survey of Warwick Town and Priory conducted with James Fish (WO CR.26.2.2), and those for Hampton Court (NA MPD 1/23/3) and Richmond Gardens (NA MR 1/696), for example. The presence in Gough Drawings of estate surveys for the landscapes on which Bridgeman worked, such as for Ledston Hall or Wolterton Hall, suggests that he was also familiar with the work of other surveyors.

Bridgeman would also have known the symbols in common use by his fellow practitioners to depict their designs, especially as he seems to have worked closely with Henry Wise and with Sir John Vanbrugh, and had some association with Stephen Switzer. Presumably Bridgeman's clients would also have seen the landscape designs of other practitioners so that a knowledge of the codes used would have been common to both parties. While each designer probably had a recognisable graphic style which identified their work, there was – unsurprisingly, given the need to communicate with a client in an easily understood code – a strong sense of a shared symbolic coding, albeit modified by the artistic ability of individual draughtsmen. Also, perhaps unsurprisingly, given the likely cultural cross-fertilisation between separate disciplines caused by the blurring of professional boundaries, it is also a code shared with estate maps and surveys.

There is certainly a degree of homogeneity about the symbols used by Bridgeman, his immediate predecessors and almost all of his contemporaries, and they are very similar to those used in estate mapping. Drawings by André Le Nôtre and his atelier for Versailles and the gardens of other chateaux, by George London, by Henry Wise (where it is possible to distinguish his hand from Bridgeman's or some other draughtsman), and by Stephen Switzer all share the same code, so that it is instantly obvious even to the modern eye what the designer intends and must have been even more obvious to contemporary clients. Even so, there are some idiosyncrasies which mark out the work of a particular artist. For example, Le Nôtre's designs use a mixture of plan and elevation: trees, fountains, and landscaped features such as amphitheatres, steps and sometimes garden buildings, are universally shown in elevation, while pre-existing buildings, designs for parterres, the elements of the understorey or coppicing, and the outlines of allées, basins, canals and rond-points, are shown in plan (Notebooks 1 & 2, Bouchenot-Déchin and Farhat, 2013). By contrast, London's depiction of features is more perfunctory. Similar coding is used on his watercolour, ink and pencil plan for Castle Howard. For example, on his plans for Castle Howard, held in the V&A, trees are depicted as dots, and buildings are shown in plan (V&A E.433-1951; E. 434-1951). Wise's plans show trees and fountains within his parterres in elevation, and the patterning of the parterres and pools in plan. Any buildings are drawn in plan, with internal walls marked in; other geographical features, such as water, appear in pen and ink, or in pencil, usually accurately drawn. Switzer's three drawings show water with uneven strokes of a brush, and fountains in elevation. The trees are drawn realistically and in elevation, although without elegance, and in the plan for Exton Park (BoL MSGD a4 fo.7) their apparently random distribution may indicate accurate locations. Buildings are in plan.

Only William Kent's work takes a different approach. From Dixon Hunt's catalogue in *William Kent Landscape Garden Designer* it is clear that Kent never produced a surveyed plan for a garden design. Some of his designs for buildings are in plan and elevation, such as those on plates 90, 91 and 92 (Dixon Hunt 1987, 159), and one, a very rough sketch for the Hermitage in Richmond Park, has a measurement, '16ft' (Dixon Hunt 1987, plate 57). Only one, 'A garden plan with boathouse' (Plate 94), is in plan, although the garden buildings and trees are in elevation. Most of Kent's proposals for gardens are in the form of painterly scenes in elevation in black ink and pencil, with outlines washed in yellowish-brown. Dixon-Hunt suggests that there is a strong influence both of the painter Claude and of Kent's involvement in theatre designs in his depictions (Dixon-Hunt 1987, 29, 42). Kent provided the settings and costumes for a production at the Theatre Royal in Drury Lane in 1724 and Dixon-Hunt considers this to be 'the tip of the iceberg' as far as Kent's theatrical involvement went (Dixon-Hunt 1987, 30). His proposals are often filled with characters, as might be a stage set. For example, his proposal for the Exedra at Chiswick shows four figures in the bowling green (Chatsworth 26A, item 24), and his 'proposal for a seat on the mount' at Holkham Hall in Norfolk shows a gondola with three people in it. Although Sir Thomas Robinson, writing to the Earl of Carlisle in 1734, suggested that Kent laid gardens out 'without level or line …' (Williamson 1995, 59), it cannot have been the case that, when the landscape was created, no surveying was done. This suggests that Kent had some different *modus operandi*. It is probably the case that there was no necessity for Kent to produce competent, surveyed garden plans because he was not responsible for the moving of earth, or the creation of waterworks. Kent's proposals allow the client to visualise the design as though looking at a painting or a stage set. He was creating something akin to an advertising image which did not rely on a shared knowledge of signifiers and would be instantly accessible. We might assume that Humphrey Repton's red books, with their depiction of 'before' and 'after' scenes, fulfilled a similar function.

The wide diversity of character in Bridgeman's plans is matched by those of other designers, too. Bouchenot-Déchin and Farhat have divided their sample of Le Nôtre's work into two Notebooks, precisely to demonstrate what they see as the reason for this diversity. They contend that the 'first notebook contains preliminary graphic items, while *Notebook 2* is the 'final design stage' (Bouchenot-Déchin and Farhat, 2013). In *Notebook 1*, even though the medium of watercolour is used extensively, the drawings are rough sketches. Some, for example no. 19, 'A Sketch for a Demi-Lune at the End of a Garden', are in ink and Le Nôtre's characteristic red chalk; others, for example no. 8, 'Design for a New Access to the Chateau of Saint Cloud', are in red chalk only (Bouchenot-Déchin and Farhat, 2013). In several sketches a new design has been superimposed, in a different medium, on the existing landscape. In *Notebook 2*, all are in watercolour and ink. Switzer's plans also show a division between plans intended as finished drawings and those which were intended as working drawings. The plan for Claremont, published in *An Introduction to a General System of Hydrostaticks and Hydraulicks*, is the most polished drawing, clearly designed for publication as an exemplar. The implication is that it improves Bridgeman's design, as Switzer himself explained: 'The upper Part of the Work may very easily be seen to be a Sketch of the fine Amphitheatre at *Claremont* … The Design of the very ingenious *Mr Bridgeman*; and the lower Part, where the Water Spouts out, is an Addition of my own, from a Work of that kind I have done for the Right Honourable the Earl of *Orrery* at *Marston* in *Somersetshire*' (Switzer 1729, 405). The drawing of Exton Park (a4 fo.7) on the other hand, in ink, pencil and wash, appears to have been drawn as a working drawing from which the cascade might be constructed. Its character is rough.

Interestingly the extant plans of London and Wise do not reflect this division. They seem universally to be distinctly functional, rather than decorative. They show, in watercolour, only the parterres to be constructed. London's drawing for Herriard House is annotated with planting instructions (Jeffrey 1985, Plate 14 No.16). The shorthand of dots for trees may also have been dictated by the need for speed. The Soane Museum website indicates why this might be with regard to the drawing for Hampton Court Palace (SM 111/39): '[t]he main purpose of this drawing appears to have been to provide an exact survey of the palace at ground level and illustrate the boundaries, occupancies and access points in all areas of the walled garden and building adjoining the palace but excluding the parks' (http://collections.soane.org/OBJECT462). Perhaps it is that, because both London's and Wise's plans are usually of parterres – relatively small, simple to construct, close to the house and without the need to identify natural features such as slopes and springs – it was largely unnecessary to produce more than a functional drawing that identified the relationship of features to each other.

The coding used in a plan, and its character, then, reflect its purpose and function. Estate surveys, having limited function beyond the recording of the value of land and other assets on an estate, or the relationship of parcels of land to each other, need clarity, but require no particular artistic ability. A drawing which has the functional purpose of conveying a pattern to be produced on a small piece or pieces of land, such as the parterres designed and executed by London or Wise, for example, needs only rudimentary symbols, and probably shows only the area to be created. The visualisation of a large designed landscape which does not yet exist, and if it did could not be encompassed in one view, on the other hand, requires drawing which reveals what is in the designer's mind in a way that is visually accessible to its audience. It is likely to use some degree of three-dimensionality and to anchor the design within the landscape that is its wider context. This can be achieved, as it was by Kent and Repton, through a fully three-dimensional picture. However, if it is necessary to use the drawing for building work, then there has to be a compromise. Le Nôtre, Switzer and, as we shall see, Bridgeman were adept at producing drawings, sometimes several for the same landscape, which could both depict a design visually, and be adapted to provide a master plan for construction. It is this that accounts for the diversity.

Bridgeman's watercolour plans were clearly intended for presentation, either to or by a client; four, two for Eastbury in Dorset (BoL MSGD a3 fo.9 and fo.10), one for Amesbury in Wiltshire, and one for Lumley Castle in County Durham, also have a cartouche, although it is empty on the plan for Lumley Castle. All are beautifully executed, with similar iconography. Trees, carefully drawn in a characteristic stylised triangular shape with shadows to the right, are depicted in groves, arranged on a regular grid pattern, and picked out in a darker green. The space around them is filled, often also on a regular grid, with ghostly partial representations of the same symbol, the whole coloured with a mottled green wash. Only on the watercolour plans for Sacombe and Ledston is the depiction different. On these two plans the groves are depicted by a much more thickly painted mottled green background without the addition of standard trees. Houses are shown in red or pink, and are all presented in plan; the footprint is accurately represented. Garden buildings are also shown in plan, making it difficult to interpret what they are intended to be. Other structures and earthworks are treated in a way that suggests a three-dimensionality. Water, where it is presented, is shown in blue. The design is often fixed in its geographical space. At Brocket Hall (if indeed by Bridgeman), annotations suggest the towns which might be seen from viewpoints to the north of the site, and in the plan for Lumley Castle the 'River Were' is labelled. Topography is indicated with hachures, shaded in pencil. Audley End shows the fields and hedgerows of surrounding farmland. Warwick Priory sets the design for the garden in the context of the town of Warwick.

It would be reasonable to assume that these watercolour plans, which span Bridgeman's whole career from Sacombe in 1715 to Amesbury Abbey in 1738, were intended to present a design to the client, once the work had been commissioned. Perhaps those with a cartouche –Amesbury Abbey, Eastbury, Marble Hill and Lumley Castle– echo the estate map tradition and were intended for display purposes; one of the two plans for Lumley Castle currently hangs, framed, in the study of the Earl of Scarborough (Earl of Scarborough pers. comm. 2019). It is clear that it is now considered an artefact in its own right, whether or not that was Bridgeman's original intention. Perhaps we might have expected the presentation of both the house at the centre of the design and the garden buildings to be in elevation, if the purpose was to enable the client to visualise Bridgeman's imagined landscape. The absence of this in almost all the watercolour plans may reflect the extent of Bridgeman's responsibilities. He was the garden designer, not the architect of the buildings. It may simply be consistent with the early eighteenth-century trend in estate maps towards presenting buildings in plan.

However, these plans seem to have had a purpose beyond display. Many of them seem to have become working documents, too, in the manner of estate maps or surveys. There is evidence that, at the very least, they facilitated discussion. This certainly seems to be the case with Brocket Hall, where an alternative to the course of the river is shown, at Wolterton, where there are several plans showing small alterations in design, and at Eastbury, where the plan (BoL MSGD a3* fo.9) offers a flap with alternative versions of the mount. More importantly, there is also evidence that they were able to double as designs from which other, more functional plans could be derived. Several have pinpricks along the lines of the principal features, as for example do the plans for Gunton, for Sacombe and for Audley End; these show that other plans were copied from them, or that they themselves are copies (Stephen Astley pers. comm). It may be that this is why most of them remained in Bridgeman's workshop, and are found now in Gough Drawings. It is possible that the plans copied from these presentation plans disappeared when the landscape was being built. On the most accomplished plan for Wolterton, (BoL MSGD a4 fo.20), pencil measurements,

'196' and '301', have been added to the geometric grove to the west of the house, suggesting that even this immaculately presented plan was used, in some way, during construction. Perhaps the use of hachures to show topography, where it was significant, also reflects the practical purpose that these plans fulfilled. Some, though not all, also have a scale: those for Eastbury (BoL MSGD a3 fo.9 and fo.10), Wolterton (BoL MSGD a4 fo.18 and a4 fo.20) (Figure 10), Gunton, Hampton Court and Kensington Gardens (NS CC.2753); the plans for Lumley Castle (1 and 2) have scales in feet, while Brocket Park and Amesbury have scales in feet and in chains, again perhaps reflecting their purpose to be both presentation drawing and survey.

A large proportion of Bridgeman's plans were executed in brown or grey ink and pencil, with additional wash. In spite of the similarity in their medium, these drawings are not by any means completely homogenous. However, a group of twelve, all in Gough Drawings, are so similar in their characteristics that they were probably done by the same hand, and, since one of them, of an as yet unidentified landscape (BoL MSGD a4 fo.25) (Figure 13), has the initials 'CB' at the end of an extensive note on the right-hand side of the plan, it seems likely that they are all the work of Bridgeman. They are the plans for (with approximate dates): Hackwood (BoL MSGD a4 fo.24), c.1720; Hackwood (BoL MSGD a4 fo.34a), c.1720; Houghton (BoL MSGD a4 fo.7), c.1722; Lodge Park (BoL MSGD a4 fo.68), c.1725 (Figure 9); Moor Park (BoL MSGD a4 fo.58), c.1720; Purley (BoL MSGD a4 fo.54), c.1720; Rousham (BoL MSGD a4 fo.63), c.1720; Tring (BoL MSGD a4 fo.78), c.1720; the unidentified plan (BoL MSGD a4 fo.25); and three for Wimpole (BoL MSGD a4 fo.30, BoL MSGD a4 fo.31, BoL MSGD a3 fo.69). As far as it is possible to date these plans accurately, they appear to come from the earlier part of his career, before, or just after, his appointment as Royal Gardener.

These plans look very similar. Almost all show buildings, regardless of status, in plan; only in two instances is this not the case: Hackwood (BoL MSGD a4 fo.34), where the roof of the house is shown faceted, and Moor Park where some peripheral buildings beyond the edge of the designed landscape are shown as rough drawings, in elevation. Earthworks are shown with pencil shading giving a sense of three-dimensionality. Groves are shown using the same unformed tree symbols as in the watercolour plans. On the other hand, avenues of trees are generally shown as dots, rather than in elevation, except at Houghton and Lodge Park. Water is shown either in a grey wash, or sketched in with short strokes in ink.

Most significantly, all have annotations of some kind which are to do with the practicalities of creating the design depicted. On some there are measurements – apparently of distances – in feet, for example on the plans for Hackwood (BoL MSGD a4 fo.34). On some, there are specific planting instructions. The plan for Wimpole (BoL MSGD a4 fo.31) details the 'Number of trees in this plantation': 'From the further end to the Circle round the Great Bason 358/Round the said Circle 98/From the Circle to the Great Parade 456/Rund the said Parades

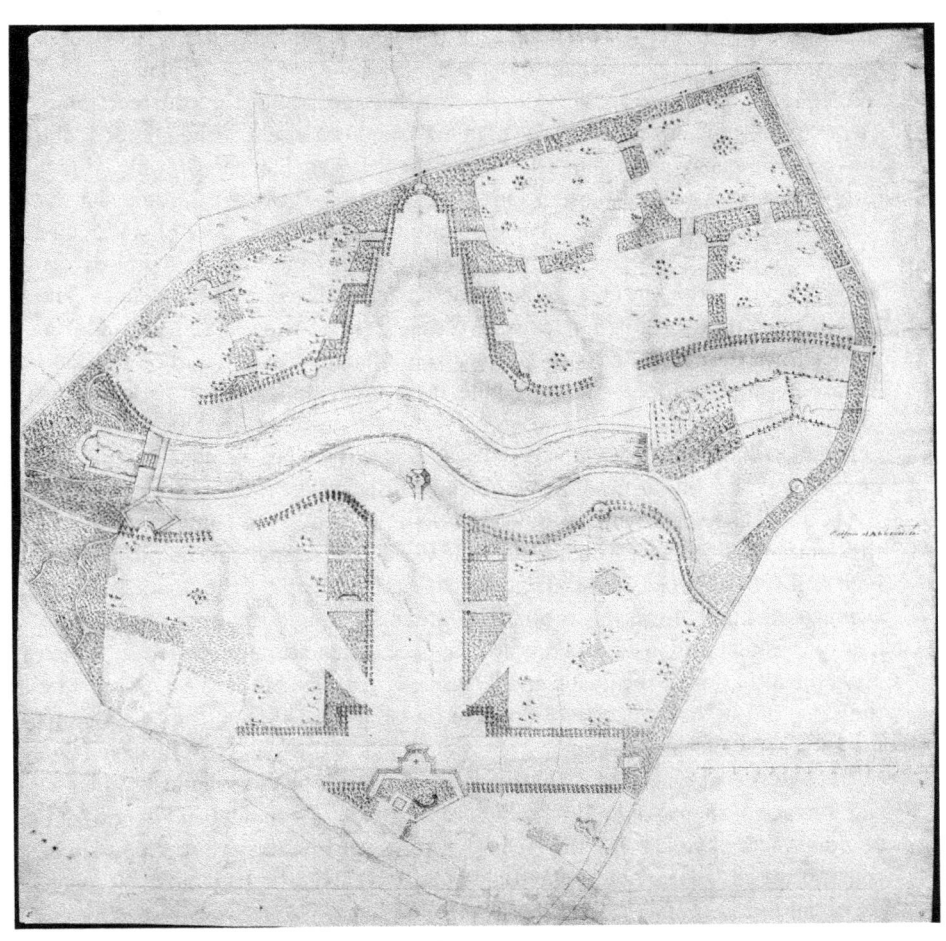

Figure 9. Lodge Park. MSGD a4 fo.68. The Bodleian Libraries, University of Oxford.

304/1216'. The plan for Tring has an annotation which reads '106 Standard Yews for the/2 Inward Lines &/106 Standard Elms for the/outward Lines'. There are also detailed instructions about building. Sometimes, as on the plan for Lodge Park (Figure 9), this is a single sentence: 'Platform at A to be rais'd. 10ft.'; or for Tring (MSGD a4 fo.78), two sentences: 'Bason remov'd within 32 feet of the walk near ye Gt. Elms/ fall of ye Theater from * to * 34 feet'. (Here, Bridgeman uses asterisks to refer to two points on the plan.) In others, notably Hackwood, Tring (MSGD a4 fo.32), Rousham and, particularly, the unidentified plan MSGD a4 fo.25 (Figure 13), there are very detailed instructions about the construction of elements of the landscape. On the plan for Tring, the levels of the stepped land down to the canal are given: 'The Canall 3 feet lower than the Gravell Garden', '3 foot below ye Gravell Garden', and 'the Levell of ye Gravell Garden'. On the plan for Rousham, there are measurements to do with the flow of water into the square pools: 'The Current or Fall of the Water from the place propos'd to bring it from further springs to the great square pond is 15 foot 6 inches – The length from ye s[ai]d further springs to the Nether Spring is 890 foot & from thence to ye Garden water is 300 foot & from thence cross the Garden to the sd Square pond is 480 foot – in the whole 1670. foot'. On the plan for Hackwood (BoL MSGD a4 fo.34), there are two sets of instructions. One, above a section entitled 'A Section of the Terrace, Stocades/& Fossee', is for constructing the ditches and bastions around the woodland garden: 'The stocades are to be each 6 feet 6 inches long & 4 Inches Square/ & to be placed in the Slope according to the Section at 6 Inches assunder/ [illegible word] is a parapet yew hedge of 2 feet high that seperates the Terrace from Stocade'. The other is at the top of the plan. Damage means that there is probably a line missing, and the words of the first half of the next line are obscured. It is about construction of walks: ' ...Which gives the Situation of the Bason and [illegible] /the Levell of the Walk AA must be the Level of the Walks/of each Side of ye Canall as farr as from the Letters/A to the Letters B which are the ends of the Side Walks of the /parterr./The inside line of trees of the sd Walk AABB are to be ... /same lines as ye pyramid yews on ye side Tarrace of the Parterre & ye Walks are to stand ... / a parelell of 7 feet within ye side Walks of ye Parterr/ the trees that form ye sd Walks are to stand 2 feet apart/ in ye lines'. The unidentified plan MSGD a4 fo.25 has the most extensive set of annotations of all (see Chapter 5) (Figure 13).

These plans appear to have been more or less accurately surveyed and, where any of the landscape has survived into the 21st century, it is clear that the instructions were followed. This is certainly true of Lodge Park. Here georeferencing with the 1st Edition Ordnance Survey 1887 reveals a very close, almost perfect, correlation between Bridgeman's plan and the stands of trees, particularly on the west of the deeply incised valley (Figure 9). A palimpsest of the tree lines in Bridgeman's design is still visible today. It is hard to avoid the conclusion that these 12 plans represent working drawings, the result of discussions with the client, from which a landscape might be constructed, with or without Bridgeman's direct and continuous supervision. There is evidence that at Lodge Park, at least, the intention was to use the plan to construct a landscape without the continuous presence of Bridgeman or his workforce. The design is mentioned in Sir John Dutton's will (1742):

> I strictly enjoin and desire every person in whom my estate shall vest this my will to finish and perfect the plantations I have begun at my new park and all other work I entended there pursuant to a plan made by Mr Charles Bridgeman for that purpose which plan I desire may be strictly pursued excepting only those particulars which I shall direct to be varied from in a paper in my own handwriting which I leave enclosed in this my will and when the same are finished I desire they may be always kept on good order. (GA D678 FAM 57)

The phrasing of this section of the will suggests that the work at Lodge Park had been begun by Sir John Dutton himself, working from a plan by Bridgeman. Two payments to Bridgeman were made from Dutton's accounts on 22 December 1729: 18s 6d was paid for 'Expenses at Oxford Fetching Mr Bridgeman to make a plan for my New Park', and £70 paid to 'Mr Bridgeman for his journeys to Shireborn and making a plan for my New Park' (Smith 2006, 237). These payments suggest a visit to make the plan, rather than a prolonged supervision of work.

If that was the case, it is not entirely clear why they should have remained in Bridgeman's drawing office and come to us as part of Gough Drawings, but perhaps copies were taken from them, as probably happened at Moor Park (see MSGD a4 fo.48 in the following section), perhaps in pencil, for easier use in the field. The plans for Houghton, Moor Park, Purley and Wimpole (BoL MSGD a4 fo.69) all have a series of pin pricks along the ink lines, also noted on some of the watercolour plans discussed above and presumably for the same purpose: that of making accurate copies (Stephen Astley pers. comm. 2013). Indeed, the pencil drawing of Moor Park (BoL MSGD a4 fo.48) appears to be an almost identical copy of the ink drawing (BoL MSGD a4 fo.58), although on a bigger scale. Perhaps Bridgeman retained oversight, as well as a copy of the design, from which other functional drawings might have been taken. None of the 12 appear to have an accompanying watercolour presentation plan, which may be significant, suggesting that they were in some way the finished product rather than a stage in the design process. While they are detailed and rigorous in their practical presentation of the landscape, the absence of trees presented in elevation suggests a tension between the need for speed and the need for clarity. Tree symbols in elevation, drawn to the standard of Bridgeman's presentation work, must have taken a long time to produce. The need for speed may also be the reason why the drawings are executed in ink and pencil, which was surely a much quicker process. Six of the ink plans, two for Boughton House and four for Wimpole Hall, appear to have been retained by Bridgeman's clients and remain in estate archives. This provenance makes it less likely that they were Bridgeman's master copies, but it is not impossible.

These plans can probably stand for the purpose of all the drawings executed in ink and pencil in Bridgeman's corpus. They were specifically created to act as working drawings of one kind or another, even the pen and ink plan for Gobions, which is so much bigger than any of the others and therefore rather an anomaly. As Rowe and Williamson note (Rowe and Williamson 2012, 86), although apparently unfinished, the earthworks in Gobions Wood, mapped and recorded by Tom Williamson, still follow accurately the plan Bridgeman drew (Rowe and Williamson 2012, 88). It follows then that, in spite of its size, the Gobions plan must have been effective enough in conveying the layout of the site for construction to take place. Its large size may have been necessary because the design shows a wilderness detached from the house, and at a distance from it, containing a large number of features, and then avenues which fan out a surprising distance into the park and terminating in focal points. If we imagine that Sambrooke intended to create the garden without continuous supervision from Bridgeman, he would have needed detailed drawings in elevation of the summerhouses and other garden buildings, careful, scaled drawings of the earthworks in the wilderness, and accurate depictions of the ends of long avenues. The size of the map and its nature are then less surprising.

There are also a small number of drawings in the collection which are entirely, or almost entirely, in pencil. These are probably also part of the practical process of creating a landscape. Three, those for Audley End, Wimbledon and Moor Park, are copies of drawings in watercolour or ink. Audley End has an exact equivalent in watercolour, and pin pricks suggest one was copied from the other (see above). The plan for Wimpole (BoL MSGD a4 fo.35) also has an exact equivalent in ink (BoL MSGD a4 fo.69). These seem to suggest either that the original drawing was done in pencil, which might well be the case if these drawings represent a survey taken in the field using a plane table, or that a copy was made of the original drawing for use by the client, and others, while Bridgeman retained the original. Some, such as the pencil drawing of Wolterton (BoL MSGD a4 fo.56), appear to be rough sketches of a possible design for the landscape. The arc of trees shown stretching out to the east of Wolterton Hall seems to be a tentative proposal, and one that was not executed. The pencil drawing of Moor Park (BoL MSGD a4 fo.48) suggests revision of ideas. While pin pricks in it suggest that it was a copy or was used to make a copy, there are significant differences between it and the similar ink drawing of Moor Park (BoL MSGD a4 fo.58). It ignores the wider park, which is shown in the ink drawing. It also shows a reworking of ideas for the south-eastern triangle. Serpentine paths have been superimposed over straight ones, and cabinets re-sited. In other places, steps have been roughly sketched in over the existing walls, and terracing added and then crossed through. The pencil plan for Wimbledon Park in Surrey, bought by the Duchess of Marlborough in 1731 (BoL MSGD a4 fo.44), has some major lines inked in, and appears to be a survey, or an early plan, for the finished watercolour drawing of Wimbledon (BoL MSGD a3 fo.31). It shows surveying lines and a grid. It is annotated with measurements and the curves of the turning circle on either side of the house, which are shown on the watercolour version. It probably shows the scaffolding of earth works which underpins the dramatic curving bowl through which the house is approached in the watercolour version of the plan (MSGD a3 fo.31). It is possible that it was the result of Bridgeman's visit to Wimbledon with the Duchess of Marlborough on 21 August 1732, of which she wrote 'I was yesterday at Wimbledon from 10 in the morning till eight at night, and I want but very little to make the place complete according to my own taste. Mr Bridgman went with me to take measures to make the way from the common to the house. He says it will be done in a month, and will be a vast addition to the place' (Scott Thompson 1946, 169).

It is unusual for the working plans of a landscape designer, if that is what they are, to have survived in such numbers. As Dixon Hunt suggests (in relation to Kent's drawings, but it is as likely to apply to all designers): 'This absence of instructional drawings may, of course, be explained by the fact that any papers used on site by gardeners are likely to be in no state for retention' (Dixon Hunt 1987, 42). This may also, incidentally, explain the general absence of evidence of plans taken from Bridgeman's master drawings, although some of the pencil drawings discussed in the next section might derive from this source. Plans were often drawn on an *ad hoc* basis to solve problems on site. There is certainly evidence that Le Nôtre worked in this way: 'Once a project was validated, its actual realization on site gave rise to further working drawings that could be modified at will' (Bouchenot-Déchin 2014, 146). This was apparently quite common practice amongst seventeenth-century architects, including Sir Christopher Wren and his draughtsman in the building of St Paul's Cathedral in London (Gerbino and Johnston 2009, 102). It may be that they were not created in the first place, or that they were so ephemeral in nature that they were lost. It may also be that Bridgeman developed *modus operandi* which were different from those of his contemporaries, facilitated by the ink drawings.

This analysis suggests that there are, broadly, three types of plan in Bridgeman's corpus fulfilling three essentially separate but probably, in practice, overlapping functions. The first type, watercolour plans, were designed for presentation, either to help the client envisage Bridgeman's proposal or to be hung in the client's house – or both. The second type were ink master plans designed to provide practical instructions for building (especially useful in the absence of Bridgeman), or as tools for consultation, and from which it is likely that other plans in pencil, a medium more suitable for outdoor work, were devised. The third type were working sketches in pencil, some of which must have been preparatory for the other two types, and some of which must have been derived from them. They were probably designed for use in the field, since both ink and watercolour would have been impractical outdoors. As suggested in Chapter 2, there were also surveys done by others and given to Bridgeman as a starting point for his own work. It seems that he rarely produced a survey of his own which preceded a design, although he certainly surveyed existing landscapes, for example the bank of the Thames at Hampton Court (BoL MSGD a4 fo.74). The design and the survey were incorporated into one plan, although, as at Hackwood, he seems sometimes to have resurveyed a landscape and annotated the estate survey with his own amendments. These three loose categories of plan do not necessarily represent stages in any kind of formulaic linear process, especially since there is currently only one site, Scampston, with both a watercolour plan and an ink plan. It is simply a way of considering the function of different kinds of plan within a process from commission to execution.

The loose process this represents is probably best seen in the extensive set of seven plans that exist for Wolterton, Horatio Walpole's house in Norfolk. The plans probably date from between 1722 and 1725; in 1722 Horatio Walpole bought the estate at Wolterton in Norfolk and began remodeling the existing house with Thomas Ripley, the Palladian architect. He seems to have commissioned Joseph Carpenter, gardener and partner at Brompton Park Nursery, to redesign the landscape at the same time. In November 1724 the existing house burnt down. William Britiffe, Walpole's chief steward at Wolterton, wrote to Walpole to inform him of this on 29 November 1724:

> Today the 11th instant about Eleven a Clockatt night a ffire hapned in your House att Woolter-ton which Demolished the Dwelling House the Gardiners Boy was Burnt ... The whole House as Farr as the Brew House was burnt ... Mr Bayfield sends me word there is not a piece of timber left in the whole House worth anything, very Little of the furniture saved ... (WH 8/5A Box 73L)

At the suggestion of Ripley, the site of the house was moved a little to the west and north. Ripley wrote, in a letter to Walpole on 17 December 1724: 'I think you should put an Entire Stop to all your works at Woolterton; Because I believe you will find a More Convenient Place to set your House in then were it now is' (WH 8/5A Box 73L). It is clear that planning a new landscape to go with the new house began at roughly the same time, although apparently not with Joseph Carpenter. Britiffe reported to Walpole on 9 December 1724 in the immediate aftermath of the fire that he had met 'Mr Ripley & Mr Bridjely' so that he could 'Impart to them what [Walpole] desired'. The letter contains the following: 'P.S. Since the writing of this Mr Badjely have been with me, he saith that he have his old draught from whence he will prepare you a Plan to Answer the Severall matters wherein you desire satisfaction he wd deliver itt to Mr Ripley to be sent to you Mr Ripley now with me wee have talked the matter over and he will write to you the next week' (WH 8/5A Box 73L). There is some ambiguity about the identity of Ripley's companion, but it does seem likely, given the fluid approach to spelling in the early eighteenth century, that 'Mr Bridjely' and 'Mr Badjely' are both, in fact, Bridgeman.

The first in the series of plans (BoL MSGD a3 fo.33) probably comes from the period when Carpenter was in charge of remodelling the landscape; it is a survey of the estate and may well be by Carpenter himself, because, in addition to showing measurements pertaining to the size of each parcel of land, it depicts the canal, the design and construction of which he was responsible for, as shown by estate records (see Chapter 2).

The remaining six plans probably come from the period following the fire and may be directly connected to the visit of Ripley and Bridgeman to Britiffe in December 1724. The survey, although unaltered by Bridgeman, seems to provide a base map for a pencil drawing (BoL MSGD a4 fo.56) which is derived from it. On flimsy, light paper, and superimposed over ponds and plant nurseries shown on the Carpenter survey to the east of the house, it shows a semi-circular area with a belt of trees, tapering towards the west. The design shown extends into the land which was, at the time, leased to a tenant named Mr Jackson, suggesting that it is a tentative idea, sketched in, probably by Bridgeman, rather than any kind of concrete suggestion. It is possible that, since it does not show the canal, it predates Carpenter's survey and might be a preparatory sketch for it, but the presence of what appears to be a design idea, the semi-circular feature with trees, would tend to contradict this.

All the remaining plans seem to postdate this pencil drawing, since they do not show the original house that was destroyed by the fire; however, they all appear to predate 1729 because none show the stable block, the foundations of which were laid in that year (Peters 1991). The next plan in the sequence seems to be an ink and watercolour drawing of the more northerly half of the garden, immediately adjacent to the house (MSGD a4 fo.18). It is annotated with a key which explains how the proposed features of the new landscape have been superimposed on what remains of the original one. The relict features are labelled: 5 is 'Firr trees to be took away', 7 is 'The hole that was before the old House, Planted round with evergreens', 11 is 'Present Stables' and 12 is 'Kitchen Ground now'. New work is also indicated: 1 'Is your House', 8 is 'New Grove of Firrs which is at present Kitchen Ground', and 13 is part of a new kitchen garden 'took out of Jacksons Field'. A very much larger plan in watercolour and ink (BoL MSGD a3 fo.55) may be next in the sequence. There is no attempt now to show the remains of the relict landscape and it offers a pared-down version of the area around the house, although there are light pencil annotations – 'For ye Citchen Garden' and 'Nursery' – in the relevant locations. There are significant new features in the drawing: an avenue axially aligned to the eastern boundary of Brick Kiln Close, running south towards the lake and ending in a small apsidal cabinet with some kind of building at its southern end; and the first depiction of the lake itself. Again, this may well be a plan designed for discussion with the client.

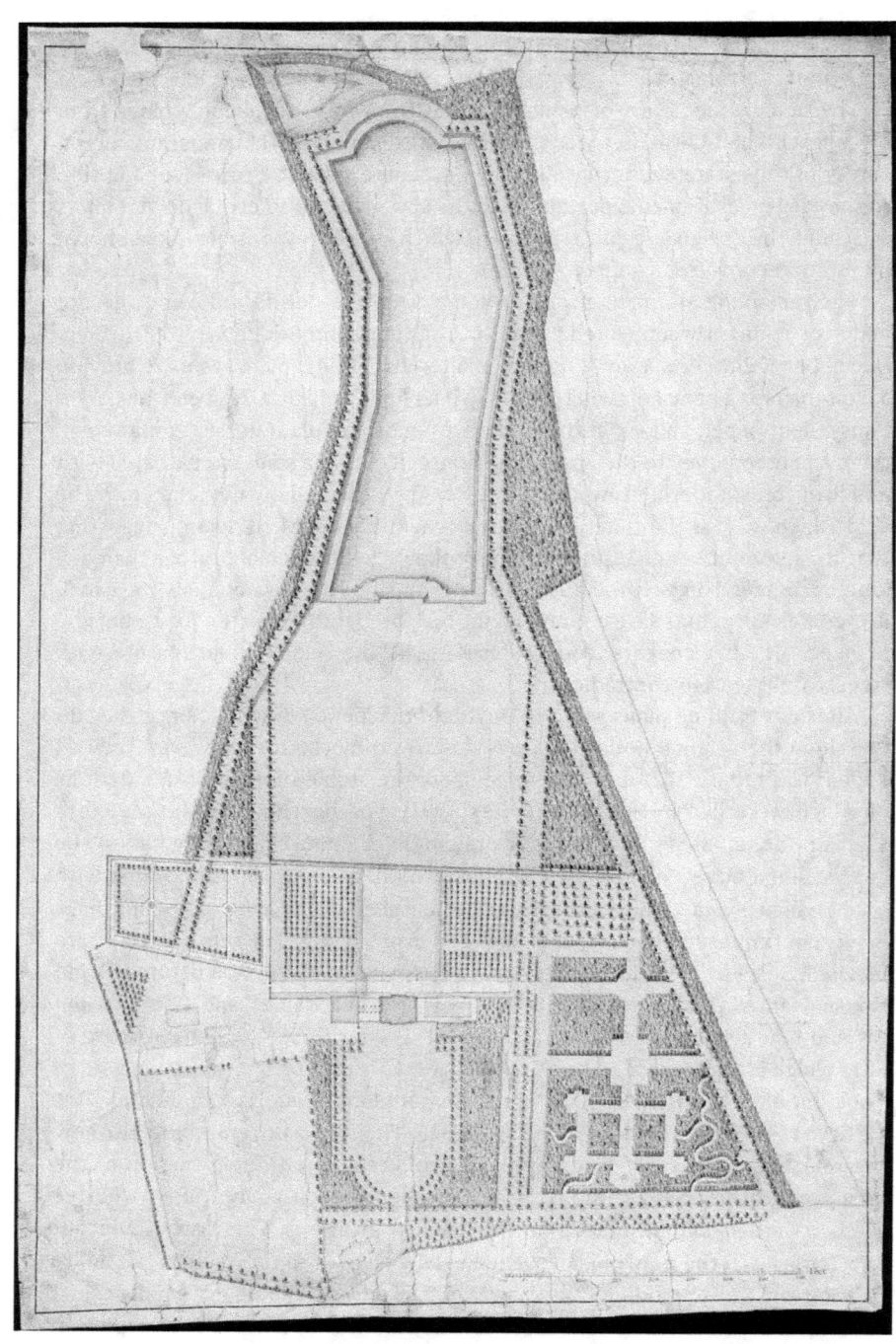

Figure 10. Wolterton Hall. MSGD a4 fo.20. The Bodleian Libraries, University of Oxford.

The last three plans, MSGD a4 fo.10, MSGD a4 fo.61 and MSGD a4 fo.20, are all identical in size. MSGD a4 fo.20 appears to be the final presentation copy, perhaps prepared for final approval by Horatio Walpole (Figure 10). It is a beautifully executed watercolour. To the north is an apsidal ended lawn, to the south the bowling green is flanked by plantations of trees, and beyond it there is the lake. To the west, a wilderness of geometrically arranged broadwalks and serpentine paths is depicted in three dimensions. It is the garden much as it appears on the Corbridge survey of 1732, except that the grove in Corbridge is less intricate. The other two clearly show the preliminaries to achieving this. Perhaps MSGD a4 fo.10 is the earlier because it still shows oval avenues on the bowling green to the south of the house, a feature of the earlier design (MSGD a4 fo.55). Its function, however, seems to have been to facilitate the construction of the lake. Along one side there is a section of the lake to scale, extending from the terrace immediately to the south of the house to the end of the lake. It is annotated with measurements: 'Fall from the Terras before the house to ye Ferosee 10 feet' and 'Fall from the Ferosee to the Water 21 feet', and shows the depth of the lake tapering towards its southern end. MSGD a4 fo.61 also shows the lake, but its purpose seems to be the design of the wilderness to the west of the house. It appears exactly as in the final design (MSGD a4 fo.20), but drawn carefully in pencil with pin pricks for transferring the design.

We are lucky that what we might loosely call a complete set of plans has survived for the landscape at Wolterton. The plans provide a record of what was probably the case at most other Bridgeman sites: a variety of drawings executed for very specific purposes in the process of taking a landscape from commission to completion. So, far from presenting us with inexplicable variety, the diverse forms taken by the drawings in Bridgeman's corpus simply have to do with their purpose. Bridgeman's contemporaries almost certainly created both presentation and working drawings in the same way. Unfortunately a large proportion of theirs have been lost, discarded as of little value or damaged, while Bridgeman's have survived, mostly in a packet of drawings passed to Clement Lemprière and collected by Richard Gough. This lucky accident has allowed us to probe beyond the existence of the artefact and its place in art history to the real processes behind the creation of a designed landscape.

CHAPTER 5

THE ART-HISTORICAL CONTEXT REVISITED

AS WITH MOST artists and designers, an effort has been made by subsequent academic writing to fit Bridgeman into the cultural and artistic context of his period. In the early eighteenth century, the period in which he was working, the elite – the rich, the intelligentsia, the literati – were preoccupied with defining themselves in the light of several essentially separate but closely related ideas. They discoursed in print, in correspondence and in conversation on the relationship between nature and the garden, the culture and politics of ancient Rome, the art, architecture and landscapes of Europe, and the development of a sense of Englishness which was distinct from the Europeaness of the near continent. So pervasive and persuasive did this discourse become that it has stood for the cultural life of the early eighteenth century ever since. Bridgeman was certainly more than peripherally involved in the elite and artistic circles where these topics were the badge of belonging, so perhaps it is no wonder that he was considered part of it. What is less clear is how it affected his work.

Bridgeman was both personally and professionally connected with those fashionable artistic circles. In 1726 he was elected a member of the Society of the Virtuosi of St Luke (c.1689–1743), 'the Tip top Clubbs of all, for men of the highest Character in Arts & Gentlemen Lovers of Art' (see Chapter 1), presumably following his appointment as Royal Gardener (Vertue, *Note books*, 3.120).[1] His fellow members included architect James Gibbs and writer George Vertue, the painter John Wootton, the enamellist Christian Friedrick Zincke and the sculptor John Michael Rysbrack, all of whom were elected in the same year as Bridgeman. Sir James Thornhill was also a member. His importance in these artistic circles is also implicit in his appearance in the painting *A Club of Artists* (1735), attributed to Gawen Hamilton, in which he appears with, amongst others, George Vertue, Michael Dahl, James Gibbs, John Wootton and William Kent, and in his appearance in Hogarth's *The Rake's Progress*. He was on visiting terms with the poet Alexander Pope.

---

[1] See online at https://doi.org/10.1093/ref:odnb/96316

Through the Office of Works, these connections were reinforced. The Office of Works was in charge of building for the monarchy from the medieval period. By the early eighteenth century this effectively meant all work on the royal palaces, buildings and land. The Offices within it were sinecures and, during Bridgeman's period as Royal Gardener, were held by artists, architects and master craftsmen well known to him. These men seem to have worked together, in loosely configured groupings, on a variety of public and private projects.

Bridgeman had worked with Sir John Vanbrugh, Comptroller of The King's Works from 1702 to 1726, and with his successor, Thomas Ripley (with whom he had also worked at Wolterton). He worked with William Kent, Master Carpenter from 1726 to 1735, and then Deputy Surveyor, with Sir James Thornhill, Serjeant Painter from 1720 to 1732, and with Henry Flitcroft, Clerk of Works at Richmond and Kew until 1728, and Roger Morris, who was Clerk of Works at Richmond New Park Lodge from 1727 onwards. He had also worked with Christopher Cass, Master Mason. Bridgeman's subscription to *Vitruvius Britannicus II* and *III* by Colen Campbell, published in 1717 and 1725 respectively, suggests that he was interested in, and in touch with, fashionable landscape and architectural design, as well as having a sufficient degree of business success to facilitate the subscription. It is significant that Bridgeman was the only gardener to subscribe to *Vitruvius Britannicus II* and one of only two to subscribe to *Vitruvius Britannicus III*. Rumble has suggested that 'the subscription lists for *Vitruvius Britannicus* show that it was neither priced to be, nor received as, a builder's manual, nor was it a stylistic manifesto. Rather it was a celebration of contemporary British architecture that gave pleasure and some instruction to polite society' (Rumble 2001, 3). Bridgeman appears to have been part of this audience.

The rise of the 'natural' garden is particularly pertinent to Bridgeman's work, because it is the only movement with which Bridgeman has been explicitly linked, both in the later eighteenth century, and by more modern scholarship (see Introduction). In the teleological narrative, summarised in the Introduction, for which Horace Walpole, the son of Sir Robert Walpole, is largely responsible, Bridgeman's work is made to fit into a model in which it is a forerunner of the English landscape garden, which found its apotheosis in Kent's vision that 'all nature was a garden' and which culminated, ultimately, in the work of Lancelot Brown. Walpole's exposition of this theory is to be found in a carefully constructed argument in *The History of the Modern Taste in Gardening* (Walpole 1995).

In fact, any reading of Walpole's elegantly argued essay needs to be mediated by attention to its purpose: a patriotic desire to prove that 'the imitation of Nature in Gardens, or rather in laying out Ground, still called Gardening for want of a specific term to distinguish an Art totally new, is Original and indisputably English' (Walpole 1995, 7). His further political agenda was 'linking the freedom of the new "natural" garden style with British liberty', as achieved under the Whig regime of his father Sir Robert Walpole, 'and pitting it against all foreign systems of oppression' (Walpole 1995, 14). The message is made explicit in his condemnation of European gardens, particularly French and Dutch, and implicit in the pejorative language he chooses to describe those gardens. For example, French gardens are full of constriction: flowers are in 'knots', every walk in 'buttoned' with flower pots, and of ridiculous frivolity 'parterres embroidered in patterns like a petticoat' (Walpole 1995, 26–27). This purpose is also clear in the way he presents Bridgeman as straddling the maligned formal style and the new, freer naturalness; the sentences and words are balanced between the two movements, as is Bridgeman's style: '… He enlarged his plans, disdained to make every division tally to its opposite, and though he still adhered much to strait walks, they were only his great lines; the rest he diversified by wilderness, and with loose groves of oak, though still within surrounding hedges'.

In spite of this, some modern garden historians have chosen to follow Walpole's assessment of Bridgeman. Willis, writing in *Charles Bridgeman and the English Landscape Garden*, suggests 'Horace Walpole gives Bridgeman a prominent place in these changes …' (Willis 2002, 18). Mavis Batey also implies that Bridgeman had some understanding of the 'natural style': 'Charles Bridgeman was eventually chosen to carry out Caroline's idea of helping Nature and not losing it in art' (Batey 2005, 205; 'Caroline' here refers to Queen Caroline). However, it is actually quite difficult to show that Bridgeman's gardens were part of the movement towards the 'natural' garden, as other modern scholars have found. Jacques, in *Georgian Gardens: The Reign of Nature*, sidesteps the difficulties of fitting Bridgeman into the 'natural' garden trajectory by acknowledging, in passing, his importance in garden design in the early eighteenth century, but choosing instead to concentrate on the gardens' cost rather than their design: 'Bridgeman's vast gardens, admired as they were, could be enormously costly' (Jacques 1983, 18). The problem with fitting Bridgeman's work into the 'natural' gardening narrative may have led to his relative absence from many important books which consider the rise of the English landscape garden. For example, there is no extensive consideration of his work in *The Genius of the Place* (1975) by Dixon Hunt and Willis, or in *Garden and Grove* (1986) by Dixon Hunt.

Perhaps some modern scholarship has been too reductive about the philosophical meaning of 'Nature' in the early eighteenth century, together with its meaning in a garden context. For example, Mavis Batey writes: 'Queen Anne's England suddenly learned that gardening was "near akin to Philosophy" when Anthony Ashley Cooper, 3rd Earl of Shaftesbury, Joseph Addison and Alexander Pope told them in quick succession that unadorned Nature was vastly superior to the "formal Mockery of Princely garden" they were then enjoying' (Batey 2005, 1). Her viewpoint is echoed by Jacques. He suggests that 'Joseph Addison and Alexander Pope both meant that bringing Nature into gardens was to apply Her precepts in *regular* gardens' (Jacques 1983, 11).

If Walpole's narrative has been the driver of this more modern discourse, it is perhaps because, by the time he was writing in the later eighteenth century, a clarity seems to have emerged about the meaning of 'Nature' in garden discourse.

It had been distilled into something coherent, which symbiotically reflected, and drove, the progress of the landscape garden. The words 'Nature', and 'natural' are ubiquitous in written garden discourse after about 1745. *The Genius of the Place* (Dixon Hunt and Willis, 1975), an anthology of writing from the seventeenth and eighteenth centuries collected together explicitly to chart the rise of the English landscape garden in writing, shows this. In a semi-fictional interview between William Shenstone and James Thomson (1746), Thomson is made to remark: 'You have nothing to do … but to dress Nature. Her robe is made ready'; in 1751, Joseph Spence writes: 'Gardening is an imitation of "Beautiful Nature" … Nature never plants by the line, or in angles'; in 1751, William Chambers writes of China: 'Nature is their pattern, and their aim to imitate her in all her beautiful irregularities'. This is a small sample of the examples found in extracts in the book, taken from the period after 1745 (Dixon Hunt and Willis, 1975). They make clear what is meant by 'Nature' in this later period: it is random and unregulated, but good, and gardens should echo this in their design. In fact, the meaning of 'Nature' in the context of gardening lacked this clarity in the early part of the eighteenth century. The writing of Shaftesbury, Addison and Pope, which Batey and Jacques rely on for their argument, is rather more complicated. Williamson has argued that Addison and Shaftesbury might have been 'misinterpreted in [an] eagerness to fit the whole of eighteenth-century garden history into a single minded quest for "nature", reading into these rather vague aspirations the seeds of a naturalistic gardening style which the authors would, in reality, have neither recognised nor liked' (Williamson 1995, 49). Perhaps Bridgeman's work cannot be made to fit the trajectory because it did not exist in the form Batey and Jacques suggest.

In the late seventeenth century and the early eighteenth century, the terms 'Nature' and 'natural', in the garden, can in part be defined in a Neo-Platonic sense: a series of universal and perfect forms which underlie the visible world, denoted by the word 'Nature', accessible through thought, and best represented by 'Art'. Garden design of the late seventeenth century was inspired by this idea. 'The gardens of Versailles … represented the natural world and man's place in it less by imitating the perceived face of nature, "the semblance of things", than by exhibiting, architectonically in the layout and emblematically through the sculpture programme, the forces that compose and sustain it' (Myers 2010, 4). Some modification of this philosophical position, and a subtle shift in the way 'Nature' and 'natural' are used, appear in the writing of Shaftesbury in 1709. Shaftesbury, in the passage most often quoted to support his supposed part in the rise of the English landscape garden, suggests that the essence of 'Nature' is better represented by wild nature than by art:

> Your genius, the genius of the place and the Great Genius have at last prevailed. I can no longer resist the Passion growing in me for Things of a *natural* kind; where neither *Art*, nor the *Conceit* of *Caprice* of Man has spoil'd their genuine

Order, by breaking in upon their *primitive State*. Even the rude *Rocks*, the mossy *Caverns*, the irregular unwrought *Grottos*, and the broken *Falls* of Waters, with all the horrid Graces of the *Wilderness* itself, as representing NATURE more, will be more engaging, and appear with a Magnificence beyond the formal Mockery of princely Gardens.

Here, although 'Shaftesbury was a Platonist', and 'for him the form of a thing, its constitutive essence, was crucial, and always signified the agency of the mind' (Myers 2010, 5), as Chambers has argued, he has his two protagonists 'not expressing a preference for wild gardens over "formal" gardens; instead they are caught in the act of preferring wild places rather than any kind of garden', since 'formal' in this context is used in the platonic sense of relating to 'forms' to qualify 'mockery', not 'gardens' (Chambers 1993, 52). Myers contends that Shaftesbury considered there was a 'hierarchy of landscapes' representing Plato's forms, and that 'untouched original landscape' represented 'the highest order of form' (Myers 2010, 10). Shaftesbury seems to be arguing that 'Nature', in a garden context, is still a reflection of an inner perception of the ideal forms, but was best represented by a nod to wild nature, a grotto or rocks, which most closely represents those ideal forms on earth; as Myers has argued, 'Shaftesbury found grottoes or rocks more "true" than the rest of the garden because they not only represented, but also resembled original nature' (Myers 2010, 11). So, as Myers suggests, the link between Shaftesbury and 'Nature' in the garden is rather nebulous and, although his celebration of the wilderness 'did eventually feed into the concept of the landscape garden', it was 'an unintended consequence' of his writing (Myers 2010, 5). In any case, it is clear that Shaftesbury's writing has little to do with how nature is manifested in either the English countryside or in gardens of the period, and it is important to note that he is not suggesting that gardens be left to wild nature. It is the act of the creation of artifice in imitation of what is wild that is important.

We can see the evolution of Shaftesbury's ideas in the writing of Alexander Pope. Pope is generally considered to be a Neo-Platonist and, as Myers has argued, 'is often linked to Shaftesbury in his philosophical outlook' (Myers 2010, 13), although Maynard Mack considers a direct link between Shaftesbury's and Pope's views to be debatable, arguing that Pope's neo-Platonic ideas might 'equally well be owing to the Stoic and Platonic writers ... whom every educated neo-classicist knew' (Maynard Mack in Myers 2010, 13). Pope's most often quoted passages reflect the view that ideal Nature is accessible through the intellect, and there is again a strong sense that it is wild nature that best embodies a sense of the ideal essence. In his essay, published in Richard Steele's short-lived newspaper *The Guardian* in 1713, he argues for the superiority of Nature: 'How contrary to this Simplicity is the modern Practice of Gardening; we seem to make it our Study to recede from Nature, not only in the various Tonsure of Greens into the most regular and formal Shapes, but even in monstrous Attempts beyond the reach of the Art it self' (Pope in Dixon Hunt and Willis 1975, 207). In his 'Epistle to Burlington' (1731), it is wild 'Nature' and 'the Genius of the Place' that best echo their ideal essences, and are responsible for the inspiration the gardener, and the artist, needs:

> In all, let Nature never be forgot…
> Consult the Genius of the Place in all;
> That tells the Waters or to rise, or fall,
> Or helps th'ambitious Hill the heav'ns to scale,
> Or scoops in circling theatres the Vale;
> Calls in the Country, catches op'ning Glades,
> Joins willing woods, and varies shades from Shades;
> Now breaks, or now directs, th'intending Lines,
> Paints as you plant, and as you work, Designs.
> (Pope's *Epistle to Burlington* lines 50 and 57–64, in Davis 1966)

While Pope's influence on the development of 'taste' in gardening in between 1720 and 1740 is significant, his contribution to the perceived roots of the 'natural' movement in his *Guardian* essay of 1713 has probably been exaggerated, perhaps with teleological insight. Martin has suggested that 'There is little sign in the essay that he had wrestled with the practical problems of garden design' (Martin 1984, 4).

Addison, who Batey and others place with Shaftesbury and Pope as being influential to the rise of the 'natural' garden, was in fact a disciple of the seventeenth-century philosopher John Locke; with Locke, Addison rejected the neo-platonic idea that art and nature imitated each other because of some 'supra-sensible reality apparent only to thought', arguing instead that the beauty of nature was perceived through the senses – in particular, as Myers has argued, through sight (Myers 2013, 1). In Addison's writing, the terms 'Nature' and 'natural' are used to denote the way in which a landscape evolves its own patterns and beauty. He explores, in essays in the *Spectator*, this idea in relation to the presentation of nature in art and, in particular, in painting. He argues for the superiority of 'the Works of Nature' over 'Art': 'If we consider the Works of Nature and Art, as they are qualified to entertain the Imagination, we shall find the last very defective, in Comparison of the former; for though they may sometimes appear as Beautiful or Strange, they can have nothing in them of that Vastness and Immensity, which afford so great an Entertainment to the Mind of the Beholder' (Addison 1710–1712, No. 404). In these essays, there is a perceptible shift in meaning in the terms 'Nature and 'natural'. Addison's ideal 'natural' landscape is one in which design comes about by serendipity, as outlined in his paper No. 417 (Addison 1710–1712): it is 'a Prospect which is well laid out, and diversified with Fields and Meadows, Woods and Rivers; in those accidental Landskips of Trees, Clouds and Cities … in what we call the Works of Chance' (Addison 1710–1712, No. 417). Here Addison is not writing about wilderness or pristine 'Nature', as his inclusion of 'Fields and Meadows' and even 'Cities' makes clear. His conception of 'Nature' is clearly of something man-made, but within which the natural world has been allowed some freedom, so that the appearance is of wildness. In his paper No. 477 (Addison 1710–1712) he describes his garden as 'a Confusion of Kitchin and Parterre, Orchard and Flower Garden, which lie so mixt and interwoven, that if a Foreigner who had seen nothing of our Country should be conveyed into my Garden at his first landing, he would look upon it as a natural Wilderness ...', and suggests that plants grow in it where they are most comfortable: 'There is the same Irregularity in my Plantations, which run into as great a Wildness as their Natures will permit. I take in none that do not naturally rejoyce in the Soil ...' (Addison 1710–1712). Addison seems to be clearly framing 'Nature' within the confines of a man-made environment, whether that be a garden or a pastoral landscape.

These complex threads of philosophical thinking about 'Nature', once accessible only to an elite of intellectuals and fashionable people of taste, and to the craftsmen and artists who carried out the work, appear to have begun to emerge into published writing of a more practical kind. Switzer, Langley and Bradley all develop Addison's vision into a gardening style guided by his conception of nature. Switzer consciously and deliberately echoes Addison's views to support his own version of garden design, 'Rural and Extensive Gardening', in *Ichnographia Rustica* III, first published six years later in 1718 (Switzer 1718). He quotes an extensive passage from Addison's paper No. 404 (Addison 1710–1712), attributing it to 'the ingenuous Author' in his vision of 'extensive and rural gardening':

> ... the Beauty of the largest and finest of Regular Gardens is easily discover'd, whereas were they laid out in a more Natural and Rural Manner, the Eye would always be discovering new Objects, and be lost in that inexpressible somewhat to be found in the Beauty of Nature, in a Rude Copice or amidst the Irregular turnings of a wild Corn Field. (Switzer 1718, 5)

Here we see that 'Natural' and 'Rural' qualify each other, juxtaposed with 'Regular Gardens'. Batty Langley, in his *New Principles of Gardening*, also appears to echo Addison when he considers that 'There is nothing adds so much to the Pleasure of a Garden, as those great Beauties of Nature, *Hills* and *Valleys* ...'; this passage is about their destruction by 'our *regular Coxcombs*' who 'to their great Misfortune ... always deviate from Nature, instead of imitating it' (Langley 1728). For all three, the making of a 'natural' garden also has the practical advantage of saving money. Langley comments on the '*regular Coxcombs*', who have gone to 'a very Great Expence in Levelling' (Langley 1728, 194). Bradley writes of 'Benjamin Townsend' that 'his Works convince me of his Capacity of doing great Things; and of his considering how to contract the Expence which is no less Commendable; his Designs shew us his Judgement in Preserving and even Improving the natural

Beauties of irregular Ground ...' (Bradley 1725, 360). For Switzer, it is a guiding principle, and *Ichnographia Rustica* is peppered with the word 'Expence'. For example, here it is used in relation to walls: 'What I would advise chiefly, is, by all Means to avoid the Expence of long Court-Walls, especially in Rural and Forest Seats' (Switzer 1718, 149).

In spite of the popularity of, and the fascination with, the concept of 'Nature' in elite circles, and its undoubted emergence in practical writing of the time, there is very little evidence in gardens built before 1740 that a deliberate effort was made to create a 'natural' garden. Williamson has argued that, from 'the actual layout of gardens in this period ... there is little evidence on the ground for the creation of more "natural" scenes' (Williamson 1995, 49). He continues: 'At all social levels, square level lawns, straight walks flanked by topiary, wildernesses criss-crossed with allées, and avenues focused in the main façade of the house continued to be popular into the 1730s and '40s, and indeed beyond' (Williamson 1995, 49). Williamson also points out that, while Switzer was writing with conviction about a natural gardening style from 1718 onwards, he designed a formal garden at Caversham in the same year, and that, when in *Ichnographia Rustica II* Switzer writes instructions for the construction of parterres, 'it is with an embarrassed recognition that these were contrary to the "simple, plain, and unaffected Method I have propos'd myself"' (p. 190) (Williamson 1995, 49).

It is perhaps, then, unsurprising that there is no written commentary, before 1730, to link Bridgeman's style to the discourse on natural gardening. For example, Switzer does not refer to Bridgeman at all in the first edition of *Ichnographia Rustica*. He praises Bridgeman in *Hydrostaticks* (1729) as 'now deservedly advanc'd to be one of His Majesty's Gardeners' (p. 91) and the 'very ingenious Mr. *Bridgeman*' (p. 405). However, after 1730, it is easy to find in Switzer's writing explicit and implicit criticism that Bridgeman's style is not 'natural' enough, although largely this is linked to the extravagance of his landscapes. In A Proemial Essay in the 1742 edition of *Ichnographia Rustica*, Switzer criticises Bridgeman for this, in contrast to his own precepts of 'rural gardening'; he is referred to as 'a late eminent Designer in Gardening whose Fancy could not be bounded' and 'that otherwise ingenious Designer' for 'aiming at an incomprehensible Vastness, and attempting at Things beyond the reach of Nature'. And he is criticised for the size of his lawns: 'no Parterre or Lawn that was not less than 50 or 60 Acres, some of them 80, 90 or 100' and for 'his Plan of Lakes' which were constructed 'without any regard to the Goodness of the Land, which was to be overflowed, but which he generally designed so large, as to make a whole Country look like an Ocean' (Switzer 1742, I, 11, 12). Pope's *Epistle IV* to Burlington (1731) refers pejoratively to Bridgeman's style because of both its expense and its failure to follow 'Nature', although in later versions of the poem Bridgeman's name was changed to 'Cobham' because, apparently, Bridgeman objected, and possibly also because the same criticism could now be applied to the work at Stowe, showing how gardening taste was shifting. The passage immediately preceding the one in which Bridgeman's name appeared is often quoted, and forms part of an endorsement of Burlington's taste, and, most particularly, his sense. This is demonstrated by his lack of extravagance in terms of both the size and the cost of his works, and Pope draws negative comparisons with 'Le Nôtre', with 'Versailles', and also with Bridgeman. At least four lines originally explicity referred to him:

> The vast parterres a thousand hands shall make
> Lo! *Bridgeman* comes, and floats them with a lake:
> Or cut wide views through mountains to the plain,
> You'll wish your hill or shelter'd seat again
>
> (Davis 1966, my italics)

The last two lines probably refer to Moor Park, where the landscape was designed by Bridgeman for Benjamin Styles.

The intellectual constructions of Nature clearly fascinated the intellectual elite of the day and, possibly as a result of Horace Walpole's essay, have continued to fascinate garden historians. However, the difficulty of finding any link between this fashionable discourse on gardening from the early years of the eighteenth century and commentary on Bridgeman's work in the same period suggests that, although these ideas were clearly popular with the literary elite who published them, they had less effect on the general practice of garden design. The evidence for its influence is based on a very few well-known texts by a very few well-known writers. The paucity of this written evidence is suggestive of what little importance was placed on the idea of 'Nature' by garden practitioners in the early eighteenth century, especially before about 1730, so that, although it looms large in garden history, it is probably of very little importance as an influence on Bridgeman.

But if we can largely dismiss the rise of the natural garden as a determiner for Bridgeman's work, the picture is more complicated when we consider the influence of Europe. From the late seventeenth century until the early nineteenth century a trip to Europe, and in particular to Italy – often termed 'the Grand Tour' – was considered an essential part of a rich, fashionable young man's education. As result there was a fascination with Italian gardens, which were viewed through the lens of both Ancient Rome and the Italian art of the Renaissance, and with the gardens of other European countries, with the Netherlands and Germany with whom the English had shared a monarch, and with the nearest neighbour, France.

Classical discourse also seems to have pervaded all aspects of intellectual and artistic life in the first part of the eighteenth century. The ruling Court Whigs appear to have seen themselves as the heirs to ancient Rome's Augustan age. Theirs was '[t]he dominant political discourse of the beneficiaries of the Glorious Revolution' which 'was appropriate to an oligarchy intent on maintaining power and privileges won at the expense of the crown and the Stuart cause' (Ayres 1997, 1). The political analogies they drew between themselves and the Augustans pervade the early eighteenth century. For example, at Houghton, 'Walpole was imaging himself as a Roman in his busts and in the iconography of the interior of his own house...' (Ayres 1997, 49). However, as Ayres has pointed out, '[t]his discourse, whose key terms were "liberty" and "virtue", was not the preserve of the ruling Whigs, though they might think of it as peculiarly theirs, but was current within most of the political tendencies of the first half of the eighteenth century, including Court Whig, dissident Whig (or "Patriot") Opposition, Tory and even to an extent Jacobite' (Ayres 1997, 1).

Classical allusion provided the shared language by which gardens were read. In the garden, it provided a 'labelling' to denote meaning (Paulson 1975, 20). Paulson suggests that statues which alluded to classical stories created meaning for visitors: 'In effect, these known elements were used like words to make new sentences. Venus plus Mars in a garden setting equals the fruitful marriage of Love and War ... To judge from the accounts we have of visitors of the 1730s and 1740s the emblem was primary ...' (Paulson 1975, 21). This seems to have been largely deliberate, especially in gardens such as Stowe or Chiswick. As Whatley wrote, in *Observations on Modern Gardening*, of 'emblematical' devices: 'through an illusion to a favourite or well known subject of history, poetry, or of tradition, [they] may now and then animate or dignify a scene ...' (Whatley 1770, 151). Dixon Hunt has argued: 'While it would be absurd to claim that all emphases upon variety, natural appearance of ground, rural imagery, statues and temples signalled a conscious classical meaning, it must nevertheless be apparent that during the 1710s and 1720s such equations were frequently and clearly made' (Dixon Hunt 1986, 191). Classical allusion was also used as a lingua franca pervading all writing about gardens, published or private, practical or literary.

For example, in published work, Pope illustrates how strict adherence to fashionable design principles leads to the destruction of Nature with a reference to a story from Virgil's Aeneid. In it, Sabinus's son cuts down the woods his father delighted in to form vistas:

> Through his young Woods how pleas'd Sabinus stray'd
> Or sat delighted in the thick'ning shade,
> With annual joy the red'ning shoots to greet,
> Or see the stretching branches long to meet.
> His Son's fine Taste an op'ner Vista loves,
> Foe to the Dryads of his Father's groves...
> (Pope's *Epistle to Burlington* lines 89–94, in Davis 1966)

In Switzer's first two paragraphs of the Preface to *Ichnographia Rustica I*, essentially a practical publication, Apollo, the Muses, Minerva and Diana are listed as patrons of the garden, (Switzer 1715, i); and in a private letter written by Matthew Prior to the Earl of Oxford, Prior compares himself to Tully or Horace: 'But Down in it self considered I love more than Tully did his Tusculum or Horace his Sabine Feild, nor would quit it for anything but to be with You or to serve you' (LL HMC58: Bath III, 492).

The representation of Roman gardens, to which Prior alludes, was an eighteenth-century construction based on descriptions of gardens and nature in classical poetry and prose. Switzer makes reference to the gardens described by 'Virgil and other Authors' in *Ichnographia Rustica II*, but the most significant writing was the description of Pliny's garden at Tuscum as translated, annotated and visualised, in plan, by Robert Castell in *The Villas of the Ancients Illustrated*, in 1728. It is interesting that a fascination with Pliny's garden predates Castell because, as Liu has pointed out, he was by no means the first to translate Pliny's description: 'Long before 1728, there already had been attempts to piece together a classical idea of a country estate on the basis of what Pliny said about his country houses'. Liu has suggested that Vincenzo Scamozzi published a study in 1616, Jean François Félibien published an annotated translation of Pliny's accounts of Laurentium and Tuscum in 1707, and an anonymous translation was published in 1724 (Liu 2010, 247). However, Castell's translation and illustration was far more influential. The model he presents is one in which three elements play a part; the first is the choice of 'well-water'd Spots of Ground, irregularly producing all sorts of Plants and Trees … and refreshed by Shade and Water' as the first villa builders did, '[t]heir whole Art consisting in little more than in making those Parts next their Villas as it were accidentally produce the choicest Trees, the Growth of various Soils, the Face of the Ground suffering little or no Alteration'. To this was added a more regular plan, 'A Manner of laying out the Ground and Plantations by the Line and Rule, and to trim them up by an Art that was visible in every part of the Design' and by so doing create a third element 'whose Beauty consisted in a close Imitation of Nature; where tho' the Parts are disposed with greatest Art, the Irregularity is still preserved' (Castell 1728, 115). It is interesting that Castell linked Roman gardens to those of the Chinese: 'By the Accounts we have of the present Manner of Designing in China, it seems as from the two former manners a Third has been formed, whose Beauty consisted in a close Imitation of Nature' (Castell 1728, 115). Both Roman and Chinese gardens offered eighteenth-century intellectuals a space so far removed from their lived experience that they served as fantasy lands where theory was undisturbed by gardening reality. Perhaps the appeal of Castell's translation and plan was that it constructed an idealised landscape that was distant and other, while, as Dixon Hunt has pointed out, it also transformed Pliny's garden into one that seemed English: it 'unobtrusively transforms the Plinian texts into images which (necessarily) invoke the syntax of contemporary English and modern Italian designs and into language which tends to approximate (again, inevitably) an English rural scenery' (Dixon Hunt 1986, 194).

There is considerable evidence that emulation of Ancient Rome affected the design of garden buildings and statuary, intended to enhance the landscapes in which they were set. As Paulson suggests, 'The statues were invariably copies of known antique originals, and the temples drew on the vocabulary of Roman buildings' (Paulson 1975, 21). How many gardens were a conscious attempt to recreate Pliny's is more difficult to determine. Mowl suggests that Burlington's garden at Chiswick is closely similar to Castell's plan of Pliny's garden in Roque's engraving of 1736 (Mowl 1999, 54), and Worsley suggests that Rokeby was also a conscious attempt by Sir Thomas Robinson, an avid collector of Roman statuary, to reproduce Tusculum (Worsley 1995, 78), but it is hard to find other examples.

It is certainly not clear whether any of Bridgeman's designs represented a conscious decision to replicate the gardens of Ancient Rome, in spite of Matthew Prior's assertions about Down Hall. They do contain features which might have been derived from Roman architecture, such as the amphitheatre at Claremont, although the inspiration is more likely to come from contemporary European gardens, perhaps seen on the Grand Tour, or mediated through the libraries of Bridgeman's clients. Roman-inspired statuary and buildings are present in many of Bridgeman's landscapes, such as at Tring, where there is a pyramid and an obelisk designed by Gibbs, or at Amesbury Abbey where a quasi-Roman grotto is flanked by earth terraces (see Figure 4), but these buildings are unlikely to be Bridgeman's designs. Indeed, at Amesbury Abbey the western part of Bridgeman's design occupies the Iron Age hill fort known in the eighteenth century, as it is today, as Vespasian's Camp. The antiquarian William Stukeley had published an account in 1724 that identified the hill as Roman: 'Vespasian's Camp ... 'tis a famous camp properly and by universal consent attributed to him ...' (*Itinerarium Curiosum* (1724) cited in Haynes 2012, 28), and yet there is no nod in Bridgeman's design to, for example, Pliny's garden. Although Roman discourse might be the lingua franca of contemporary discussion about gardens, there is no evidence that Bridgeman intentionally included specific Roman elements in his designs.

Both Baroque and neo-Palladianism, the architectural styles popular with the ruling elite in the late seventeenth and early eighteenth centuries, have their origins in Europe. English Baroque architecture is usually presented as short-lived, and is closely identified with the taste of the Stuart kings from the mid-seventeenth to the early eighteenth centuries. Sir John Vanbrugh, and Sir Christopher Wren, William Talman and Nicholas Hawksmoor, are identified as the principal architects of the style which is exemplified by houses such as Chatsworth (designed by Talman), Blenheim and Castle Howard (designed by Vanbrugh), and Easton Neston (designed by Hawksmoor). Although the style originated in Europe in the Renaissance, English Baroque country houses tend to have less heavily ornamented façades than their European counterparts. Palladianism, on the other hand, disseminated through the three volumes of *Vitruvius Britannicus* published in 1715, 1717 and 1725 respectively by Colen Campbell, is seen as a rejection of the court taste of the Stuarts and of the architectural style of Wren (Summerson 1969, 197). Summerson identifies the 'three main loyalties' of the neo-Palladian architectural revival of the early eighteenth century as 'loyalty to Vitruvius; loyalty to Palladio himself; and to Inigo Jones' (Summerson 1969, 197). Gibbs, Campbell, Ripley, Flitcroft, Morris and Pembroke, all of whom Bridgeman worked with, are usually considered neo-Palladian architects. Williamson suggests, in his analysis of Bridgeman's landscape design at Houghton which, 'in its vastness and its simplicity, served to complement the crisp Palladian lines of the hall ...' (Williamson 1998, 55), that if Bridgeman had mirrored the architectural style of the house in his landscape, we might assume that his landscapes for Vanbrugh's Baroque architectural projects, for example at Lumley Castle or Claremont, would differ from those for neo-Palladian projects, for example, Wolterton Hall or Moor Park, and this does not appear to be the case.

This may be because the terms English Baroque and neo-Palladian themselves need to be treated with some caution since, as Garnham has suggested, '[o]ur modern understanding of architecture as a succession of styles was not formulated until later in the eighteenth century' (Garnham 2013, 15). Johns suggests the term Baroque was itself not in use until the nineteenth century (Johns in Peters Corbett and Arnold 2013, 97). It is not likely that the architects defined themselves or their work by these categories, and there is some scholarly discussion about how far these terms are helpful in understanding the buildings they produced. As Downes has suggested, 'the ambiguities between *Baroque* as a style-label and as a date-bracket are more numerous and more confused than ever' (Downes in Ridgeway and Williams 2000, 2). There is general agreement that Vanbrugh's Castle Howard was 'the first great house in England that could reasonably be described as Baroque', but there is less unanimity about other houses (Mowl 1999, 2). Little notes that Gibbs's *Book of Architecture* was published in 1728 at 'the heyday of the Palladian movement'; he contends that 'Palladianism, in the 1720s was what patrons liked and expected, and for Palladianism alone were many of them prepared to pay' (Little 1955, 89).

There is a clear cross-fertilisation between the gardening tradition in Italy, France and Holland in the seventeenth and early eighteenth centuries and that in England. There were clear connections between those working on gardens in France and England from the middle of the seventeenth century to the period in which Bridgeman was working. Willis notes that, in the later seventeenth century, André, Charles and Gabriel Mollet worked at St James's Park for Charles II (Willis 2002, 13), and André Le Nôtre, at the request of Charles II, was responsible for the design of the formal garden immediately to the north of the Queen's House at Greenwich Park (Bouchenot-Déchin and Farhat 2013, 6). John Rose, the King's Gardener from 1661 until his death, was a pupil of Le Nôtre (Green 1956), and George London visited Chantilly, Fontainebleau, Vaux-le-Vicomte and Versailles, and may have met Le Nôtre (Green 1956). London's library contained books on French gardening (Willis 2002, 16), and his own designs, particularly for parterres, show a strong French influence; for example, the miniature garden he designed for Marshal Tallard at Nottingham (Dixon Hunt and Willis, 1975), and his original designs for Castle Howard in Yorkshire (V&A E433-1951/E434-1951). The landowners who employed these gardeners also had strong connections with France. For example, Ralph, 1st Duke of Montagu, who had spent time in France as an ambassador between 1669 and 1672, and then as an exile between 1682 and 1685 (Heward and Taylor 1996, 94) remodelled Boughton House, building a large new block against the north side of the original Great Hall, turning it into something 'more like an urbane chateau in the Ile de France, transported to the more domestic landscape of the English Midlands' (Jackson-Stops in Murdoch 1992, 59), and employed the Dutch gardener van der Meulen to create a French water garden. There were also publications through which French ideas of gardening were disseminated, for example in the translations of *Le jardinier solitaire* and *Le jardinier fleuriste et histiographe* by London and Wise, *La théorie et la pratique du jardinage* by D'Argenville, translated by John James.

The true relationship between garden design in England and that in Europe in the early eighteenth century is quite difficult to tease out. This is partly because both contemporary and modern commentators have gone to great lengths to establish a separate and very different tradition in Britain. There was, particularly in the later eighteenth century, a denigration of European gardens in comparison to English gardens, because 'Englishness became defined as the rise of the English landscape garden which for them symbolised the English constitutional regime, and was contrasted with formal European gardens which were made to symbolise despotic, autocratic monarchies' in writing by Horace Walpole, William Burgh and William Falconer (Bending 1994, 215–216). Modern garden historians have refined this by creating a loose taxonomy of implicitly derogatory terms to define the gardening styles of European nation states. In this categorisation, Dutch gardens were 'compact' (Jacques and van der Horst 1988, 1), and had 'a sense of enclosure, an inward-looking orientation' and reflected 'strong horticultural traditions' (Laird 1992, 43). They were 'essentially piecemeal and [of an] incremental nature' (Dixon Hunt quoted in Laird 1992, 42–43) with a 'highly mathematical ... approach to the overall layout' (Jacques and van der Horst 1988, 10), and a 'fussier' use of evergreens (Dixon Hunt and Willis 1975, 8). French gardens are differentiated from this by their 'sense of grandeur and vast scale', 'an extension of the palace proper, providing a majestic setting for the firework displays, theatrical performances, and all the arts of the *fêtes galantes*' (Dixon Hunt and Willis 1975, 6), with 'grandiloquent ornament and statues' (Dixon Hunt 1975, 8). They were 'resplendent and autocratic' (Dixon Hunt and Willis 1975, 7). Both styles are said to derive from Italian gardens which, in addition to those characteristics listed above, are said to have had a 'certain intricacy and a delight in waterworks' (Dixon Hunt and Willis 1975, 7).

Both the writing of the later eighteenth century and modern scholarship have produced a clear, but arguably misleading, distinction between the evolution of English gardens and the gardens of separate European nations in the early eighteenth century. In fact, the development of European gardening styles, and that of English gardens, was probably more organic and haphazard than any of the opinions above suggest. Rather than a linear development of purposeful, stylistic choices, it is probably more helpful to think of a shifting, fluid and probably unmeasurable system of cross-fertilisation, backwards and forwards across national borders, which in any case had different resonances in the eighteenth century. What stylistic divisions there were are just as likely to have been dictated by the topographical, meteorological and geological constraints of the regions in which the gardens were built, and by affordability. Although Dixon Hunt maintains that 'garden connoisseurs in the late seventeenth and early eighteenth centuries were able to discriminate, seeing Italianate or Dutch or French characteristics in any given garden and having distinct associations with each' (Dixon Hunt 1986, 8), Jacques is unconvinced. He considers it more sensible to 'dismiss the utility of stylistic labels like "Dutch" and to emphasize that international design fashions are adapted regionally by factors such as topography and cultural landscape patterns' (Jacques 2002, 125). Jacques contends that, for example, the '[d]ifferences between Dutch and French gardens occur more because of the imperatives of geography and climate than because of the stylistic preferences of garden designers' (Jacques 2002, 125). This has skewed our perception of the influence of European gardens and gardening on Bridgeman's style.

Yet there was certainly a growing sense in the early part of the eighteenth century of a garden that was peculiarly English. Exactly how this sense of Englishness worked as a determiner of fashion in gardening styles for Bridgeman and his contemporaries is more difficult to determine because our perception of what constitutes Englishness in a garden has, to a large degree, been influenced by the writing of the 1760s to the mid-1790s, and this has obscured our perception of what Englishness meant to Bridgeman's generation. In fact, writing contemporary with Bridgeman's career can be interpreted as presenting a subtly different picture of the relationship between English and European gardening. There was a sense in which, as discussed above, the horticultural model of the gardens of the Ancients was copied and used emblematically for the superiority of the English political system, after the accession of the Hanoverians. Englishness in the garden was also linked to a lack of extravagance (see above). There is also a sense of the superiority of the English soil and climate for gardening in contrast to those of European countries. Batty Langley, in *The New Principles of Gardening*, argued: 'we abound in good soil, fine Grass, and Gravel which in many Places Abroad is not to be found, and the best of all Sorts of Trees' (Langley 1728), while Bradley considers 'England to enjoy a Climate much more favourable to the Health both of Plants and Animals, than Italy, which on a sudden Start, changes from hot to cold' (Bradley 1725, 288). The movement away from rigid formality, discussed above in relation to the pervasive discourse about the 'natural garden', seems largely to be framed in an overt rejection of Dutch gardens. Batty Langley singles out Dutch gardens for criticism: 'These regular Gardens were first taken from the Dutch, and introduced into *England* in the Time of the late Mr *London* and Mr *Wise*, who being then suppos'd to be the best Gardeners in *England* (the Art being in its Infancy) were imployed by the *Nobility and Gentry of England* to lay and plant their Gardens in that *regular stiff, and stuft up Manner*' (Langley 1728, xi). Bending suggests that a passage in Bradley's *Survey of Ancient husbandry and*

Gardening is also, in fact, an attack on the Dutch style (Bending 1994, 211). It is hard to explain this antipathy towards Dutch gardening, in both Langley and Bradley, given its common roots with, and stylistic similarity to, French gardens in particular. The argument is further confused when we consider that Wrest Park, a garden of exactly this period, was probably modelled on Dutch gardens by Henry Grey, who had visited Holland in the 1690s, and explicitly linked through iconography to the principles of the Glorious Revolution and the reign of William III (Halpern 2002, 139). It is possible that the antipathy towards Dutch gardens was simply based on their relative smallness, since land remained a powerful signifier of power in the early eighteenth century (see Chapter 8).

However, while condemnation of Dutch gardening is explicit and largely universal in print by the time Bridgeman began to work alone, it is difficult to find overt criticism of French gardens in any written text contemporary with Bridgeman's career. In fact, the reverse is often true. Addison, in 1712, compared English gardens adversely to those of France and Italy: 'On this account our English gardens are not so entertaining to the Fancy as those in France and Italy, where we see a large Extent of Ground covered over with an agreeable mixture of Garden and Forest, which represent every where an Artificial Rudeness, much more charming than that Neatness and Elegancy which we meet in those of our own Country' (Addison 1710–1712, No. 414). Switzer, in 1718, also wrote in praise of French gardening: 'By Ingentia Rura (apply'd to Gard'ning) we may understand that Extensive Way of Gard'ning that I have already hinted at, and shall more fully handle; this the French call *La Grand Manier*, and is opposed to those crimping, diminutive, and wretched performances we every-where meet with' (Switzer 1718, xviii). Bradley, in 1725, suggests borrowing ideas from Versailles, albeit on a smaller scale: '... if we were to borrow so much from the *Versailes* Gardens as one might take in at small Expence, such as the Fables of *Aesop*, to be here and there intersperc'd in our Woods, represented by figures as big as the Life, of men, Birds and Beasts, painted in their natural Colours ...' (Bradley 1725, 360). This praise for, and emulation of, French gardens is also seen in the popularity of *La Théorie et la Pratique du Jardinage* by A.J. Dèzailler D'Argenville (1680–1765) (Dèzailler D'Argenville 1709), translated by John James in 1712. The gardens of the French elite were fashionable in Europe and England well into the eighteenth century.

This, then, is the cultural and artistic world within which Bridgeman worked. It is easy to dismiss some of it as an influence on him. However, such was the prevalence in early eighteenth-century England of gardens which imitated those in Italy, France, and even Holland, it is impossible to believe he remained uninfluenced by European style. This was the visual and intellectual milieu in which he was immersed. We have sound evidence that he had seen, for example, the French-derived design for Greenwich (see Chapter 2). It would then be very surprising if he had not absorbed some of it into his style.

CHAPTER 6

THE 'INGENIOUS MR BRIDGEMAN'

AS WE HAVE seen in the previous chapter, Bridgeman's work sits on the cusp of the decline of the formal geometric garden and the rise of the 'natural' garden. The geometric garden had not quite died, and the 'natural' garden was still in the throes of its birth. It was a period when coexistence was possible. This seems to have made defining the precise nature of Bridgeman's style problematic for modern scholarship. Dixon Hunt, for example, dismisses the idea that Bridgeman had any clear style at all: 'Bridgeman seems to have had little interest in design theory or in annexing his work to any cultural or political cause; he seems to have been very much at the mercy of specific commissions, so it is hard to determine exactly what is truly *Bridgemanick*' (Dixon Hunt 1986, 189). Mostly, though, as we have seen, the loose orthodoxy that Bridgeman's style in some way prefigures the rise of the 'natural' garden has been perpetuated, generally, as a deficit model. Bridgeman is seen as a pale and rather incompetent imitator of the pioneers of the natural garden style; Peter Willis has him 'taking his cue from Switzer's advocacy of a Farm-like Way of Gardening' (Willis 2002, 132) while Mowl considers he had 'not mastered [the] style or captured the spirit of an Arcadia' (Mowl 2000, 77). However, we can perhaps now dismiss the idea that Bridgeman was a forerunner of the 'natural' garden. It is hard to imagine that any examination of his style is helped by attempting to retrofit Bridgeman's designs into models that often postdate his work by 40 years. It is more helpful to find his roots in a late geometric style which derives directly from the later part of the seventeenth century, and then consider how he loosened the formality which bound it. As Mowl (in some contradiction of the remark quoted above) also suggests: 'Bridgemanesque – symmetry modified by art' (Mowl 2000, 104).

In fact, the majority of the individual components of Bridgeman's landscapes are found in the gardens of seventeenth-century Europe, particularly in France and Italy. Willis suggests that 'we should not rule out Italian inspiration for much of Bridgeman's work – partly through the foreign travels of such friends as Gibbs, Wootton, and Kent, and partly through a visit Bridgeman himself may have made to the Continent in 1732 or so' (the name 'Bridgeman' was among a list of those Joseph Spence met in Paris in 1732) (Willis 2002, 133 and 133 n. 31;

BL Add MS 2235 fo.94). Although there is no other evidence that Bridgeman visited France or, indeed, any other European country, circumstantial evidence strongly suggests that he must, at the very least, have seen French landscape designs on paper, if not in France. Perhaps it is relevant that amongst the plans in Gough Drawings, catalogued as MSGD a3 fo.13, there is a plan for the bosquets at the chateau of Choisy in France. It is identical in layout to the plan of Choisy published in Bouchenot-Déchin and Farhat (2013), in Notebook 2 by 'Desgots pere et fils', although it appears to be a rougher drawing. It is labelled 'Choisie' on the reverse. Since it is in Gough Drawings, it is tempting to think that, if not copied by Bridgeman himself, it formed part of his library of drawings. He also worked as a draughtsman for London and Wise at Brompton Nurseries, and appears to have drawn a plan, perhaps a copy, of Le Nôtre's design for Greenwich for Wise in 1711. It is likely, then, that French landscape design influenced Bridgeman's style although, obviously, the gardens at Versailles and other French grand houses were also influential in England in the seventeenth century and were reproduced in fashionable English landscapes into the eighteenth century. As Williamson notes: 'the late geometric theme continued to dominate garden design until the years around 1730' (Williamson 1995, 52).

Certainly, the most recognisable component of a Bridgeman landscape, sculpted and turfed earth, can be traced first to Europe, and in particular to France. As Jacques and van der Horst suggest, 'Where an earth terrace was made in a garden the usual practice in France as elsewhere was to form a turf *glacis*, or slope', although they also suggest that 'the English were ... pre-eminent in the decorative sculpturing of such slopes', as the terraces in the Maestricht Garden, maintained by both Wise and Bridgeman in their capacities as Royal Gardener, show (Jacques and van der Horst 1988, 126). There are so many examples of turfed and stepped structures in late seventeenth- and early eighteenth-century gardens, both in England and in Europe, that, anyway, it is probably safe to say that they are not an innovation of Bridgeman's, although with one caveat: turfed amphitheatres do seem to be largely an invention of his own. Their stone antecedents may well be from Italy where they were originally derived from Roman structures. Dixon Hunt has shown that, in Italy, the 'descending concave set of steps leading to a circular platform from which an answering set of convex steps descended further – became a distinctive garden form' (Dixon Hunt 1986, 61). It seems unlikely that Bridgeman visited Italy, but these structures were present in engravings by influential architects, including Palladio, and the books were probably accessible to him in the libraries of his clients, such as Edward Harley, the Earl of Oxford. Harley was a bibliophile and had a very extensive library. Bridgeman is recorded by Humfrey Wanley as visiting Harley's library on a number of occasions between 1721 and 1725 (Willis 2002, 69). Dixon Hunt points out the similarities between Bridgeman's Claremont and the theatre in the gardens of the Isola Bella in Lake Maggiore, and Serlio's illustration of the exedra in the Vatican Belvedere which Bramante had adapted from the Roman Temple at

Palestrina (Dixon Hunt 1986, 61–62). It is hard to say what led Bridgeman to turf them instead of creating them in stone. There is a strong tradition of sculpted, turfed earth in England, from Neolithic and Bronze Age burial mounds onwards, so perhaps he was also influenced by these in the English landscape. It is also true that in England, where turf grows well in a mild, wet climate, they were certainly considerably cheaper to construct than stone.

Bridgeman's bastions, terraces and ditches may have their origins in European military architecture, particularly in the Low Countries. Williams has argued persuasively that the fortified gardens designed by Vanbrugh have their roots in the military campaigns of the late seventeenth- and early eighteenth-century campaigns in Europe (Williams in Ridgeway and Williams 2000). Vanbrugh might well also have been Bridgeman's principal influence here. He created bastion gardens at Blenheim (see Bridgeman's plan for Blenheim Palace 1709) and at Sacombe (Milledge 2009, 41). Both are sites where Bridgeman also worked. Bridgeman uses the language of fortification in his description of the structures to be created at Hackwood, his most obviously fortified garden: a 'Tarrace, Stocade & Fossee' (MSGD a3 fo.34). It may even be that Vanburgh is actually responsible for the structure of the bastions which enclose the garden at Eastbury, even though Colen Campbell attributes the design to Bridgeman in *Vitruvius Britannicus III* (1725). Dalton points out that a rough sketch of the bastion garden appears on the reverse of a plan in Gough Drawings (MSGD a4 fo.80-81), a plan attributable to Vanbrugh.

Lakes and canals are an important feature in any designed landscape. They add sound when the water is channelled through a cascade, and still water reflects light, a mirror to the sky. Bridgeman's landscapes made considerable use of them, although there are fewer lakes than the assertion made in *Hue and Cry*, a poem allegedly by Sir James Thornhill, would suggest: 'They say he makes water for miles altogether'. Bridgeman's lakes and canals are largely designed to a formula found in many gardens of the late seventeenth and early eighteenth centuries, in both England and Europe. The probable inspiration for most of Bridgeman's geometric ponds and canals are those designed for French gardens in the late seventeenth century, particularly those of André Le Nôtre for Versailles and other chateaux; it is possible to find identical patterns in the plans in Bouchenot-Déchin and Farhat's extensive retrospective work on Le Nôtre *Le Nôtre in Perspective*. For example, the basin at Sacombe in Hertfordshire is identical to one on a 1665 plan for Versailles from Le Nôtre's workshop (Bouchenot-Déchin and Farhat 2014, 215) and the octagonal basin at Down Hall in Essex is closely similar to the design for the Grounds at Choisy 1680-85 (Bouchenot-Déchin and Farhat, Designs and Drawings II, 14). These shapes of bodies of water are also echoed in Dutch gardens of the same period, for example in the plan for Het Loo drawn by Christiaan van Staden c.1700 (Jacques and van der Horst 1988, 57), and in the ponds and canals in the 80 plates in *Britannia Illustrata* published in 1707.

In some of Bridgeman's landscapes, however, there is a looser treatment of water. For example, the stream which runs through the garden at Gobions has been allowed, largely, to follow its natural course, although there is probably some evidence that artificial embankments were created. But even this is not without precedent. Le Nôtre's drawing for the Trianon Garden at Versailles where The Garden of Natural Springs (*Le Jardin des Sources*) is shown as a series of irregular-shaped pools linked by serpentine streams within what is clearly an otherwise relatively formal garden (Designs and Drawings II, 6, in Bouchenot-Déchin and Farhat 2013). Sally Jeffrey has shown that a similarly styled watercourse, although artificially constructed, was designed by Nicholas Hawksmoor for Lord Carlisle's garden in Wray Wood at Castle Howard in North Yorkshire (Figures 2 and 4 in Jeffrey 2018, 39 and 41). It may be that these are all style innovations, or perhaps, in the Trianon garden and at Gobions, at least, they were a response to an area of saturated ground in which canals with straight sides were much more difficult to construct. It is also possible that the straight-sided canalisation of existing rivers or brooks that appears on so many of Bridgeman's designs are a visual trope rather than a practical suggestion.

Bridgeman was, to all intents and purposes, a designer of woodland gardens. Almost all his designs contain some formal or informal groves, often over extensive areas. The formality and structure of many of these closely resemble the formal bosquets created in France in the seventeenth and early eighteenth centuries. Dézaillier d'Argenville's *La theorie et la practique du jardinage* (Dèzailler D'Argenville 1709), widely available in a translation by James, reflects the practice of woodland design in France. Squares of woodland are formulaically laid out with trees in the quincunx pattern, or in straight lines, or contained within geometric shapes created by hedges with a fountain or menagerie at the centre. A quick scan of the landscapes depicted by Kip and Knyff in *Britannia Illustrata* (1707) shows the influence in England of what we might term typically French treatment of woodland. Great houses sit in the centre of designs in which, except in the immediate vicinity of the house, compartments, planted geometrically and more or less densely with trees, are divided from each other by straight allées. It is impossible to prove whether Bridgeman had seen Le Notre's designs for woodland, either in plan form or in actuality, or indeed whether he had read Dézaillier d'Argenville's *La theorie et la practique du jardinage* either in the original or in translation, but it is hard to avoid the conclusion he was influenced by both, or, at the very least, was influenced by the English equivalents. Eastbury, for example (c.1725), conforms to a formal grove structure axially arranged. The garden to the east of Vanbrugh's house contains, within its hahas and bastion walls, wooded groves more or less symmetrically arranged around wider allées, bisected by straight and serpentine paths. At Wolterton c.1725 (MSGD a4 fo.20) there are also formal groves: to the west a more complicated design of a double cross with square cabinets connected by straight and serpentine paths.

However, Bridgeman did not always design formal woodland. In common with Hawksmoor at Wray Wood at Castle Howard (Jeffrey 2018, 61–62), and Switzer (in print, at least), a number of designs show less formal woodland. Switzer's suggestion, 'When you find a Wood that has a great many Hills and Dales, and is almost all of it compos'd of Irregularities, 'tis there one should not strain either the Fancy or the Purse, but follow those little Shelvings and natural Turns and Meanders' (Switzer 1718, 198) was published in 1718. An estate map in Castle Howard archives dating from 1773 shows a number of serpentine paths linking cabinets in the wood (Jeffrey 2018, figs 13 and 14) and, while Jeffrey admits it is impossible to be certain the design is Hawksmoor's, she makes a plausible case for his authorship in her exploration of his drawings for the design of the watercourse and cascade in the interior of Wray Wood (Jeffrey 2018, fig. 3, 4 and 5). At Sacombe in 1715 Bridgeman's design cuts a *patte d'oie*, axially aligned on the house through an irregularly shaped piece of woodland; the main axis leads through the trees on a raised walk to a canal, while to the north-west an arm leads to a cabinet with terraces and a pool, and another straight walk runs south to the edge of the woodland. Otherwise Bridgeman's design leaves the interior of the woodland undisturbed. He repeats a version of this idea at Down Hall in 1720. Here the central arm of the *patte d'oie* runs through pre-existing woodland on a north–south axis to an octagonal basin. The arm to the north-west walk terminates at the canalised stream, while to the east, a shorter arm terminates in a pool. In the British Library version of the plan (BL Loan 29/357), the two cabinets embedded between each of the arms of the *patte d'oie* are linked by serpentine paths. Again Bridgeman leaves the remaining woodland undisturbed. It is tempting to try to guess at a chronology for the development of more informal woodland, especially as Bridgeman almost certainly worked with Hawksmoor at Blenheim and it is probably Hawksmoor's plan that forms the basis of Bridgeman's plan of Greenwich (CL CMP/30). In fact, it is impossible to say which of these three began to move away from the idea of formally compartmentalised woodland first (see Chapter 3). It is also probable that this apparently innovative design, which might have originated with either Bridgeman, Hawksmoor or Switzer, was actually inspired by French gardens. Jeffery suggests, very plausibly, that Hawksmoor's inspiration might have come from France, and cites in particular Le Nôtre's 'Labirinthe' (Jeffrey 2018, 29). Switzer admits that James's translation of Dézaillier d'Argenville might have been his inspiration:

> Tis in large Hollows and low Grounds, and in the Middle or Center of Woods, that we make our little Cabinets and Gardens, of which some are to be found in this Book, and others may be taken out of Mr James's, besides an infinite Variety that may be contriv'd ... (Switzer 1718)

Horace Walpole is unequivocal in crediting Bridgeman with the invention of the ditch or haha (Walpole 1995). If it were entirely Bridgeman's invention, then it would clearly have been a significant contribution to garden design, since, in Walpole's view, it was an important marker in the emergence of the 'natural' garden. A haha usually involves a deep ditch with a brick or stone wall dropping vertically from the level of the lawn on the garden side to its bottom. On the opposite side the ditch rises steeply to join the parkland again at ground level. The result, from the garden side, is that an uninterrupted view of the countryside is offered, but a barrier to stock is created. However, in spite of what was written by Walpole, the idea of the haha predates Bridgeman. Again, the influence is probably French. James's translation of Dézaillier d'Argenville's 1709 work (both of which predate Bridgeman's known design career) offers them as an alternative to a grill: 'At present we frequently make thoroughviews, called Ah Ah, which are openings in the walls, without grills, to the very level of the walks, with a large and deep ditch …' (Dézaillier d'Argenville 1709, 77). Bridgeman does, however, seem to have created a very successful haha at Houghton Hall in Norfolk for Sir Robert Walpole. The ditch at Hackwood seems to have been intended for that purpose; the insertion of pieces of wood 'each 6 feet 6 inches long & 4 Inches Square/ & to be placed in the Slope according to the Section at 6 Inches assunder section of the Tarrace, Stocade, & fosse', very much in the manner of a military fortification, seems to be a deliberate stock barrier. Perhaps it is only possible to be certain that Bridgeman created a haha at Wolterton where his letter to Walpole in 1736 makes it clear that he intended to replace a hedge with a ditch in which a wall would be built:

> … wee opend the Laurell hedge on furtherest side of the Grove to the width agreed on which takes in the width of the South Terrace … & the Western end of the house … Wee have likewise agreed upon the fencing in the Garden on the western end; which is, by placing a common pale behind the lawn hedge before mentiond, immediately west of the grove before mentiond, except where the opening is before the western end of the house, and in that space 'tis proposed to be a wall of 4 feet high set in a fosse… (WH 8/12 box 3LX)

It may be significant that this is towards the end of his career, when the fashion for 'natural' gardening, which Walpole is specifically referencing, was becoming established.

However, if we are looking for what is genuinely innovative in Bridgeman's work, what marks him out from his contemporaries in terms of design, then we have to turn to the way he organised and manipulated space. His designs were enormous, Willis calls it his 'predisposition for vastness of scale' (Willis 2002, 130): his design for Lodge Park, for example, largely restored by the National Trust, measures 1.16 km^2 (287 acres) with a main axis of 1050 m x 1450 m, and Wolterton, where the lake, at least, survives, is 0.31 km^2 (76 acres) in area and its main axes measure 950 m x 400 m. But although his designs recognised the importance of the macro – that the point of a creating a vast landscape is to be able to see it stretching into the distance from a number of different vantage points, and, sometimes, to see the edges of it, and how it fits the wider landscape – he also understood the micro, the journey from one intimate space to another and the changes in perspective this brings. His landscapes demonstrate an implicit understanding of what Tilley explains here:

> Landscapes are thus structured in terms of the relatedness and relative depths of places within them. Their experience includes the body as it is animated and moves, what spreads into the distance, a region where some things are sensible and other things hide themselves at one moment to reveal themselves to the ambient body at another. Places and landscapes are created and experienced through mobility as much as stasis ... (Tilley 2004, 25–26)

In the deft placement of built features, and the incorporation and enhancement of natural ones, Bridgeman achieved landscapes that rolled away from the eye in vast panoramas while at the same time allowing and inviting journeys through the intimate spaces. Deconstruction, taking the landscape apart to see its working parts, allows us to see precisely how Bridgeman achieves this.

In fact, the structure of a Bridgeman landscape, regardless of size, is hung on scaffolding provided by the ratios, angles and geometric proportions of late seventeenth-century garden design, albeit on a grand scale. This must have presented practical challenges, since accurate surveying was problematic over such distances in the early eighteenth century. Presumably the need for such a structure was partly dictated by his clients, who expected and understood a garden of overt geometry. It was also the model presented to Bridgeman by the generation of gardeners that preceded him in the late seventeenth and early eighteenth centuries, and in large sections of gardening manuals and books of the period. For example, in the Introduction of *Ichnographia Rustica* Vol. 2 (1718) Switzer writes 'Amongst the several Businesses to which Mathematics is turn'd, 'tis certain that 'tis no where and in no Case more useful, plain and diverting, than in the Laying out of Gardens ...' (Switzer 1718). However, it is clearly simpler to create a stiff geometric framework in a relatively small space, and to produce 'regularity and congruity' by building up small regular units around a central axis, each with a geometric design within it, within a larger rectilinear enclosure (Phibbs 2006, 4). As Phibbs points out, these designs were most suited to smaller, rectilinear, flat sites, of no more than two acres, because, he suggests, it was much easier to accurately replicate the design on the land. Holland, in particular, was, as Jacques and van der Horst have noted, 'well suited to drawing-board designs' (Jacques and van der Horst 1988). There, as De Jong points out, the price of land and the need for drainage dictated the size and design of gardens, and their boundaries (De Jong 2000, 24). It is, though, clearly possible to achieve a geometric landscape over a vast area, as the gardens at Versailles demonstrate, although setting it out clearly required superior surveying skills. Le Nôtre created a 'spreading geometry of landscaped circles, squares and intersecting walks – all centred on the main axis with several transversal lines' (Howard Adams 1979, 86). Adams suggests that, for Le Nôtre, this was for practical reasons; the technique 'provided the basic ordering devices which enabled Le Nôtre to maintain unity and continuity in the face of unpredictable expansion ... It was additive and could be extended endlessly as the King's obsessions and growing power might require' (Howard Adams 1979, 86). Creating a vast, loosely geometric landscape in the relatively densely settled and closely woven English countryside was clearly more challenging. As Jacques and van der Horst point out: 'in England it was often difficult to perfect the organisation of a layout because of existing roads, rivers, topography and all the other inherent irregularities of the English countryside' (Jacques and van der Horst 1988, 24).

Of course, with areas of the magnitude of a Bridgeman landscape, geometry perforce becomes a subordinate design parameter, to be relaxed to fit the landscape. It is sometimes difficult to be precise about the angles since it is not clear exactly where Bridgeman intended that angles or distances should be measured from, but with some approximation it is possible. At Sacombe (c.1715) the design is obviously geometric, a *patte d'oie* forming isosceles triangles; measuring reveals that the main axis, measured from the house to the end of the canal basin, is divided exactly in half at the end of the walk, where, Milledge suggests, the grotto was situated (Milledge 2009, 45). The isosceles triangle itself is roughly proportioned so that one side is one fourth of the main axis and the other two are one fifth. The walk to the south is three-fifths of the main axis. At Lodge Park (Figure 9) the structure is less obvious but, although the landscape was arranged without any formal walks, a similar structure of geometric ratios, proportions and angles is measurable, holding the landscape together through invisible lines. Bridgeman's design is underpinned by angles and ratios from this axis. Closest to the Lodge, two wide symmetrical vistas are cut into the avenue at 45 degrees, allowing a vista to the small cascade at the southern end of the lake. On the eastern lip of the valley there is a small platform, raised, as Bridgeman's instructions make explicit, '10ft', and placed exactly at the half-way point of the main axis, while the width of the terrace to the east of the river is one eighth of it and the width of the ziggurat to the west is one quarter of it, at its widest point. The dimensions at Lodge Park are only visible on a plan and only quantifiable by measurement. Once the design was built and planted and visitors perceived it either statically or moving, the proportions of the landscape were probably sensed rather than measured.

To understand how Bridgeman worked with a geometric structure, individual elements of garden design and the naturally occurring features of a landscape, we might deconstruct two projects in detail: Amesbury Abbey in Wiltshire, designed for the Duke of Queensberry and dated 1738 on the cartouche of

Bridgeman's plan (MSGD a3* fo.32) (Figure 4), and Gobions in Hertfordshire (Herts a1), undated, but probably designed sometime in the early 1720s for Jeremy Sambrooke. In both cases, at least some of the landscape has survived in earthwork form. Both are very big.

At Amesbury Abbey, the site covers 0.26 km^2 (64 acres), its two major axes measuring roughly 700 m and 550 m. At Gobions the site is 2 km^2 (494 acres) in total. Bridgeman's design for the wood at Gobions covers 0.16 km^2 (39 acres), with two major axes which measure 1000 m and 300 m respectively, although significant features are placed in the surrounding estate.

The river Avon bisects the site at Amesbury Abbey. To the west of it the garden is on the eastern slope of a roughly oval chalk hill on which the univallate Iron Age hill fort also stands (see Chapter 5). It rises to around 90 m at its highest point, falling precipitously to the Avon on its eastern flank and more gently to the south towards the water meadows created by the river as it becomes braided. To the east of the river, the garden is largely flat, on the sand and gravel river deposits laid down by the river. The landscape that Bridgeman worked on appears to be the one shown in a survey by Henry Flitcroft, executed for the Duke of Queensberry in 1726. The survey shows the mansion house, designed in the late seventeenth century by John Webb. It replaced the buildings of the Benedictine nunnery from which the house takes its name. It too was replaced in 1834, but on a similar footprint. To the south-east, and within 220 m of the house, is the old precinct wall of the nunnery and, immediately behind it, the back gardens of houses in the High Street and the town of Amesbury. Flitcroft's survey shows some of the walls which remained from the Abbey and a medieval canal which bisects the site from south to north, roughly parallel to the river Avon (WRO 944/1). Only the flat summit of Vespasian's Camp is shown, which, although owned by the estate, was in 1726 under open field cultivation and known as 'The Walls'. The cliff facing the house is not shown because it was not, in 1726, part of the Amesbury Abbey estate: the land was only finally bought in 1742, although the Duke of Queensberry had signalled his intention to buy and keep in hand the land to the immediate west of the Avon in 1726 (WRO 944/2).

Bridgeman's treatment of this landscape is shown in the beautiful and accomplished watercolour plan held in Gough Drawings, catalogued as MSGD a3* fo.32 (Figure 4). He has created an axis focused on the juxtaposition between the hill fort and the river Avon beneath it, rather than on the mansion house with its rather inconvenient proximity to the town. Bridgeman's axis runs from a rond-point almost at the top of the hill, through a tapering ziggurat-like figure of trees, down the east-facing cliff above the Avon, to the midway point of where, in the poetic words of the site's guardian, Mike Clarke, 'the river kisses the ramparts' (pers. comm. Mike Clarke) across the river, then through a bastion at the corner of a kite-shaped kitchen garden, over the bridge across the medieval canal, and, by-passing the house, arrives at an obelisk almost at the perimeter wall, which is screened from the town by three rows of trees. The centre of the kitchen garden, although probably never built, provides the exact half way point on this axis. Bridgeman places a small neo-classical hermitage, known locally as Gay's Cave, on the steep cliff face above the Avon equidistantly between the two ends of the straight stretch of the river, and frames it with a diamond of terraces cut into the rampart of the hill fort. The circular rond-point on the summit of Vespasian's Camp is identified by the Ordnance Survey as a barrow on all maps from the 1878 1st Edition. It seems much more likely to have been deliberately created by Bridgeman as the western terminus of his axis, unless, by some happy coincidence, a barrow happened to be sited on exactly the right axial trajectory (Haynes 2012, 34; Bowden 2016, 23). From the rond-point on top of Vespasian's Camp, a triangular vista sweeps down the gentler slope of the hill to the south. Bridgeman effectively uses Vespasian's Camp to limit horizons from within the garden, creating a sense of enclosure and exclusivity. The medieval canal becomes a decorative canal, punctuated by a pool midway along its length. The precinct wall is screened in its entire length by trees, and the view of the north elevation of the house, clearly visible in a drawing by Stukeley which predates Bridgeman's plan, is also obscured by a plantation of trees. The view of the hill from the house suggests a protection from the land beyond it, while, from the rond-point on the top of the hill, there are vistas to the south and east. Intimate spaces are created within the woodland on the cliff. Narrow paths lead along it above the river to Gay's Cave, and a walk screened by trees follows the river on its eastern bank. Willis's assertion that the design is 'fragmented and lacks a dominant, cohesive idea' clearly misses the point (Willis 2002, 54).

There are no contemporary accounts by which we can judge the effect of all this on those who visited Amesbury. A diary entry by Lady Sophia Newdigate while on a tour of the area, probably in 1747, records her visit to Amesbury, but her impression is coloured by the fashion for natural gardening: 'here is about 40 acres part of which is very well disposd there is a high hill in ye Garden in a very stiff formal taste at present but going to be altered' (WRO CR1841/7). However, enough of it has survived on the hill fort, where there has been much less modern disturbance, to give some sense of the landscape as Bridgeman intended it. Although largely covered in dense woodland, Gay's Cave, and the diamond terraces which frame it, have survived, and their effect when viewed from the house is clearly visible in a photograph from the 1915 sales catalogue (WRO 798/2). The low terraces which formed the banks of the ziggurat-shaped tapering terrace leading to the rond point are still visible. A narrow path now runs through the centre of this space, which is dense with long grass and nettles in summer. Although saplings of ash and sycamore are beginning to colonise the space, it is still clearly identifiable as Bridgeman's rising terraces, and, in winter, the straight edges of low banks are faintly evident on both sides towards the southern edge of the space, although they are degraded and no longer right-angled.

Gobions was a small estate bought by Jeremy Sambrooke from Richard Beachcroft in 1708 (Rowe and Williamson 2012, 2). Sambrooke's wealth came

THE 'INGENIOUS MR BRIDGEMAN'   105

Figure 11. Gay's Cave and the Diamond in 1915. WRO 798/2. Reproduced by kind permission of Wiltshire and Swindon Record Office.

from the East India Company. At some point after its purchase, but before 1732, Sambrooke commissioned Bridgeman to design a landscape. The plan, discovered by Anne Rowe in the Bodleian Library (BL Gough Maps Herts a1) (see Chapter 3) is by far the biggest existing plan of a Bridgeman landscape. There is a palimpsest of the earthworks which formed Bridgeman's design in the wood at Gobions, now a nature reserve owned and managed by Herts and Middlesex Wildlife Trust. Both the earthworks and the history of the landscape have been extensively documented by Anne Rowe and Tom Williamson in 'New Light on Gobions' (2012). The edges of the Bowling Green, the platform for the Bowling Green Summerhouse, the amphitheatre and the avenue from the Bowling Green to the canal are all visible and have been shown in an earthwork plan by Tom Williamson (pers. comm. Tom Williamson). It is also possible to see the remains of the grotto and the site of the cascade. Avenues not visible on the ground make a ghostly appearance on LIDAR, which shows an avenue running south-west from the site of the house, an avenue south to the Folly Arch, a brick-built castellated arch, attributed to James Gibbs (although with no evidence for the attribution), and a rectangular basin to the north of the wood (2 m resolution; https://www.geomatics-group.co.uk). There is plenty of cartographic, pictorial and documentary evidence of what was built. A map surveyed by Thomas Holmes, held in the Gloucester Record Office (GA D1245/FF75), shows the features. The map of Hertfordshire by Dury and Andrews (1766) shows Gobions, and plans of the estate from 1815 (HALS 34137), 1833 (HALS 66507) and 1836 (HALS 34188), and the Tithe map from 1844 (HALS DSA4/62/2), show the evolution of the landscape as it degraded. Crucially there are enough contemporary accounts and engravings of it in the eighteenth century to give us some understanding of how it might have been experienced when it was new. Two written records of the landscape survive: George Bickham described it is his appendix to *The Beauties of Stow* (1750), and William Toldervy describes the landscape in great detail in an extended paragraph in *England and Wales described in a series of Letters* (1762). Jean Baptiste Chatelain produced two engravings, one of the Bowling Green and one of the Canal and Temple in 1748, and a drawing of the Grotto entitled 'Gubbins Park – In the Woods' (HALS North M.27) was done in 1814. There are also prints of the house and of the Folly Arch in the Gerish Collection (HALS DE/GR/56/2/9).

An undated estate map held in a collection at Hatfield House depicts the site before Bridgeman's work. The map shows the house (demolished in 1836), and a small formal garden, from which an avenue of trees runs down to the south-west into a shallow valley until it meets the boundaries of a wood, Denn Wood, which, together with Greate Wood, occupied the valley bottom in a roughly east–west direction. It is hard to say how long the two woods within which Bridgeman's design sits had occupied the site; they were certainly present when Bridgeman began work and are shown as separate blocks of woodland on the Hatfield map of c.1708, separated by a narrow neck of land; georeferencing and existing wood banks suggests that Bridgeman retained the boundaries. Presumably, then, as now, a tributary of the Mimshall Brook, known as Ray Brook, ran through the woodland in the valley bottom, disappearing in a number of swallow holes in Denn Wood, to the west. The ground rises from 90 m above sea level in the valley to 110 m at the Folly Arch on Swanley Bar in the south and to 125 m on the valley rim to the north. The geology is predominantly London Clay, and the presence of pre-existing woodland often indicates poor soil on which it is likely little else will grow successfully. Williamson, Barnes and Pillatt argue that '[b]oth coppiced woods and commons (wooded or otherwise) were most extensive on the more agriculturally 'difficult' soils – acid gravels or poorly draining clays' (Williamson, Barnes and Pillatt 2017, 20).

Bridgeman's design is depicted in the plan, discovered in 2011, in the Bodleian Library. The character of the map is rather dirty and in some areas there are holes. Because of this, the design is depicted here in schematic form by kind permission of Tom Williamson and Anne Rowe, in whose article (Rowe and Williamson 2012) the following plan appears.

The design occupies the land to the north, east and south of the house. What has been created is a detached landscape with no axial alignment to the house (at (b) on the plan); in fact, it is not clear whether the garden could be fully seen

THE 'INGENIOUS MR BRIDGEMAN'

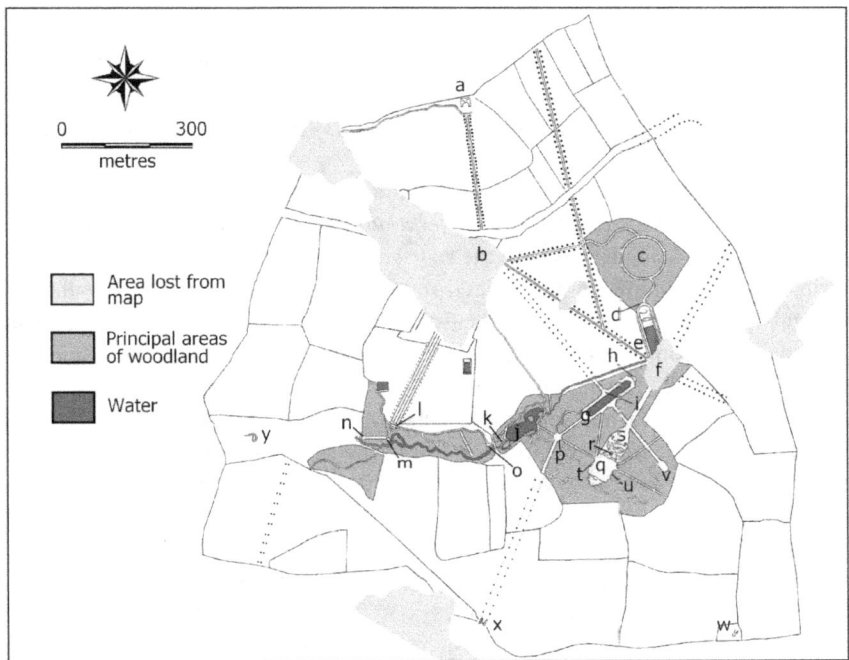

Figure 12. Location of the principal garden features at Gobions based on the Bodleian Map. Reproduced by kind permission of Dr Anne Rowe and Professor Tom Williamson.

Key: The position of features described by William Toldervy (1762), but not shown on the map, are described as 'site of': (a) seat at end of a walk running north from the house; (b) site of the house (not shown on the Bodleian map due to damage); (c) 'rotunda'; (d) 'large alcove'; (e) basin; (f) site of the figure of time (not shown on the Bodleian map due to damage); (g) canal; (h) site of the canal temple (not shown on Bodleian map); (i) site of the figure of the 'Roman gladiator'; (j) lake; (k) cascade; (l) lattice-work summer house (see Figure 9); (m) obelisk; (n) viewpoint overlooking the swallow holes; (o) horseshoe-shaped feature (site of grotto?); (p) Hercules rotunda; (q) bowling green; (r) bowling green summer house; (s) terrace below the summer house; (t) site of the figure of Venus (not shown on the Bodleian map); (u) site of the figure of Adonis (not shown on the Bodleian map); (v) oak tree; (w) sham ruin; (x) Folly arch; and (y) seat on a bastion.

from the house. However, within this space, Bridgeman creates a unified design focused on the wooded valley. To a very large degree, the position of the wood dictates the way the design uses space. The landscape created uses the modest rise from the wood to both the south and the north, to tie the landscape together and to create an illusion of seclusion and privacy. From the valley garden, cradled in the bottom of this shallow bowl of hills, the low ridges both to the north and the south are the horizon. To emphasise this, Bridgeman creates focal points in the rim from which the garden can be viewed: a bastion with a seat on the 110 m contour line (a), the Folly Arch at F on the 120 m contour line (x), and the sham ruin on the 105 m contour line (w), all of which may have been intended to fulfil this purpose (Rowe and Williamson 2012, 89). Avenues lead down from the bastion and from the Folly Arch.

The intimate spaces are reserved for the wood, to which the eye is drawn from all these vantage points. Inside the wood, the straight and serpentine paths create a journey which plays with the space in what is actually a relatively narrow strip of woodland. The plan is divided so that, in the wider part of the valley, to the east, the garden follows a geometric model with walks at 45 degrees and 22.5 degrees from the allée that runs north–south to the Folly Arch and the canal (g), the oak clearing (v) and the bowling green (q), and are connected to each other by straight and serpentine walks within the woodland. To the west, as the Landscape Design Associates point out, 'the layout appears to lack any basis in geometry' (cited in Rowe and Williamson 2012, 94); where the valley becomes more deeply incised, Bridgeman appears to have responded to the topography by abandoning any attempt to create a geometric design and, instead, including more winding paths and allowing the stream to largely follow its natural course, from a naturalistic lake (j) with cascades (k) to deal with the downward trajectory of the stream to the swallow holes, where a seat is placed (n).

The effect is clear in the description Toldervy (1762) wrote when he visited the garden in 1762. His account is carefully judged to accentuate the mystery and excitement of the place, but if we look past the coded language in which much of the writing about gardens in the later eighteenth century is couched, we can see how Bridgeman's landscape had matured and how cleverly his manipulation of space worked to create intimate spaces which invite exploration. Toldervy enters the space through a 'pretty sort of Labyrinthe' of oak trees, which are 'very strait and vastly high'. He continues 'through meandering Walks, cut through the Underwood ... to a very affecting Grotto ...', and beneath 'a large Arch ... beheld a ravishing Cascade', the sound of which remained with him as he walked on. He arrived at a 'beautiful canal; at the End of which is a handsome Temple, whose Front is supported by four Pillars', the beauty of the scene enhanced by the statues placed around the canal. Turning left, he comes upon 'the neatest and most retired Bowling-Green I ever saw', on one side of which is an urn, on the other 'a Summer-House, full of Orange and Lemon-Trees'. Toldervy's account also makes clear that, though the valley and the wood were the destination of the design, the quiet heart of a secluded space, the views out were part of the intention of the designer and certainly noticed by the visitor. He writes that 'the Eye is infallibly led to an Obelisk, at a considerable Distance, beyond the Gardens ...' and draws attention to the statue of Cleopatra: 'I ascended a strait Walk, which brought me, on the Left-Hand, to a Cleopatra, as stung with an Asp. This Figure stands upon a Pedestal, in a Meadow, at some Distance'. In fact, the statue of Cleopatra was placed just beyond the eastern boundary of Greate Wood; the word 'Cleopatra' or 'Cliopatra' has been written lightly in pencil on the Hatfield Map in a place now occupied by a small garden, incorporated into the wood. Even today, standing within the Gobions Wood, there is a sense that the garden as a secret place, and there is drama in the view of the Folly Arch.

It is possible to deconstruct all of Bridgeman's better documented landscapes and find there the alchemy he creates with a loose geometric structure, the careful placing of built features, and an understanding of the topography and geology of the landscape. What follows is a series of snapshots of the process at work at other sites. At Sacombe (c.1715), where the soil is a chalky till characterised by its flint content (mapapps.bgs.ac.uk/geologyofbritain/home), the design itself is relatively simple, and based on geometric proportions. However, the length of the two arms of the isosceles triangle which form the outer edges of the *patte d'oie* is determined by the boundary of a piece of pre-existing woodland. Although no earlier plans of the site exist, the irregular boundary of the wooded area is partly the result of the presence of the parish boundary (OS Digimap 1:10,000) and so it is likely to be older than Bridgeman's design. Because it is a regular geometric form, this distance dictates the length of the other arm and the siting of the small theatre; the position of the oval pond is therefore also determined by this distance as well as the gentle slope of the hill, immediately to its north between the 105 m and 110 m contour lines, which must drain into it. Presumably, though, this natural drainage did not produce sufficient water to fill it, and Milledge suggests that the triangular reservoir to the north of the pond and several metres higher, was used to feed it; the OS map at a scale of 1:2500 shows a drain which could have fulfilled this function (Milledge 2006, 43).

At Moor Park, Bridgeman's design uses the natural topography of the land as it descends to the river Colne. On the roughly level ground to the north-east of the house, and axially aligned to it, steps from a terrace lead down to square bowling green bisected by a broad path, beyond which is an octagonal basin from which a canal extends some 250 m to a man-made bastion. To the north and south of this central structure, the design places two roughly triangular, bastion-like structures each bounded by a terrace. To the north, down the slope towards the river Colne, this terrace follows the 85 m contour line almost exactly, following the bend in it. Within it are cabinets and straight and serpentine paths. To the north, as the land slopes up, the terrace climbs the hill and is extended beyond the end of the triangle towards the highest point in the park on the 110 m contour line. Within this triangle, there are again cabinets, linked by straight and serpentine paths, and, of particular interest, three radiating and tapering vistas pointing out towards the boundary of the park. The terrace running from the apex of the triangle towards the top of the hill terminates in an octagonal space which is linked to a basin in the shape of a cross cut into the slope. The summit provided (and still provides) breathtaking views: Sir John Evelyn commented in 1726 on the 'greatest addition ... a terrace of a vast length looking directly on Cashiobury 3 miles off, & into the country towards Harrow ...' (Jeffery 2014, 15).

At Hackwood, Bridgeman transformed Spring Wood for the Duke of Bolton. The pre-existing large wood, steeply sloping to the east and probably medieval in origin, was, by the early eighteenth century, crossed by rides and surrounded by a perimeter walk (https://historicengland.org.uk). The wood became a coherent design in which compartments filled with fountains, cabinets, terraces and a menagerie were linked by straight and serpentine paths and surrounded with bastions and canals. Here, Bridgeman's fountains and pools are fed by the springs emerging from the chalk, from which the wood takes its name, and the canal which occupies the ditch immediately to the east of Bridgeman's bastions at the bottom of the slope occupies a small curving band of silt and gravel.

It is impossible to tell how much, if any, of what is covered in this chapter was actually a deliberate expression of an artistic vision. It is tempting to try to impose some kind of conscious aesthetic on Bridgeman's work, perhaps in response to the social and artistic currents of eighteenth-century society. There are a number of well-rehearsed frameworks which might be applicable to such an idea. For example, we might see a gradual relaxation of geometry as the result of the rising popularity, if not of the 'natural' garden, then at least of an interest in nature, especially after 1730. We might also see the creation of detached gardens, not axially aligned to the house, as coinciding with the beginning of a growing informality in society as the eighteenth century progressed. Williamson has argued that '[a]t one level, the elegant serpentine gardens and the careless, yet structured irregularity of the landscape park can be read almost as a structural transformation of the new, more informal behaviour now adopted by the rich' (Williamson 1998, 177). It may be that we could see Rousham, and particularly Gobions, with their non-axial structure which encourages different routes, as part of the trajectory towards informality. We might suggest that Bridgeman's work as a response to the way the elite 'increasingly distanced themselves from local communities and agrarian life' (Williamson 1995, 58). Williamson argues that parks came to be 'read almost as islands of gentility, of polite exclusion, within the wider working countryside' (Williamson and Spooner 2016, 206). This certainly seems to be the case at Houghton Hall, for example, where banks of trees screen the perimeter. Perimeter belts can also be read as features designed to keep the labouring classes out of the parks; indeed, the Black Act of 1723 was designed to protect not only game, but also trees, making it a capital offence to 'cut down or otherwise destroy any trees planted in an avenue, or growing in any garden, orchard or plantation, for ornament, shelter or profit (Daniels in Cosgrove and Daniels 1988, 44). A large geometric landscape can also be read as a signifier of power; as Williamson has argued, '[t]he great geometric parks and gardens of the late seventeenth and early eighteenth centuries represented demonstrations of naked power' to be read as such both by other members of the ruling elite (Williamson 1998, 66).

All of this is completely plausible, and the theories have merit, but the evidence does not support anything like a clear trajectory suggestive of a conscious design aesthetic. In fact, as shown above, we can find geometric underpinning of some kind in all Bridgeman designs between 1715, at Sacombe, and 1738 at Amesbury, and very often similar geometric structures. For example, the formal, geometric ziggurat structure within which trees are planted appears at Eastbury c.1725, is part of the proposal at Boughton c.1729, and was created in Amesbury in 1738. The detached gardens at Rousham were probably designed before 1719 when the estate map which shows them was drawn, while the gardens at Gobions were probably created in the middle of the following decade, much too early, it could be argued, to be part of a growing informality. Garden design is a messy, organic business, driven as it is by a number of factors: historical precedent, availability of plants, climate, the practicalities of a site and, crucially, client preference. With close and rigorous unpicking it generally resists any effort to turn it into a chronological logicality. What we can say of Bridgeman's style is that he understood that the elements of his design must be moulded to the topography and be appropriate to the geology of the site. Probably this sounds rather obvious, not to say prosaic, but it is hard to find another designer before Lancelot Brown who was able to create a coherent design aesthetic which embraced the practical limitations of a site with such flair, consistency and commercial success.

CHAPTER 7

BUILDING A LANDSCAPE

MUCH OF THE writing about Bridgeman, and in fact this is probably true about most other garden designers except perhaps the most modern, places him in a universe of art and philosophy where the mechanics of creating a landscape are of less relevance than the aesthetics and the ideas. Actually, though, the making of gardens is an intensely practical business. It is necessary to know what will grow and how to look after it while it does, and how to build the roads, paths, terraces, theatres and hydraulic installations that make up the skeleton of the garden. Without that, no art is possible. Bridgeman was a master of all the disciplines needed to construct what he had designed.

Any landscape must begin with an accurate survey. The business of surveying distances over a large area of land is complicated even with modern surveying apparatus; in the early eighteenth century it was far more so, although essential for the correct apportionment of land and the avoidance of dispute. Bridgeman was clearly a skilled surveyor. The methods he used must have been those of the estate surveyor whose work was the measurement of parcels of land on an estate for an employer or client. In the fifteenth and sixteenth centuries measurement of the area of these parcels was accomplished using a cord of predetermined length. By the late seventeenth and early eighteenth century this cord had largely been superseded, for measuring purposes, by Gunther's chain, introduced in 1620 by Edmund Gunther (Bendall 2009, 130). Leybourn describes this chain as 'divided into 100 Links, one of these Links being made four times the length of the other. Now, if this chain be made according to Statute, each Perch to contain 16½ Feet; then each Link of this Chain will contain 7 Inches, and 92/100 of an Inch, and the whole Chain 792 Inches, or 66 Feet'. This chain would be 'carried by two men, who working together will mark out each length of chain with sticks' (Leybourn 1653, 45–49). The chain was relatively inexpensive. Bridgeman's contemporary, and rival in the question of drainage of the fens, Thomas Badeslade, was paid £5 for one by Sir Robert Walpole in 1719. Bendall shows that this method of measuring distances was in use by surveyors working at the same time as Bridgeman. She uses the example of Joel Gascoyne, who used a chain to survey the boundaries of the manor of Great Haseley in Oxfordshire in 1701 (Bendall 2009, 131). Although postdating Bridgeman's death in 1738, the reference Bendall makes to a survey done by John Davis in 1741 for which he was paid £75, including a payment for the 'chain carriers', is probably contemporary enough to suggest that the chain method would have been familiar to Bridgeman (Bendall 2009, 131). Distances might also be measured in feet using a wheel perambulator, or waywiser, a wheel by which distances could be calculated by multiplying the number of revolutions by the circumference of the wheel. Although Richeson dismisses the measurements obtained in this way as 'highly unsatisfactory', and both Bendall and Richeson suggest the wheel perambulator was used only for road measurement, Andrew Macnair suggests that it was the instrument used most frequently by garden designers in the eighteenth century (Richeson 1966, 173; Bendall 2009, 135; Macnair pers. comm.).

Surveyors used triangulation to determine the location of a point from other known points. Bendall suggests this method was in use in the seventeenth and eighteenth centuries. It required a mastery of geometry and the use of a plane table or an azimuth theodolite. A plane table was a smooth wooden table top with a frame to hold relatively large sheets of paper, mounted on three legs. The top was connected to the legs in such a way that it could be levelled using a plumb line, or spirit level. It could easily be transported to the site and had the advantage that a plan could be made in the field. Instructions for its use were given in publications contemporary with Bridgeman's work by Laurence in 1716, and by Wyld and Wilson in 1725 (Bendall 2009, 131). A plane table was simple to use and relatively inexpensive, costing, with a spirit level, around eight guineas in 1740s. By contrast, the theodolite was a more complicated, and considerably more expensive, option, costing perhaps as much as £50 in the eighteenth century. Measurements were taken from a theodolite and entered in a log book in the field, to be worked on elsewhere (Bendall 2009, 132). During the period in which Bridgeman was working, improvements were made to the design of the theodolite, particularly by Jonathan Sisson in c.1720. His improved instrument is recommended in Samuel Cunn's revised edition of Laurence during the 1720s (Richeson 1966, 147). Because of its cost, and because it required a more sophisticated set of skills, Bendall suggests that its use was not as common as the plane table even by the nineteenth century (Bendall 2009, 134). Richeson also makes the point that, as demand for surveyors' services increased, chain surveying was often preferred to either the plane table or the theodolite, as it was a quicker process (Richeson 1966, 160–161).

It is clear that Bridgeman was conversant with these techniques and used them in the process of constructing his landscapes. His plans have scales in both chains and feet. The inventory of his possessions taken after his death shows that he had the equipment to make the geometric calculations necessary for surveying: '5 T: Squares' and 'a Foot Case of brass Instruments Three Protractors' (PROB. 3/37/95). The instruments detailed in his Inventory also suggest that it is likely that he owned a plane table, and certainly owned a theodolite. His inventory lists a 'Small Spirit Level in a Case', which may have been for use with a plane table, and 'a Theodolate in a Case nine inches over and a wooden Case for taking Prospects' (PROB. 3/37/95). Triangulation lines are also visible on a number of plans: for example, on one of the drawings for Boughton, where they have been lightly drawn on the plan to measure the land to the north of the house and the area of the lake. Many are closely annotated with measurements in what looks like his hand. The plan for the theatre at Tring (BoL MSGD a4 fo.78), for example, is covered with carefully calculated distances: the octagonal pool is 100 feet in diameter, its perimeter wall 87 feet from the walk at its terminus, the distance between the side of the theatre and the side of the pool is 28 feet. In order to fix a point on the land from which to begin the construction, intersecting lines seem to have been drawn from existing trees. A pencil calculation at the bottom of the plan adds the distances together to calculate the length of the entire theatre.

The survey formed the basis from which the plan was drawn. While it is not certain where this took place, it seems likely that the work was done in some kind of drawing office or workshop, probably located at Bridgeman's house at Broad Street in Soho. In addition to equipment consistent with surveying, there are items used by draughtsmen (NA PROB.3/37/95): '… a drawing board on Trussell … Five dozen of black lead pencils'. It was also from Broad Street that Bridgeman wrote to Alexander Pope on 28 September 28 1724, concerning plans for a location unspecified, but probably Marble Hill: 'I came home on Fryday night & had Your kind letter [O]n Saturday morning I begun on the plan & have not [lef]t it till 'tis finish'd which I hope will be about tomorrow Noon …' (BL Add MS 4809 fo.141v). It is not clear whether Broad Street functioned as a drawing office in which Bridgeman employed other draughtsman to help him draw plans, but it is highly likely. There appear to be some parallels with André Le Nôtre's working practices. Bouchenot-Déchin suggests that Le Nôtre and those who worked closely with him, working on gardens for Louis XIV, lived in close proximity to each other: '… they lived in a small area near the Tuileries, specifically between the house the king had placed at his gardener's disposal, and the home of his in-laws opposite the church of St Roch, which he and his wife had inherited …', and that while the French equivalent of the Office of Works, the *Surintendant des Bâtiments*, 'provided a framework for Le Nôtre's activities, it would appear that his home was, though not strictly speaking a workshop, an essential port of call. Colbert, Louvois and the Prince of Condé all mention visiting it to fetch plans, request a new design, or get advice' (Bouchenot-Déchin 2013, 150). Bouchenot-Déchin also suggests that Claude Desgots had set up 'a large room, that almost certainly served as a combination workshop, office, and 'school', in his house in Paris and possibly in his house in Meudon, too (Bouchenot-Déchin 2014, 151).

Once the plan was drawn, it had to be marked out on the land. A letter from Bridgeman to Thomas Hall at Goldings (here quoted in full) shows us the preliminaries for marking out the design there:

> I am very much asham'd of my Self for keeping you so long without Your plan; which I hope you will be so good as to forgive; it is done at last and very much to my own mind & good liking, & I hope 'twill be approvd by you. I have for this fortnight been laid up with a terrible broken shin & under the surgeons

hand, but hope to be well to attend you in a weeks time at Goldings, with Mr Flitcroft; in the mean I beg 3 or 4 hund. stakes of 2 & 3 feet long may be got ready, a good Garden Line beetle & 2 10 feet rods & some deal rods at about 8 feet long for Light Sticks. (NA 103 -130)[1]

A 'Light stick' is an alternative term for the offset rods which were used to measure short distances at right angles to a line. Gillespie, writing in the mid-nineteenth century, suggests that a light stick was ten to fifteen links of a chain in length, somewhere around the '8 feet long' that Bridgeman specifies in the letter (Gillespie 1855, 78). The 'beetle' is a large mallet usually used for knocking in wedges, but in this case perhaps used to knock in the stakes.

Presumably, before construction began, there must have been some communication, and possibly collaboration, between the architect or architects responsible for the design of the house and the landscape designer, whether it was new or being remodelled. Other craftsman may also have been involved in the discussions. For example, at Wolterton, where Bridgeman was creating a new landscape around a new house designed by Thomas Ripley, there appears to have been a collaboration, almost from the inception of the work there. Ripley's letter to Walpole on 17 December 1724 suggests that he and Bridgeman have already consulted with each other about the commission, and will visit Bayfield, the chief land steward, together (WH Box 73L 8/5A) (see Chapter 3). Indeed, the site of the old house appears on the plan for Wolterton (BoL MSGD a3 fo.18). Letters held in the Wolterton archive show Ripley and Bridgeman together visiting Britiffe, Walpole's chief steward in London, in December 1724, and again, this time with Christopher Cass and George Deval, in 1728 (WH Box 73L 8/5A). Ripley appears to have collaborated with him on the design for the garden. In this letter, Britiffe writes: 'Mr Ripley Design a bouling Green as far as the old ferosee' (WH Box 73L 8/5A). Bridgeman's own letter to Walpole in 1736, in which he outlines the reshaping of the garden, comes as a result of a letter to Ripley from Walpole which appears to contain a message for him from Walpole and alludes to a joint visit to Wolterton: 'Mr Ripley shew'd me Your honours Letter to him, wherein you desire to know what was done & orderd when he & I was last at Wolterton'. There was clearly another visit planned: 'I intend to go into Norfolk this next Month when Mr Ripley will be there, and see that these things by Your order in hand, be accomplished; and to do whatever else, Your honour shall command me in' (WH Box 3LX 8/12); and in 1737 both were at Wolterton drinking Walpole's wine (WH Box 29L 8/20). It is likely that this was a close collaboration, not simply because the letters hint at it, but because the new position of the house at Wolterton is axially aligned to Bridgeman's new lake; the bend in the lake, which follows the boundaries of the oddly shaped piece of land available to Walpole for the garden,

---

[1] I am indebted to Alison Cassidy for this letter, which she uncovered at the National Records Office. It is undated, but is probably from 1735.

is sited so that its terminus is not visible from the house, giving the illusion of a much longer piece of water. This was clearly also the case at Lumley Castle, where, working alongside Vanbrugh, Bridgeman seems to have designed a tapering vista which runs west towards the river Wear from Vanbrugh's new ceremonial hall on the west range of the castle (Pevsner 1983, 359–360; Dalton 2012, 180).

There must also have been some collaboration with regard to the siting of garden buildings. There is little documentary evidence for this but it seems reasonable to assume that, where a vista terminated in a statue or a building, considerable consultation occurred between sculptor or architect and Bridgeman. At Gobions, James Gibbs was probably responsible for the garden buildings. The Ashmolean Museum holds a drawing of an octagonal temple by Gibbs inscribed 'for Mr Sambrooke of Gubbins' and, although Tom Williamson and Anne Rowe point out that this is not the temple that appears in the Chatelain drawing, they make the point that there is another drawing in the same collection which shows the octagonal dovecote at Gobions, and they consider it plausible that the Folly Arch, the southern focus of an avenue designed by Bridgeman, was also designed by Gibbs (Rowe and Williamson 2012, 84). At Hackwood in Hampshire, Gibbs was responsible for the pavilion in the Menagerie and for the Rotunda at the top of the amphitheatre. Both designs appear in Gibbs's *Book of Architecture* (1728), and are shown in plan form on Bridgeman's plan (BoL MSGD a3 fo.34), although the Rotunda and amphitheatre were built in the north-east quadrant of the garden rather than the south-east as shown on Bridgeman's plan.

It is clear that Bridgeman must also have had some grasp of construction techniques, and the minutes of the Board of Works suggest that he was personally competent in the construction of roads. As Royal Gardener, his responsibilities extended to maintaining the roads in the Royal Parks. This maintenance is not specifically stipulated in his contract, and so payments for this work appear in the minutes of the Board of Works: for example, on 28 November 1729 payment of £240.2s.0d was made to Bridgeman 'in full for defraying the Repairs order'd to be done this season on His Maj[estys] Road Leading from Pimlico to Fulham, w[hi]ch was done accordingly' (NA Work 4/4). It is possible to see what the process of constructing walks entailed in the proposal submitted by Bridgeman and Wise for the work at Kensington Gardens (NA Work 6/114). The work was to be carried out by Bridgeman's workforce. The creation of the gravel walks was a major undertaking, not least because of their surface area: 'the Principall Walks of which is 80 feet wide & 2800 feet long & all the several other Walks of the same length' (NA Work 6/114). Earth was 'to be dug & taken of the Ground between the several Walks of Trees there which Earth is to be removed' and gravel laid 'in the place thereof'. Bridgeman and Wise charged £246.3s.0d for 'the Expences of digging filling onto Carts carting away disposing & laying the same in proper place in the old and new Plantations all charges included' (NA Work 6/114). The process also involved the sourcing of gravel from the site: 'the Gravell to be used for this purpose is propos'd to be taken out of several Pitts to be sunk in proper places in the said great Upper Wilderness & in Hyde Park', and there were further charges for 'the expences of opening the severall Pitts digging the Gravell Casting screening the same loading Carting laying spreading making ramming rolling & finishing' (NA Work 6/114). Bridgeman and Wise undertook to 'make good' the land from which the gravel had been removed afterwards: 'the said Undertakers are to have liberty to dig gravell & take Turf for the Works in Hyde Park it is meant and intended that neither the Gravell so to be dug not the Turf so to be taken but in such herbage of the said Park & that ye said Undertakers shall level & lay the Pitts from whence the said Gravell shall be dug in decent & comely order & sow the ground from whence the said Gravell shall be taken with hay seed at their own charge' (NA Work 6/114).

Most of Bridgeman's designs included durable flat surfaces: roads, walks, terraces and straight and serpentine paths, many of which incorporated rond-points and small cabinets. They appear to have had a number of surfaces: grass, gravel or paving stones, either separately or in combination. However, all required the creation of a surface that was long-lasting, well-drained and level, since their principal function was to facilitate movement through the landscape either on foot or on a horse, or to allow easy access around features such as lakes. It is a testament to their durability that in many Bridgeman landscapes, traces of these remain. At Down Hall, although Bridgeman's garden is largely covered with dense undergrowth, LIDAR reveals that the *patte d'oie* to the north of the house, shown on two plans, Gough Maps 46 fo.262 and BL Loan 29/357, still exists. The long, elevated terrace at Sacombe, running from the end of the parterre to the canal, is not only still visible, but still serviceable. At Amesbury, the edges of the square platform and the rond-point on top of Vespasian's Camp are visible today (Figure 4). The contours and foundations of the rond-point at Tring at the end of the King Charles Ride, recently restored by Hertfordshire Gardens Trust, have also proved durable.

Although bowling greens, grass walks and parterres may be the least ambitious elements of any Bridgeman design, their construction was a labour intensive and relatively complex procedure. Again his work as Royal Gardener shows that Bridgeman understood the practical implications of creating large areas of grass. The process of finishing the earth surface and turfing it is detailed in Bridgeman's proposal with regard to the new work at Kensington Gardens: 'For Turf to be used in laying several Walks, Verges & Divisions of Grass intended within this new Ground the Turf so used to be taken of the Walks in the new Paddock where gravell is to be taken of the Walks in the new Paddock where gravell is to be laid & and also such places in Hyde Park as lye out of sight. The Expences of cutting the Turf loading & carting the same levelling & preparing the said several Verges & Divisions to receive it laying, beating, rolling & finishing the same all charges included £318.8.0' (NA Work 6/114). This entry in Bridgeman's proposal makes it clear that the grass for the 'Verges & Divisions' is to be reused from turf cut in the making of the gravelled walks. The work on a similar stretch

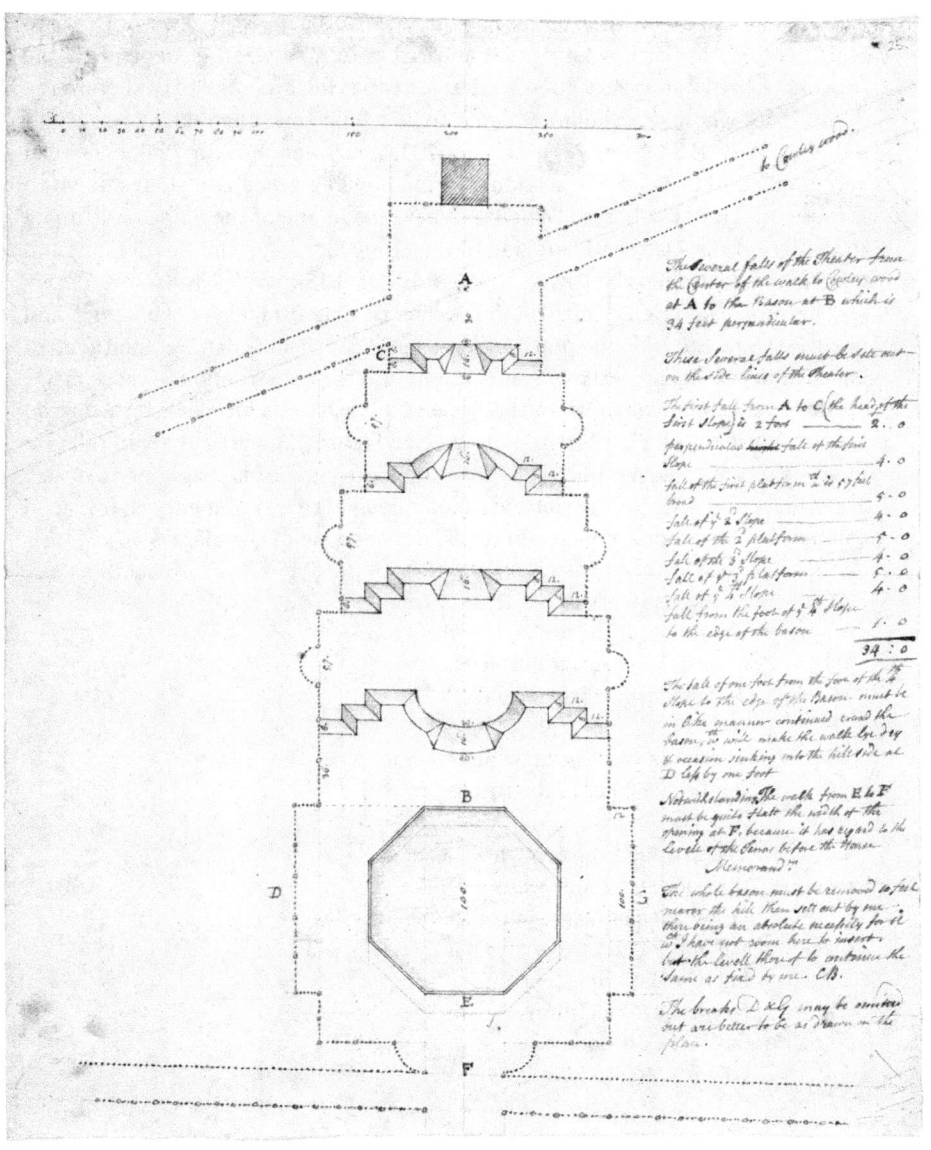

Figure 13. An unidentified plan for a theatre. MSGD a4 fo.25. The Bodleian Libraries, University of Oxford.

of grass to the south of Wolterton Hall, designed by Bridgeman, is set out in correspondence between Horatio Walpole and his land steward Bayfield. In November 1728 Bayfield wrote about the need to change the level of the area which is to form the bowling green and refers to how weather dependent the process was: that it 'is very good wether for carreying away the earth before the South Front where the Bouling Green is to be w[hi]ch must be taken down about 3 foots & ½' (WH 8/5A Box 73L). By June 1731, Will Brand, Horatio Walpole's head gardener, and his men were working on the bowling green and slopes down to it to the north of the house: 'Will Brand have made one of the Slopes & is doing the other on the Right and Left side of the Stone Slopes on the North Front and Carrying and Leveling the Lawn ...' (WH Box 29L 8/15).

The most ambitious construction projects that Bridgeman envisaged and oversaw were the monumental terraces, mounds, theatres and amphitheatres which appear in many designs. Some insight into the construction of these major earthworks can be gained from the detailed instructions for earth terracing on the unidentified ink plan MSGD a4 fo.25 (see Figure 13), particularly in relation to levels. Since these are initialled 'CB' at the bottom, we must assume that they are Bridgeman's. His instructions are meticulous but clear and easy to follow. A column of instructions appears on the right-hand side of the plan:

The several falls of the Theater from
the center of the walk to Cowley Wood
at A to the Bason at B which is
34 feet perpendicular.

These severall falls must be sete out
on the side lines of the theater.

The first fall from * to C (the head of the first slope) is 2 foot	2.0
Perpendicular height fall of this slope	4.0
fall of the first platform wch is 57 feet broad	5.0
fall of ye 2d slope	4.0
fall of the 2d platform	5.0
fall of the 3d slope	4.0
fall of ye 3d platform	5.0
fall of ye 4th slope	4.0
fall from foot of ye 4th slope to the edge of the bason	1.0
	<u>34:0</u>

The fall of one foot from the foot of the 4th
slope to the edge of the Bason must be
in like manner continued round the

bason wch will make the walk lye dry
& occasion sinking into the hillside at
D less by one foot.

Notwithstanding. The walk from E to F
must be quite flat the width of the
opening at F, because it has regard to the
level of the Terras before the house.
        Memorandm

The whole bason must be removed 10 feet
nearer the hill than sett out by me
there being an absolute necessity for it
wch I have not room here to insert
but levell thereof to continue the
same as fixd by me. CB'.

The breaks D & G may be omitted
but are better to be as drawn on the
plan.

These are meticulous instructions. Bridgeman is clearly concerned with how the earth will be moved to create the steps of the 'Theater'. So, for example: 'The first fall from A to C (the head of the first slope) is 2 feet' and 'the perpendicular fall from this first slope 4.0'. In an abbreviated form this information is repeated for each platform, with a total showing the entire fall of 34 feet at the end. The drainage of the 'Theater' is considered: 'The fall of one foot from the foot of the 4th slope to the edge of the bason must be in like manner continued round the bason w[hi]ch will make the walk lye drye & occasion sinking into the hillside at D less by one foot', as is its spatial relationship to 'the level of the Terras before the House'.

We might also consider how a pragmatic consideration of the underlying geology affected the construction of these major earthworks. At Claremont, the amphitheatre is created out of the south-western end of a steeply inclined promontory of sand and gravel (Lynch Hill gravel member), presumably relatively easy to work. This seems to have allowed the creation of a very large amphitheatre which, restored by the National Trust in c.1975, is dramatic even today (Figure 14).

The amphitheatre at Cliveden is considerably smaller, perhaps because of the difficulties posed by both the underlying geology and the topography of the site. It is built into the edge of a deposit of sand and gravel (mostly Gerrards Cross gravel) where it joins the very steeply inclined cliff formed of the underlying bedrock of chalk descending to the river Thames to the east of the site. Its construction is mentioned in a letter from the Earl of Orkney to his brother, and

Figure 14. The amphitheatre at Claremont. Photograph: Susan Haynes, 2013.

shows the difficulties inherent in the task: '... I think it will be better than was Intended (but the Amphitheatre is quite struck out) wher[e] to get the turf and trees for la grand machine, beside there is great difficulty to get the slope all that side of the Hill where the precipice was, but Bridgeman mackes difficultys of nothing ...' (MS 1033, fo.157, in Willis 2002, 427). Here archaic meanings have obscured the sense of the words: 'struck out' may well be used in a building sense meaning to remove the supporting timbers from a structure, and 'la grand machine' probably refers to the construction or edifice (www.oed.com).

Once the survey was done and the plan drawn, and the construction work was planned if not begun, Bridgeman must have turned his attention to planting. After all, Bridgeman was primarily a gardener. It is how he described himself in the subscription list for *Vitruvius Britannicus II* and *III* and how he was known to his contemporaries, and he was, of course, Royal Gardener. Although the plans themselves mostly give little away, we can probably assume that he exercised that expertise in the choices he made for the planting of his landscapes. However, there is no indication in Bridgeman's plans to suggest the planting of flowers, but, given that expertise, it seems unlikely that Bridgeman's landscapes were devoid of flowering plants. What is notable about the omission from every plan and document of a detailed planting list, or any serious indication of planting intentions, is the contrast it represents to contemporary writers and gardeners. Stephen Switzer's *Ichnographia Rustica* Vol. II contains species-specific advice on trees and flowering plants, particularly in Chapters VII, VIII and IX. Batty

Langley devotes some pages in Part V of *New Principles of Gardening* to the habit, propagation and flowering qualities of plants and shrubs: 'The first Blowing flowering Shrub is the *Mezerion* which presents its *beautiful Blossoms* in *January* and continues in Bloom to the Middle of *February* (Langley 1728, 180). In the section following this, '*Of the Manner of Disposing and Planting Flowering Shrubs in the Proper Parts of a Wilderness*', he suggests where these flowers might be best planted to produce 'a perfect Slope of beautiful Flowers'. Laird makes the point that the bills for the flowering plants delivered to John Dillman, gardener to Frederick, Prince of Wales, between 1735 and 1738, for the garden Kent designed at Carlton House, were for 'honeysuckles, jasmines, double sweetbriers, syringas and mezereons' (Laird 1999, 41). It may be that Bridgeman's landscapes were similarly planted, but, if they were, there is no evidence of it.

What evidence there is largely concerns trees. The plans indicate trees in one of four ways: by single dots, by a generic stylised symbol, by a truncated version of the same symbol which shows only the top of the tree, and, very occasionally, by a small triangular symbol which is probably intended to be a clipped evergreen, probably yew or box. With the exception of the last, none of these is in any way species specific, but three of the plans, for Tring (BoL MSGD a4 fo.32), for Purley in West Berkshire (BoL MSGD a4 fo.54), and for Scampston in North Yorkshire (BoL MSGD a4 fo.27), are annotated with precise instructions for planting. There is also some documentary evidence which indicates what was planted at Kensington Gardens, at Lodge Park, at Boughton, at Wolterton and at Rousham, but, although useful in building a picture of the plants used in Bridgeman's landscapes, these sources do not necessarily convey his intention.

Barnes and Williamson suggest that oak, beech, elm, lime and sweet chestnut were used most widely in geometric schemes in the early eighteenth century, and this is supported by the available evidence of the planting of Bridgeman's landscapes (Barnes and Williamson 2011, 123). The strongest evidence supports Bridgeman's use of elms, although because of the onset of Dutch elm disease in the 1960s, it is unlikely that any of Bridgeman's original planting of standard trees survives (Barnes and Williamson 2011, 77). Elms are the only species mentioned by name in the documents that relate to Bridgeman's remodelling of Kensington Gardens (NA Work 6/114). In 1727, Bridgeman charged for watering 'the great Elms' and requested an extra payment of £100 for '100 of the Large Standard Elms that are dead on the new part of the Gardens to be replanted The prime lost of the Trees, Carriage to the Thames, Water Carrieage, Carriage from the water to Kensington preparing the Soyl & planting all charges included' (NA Work 6/114). The claim was disallowed, probably because his contract explicitly stated that 'the said Undertaker is at his own Proper costs & charges to make good the several Plantations of Fruit Trees, Forrest Trees, Flowering Shrubs and hardy Evergreens that shall at any time happen to dye by planting others in their Places' (NA Work 6/114). In 1731, '273 large Standard English Elms' were planted 'in Grove manner on each side the water in the Circular Lawn'. Elms are also specified on plans. Annotations on the plans for Scampston (BoL MSGD a4 fo.27), and for Tring (BoL MSGD a4 fo.32), specify 'Elms etc.' on the western edge of Blakey Beck to the east of the park, and '106 Standard Elms for the outward Lines', respectively. Elms are amongst the trees to be planted at Down Hall by Stephen Bridgeman in 1729, and are being dug up to make way for evergreens at Rousham in 1739. Between 1724 and 1729, 7,000 elms and 700 wych elms were ordered for Lodge Park (Smith 2006, 242).

Oaks are mentioned less frequently as part of the planting of Bridgeman's new landscapes, although this may not mean that they were used less frequently. They were to be planted at Wolterton in January 1727 as part of Bridgeman's new plan for the garden: 'If they plant a Line of young Oaks 40 feet from the ditch it will run 10 feet into the young wood (Come up) w[hi]ch will breake that Plan of the sd Nursery, Laid Down by Mr Carpenter' (WH 8/5A Box 73L). At Down Hall, if we assume that Stephen Bridgeman's letter refers to Charles Bridgeman's planting, oaks were clearly being raised in the nursery: 'I think it will be very proper this Spring to dig ye ground Between ye Nursery of Oaks ...' (BL 70370/160). Oaks are also commented on by both Bickham and Toldervy, writing about Gobions in the 1760s: Bickham notes a 'Forest of Oaks', and 'lofty Oaks', and Toldervy writes of 'oak Trees, which are very strait, and vastly high, remain entire'. These may be the trees planted 40 years before, in the 1720s, as part of Bridgeman's planting scheme. Barnes and Williamson show that, at Houghton Hall, both oaks and beeches from Bridgeman's original avenues survive (Barnes and Williamson 2011, 123).

Other types of deciduous trees were used in Bridgeman's landscapes. Limes were very popular at the end of the seventeenth and beginning of the eighteenth centuries. As Barnes and Williamson point out, 'Lime was particularly favoured as an avenue tree, probably because of its relatively rapid growth combined with its graceful form when young' (Barnes and Williamson 2011, 121). At Kensington Gardens in 1727, Bridgeman's account records the 'planting in borders Lyme Espaliers' (NAWork 6/114). These appear to be limes espaliered to form hedges. At Wolterton two sweet chestnut trees, to the north of the house, have girths today of around eight metres, suggesting that they were part of the avenue composed of this species shown on the survey of Wolterton Hall executed by Corbridge in 1732 (Williamson 1998, 72). Williamson has also shown that there is a line of smaller chestnuts, between 5 m and 6.5 m in circumference, within the former wilderness to the west of the house which are likely to be the remains of one of the allées shown on MSGD a4 fo.20. This is supported by the instructions left to Bradshaw the gardener in May 1737, after a visit to Wolterton in April 1737 by Ripley and Bridgeman, to 'plant some more Chestnuts' (WH 8/20 Box 29L and 8/12 Box 3LX). On 3 March 1730, William White was paid for planting sweet chestnuts at Boughton.

There is evidence for the planting of evergreens, in particular of yews. They, or possibly box, are symbolised in a stylised, clipped pyramidal form in parterres in a number of plans; for example, in the parterre at Sacombe (BoL MSGD a4 fo.64), Warwick Priory (WRO CR. 56), and at Eastbury (BoL MSGD a3* fo.9). On Bridgeman's plan for Tring (BoL MSGD a4 fo.32), the planting along the edge of the canal is represented with small circles, annotated: an outer line is composed of 106 standard elms (see above), an inner line of 106 yews. At Lodge Park, between 1724 and 1729, Sir John Dutton ordered 50 yew sets. At Wolterton in 1729 yew trees were planted around the edge of the sunken bowling green (WH Box 8/13), and at Boughton in 1730 they were planted on the Mount, both presumably as part of Bridgeman's remodeling of the gardens. It is possible that some yews planted in the 1720s and 1730s during Bridgeman's reshaping of the landscape survive at Amesbury Abbey and at Sacombe. Two yew trees, framing the slope to Gay's Cave at Amesbury Abbey, might be of sufficient antiquity and girth (both are over three metres) to be original (Haynes 2012, 24), and Milledge suggests that eight yew trees at Sacombe with girths in excess of 100 inches might also be part of Bridgeman's planting (Milledge 2009, 49), though, as John White has noted, it is very difficult to accurately date yew trees, and so girth alone may not be sufficient to establish their planting as part of Bridgeman's plan (http://www.forestry.gov.uk). Other evergreens, 6,000 Scots firs, at Lodge Park (Smith 2006, 242), and silver firs at Wolterton (WH Box 8/13) were used. Holly was probably used within the groves and as a hedging material at several sites. At Wolterton a holly hedge was grown (WH Box 28L 8/14) and at Lodge Park 1050 holly sets were ordered by Sir John Dutton (Smith 2006, 242).

There is also limited evidence of the use of ornamental and fruit trees. Bridgeman appears to have provided them at Great Saxham, although whether they were part of a planting scheme is less sure (BoL MSGD a3 fo.41) (Figure 8). At Purley, the borders of the parterre are labelled '1' and '2', explained in an appended key: '1. Border for paradise apples 2. Border for dwarfs' (BoL MSGD a4 fo.54). Accounts from Purley record substantial payments for plants and for ornamental and fruit trees (Hussey 1970, 310–313). At Lodge Park, 100 flowering trees were part of Sir John Dutton's order (Smith 2006, 242). Shrubs were planted as part of the understorey at Wolterton, since, in his letter to Walpole of 1737, Bridgeman writes of 'cutting down the shrubs under the trees of the Grove', but there is no note of the species.

The size of some of these trees, when transplanted on to the site, was large enough to make an immediate impact. As Smith points out, '[b]y the 1720s and 1730s the technique of transplanting large trees was well understood and used to provide instant effects' (Smith 2006, 242). An engraving by Kleiner from 1724 shows the movement of large trees in tubs, and we can probably assume that this technique was used to place trees in Bridgeman's landscapes (Willis 2002, Plate 92a). At Wolterton, specific mention is made of 'the trees w[hich] were lately sent over in a tubb doe begin to spring and put out Leaves most of them'. These trees seem to have been intended for the 'plantation', since Will Brand, the gardener, is encouraged to 'give Yo[ur] Hon[our] and account of how the tree and plantation goe' (WH Box 28L 8/14). At Boughton, it is also likely that large yew trees were transplanted. An entry in the accounts records: 'Tho. Wright for 4 baskets to carry Yews in to Plant on the Mount £1' (NTS Account Book 430). Certainly, large trees were specified at Lodge Park; Smith notes that 'eight hundred "large" ashes and eighty-five "large" elms were ordered (Smith 2006, 242). At Kensington Gardens the trees were large enough to need a team of horses to transport them. In 1731 Bridgeman charged 'For 9 single days a Team in drawing the said kinds of ever Greens from the said Quarter at 10s per day' (NA Work 6/114).

We might question why there is so little which conveys Bridgeman's intentions in the planting of his landscapes. It may be that, in leaving no narrative or explanatory record of his work, unlike Switzer and Langley, any preferences he had about plants have been lost. It may be that, because he apparently had no nursery of his own, he merely facilitated the supply of plants from other sources and, since he had no business interest in the supply of the plants required, his role was largely advisory. Perhaps his interest and expertise lay in the structural design of the landscape rather than how it was planted.

Bridgeman was also, demonstrably, a highly competent hydraulics engineer. Much of his work involves some manipulation of water around a site or the construction of sizeable ponds and canals. His only publication, in 1724, entitled 'The two great Sewers of the Country With Considerations on the Scheme propos'd by the Corporation of Lynn for Draining the said Fens, and Reinstating that Harbour', is also an indication of his level of ability in this field. It has been largely ignored by garden historians, although its existence, and the expertise it displays, suggest both a competence in levels and water management, and a reputation for it beyond the confines of garden construction. It was prepared for the Earl of Lincoln, to whom it is also addressed, which presumably means Lincoln understood Bridgeman's expertise in this area, especially as a rival plan for the Corporation of King's Lynn was being prepared by Thomas Badeslade and John Armstrong, the Chief Engineer of England.

Bridgeman's assessment of the problem of the drainage of the fens and the silting up of King's Lynn Harbour confirms a command of both hydraulic engineering and geology. He suggests that the root of the problem lies in the tidal nature of the Ouse, and in the particular make-up of the sand and silt on the bed of the Wash: 'The Great Bay or Estuary, that lies between the Counties of *Lincoln* and *Norfolk*, and into which the Rivers *Ouse* and *Nene* empty themselves, has by Nature a very loose bottom, of perhaps the most subtle or small Sand or Silt that can be produced' (Bridgeman 1724, 2). This sand and silt are washed easily back into the harbour at King's Lynn and further on into the Ouse at every flood tide, accumulating as far up as 'the before-mentioned Places, *Germans* on the River *Ouse* and *Wisbech*, on the River *Nean*, as far as the Tides extend themselves up these Rivers,' with the consequent blocking of the sluices. Part of the problem, he suggests, is also the relative weakness of the ebb tide in comparison to the flood tide: 'for that, as the Tides in this Harbour do not employ above the Space of Three Hours in their Flux, and almost the remaining Nine in their reflux, that by such a slow reflux, they lose near two thirds of the Weight and Force the Flux is qualified with' (Bridgeman 1724, 3). The result of this is that, even with fresh water coming down the river, there is not enough force to wash out the accumulated silt. Interestingly, Bridgeman points to Holland as a place where comparable problems and solutions might be found: 'And I humbly hope the Method I shall propose for the Relief of this Country, and Lynn Harbour, will neither appear unreasonable, or unprecedented, if we cast out Eye cross the Water, on our neighbouring Country, the Provinces of Holland' (Bridgeman 1724, 5). It is possible that, at the very least, this points to some professional interest in the hydraulic engineering carried out in Holland, if not to closer contact between Bridgeman and Dutch engineers.

Bridgeman's solution proposes that the six-mile bend in the river Ouse to the south-west of King's Lynn be by-passed by a new cut '[t]wo Hundred and Fifty Foot Wide' (Bridgeman 1724, 12) taking the river almost due north from 'Ebrink' (now Eau Brink), with a navigable sluice where the new cut would join the current harbour to effectively prevent the tides from travelling up the river Ouse at all. The old course of the river would then become good marsh land, he suggests. He proposes that new cuts, each of a hundred feet wide, should bring fresh water from the river Nene to join the Ouse at the beginning of the new cut to the south of King's Lynn. The advantages of this scheme, summed up in his paragraphs 42–48, would be that the river would no longer be silted up by sand carried on the flood tide, that the flood waters would have more receptacles in which they could be held, thereby effectively saving more fenland from flooding, that these receptacles of water could also be used by fenland inhabitants to irrigate their crops when necessary, and that, most crucially for King's Lynn Harbour:

> [The] vast Stores of freshes of these united Rivers, being brought down to the very tail of Lynn Harbour, and riding within their Sluice in wet Times, Ten or Twelve Foot deep in Water, and that above the now Bottom of that Harbour, (silted up as it is) and these vast Stores being discharged through their Sluice, at the Tail of every Tide, when the Bay, or Wash, is pretty well emptied of it Tide-waters, will, I humbly conceive, in a very little Time, by their prodigious Weight and Force, effectually scour the Silt out of the Harbour ... (NRO EA 386.32, 14)

Bridgeman's plan was rejected by the Corporation of King's Lynn, rather more because of the shifting landscape of differing, and potentially conflicting, interests between 'Adventurers', Members of Parliament, landowners, fenman, bargemen and tradesmen than because of its competence. In fact, a substantial part of Bridgeman's proposal was, as Willis suggests, eventually executed (Willis 2002, 36 and n. 53). At the end of the eighteenth century Nathaniel Kindersley revived the idea, which was probably originally his father's but which Bridgeman suggested in his own proposal, that a cut be made from Eau Brink to King's Lynn. The first Eau Brink Act was passed in 1795, but, because of the Napoleonic Wars, the Eau Brink Cut was not opened until 1821 (Darby 1983, 123). Bridgeman's proposal for a sluice on the river Ouse immediately to the south of King's Lynn has never been implemented. However, in the 1930s the erection of an intermittent barrage at Freebridge, immediately to the south of King's Lynn and in a similar position to Bridgeman's sluice, was considered for exactly the reasons he gave in his proposal: to exclude seawater and silt from the river Ouse (Summers 1976, 227). The idea was rejected because of the fear that it would result in silting to the north of the barrage. There was, as there was with Bridgeman's plan, considerable opposition from the harbour authorities at King's Lynn, and, although rejected, it has remained a popular plan with those who live in the Fens. After the floods of 1947, water from the Ouse was channelled through the A.G. Wright sluice into a relief channel, built from the Ouse slightly to the south of the Denver sluice. The channel runs 11 miles along the eastern bank of the Ouse, rejoining it at a tail sluice just south of King's Lynn. This channel acts as one of Bridgeman's 'receptacles' so that, in times of flood, river water can by-pass Denver sluice and, when the tide falls, be channelled back into the Ouse and run out to sea more quickly (Darby 1983, 21).

Bridgeman brought to the creation of large bodies of ornamental water, such as lakes and canals, the expertise shown in his grasp of the complexities of fen drainage. As Roberts points out, this must have been his greatest challenge: 'The making of the lakes and rivers of the landscape park was a demanding operation that frequently involved the planning of an integrated system of drainage and supply works and which had to take account of the intended land use of surrounding areas' (Roberts 2001, 15). There are water features which required complex engineering in a very significant number of his designs: for example, at Wolterton Hall (BoL MSGD a4 fo.61 and MSGD a3 fo.55), Lodge Park (BoL MSGD a4 fo.68) and Rousham (BoL MSGD a4 fo.63). His work at Kedleston Hall was concerned only in making a water feature (SC Object 109274). Some, for example at Wolterton Hall and the Round Pond in Kensington Gardens, remain filled with water today. The making of three stretches of water, the Round Pond and the Serpentine in Kensington Gardens, and the Lake at Wolterton, is relatively well documented, allowing us further insight into Bridgeman's expertise.

The 'Great Bason', known now as the Round Pond, is seven acres in area, and measures 200 by 150 metres. Bridgeman's contract suggests that work on it had already begun by 1726: 'For finishing the Great Bason in the said semi-circular lawn ...' (NA Work 6/114). There is some ambiguity about this, since the construction of a 'Great Bason' is nowhere mentioned in the proposal presented by both Wise and Bridgeman, before 11 March 1726 (NA Work 6/114), so it is likely that 'finishing' refers to enlarging a smaller, rectangular pond shown in the same place as the Round Pond on a drawing of Kensington Gardens attributed to Wise (NA Work 32/312). It may be that it is a reference to the contention made in the

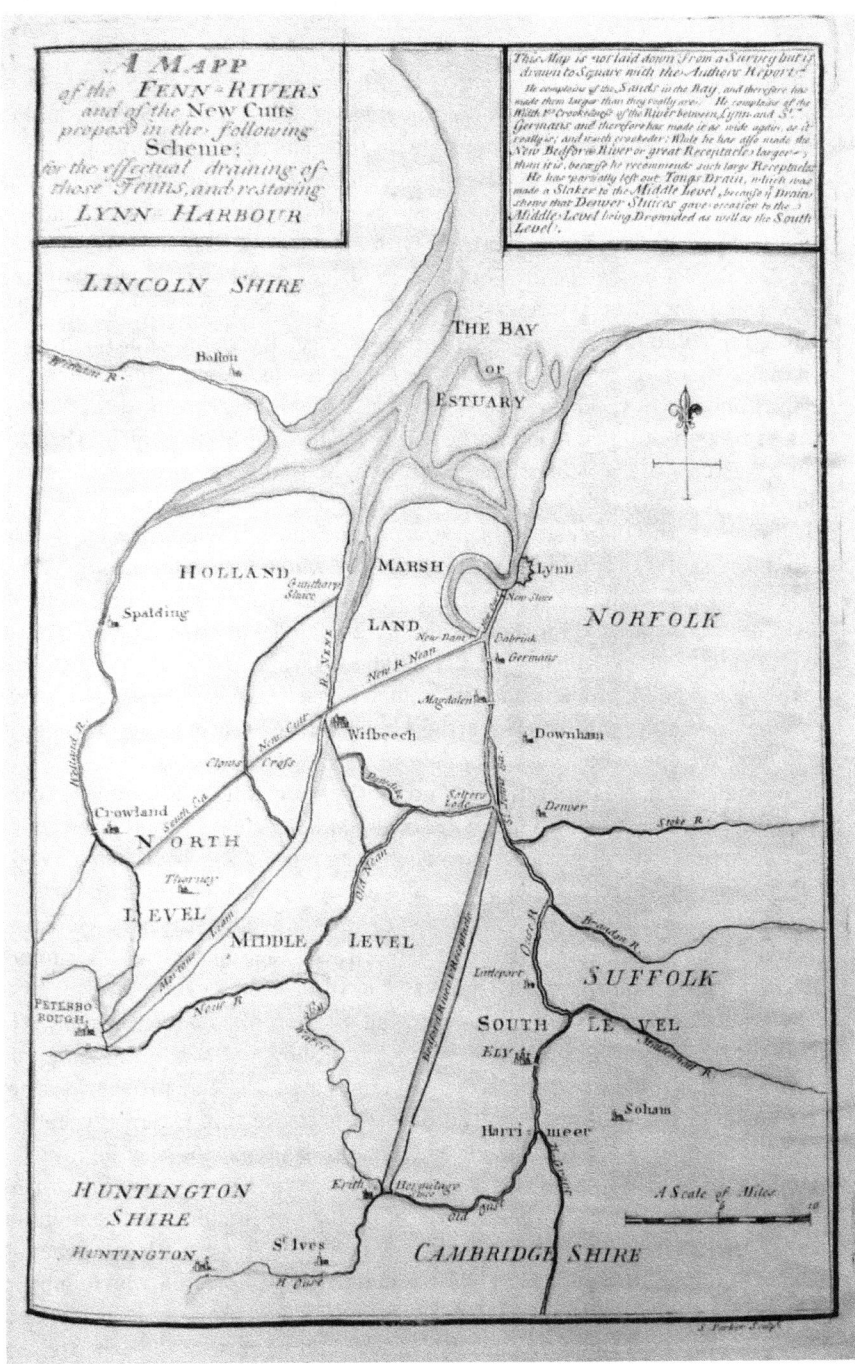

Figure 15. Bridgeman's plan for the drainage of the fens to the south and east of King's Lynn. NRO EA 386.32. Item from the collections of Norfolk County Council Library and Information Service.

Biographical Dictionary of Civil Engineers that James Horne, deputy Master Mason from 1726, began the construction of the Round Pond, although Skempton does suggest that Bridgeman was responsible for the plan, (Skempton 2002).

The new pond appears to have been constructed by digging down to the clay, in some places 15 feet below the surface of the garden, and encircling the small rectangular pond in its entirety with a trench 2,216 ft long, from which '14777 Cube Yardes of Sand' would be removed. The Round Pond is 16 feet deep. This trench would form the circumference of the new pond and be filled with 2,951 cubic metres of clay, two feet thick at its upper end, rammed in, and making contact with the underlying clay at its lower end: 'this Trench is to be thus opened to receive a wall of Clay raisd from the bottom to the Surface of the Lawn' in order to 'confine the Water in the Said Bason which otherwise would waste thro' the Veins of Sand in which the said Bason is dug to the great injury of the Beauty of that water & of the Health of the Palace'. Bridgeman is specific about the dimensions of the clay and where it will come from: 'Clay used in the said wall round the great bason the whole Circumference thereof in some parts 15 feet deep the upper end to be 2 feet thick amounting to about 2951 Cube yards the clay for this purpose to be dug deeper the upper end of the Lake in this Paddock which is now to Shallow' (Work 6/114). This would have created a clay bowl, providing, as Bridgeman himself suggests, an effective seal. Presumably, this creation of a watertight bowl before breaching the rectangular pond obviated the need for a coffer dam.

The logistics of this operation are not entirely clear. It seems unlikely that a trench 15 feet deep and two feet wide could be dug safely, in sand, even today, and ramming it with clay would have been even more difficult. It is much more likely that what Bridgeman's labourers dug was a much wider trench in the sand around the circumference of what is now the pond, and, in stages of a few feet, created a wall of clay along its outer edge, each stage of which was rammed and then encased on the inner edge with earth or sand to keep it in place. In this way, Bridgeman was effectively creating one half of a dam with a clay core of the kind common in the Roman period, and shown in section in *Early Dam Builders in Britain* (Binnie 1987, 4). At the Round Pond, the clay probably formed a right-angled triangle, wider at the base than at the top, where the upright and horizontal axes are buttressed by the earth wall and the clay floor. It is a technique of which Switzer was aware and which he writes of in *Ichnographia Rustica*. 'It has always been the Method of Stoning or Bricking, and sometimes Leading the Sides of Fountains, Canals, and Ponds ... These Walls are generally made of Stone or Brick and clay'd well behind, to keep the Water from finding its way thro' the Sides ...' However, it is likely that he had much smaller pieces of water in mind, and, in any case, he advises against it because of the expense: 'but in this respect there is so much Money buried, that I cann't but advise Gentlemen to consider if there are no nearer Methods' (Switzer 1715, 304). It also seems to be the technique used by Lancelot Brown in making the pond at Petworth, some twenty years later. Binnie cites part of the third contract, from 1753, in which 'The making of all necessary clay walls' is mentioned. He contends that '[t]he reference to clay walls suggests that Brown was learning by experience that the need to make earthworks watertight could not be ignored.' Binnie goes on to include a description of building the lake, which sounds very like what Bridgeman may have done at the Round Pond: 'Earth fill was used to build up the pond to a kidney shape on top of which a clay blanket extending not only over the inner slopes but also, possibly all of, the floor of the pond was placed. On the inner slopes, the clay in the upper parts was protected with stone pitching and in the lower parts with coarse sand and rubble' (Binnie 1987, 63).

Although there is no mention of the source of water for the Round Pond, it seems likely that both it, and the rectangular pond that preceded it, were fed by springs. Bridgeman explicity mentions drainage: '& for finishing the Mouth of the Conveyance of the Water out of the Great Bason'. There is further evidence that Bridgeman was responsible for the Round Pond and its infrastructure when repairs were needed to it: 'The Water which runs through the Ditch made by Mr Bridgeman at the side of the Great Pond in Hyde Park for carrying waste water having washed away much of the Earth in the Ditch; & thereby laid bare for several yards two large Leaden Pipes which come from the two Water Houses there, and, as I am told convey water to St James's Palace' (NA Work 1/1).

Bridgeman was also responsible for the construction of part of the Serpentine in Hyde Park. Document 26 in Work 6/114 shows how 'the Lake in this Paddock', almost certainly the arm of the Serpentine which now runs north from the Serpentine Bridge, was made (BL K. Top xxviii 10 b). Here the technique was different, and involved damming an existing stream. This part of the Serpentine was created from the first four of ten separate rectilinear ponds formed from the course of the river Westbourne (Green 1956, 77). Bridgeman refers to construction work at both the northerly and southerly ends of 'the Lake'. Clay was 'to be dug deeper the upper end of the Lake in this Paddock which is now to shallow'. This was the source of the clay used in the Round Pond and was carted 'above half a mile', roughly the distance from the northerly end of the present Serpentine to the centre of the Round Pond. In a separate item, Bridgeman estimates a cost of £200.6s.0d for 'raising & finishing the head of the Lake & the Walks round the Same to level some parts thereof is already raised by ramming them light with Clay & proper Earth will take up about 3506 Cube yards, also finishing the brickwork belonging to the same ...' (NA Work 6/114/21). Here Bridgeman's proposal seems to suggest that a dam would be raised at the end of the Longwater, before it turns through 90 degrees into Hyde Park. A dam built here would effectively have been half way down the current course of the Serpentine, and was almost certainly demolished within two years to complete the present Serpentine, when, as *The London Journal* of 22 August 1730 reported, 'The King has given orders to turn the Ponds in Hyde Park into a Serpentine River'. Skempton's *Biographical Dictionary of Civil Engineers* suggests that this was indeed the case: 'For the Long Water the valley (hitherto occupied by the four uppermost ponds) was deepened and widened by excavating 31,479 cu yd from the bottom and 6,515 cu yd from slope on the east side, most of the material being used in levelling the ground for a lawn around the Pond and building a wide embankment across the valley as a temporary dam (at the site of the present bridge)' (Skempton 2002).

At Wolterton, a private commission, a lake was constructed by damming a shallow valley to the south of the house. Four of Bridgeman's six designs for Wolterton show a parallel-sided formal lake which nearly fills the valley and bends with it. One (BoL MSGD a4 fo.10) also shows the lake in section, so that the fall in height can be seen. The lake superseded a geometric straight-sided canal, designed by Joseph Carpenter and shown on the survey held in Gough Drawings. This seems to have failed, probably because of the boggy nature of the ground. A letter from Britiffe, Walpole's steward, to his employer in August 1724 hints at this: 'I Have been at Woolterton And found your worke there about the House as forward as needful Harvest being begun your Canal works is at a Stop for the present indeed the wett Season wee had some time before prevented the workmen getting on so well as otherwise they w[oul]d ...' (WH 8/5A Box 75L). Geologically, the shallow valley occupied by the lake differs from the land around it. While it is surrounded by glaciofluvial deposits of sand and gravel which are free-draining, Bridgeman's lake occupies a north–south narrow deposit called Head, which contains clay, as well as silt, sand and gravel (mapapps.bgs.ac.uk/geologyofbritain/home). The Lake does not seem to have been puddled with clay; a 70 cm core (WOLT1) taken from the lake in November 2006 at TG16284 31222, as part of environmental research by Dr Carl Sayer from UCL, reveals only mud, suggesting that the Lake retains water naturally and is fed by several springs and a number of field drains that run into it.

Some at least of its construction is documented. The land steward Bayfield's letter to Horatio Walpole of 2 January 1726 concerns the dam at the end of the lake (8/5A 73L). The letter, in some ways Bayfield's attempt to persuade his employer to follow his advice about building it, contains interesting details about the practicalities of the process and points up the difficulty of constructing a dam when all the material has to be dug and moved by men with spades and barrows. First there is finding soil of sufficient quality for construction. Bayfield has identified some that is suitable in the relatively newly-acquired land which borders the lake site: 'there is a Hill in the Land w[hi]ch was Mr Rich. Robins's that Lay very near the Head of the New Pond & is very good stuff to make the Heading of'. He points out that it makes economic sense to move the soil the shortest distance possible: 'and will be carried to the Head of the pond for one third of the Charge that the earth will be fetched from the North end of the pond'; and that, because of the shortness of the distance, it does not matter so much that the season is winter: 'I think me it will be don almost as cheap as in sumer time'. The weather is also advantageous to the task: 'the wether frosty & Drie that we can now work upon it and easy Digging'; and the topography is in their favour: '& is Down hill & Drie Land' (WH 8/5A Box 73L). Sacombe is also illustrative of the problems inherent in creating large water features. While the construction of the 'egg pond' and its feeder triangular reservoir (see above) was relatively easy, the canal, shown clearly on the plan (BoL MSGD a4 fo.64), proved more problematic. It was apparently under very slow construction from 1722, the year in which Rolt, Bridgeman's client, died and the gardener Edward Humberstone remembered that 'all the men in the summertime were busy at work making the canal' (HALS DEAS/2180), to 1728, when Decker noted that the canal and the basin at the end of it were 'but only begun' (Decker 1728). The reason for the length of construction appears to be difficulty of finding an adequate water supply. Salmon suggests that, in addition to a supply from 'a Stream a Mile off', a spring had been 'lately discovered about the level of the Canal' (Salmon 1728). This suggests that, whatever Bridgeman's intentions for filling the canal, they had clearly been geologically frustrated until the discovery of the spring.

There are many Bridgeman landscapes in which running water is made to feed pools and fountains; mostly these seem to be dependent on water piped from springs on higher land. Sichet notes that the placing of water features in seventeenth-century gardens was largely dictated by the geographical location of water courses and springs. As he puts it: 'Hence the layout, apparently composed of freely designed forms, was in fact dictated by what it was technically possible to do' (Sichet in Bouchenot-Déchin and Farhat 2013, 206). Rousham is one where this is true. An intricate system of pipework fed the pools and fountains of his design. The ink drawing for Rousham shows Bridgeman's instructions for the construction of the pools and rivulets running between them (BoL MSGD a4 fo.63). Bridgeman piped water from springs on the upward slope to the west of the garden to the western boundary of the garden and then by way of a small conduit to the Square Pond, now the Octagon Pond. The conduit shown on Bridgeman's plan is still in use today, running into the north-eastern corner of the Octagonal Pond. His instructions read: 'the Current or Fall of the Water from the place propos'd to bring it from the furthest springs, to the great square pond is 15 foot 6 inches. – The length from ye further springs to the nether springs is 890 feet & from these to ye Garden water is 100 feet and from thence cross the Garden to the square pond is 480 feet – in the whole 1670 feet'.

It is not possible to be specific about the piping used by Bridgeman in such an enterprise. Sichet has shown that, while cast-iron pipes were invented during the reign of Louis XIV, and manufactured from 1671, they had little impact on the way water gardens were conceived and constructed, even though they could be made in larger diameters and withstood water pressure better than did existing materials (Sichet in Bouchenot-Déchin and Farhat 2013, 206). So although this new technology was available, it is most likely that the pipes Bridgeman used to pipe water from springs at Rousham and at other sites were made of clay, wood or lead. Chapter IX of Switzer's *An Introduction to a General System of Hydrostaticks and Hydraulicks* (1729) is entitled 'Of several Kinds of Pipes for the Conveyance of Water, whether Lead, Iron, Earth or Wood', and discusses the relative merits and expense of each kind of pipe. He makes it clear that all four materials were in regular use in England, and contemporary accounts show this. John Rowley's instructions to Rowland to improve the running of the Water Engine at Windsor in 1722 include the replacement of lead pipes: 'the Great Lead Main ... & to lay a new One of 4 Inches bore to be laid as straight as possible, and the Lead to be 3/8 of an inch thick at least (NA Work 4/2 ff.50v.63, 64 cited in Appleby 1996, 19), and his bill for the piping for water to the cistern in the White Tower in the Tower of London includes £37.5s.7d for elm piping (WO 51/102 (Bill Book) f.49 cited in Appleby 1996, 19). Archaeological evidence from excavated water gardens indicates the same. At Boughton, bored elm trunks were used to drain water from the water garden, which incorporates the Star Pond to the south-west of the site, to the drainage pond, and cylindrical clay pipes which carried the water to the fountain jets (RCHME 1979, 161).

If insufficient water was available to allow the artificially created watercourses to function, Bridgeman used a cistern to feed them. This was almost certainly Bridgeman's intention at Moor Park in Hertfordshire, although it is not clear whether the cascade to the south of the house was ever completed. Bridgeman's intention, shown on the plan MSGD a4 fo.58, was for a cascade fed from a cistern disguised as a cross-shaped pond on the 110 m contour. Sir John Evelyn noted, in 1726, that there is 'a design of making a Cascade on one side of ye house', which suggests that it had yet to be built. It seems likely that it might have been under construction, however, by 1728, when Sir Edward Gascoigne visited the park and commented on the great expense of building a canal and cascade, although there is little evidence on the site today. Perhaps it proved problematic to construct a cascade where the supply of water was supplied only by a cistern. Lord Halifax wrote, in 1710, to the Duke of Montagu during the construction of the water garden at Boughton for advice on the construction of a cascade: 'I desire you would write to Boughton to Monr Vandermulen to send me an exact account of the cascade, viz. how many feet the water falls, the dimensions of the steps, the breadth of each step, the distance from step to step, and, if he can, to make such a draft of the whole, by a scale, as we may follow the example as far as our ground admits of it' (Steane 1977, 404). It seems to have proved necessary at Boughton to install a windmill to pump the water for the fountains (RCHME 1979, 158). Most of Bridgeman's landscapes were constructed in the south of England where steep hills and fast flowing streams were in short supply, which may account for the shortage of cascades in his work.

Bridgeman's designs often include the canalisation, or at least the regularising of the banks of existing waterways, although this proposed treatment was generally restricted to small, slow flowing waterways. The designs for Down Hall, Rousham and Lodge Park show some variation on the idea of canalising existing waterways. As suggested in Chapter 5, it is hard to tell whether this is integral to the geometric concept of the design, or whether Bridgeman planned to, or did, straighten the earth bank of the river, or build a masonry retaining wall to hold the river bank and a terrace on top. At Down Hall there is no evidence at all, either on site or from 50 cm resolution LIDAR, that the banks of Pincey Brook were straightened or, indeed, altered in any way. At Lodge Park (BoL MSGD a4 fo.68), it is possible to see, in earthwork form, the small, straight-sided canal, fed by the river Leech, which Bridgeman's proposal also shows (Figure 9). Bridgeman's design replaces this canal with a much wider, parallel-sided canal, created by an artificial dam at the southern end of the river. It seems unlikely that this was ever built. At Rousham, there is evidence that, if the garden bank of the river Cherwell was straightened, as Bridgeman's design (BoL MSGD a4 fo.63) shows, it was not rendered in masonry. In letters to General Dormer, Dormer's Steward, William White, writes in May 1738, when the garden at Rousham was being prepared for Kent's remodelling, that 'Some Men are now employed, in Conveying into ye Garden, by boats, the Earth taken out of ye river, and par'd off ye Banks', which suggests that neither side of the bank had been faced with masonry (Müller 1997, 181). Presumably, to do this in a flowing river would have been difficult and expensive, involving either the rerouting, albeit temporarily, of the waterway, or the building of a coffer dam to keep the mortar dry if it extended below the water line. It must be said that, at Rokeby Park in County Durham, built by Sir Thomas Robinson between 1725 and 1730, the sharp bend in the course of the river Greta, to the immediate east of the house, is faced with large blocks of dressed ashlar, presumably limestone given the geological strata on which it sits (http://mapapps.bgs.ac.uk/geologyofbritain). However, it appears that no mortar is used and the retaining walls appear to sit on existing limestone rock formations which form a solid foundation.

Bridgeman also made use of the water systems of the landscapes that preceded his own designs at some of the sites on which he worked. We might see Bridgeman's pragmatism in his exploitation of what was already on the land when he began work on a site, although it was presumably common practice for all designers to make use of relict features. At Amesbury, the survey executed by Henry Flitcroft in 1726 shows the medieval canal which runs through the site on a roughly north–south axis (WRO 944/1 and 944/2). The southern opening of this canal is still visible in the river Avon, although the canal itself is marked only by a path. Bridgeman's design reuses this canal, making it a waterway through the eastern garden, and adds a round pool axially aligned to the house. At Moor Park, Bridgeman may also have reused a hydraulic system which was already in place: Temple writes about 'Two fountains' in the parterre and 'Fountains' and 'Water-works' in the grotto (Temple in Dixon Hunt and Willis 1975, 98). Jeffery suggests, in relation to the seventeenth-century garden, that 'Moor Park was evidently well supplied with water features, in the fashion of the day, both on the parterre and in the grotto, and must have had a hydraulic system that raised water from the river below and no doubt stored it in a cistern at high level from which the fountains and waterworks were supplied by gravity.' She notes that, in 1739, an inventory recorded that the 'south pavilion contained "A small Water Engine", perhaps from the early days of the gardens and no doubt for this purpose' (Jeffery 2014, 7). It is possible, then, that Bridgeman's basins, canal and putative cascade used, and possibly updated, these hydraulic systems.

This is an aspect of eighteenth-century garden design which is often ignored: the way in which the gardens were constructed, and the problems which topography and geology must have posed when translating a design from drawing board to execution on real land. It is clear that Kent was almost never responsible for the building of what he designed, and although Switzer and Langley both wrote books which contained practical advice and methodology, there is considerably less evidence that they used those skills themselves. In many ways, Bridgeman's expertise singles him out amongst his contemporaries. He had the vision required to create change in a landscape, and a grasp of the aesthetics needed for the design, but he was also capable of overseeing every aspect of the design's construction. It is probably why he, and not Kent, or Switzer or Batty, was appointed Royal Gardener and why he was so popular in his lifetime.

CHAPTER 8
A COMMERCIAL ENTERPRISE

OF ALL THE aspects of creating designed landscapes, perhaps the one most regularly ignored is the intricacy of financing them. This is partly because art history, in regard to gardening at least, finds the philosophical and design aspects of gardens more interesting than how much they cost. It is also because, particularly before the mid-eighteenth century and the gentlemen improvers, it is almost impossible to find systematically costed accounts in the archives of either the clients or the practitioners, and therefore quite difficult to be precise about the money that changed hands. However, it is obvious that creating these landscapes was spectacularly expensive, and required a provision of goods and services which had to be paid for.

Yet the idea of Bridgeman's clients as consumers is completely missing from the writing about Bridgeman, and rarely makes more than a footnote in the writing about his predecessors and contemporaries. Most commentary on the rise of consumerism in the eighteenth century has tended to concentrate on the lower and 'middling' classes; as Weatherill puts it, the desire 'to emulate those of higher social rank, in order to keep up appearances' was the main driver of this significant change in behaviour (Weatherill 1988, 194) Clearly the emulation of the rich and powerful by the 'middling sort' is of less interest here, since Bridgeman worked exclusively for the rich and the powerful, the 'propertied people' who Langford characterises as trailing 'their possessions before the gaze, fascinated, awed, resentful, of the unpropertied people who were their employees, servants, or merely spectators' (Langford 1991, 11). Bridgeman's clients were drawn from the nobility with inherited wealth and land. These clients were the 'rich who led the way' and 'indulged in an orgy of spending' (McKendrick et al. 1983, 10); they were the powerful men, and occasionally women, who saw themselves as the arbiters of fashionable taste. However, Bridgeman's clients were clearly not immune to 'the compulsive power of fashion begotten by social competition' (McKendrick et al. 1983, 10). An understanding of 'taste' was a badge of belonging to, and remaining within, the elite.

Paradoxically, the notion of art and taste, which has largely concealed the understanding of Bridgeman's clients and consumers, was generated by them. A rather complicated mechanism for defining what constituted fashionable taste was in operation, one that seems to have had a direct impact on our perception of Bridgeman and his relationship with his clients. Fashionable 'taste' might have originated at court, in particular with Queen Caroline. Although Pope denounced Queen Caroline's taste in *The Dunciad*, she was a patron of the arts, and 'the early Hanoverian court created a distinctive court culture in order to cement its relationship with the British people' (Jay 2014, 75). Caroline certainly supported poets such as John Gay and the labourer poet Stephen Duck, artists such as Wootton and Rysbrack, and musicians such as Handel, and created a significant library (Langford 1989; Willis 2002; Jay 2014). There seems to have been some close contact between Queen Caroline and Bridgeman. Although no letters between Bridgeman and his royal clients survive, there are documents from the Office of Works, collected together in the National Archives, which signal the direct involvement of Queen Caroline: the first is for 'reforming the Southern parts of the Gardens from the Orangery down to the Road according to plan thereof drawn by Her Majestys direction', the second for 'repairing the Gardens according to a Plan thereof as directed by Her Majesty from the Orangery down to the Southern Extent next the Town the grass part thereof to be laid with Turf and for replanting the Ever greens taken out of the Quarters to be layed into lawn as specified in the said Plan', and the third states: 'It being Their Majestys farther pleasure that a Berceau or Walk for shade be planted in the Spineys next the boundary Walks the Trees for the same to be taken out of the Quarters & that Serpentine Walks be made in those Quarters and that the Wood Quarters in the Upper Wilderness (?) (or in the upper Walks) be opened as Her Majesty shall direct ...' In 1731 Bridgeman charged for work 'he alledges' is 'by Her Majestys Order and Directions in carrying on the works in the Paddock at Kensington which by agreement were to be finished in the manner therein mentioned for £5000' (NA Work 6/114).

However, what Stella Tillyard has called 'cultural authority' was less likely to reside at court under the Hanoverians than under their Stuart predecessors (Tillyard in Postle 2005, 23). Royal patronage was no longer necessarily an arbiter of fashionable taste in the early part of the eighteenth century. Some of Queen Caroline's garden projects, for example the grotto and library in Richmond Park, were the subject of ridicule (Langford 1989, 35). Colley suggests that 'the court was never the only focus for fashionable society, though it was always an important one' (Colley 1992, 200). She uses the example of the Duchess of Queensberry, one of Bridgeman's clients, who was banished from court for her support of John Gay and Gay's play *Polly*, in which Gay lampooned Walpole. The Duchess left court, and her husband resigned his post as Gentleman of the Bedchamber, but both continued to move in fashionable circles and *Polly* was a great success.

Rather than the simple imitation of court fashion, a symbiotic relationship seems to have developed between those members of the elite who wanted, consciously or not, to define their own status by their 'taste', and those who provided the means for them to do it. Inglis argues that those with money 'needed architects, writers, painters, landscape gardeners, interior decorators' to create what was fashionable for them, 'and where once, at court and in its satellite mansions, such artisans would have been entirely subordinate to the rule of the master, in the much more open market created by new cities ... success depended on sufficient patrons finding what he (and gradually at least in fiction writing, she) created to their taste, made in the name of style' (Inglis 2010, 41). As Lilti and Jeffress note, 'Reputation ... corresponds to the judgement that the members of a group or community make collectively regarding one of their own ...' (Lilti and Jeffress, 2005, 11), and in this case it seems that a collective, though perhaps unconscious, decision was made by both the artistic community and the elite who paid them, ensuring that both the artists and the elite remained part of an exclusive coterie.

This appears to have been true regardless of where the wealth came from. The elite in the early eighteenth century was not simply made up of the aristocracy who had inherited land, money and titles, but also included those who had bought land and property with the vast fortunes made either by themselves or by their parents and grandparents, in trade and in other commercial enterprises. The origins of the wealth of Bridgeman's clients whose money came from trade is detailed in the Introduction, but two examples will serve as a reminder. Francis Hawes bought Purley in Berkshire in 1720 with wealth acquired as a director of the South Sea Company, while Sir William Gore, a director of the South Sea Company and of the Bank of England, had inherited Tring Park in Hertfordshire from his father, also a banker. Bridgeman worked extensively for this group of clients. It is generally assumed that this 'new money' was simply emulating the aristocracy in a slightly pathetic attempt to enter their world. As Harwood suggests, 'One of the recognised ways of buying into the establishment ... was to buy estates, particularly if they were close to centres of population – and especially London' (Harwood 2007, 52). In fact their employment of Bridgeman, and the work he did for them, suggests it was rather more complicated. The gardens Bridgeman created for these men were not a pale imitation of the taste shown in the gardens he created for his noble, landed clients. Some were amongst those most admired by both their contemporaries and held up as examples of exquisite taste: Queen Caroline visited the garden at Gobions in 1732; it was described by Bickham in 1750 and Toldervy in 1762; and indeed, the landscape received a ringing endorsement from Horace Walpole for the taste it displayed. These clients were men who, with the same resources as the aristocracy and, crucially, a sense of the new potency they represented in a changing society, were as susceptible as their aristocratic peers to the notion that 'taste' was what defined membership of the ruling elite.

We might see the creation of this symbiotic relationship between the elite and the artistic community at work in the letters and published literary works of the period. For example, in a letter written in June 1720, by Matthew Prior to his friend, supporter and patron of the arts, Edward Harley, Prior casts a number of artists, all of whom had worked for Harley and other mutual friends, as characters in a narrative which serves to reinforce the interdependence between them and Harley:

> I invited the *virtuosi* t'other day; Gibbs, Wanley, Wootton and Christian; the two first could not come, and the two last could not be got away till midnight. Dirty Dibben, of Dorset-shire, and the Archdeacon of Bath were of the company, as well to bless the meat as to drink great share of the claret; Morley assisted in tea. It was conversation about five o'clock, a disputation towards seven, and a bear-garden about ten. We drank your health over and over, as well in our civil as bacchanalian hours. (Bath Papers III 482–483)

This process is particularly clear in the poetry which has to do with fashion in gardening and landscape design. There is a mutual dependence between the members of the elite who own the gardens and pay for the transformations, the artists who provide the designs, and the poets who write about them. Take Pope's poetry, for example: in *Epistle to Burlington* (1731), Lord Burlington's 'taste' as both facilitator and designer is explicitly praised in Pope's own creation, the poem:

> Who then shall grace, or who improve the Soil?
> Who plants like BATHURST, or who builds like BOYLE.
> 'Tis Use alone that sanctifies Expence,
> And Splendor borrows all her rays from Sense.
> (*Epistle to Burlington* lines 177–180, in Davis 1966)

In *Epilogue to the Satires, Dialogue* II, William Kent, the designer, and Henry Pelham, the brother of the Duke of Newcastle, are mentioned in adjacent lines of another of Pope's poems:

> Pleas'd let me own, in *Esher's* peaceful
> (Where *Kent* and Nature vie for PELHAM'S Love).
> (*Epilogue to the Satires*, Dialogue II, Davis 1966)

In Summer, from *The Seasons*, Thomson includes the gardens at 'Twit'nam', 'Hampton', 'Clermont', 'Cornbury' and 'Esher', the poets 'Gay' and 'Pope', and the aristocrats 'Queensberry' and 'Pelham' in the space of ten lines (Thomson 1730). While it could be argued that these examples simply express the deference due to an aristocratic patron, the slightly uneasy combination of over-familiarity, deference and admiration suggests that they function more as the reinforcement of a shared conception of taste.

Bridgeman appears on the periphery of this discourse. In Prior's letters of 1720 and 1721, during the work on both Down Hall and Wimpole, he appears as one of what Prior terms Harley's 'virtuosi': 'I invited the Virtuosi t'other day,

Gibbs, Wanley, Wootton and Christian...' (16 July 1720) and 'I believe you have Your Virtuosi by You, while you receive this Letter ...' (18 March 1721). Here he is presented as 'Friend Bridgeman', whose 'Devotion has consisted chiefly in contriving how the Diagonal may take Waddon Steeple exactly in the middle'. He also appears in Thornhill's 1721 ballad *A Hue and Cry* (see Chapter 6). He is mentioned in the correspondence of the elite in relation to design. In a letter to the Duchess of Suffolk written in August 1735, the Duchess of Queensberry compares the countryside around Brussels to his work: 'Adieu, my dear Lady Suffolk. Did you ever see Brussels? The whole country round about it is like the best-natured ground that ever was seen, laid out by a Bridgeman some years ago' (Murray 1824, Vol. 2, 134). In the Duchess of Beaufort's letter to her son, his work is praised: 'The draught Bridgeman sent down for Badminton is one of the Grandest things I have ever seen' (Willis 2002, 427), and in 1735, Lady Burlington even reports a friendly stylistic disagreement, and casts her husband as arbiter in it: 'There is a new design going forward at Richmond in ye garden, & a building of Kent's design ... I took ye liberty to differ with Mr Bridgman & I daresay you wd be of my opinion' (Willis 2002, 103). Bridgeman's inclusion in this exclusive set of artists and aristocrats is demonstrated by his inclusion in Edward Harley's list of those to be invited to Prior's funeral and his election to the Virtuosi of St Luke.

This discourse is largely responsible for the notion that gardening existed only in this artistic milieu, in which artists were supported by their patrons, although, clearly, patronage was a significant part of the business of garden design in the early eighteenth century. Coulton highlights this in relation to the foundation, and continued trading, of Brompton Park Nurseries. John Evelyn, whose original translation of la Quinitie's *Instructions pour les Jardins Fruitiers et Potagers* London and Wise drew heavily on, endorsed their business in an 'Advertisement' (Green 1956, 25), and Coulton points out that the 'Advertisement' printed in 1681 was designed to flatter Henry Capel, Brompton Park Nursery's most important patron (Coulton 2005, 54). In Bridgeman's period, Kent seems, certainly in his early career, to have been dependent on patronage. Mowl lists Talman Massingberd, Coke and, of course, Burlington as amongst Kent's patrons in Rome (Mowl 2006, 44 and 45). It is certainly true that Bridgeman's work was also, to some degree, governed by patronage. Willis refers to 'Three of Bridgeman's patrons ... Cobham, Burlington, and Edward Harley, 2nd Earl of Oxford', suggesting that not only these three were Bridgeman's patrons, but that there were others too (Willis 2002, 69). We might add Queen Caroline and Charles Townshend to the list. One of the surviving letters in Bridgeman's hand, to Charles Townshend, on 29 September 1733, refers explicitly to it: 'My Lord – Just after your Lor[shi]p spoke to me at Hamp[ton] Court on Sunday last, my good Friend and Patron orderd me to desire my Cosin Bridgeman not to engage his Vote, & this was his whole order to me at the time: I was since down with my Cosin at Hartford, & he kindly promis'd me he would not ...' (Willis 2002, 156). Bridgeman's letter to Harley in 1734 is written in a similar tone: 'My Lord/ I hope Your Lord[shi]ps. Goodness will permit me in this manner, 'tho late, to congratulate Your Lord[shi]p, and my Lady Oxford, on the marriage of Lady Margaret with his Grace the Duke of Portland; I heartily wishing them a long & a happy life; and Your Lord[shi]p. and my Lady Oxford, all the pleasures and Satisfactionn You [c]an hope thereby, humbly begging leave to signify to Your Lord[shi]p. that nobody can have a greater honour for Your Lord[shi]p, & family than I have, not feel more sensibly any good enjoy'd, or hop'd for in it ...' (Bl Loan 29/20). While these letters demonstrate that Willis is justified in his assumption that Bridgeman had patrons, the importance of patronage to him in his work is more difficult to determine. It is probably true to say that Bridgeman relied considerably less on patronage, than did, for example, Kent.

The idea of patronage has tended to obscure Bridgeman's activity as a commercial operator. Bridgeman's professional operations were effectively proto-commercial, and we might place him within a framework of entrepreneurs, some who predated him, some his contemporaries, whose businesses in the garden trade capitalised on a burgeoning consumer demand. Perhaps Bridgeman was one of those men who, as McKendrick puts it, 'had not only responded to those changes; they had, as a result of their earnest endeavours, played a substantial and positive role in bringing them about' (McKendrick et al. 1983, 2).

This is because Bridgeman also inhabited another, fast emerging, world. In the early eighteenth century, trade and commerce were an increasingly important engine in the economy. Trade was 'the mainspring of Britain's economy and a vital part of its identity'. A government pamphlet of 1731 stated categorically: 'Whenever our trade perishes so must our public dignity and strength' (Colley 1992, 60). Highly lucrative trade with India and the Far East, with the west coast of Africa and with countries at the eastern end of the Mediterranean had been established by the end of the seventeenth century, through companies chartered by the Crown and therefore granted a monopoly of trade: the East India Company, the Royal African Company and the Levant Company, and early in the eighteenth century the South Sea Company, formed to trade with what is now known as South America. Much of the trade was in desirable, aspirational consumer goods such as tea and silks, but they also dealt in slaves (however inconvenient and painful that is to acknowledge).[1] Trade also provided the bulk of the state's revenue which came through taxation (Colley 1992, 65). Even more importantly in national economic life, the majority of loans to the government, the National Debt, for the funding of expensive wars like the War of the Spanish Succession, came not from the landed classes but from these vast trading companies who had considerably more liquidity of capital (Colley 1992, 64). The Bank of England

---

[1] Britain's colonial past and its role in financing the building of mansion houses and, of course, the designed landscapes around them, has rightly become a topic of some concern. Clearly the landscapes on which Bridgeman worked were almost certainly financed in this way, but there is no space to consider the issue here other than to acknowledge it.

was created in 1694 to manage the National Debt, although it also operated as a private bank, accepting deposits from the public. The disaster that befell the South Sea Company provides a clear picture of the reach of trade in the economic life of the early eighteenth century. The South Sea Company was set up in 1711 to consolidate nine million pounds of unsecured government debt. Creditors for this floating debt were forced to surrender their holding to the South Sea Company, where they became shareholders in an enterprise that promised profit through a monopoly of trade through ports in South America. In 1720 it was granted part of the National Debt, prompting a buying frenzy of its shares. The early eighteenth century was a diverse and burgeoning commercial world that underpinned the financial workings of the state, and, crucially, the fortunes of Bridgeman's clients on which his work was dependent.

This was a world in which most of Bridgeman's clients may also have been involved to some degree, either indirectly through stock holding and through investment in the slave trade and overseas plantations, through active engagement in the companies involved in trade, or through wealth inherited from their merchant forebears. For example, Thomas Hall at Goldings was a merchant. Born in 1692, he had made his fortune in trade, working as an independent and significant ship owner chartering ships to the East India Company, and trading on his own behalf with China and India (Gill 1961). Sir William Gore at Tring was the son of one of the founding directors of the Bank of England, and was himself Governor of the Bank of England between 1709 and 1712 and of the South Sea Company between 1712 and 1715. Whether they came from a landed or a mercantile background, commerce generated at least some of the wealth Bridgeman's clients were able to invest in the landscapes he created for them, because for all of them the most conspicuous marker of taste and wealth was the country estate: '[t]he ability to spend lavishly, combined with the discernment required to identify and acquire the right type of things, distinguished the elite and marked out the country house as a key site for luxury consumption' (Stobart and Rothery 2016, 2)

The landscape parks themselves were more than a blank canvas for artistic expression. They were economic entites in their own right. Complex economics underpin the workings of a landed estate; as Tom Williamson has suggested, the aesthetics of a designed landscape existed only because of the 'complex relationship between the productive estate land and the designed core' (Williamson 2000, 14). There were complicated interrelationships between economic trends in the eighteenth century, the economy of the landed estate and the development of a designed landscape. For example, Williamson links the rise of the large estate with the agricultural recession of the late seventeenth and early eighteenth centuries, when incomes from tenanted land fell. For a century, from c.1650 to c.1750, the population remained static (Williamson 1998, 15; 2000, 14). This, and the Land Tax of 1691, he argues, coupled with the relative political stability brought by the Glorious Revolution of 1688, favoured the growth of large estates. Their owners were less reliant on rents from tenants for income, often having alternative sources derived from the offices they held, and were able not simply to keep their own estates, but also to expand those estates into those of the local gentry, who, having less diverse sources of income, were unable to maintain their estates financially. Although clearly interested in the design of the landscape parks with which they surrounded their houses, Bridgeman's noble clients were also closely involved in the economics of the running of their estates. Although the survey Flitcroft conducted for the Duke of Queensberry in 1726 devotes one page to the garden around Amesbury Abbey and the Duke's property in the town of Amesbury, the majority of the beautifully painted watercolour pages are devoted to the tenanted land belonging to the estate, and the accompanying terrier is concerned with rent and revenue from that land (WRO 944/1/and 2). Daniels and Seymour draw attention to the way in which 'the most grandiose schemes were funded from other, still more lucrative, sources – urban ground rents, mineral leases, stocks and bonds, government sinecures, the spoils of war, overseas plantations, overseas trade' (Daniels and Seymour 1990), and that focusing on the aesthetic qualities of these parks has obscured the ways in which the aristocracy, in the eighteenth century, was beginning to participate in this much more diverse economy.

The trees which formed part of the design of the landscape park in the eighteenth century became an important source of revenue (Cosgrove and Daniels 1988; Daniels and Watkins 1991; Williamson 2000; Rackham 2004). Williamson suggests that, after the Restoration, tree planting accelerated and was seen as 'a more attractive form of medium- and long-term investment'. Here, not only was there economic value in the plantations, but, because of the land thus occupied for 'perhaps two generations', there was a clear statement of the status and wealth of the landowner (Williamson 2000, 17). Woods planted as part of the landscape design were sometimes coppiced to provide a source of revenue. Daniels and Watkins demonstrate how, on the Foxley estate, the property of the Price family, woods for both timber and coppice purposes were sown throughout the eighteenth century (Daniels and Watkins 1991, 146). Plantations in parkland were a valuable source of revenue, yielding timber for such products as pit props and hop poles (Daniels and Seymour 1990). The growing of oak trees for ship building predates the eighteenth century and is encouraged in John Evelyn's *Silva*: 'Those sapling oaks, which at Britannia's call/May heavy their trunks into the main/And float the bulwarks of her liberty' (Evelyn and Hunter 1786, 3). Revenue was also produced through the grazing of livestock in the landscape park. Deer, although prohibited from open sale, were economically profitable precisely because of it. Venison was highly prized as a gift, and also, after a cull, changed hands at high prices (Daniels and Seymour 1990, 492). This interest in deer is reflected by the relocation of the deer park from c.1660 onwards, away from its medieval position separate from the main house, to one surrounding the owner's main residence (Williamson 2000, 21).

Sheep, too, were grazed on parkland and provided saleable products of mutton and wool (Daniels and Seymour 1990, 492).

Landscape design was also already part of this commercial engine. There was a burgeoning embryonic infrastructure to support any proto-commercial enterprise in landscape design by the end of the seventeenth century, and certainly by the beginning of the eighteenth. Harvey has shown that 'we can place the beginnings of the garden trade' in the middle of the seventeenth century, and that (significantly for an evaluation of his business) during the period of Bridgeman's lifetime this development of a 'garden trade' was manifested in a significant increase in the number of nurseries and seed merchants, initially in London, and then in the provinces. By 1685 there were five commercial nurseries, of which Brompton Park was the largest, and by 1688 three commercial seed merchants in and around London (Harvey 1974b, 5); by the time the Society of Gardeners published their *Catalogus Plantarum* in 1730, when 14 gardeners were included in the Society and five others signed the Preface, the number of nurseries had swelled to 15 in and around London, and the number of seed merchants to at least five. By the 1730s provincial nurseries had been established at Colchester, Exeter, Newark-on-Trent, Oxford, Pontefract and Gateshead, and in York, where at least four firms were in being (Harvey 1974b, 5). Coulton suggests that we should treat 'the hypothesis that the turn of the eighteenth century witnessed a significant shift in the cultural organization of nursery-keeping' with some caution, since it is 'tentatively grounded upon the fact that from this point onwards there survives a growing number of documentary sources (manuscript and published, cartographic and pictorial) which can be invoked to verify the existence of more and more trading plantsmen' (Coulton 2005, 21). However, in spite of this caveat, it is clear that commercial nurseries and seed merchants were increasing to meet this new market's needs. Coulter quotes Peter Collinson, writing in 1768, about the period between 1710 and 1730: 'the taste of gardening increased annually [... and] as the taste increased, nursery-gardens flourished' (Coulton 2005, 22).

We might see Brompton Park Nurseries, from 1681 until the first two decades of the eighteenth century (during which time Bridgeman was almost certainly working there), as an example of how the supply of plants, seeds and gardening expertise was turned into an embryonic but highly successful business. As shown above, George London, with his early partners, and then with Henry Wise, built a nursery which became the most influential of the period, able to supply thousands of plants to estates all over the country, and offering a design service too. Coulton considers that these gardeners were able to understand not only what consumers wanted but how to present themselves as the foremost suppliers of those commodities. Even from its inception, he argues, the founders of Brompton Park Nurseries marketed themselves, their plants and their expertise in an 'Advertisement' of sorts, which emphasises their personal credentials, lists the plants, describes their arrangement according to species within the 24 walled acres of the nursery, and emphasises their hope that their 'Compleat Nursery' will be 'fitting to serve and give content to all sortes of planters whatsoever'. As Coulton points out, 'From the very beginning the principal players in Brompton Park's horticultural and literary productions were keen to validate the quality not only of its nursery plants but also their own positions within chains of production and consumption, and the complex matrices of England's social hierarchies' (Coulton 2005, 53). He further argues that the publication of *The Compleat Gard'ner*, a translation by London and Wise, published in 1699, of la Quintinie's text *Instructions pour les Jardins Fruitiers et Potagers* with significant commentary and additions for the English gardener, represents a shrewd marketing ploy for their own business: in *The Compleat Gard'ner* 'George London and Henry Wise seek to shore up both the reputation of nurserymen in general and their own positions at the pinnacle of the trade. By emphasizing issues unique to their native country ... they are able to justify their amendments to la Quintinie as well as locate themselves as appropriate arbiters upon the state of British gardening' (Coulton 2005, 62).

As the eighteenth century progressed, it is possible that the emergence of diversification, established tradesmen branching out into, and specialising in, other areas of the 'garden trade', was another symptom of the emerging response to the market. Malcolm Thick notes the rise of the specialised seed merchant, using Switzer as an example. He shows that when Switzer, initially a garden writer and designer, set himself up as a seed merchant in the 1720s he was met with some hostility (Thick 1990, 109). London and Wise noted the new tendency of seedsmen to stock plants, and 'acidly remarked on "Gentlemen coming to London at the Seasons of Planting, and observing often that Bundles of Trees are standing at the Seed-Mens Shops, or at least meeting with some of their printed Catalogues, in which they make large Offers of the Sale of all their Sorts of Fruit trees, Ever-greens, Flowering Shrubs, and Roots; but with what Certainty any one may depend upon the Truth of what is offered, or what Reason they should have to buy them rather than of a Gardener, we leave them to judge"' (Thick 1990, 109).

Bridgeman's activities sit comfortably within this burgeoning commercial world. In spite of the paucity of documentary evidence about his business dealings, we can see the emergence of a quasi-commercial operation, although one still to some degree reliant on patronage. Apparently Bridgeman was able to offer a service which provided everything necessary for the creation of a new landscape, from survey to construction, rather on the model of the generation of gardeners who followed him. There is evidence, although sometimes only from one or two clients, that Bridgeman was engaged in all the activities that might accompany such a proto-business enterprise: contracts and estimates were produced; labour employed, and foremen engaged to supervise; plants and trees ordered and purchased; and payments made by the client. However limited the evidence, it offers us an insight into the way Bridgeman worked.

A COMMERCIAL ENTERPRISE

The number of projects he was involved in make it obvious that some serious organisational planning would have been required to support this level of activity. Any attempt to quantify the number of projects on which Bridgeman worked in any one year is problematic because of the lack of reliable dates, the absence of documentary evidence and the probability that he was working on other commissions, as yet undiscovered. However, it is possible to make an estimate, using letters and estate accounts, of the number of sites with which he was involved, and from this a picture emerges of a packed schedule of projects. There is firm, dateable, documentary evidence that, between 1711 and 1738, Bridgeman was creating new landscapes, or improving existing ones, at 35 separate sites. There is also firm but undated evidence of work at a further ten sites, making 45 in total. While some sites may simply have involved providing a plan, the work at most extended over several years; for example, Bridgeman was involved at Stowe at least between 1711 and 1727, and at Wolterton between 1724 and 1735. In addition, we know of two contracts that probably simply involved maintenance of an existing garden: at Montague House from 1725 to 1730 and at Compton Place from 1728 to 1738. All of this was in addition to Bridgeman's duties as Royal Gardener between 1726 and 1738. (See Appendix III for a table detailing Bridgeman's projects by year.)

At the heart of most design operations run by the 'gentlemen improvers' of the mid-eighteenth century (and a significant source of evidence for their activity) was the estimate and the contract, drawn up and signed by both improver and client (Stroud 1975a; Cowell 2009). The only surviving contracts for Bridgeman's work are those from his role as Royal Gardener, held at the National Archives. They are bound in volumes Work 6/114 and copied in Work 16/39/1. Others are alluded to, notably in the correspondence after Bridgeman's death between Sarah Churchill, Duchess of Marlborough, and Bridgeman's widow, Sarah. However, the completeness of the documents held in the National Archives, and their comprehensive detail, makes them an illuminating source of information about Bridgeman's activities.

The contracts show that Bridgeman's work as Royal Gardener was divided into two branches: the maintenance of existing gardens, and the design and construction of new landscapes and their maintenance for a stipulated period of time. Bridgeman's contract as Royal Gardener, both jointly with Henry Wise, as Joseph Carpenter's successor, and then as sole Royal Gardener, was the former, essentially a maintenance contract.[2] In essence, the two contracts differ very

---

[2] The contract of 1726 appoints Bridgeman as successor to Carpenter and seems to ensure his appointment as Royal Gardener after Wise's retirement or death. There are three copies: one is in Work 6/114 fo.7r.–10r. and printed in Appendix II of *Charles Bridgeman and the English Landscape Garden* (Willis 2002), one is in Work 16/39/1, and a third is in Work 5/147. A second contract, in 1728, appointed Bridgeman as sole Royal Gardener. This is also bound in both Work 6/114 fo.12v.–15v and 16/39/1, and is also printed by Willis as Appendix III (Willis 2002).

little from each other. Both outline Bridgeman's and Wise's responsibility for the Royal Gardens at Hampton Court, Kensington, Newmarket, Windsor and St James's (Work 6/114, Work 16/39/1), quantifying the acreages of the parcels of land located either in the formal gardens at each site, or in the kitchen gardens or glass houses within those gardens. There is a detailed list of the practical daily gardening work to be undertaken in each garden, an extensive list of tools to be provided by the two men; the contract also specifies that the replacement of any plants that die is the Royal Gardeners' responsibility. Both also state, in an appended Memorandum to the 1726 contract, and as part of the text in the 1728 contract, that the contract covers only maintenance of what already exists, and not new work. In the 1726 contract this is covered by the phrase 'altering or new making any part of the Gardens but to keep up what is already made', while the 1728 contract is more specific: 'nevertheless that in Case his Majesty shall signify his Royal Pleasure to alter the present Disposition of or to new make the Gardens or any of them hereby meant to be maintained & kept up or any part thereof then the Charge & Expence of such Alterations or new making from time to time shall be borne by His Majesty' (NA Work 6/114, Work 16/39/1), adding that any new works will be 'performed at His Maj[es]ty's Charge'. Both also contractually oblige the King to pay for the carriage of all garden produce '... from Hampton Court to Windsor or from Kensington to Windsor' and for 'the Repairs of all the several Houses Glass cases and frames all Flower sticks painted & plain (that is without being painted) all tubs & Potts for the Orange Trees & other plants and flowers' (1728 contract NA Work 6/114, 16/39/1). There are, in fact, only two significant differences. As sole Gardener, Bridgeman's contract paid him a rate of £15 per acre, £5 less an acre than the amount paid to him and Wise. The total per annum, stipulated in his contract, was £2220 a year, from Lady Day 1728, paid in quarterly instalments of £555. The list of equipment to be provided by Bridgeman is more extensive. There was a separate contract between Bridgeman and the Office of Works for the maintenance, or 'keeping', of royal gardens, at Windsor. This was negotiated separately from his contract as Royal Gardener, apparently because it had also been the subject of a separate contract for his predecessor in the role, Henry Wise. It was negotiated on 20 December 1728 for work on the Great Court and Terraces at Windsor Castle: 'The Memorial of Chas Bridgeman Gardner to the King Most Humbly sheweth that while the Late Contract with Mr Wise for keeping the Royall Gardens at 20£ an Acre subsisted there was another Contract also with him for keeping the terraces Great Court & enclosed Slopes at Windsor Castle at the rate of one hundred & sixty pounds a year' (NA Work 6/115).

The probate inventory taken following Bridgeman's death in 1738 contains the 'Tools' and 'Materials' specified by his contract as Royal Gardener, and gives an indication of the considerable outlay and ongoing costs that Bridgeman's work as Royal Gardener incurred (NA PROB.3/37/95). At five separate locations, the Royal Gardens at Kensington, the stables at Kensington Gardens, St James's, Windsor and Richmond, the Inventory lists everything necessary to work efficiently in the gardens: a huge number and variety of gardening implements and equipment, dung and 'prepared earth', and horses, their harnesses, and hay. The total worth of these is given as £230.1s.9½d (NA PROB.3/37/95), a total of around £27,000 today (http://www.nationalarchives.gov.uk/currency-converter/#currency-result). It is not clear whether these implements were also those he used for private work, but the inventory contains no record of any other equipment of this kind, so it is likely.

However, it is the complete set of the documents, contracts, accounts and instructions for payment which have to do with the reshaping of the paddock in Kensington Gardens that is the most illuminating about the way Bridgeman managed a major project. Again the documents are collected together in the National Archives in Work 6/114 and copied in Work 16/39/1. The documents cover the work proposed by Wise and Bridgeman for George I, and the work proposed by both men, and then by Bridgeman alone, for George II and Queen Caroline, including the change in the brief, from menagerie to formal designed landscape, which occurred after the death of George I. They present a detailed picture of negotiation between Bridgeman, the Board of Works and the Treasury on the progress of a project showing the close scrutiny it was subjected to at all stages by the Office of Works. Perhaps this was because, as Crook has shown, several years of financial mismanagement at the Office of Works preceded Bridgeman's tenure as Royal Gardener and by the 1720s and 1730s the Office of Works was 'almost a model of orderly administration: an oasis of moderate efficiency ...' (Crook et al. 1976, 86).

The process by which the work was eventually completed in 1732 was closely scrutinised, complicated and somewhat tortuous. The first set of documents is concerned with Wise and Bridgeman's estimate of the work for George I. Bridgeman's estimate for the work, delivered in early March 1727, was £3997.18s. On 11 March 1727, John Scrope, Secretary to the Treasury, asked 'the Surveyors & the rest of the principal Officers of His Maj[esty's] Board of Works' to examine the estimate. On 30th March 1727, Officers of the Board of Works Richard Arundell, Thomas Ripley, Nicholas Dubois and William Kent, apparently following a close examination of Bridgeman's proposal, reduced the estimate to £3800.15s.1d. A contract for the work at this price was signed by Wise and Bridgeman, but not without some ill feeling, because 'The Board of Works' had 'reduced the prizes of the above mentioned Works as low as possible,...'. Bridgeman and Wise requested that the work be paid for in three separate instalments, £1500 immediately, £1000 on 1 June and the balance on completion of the work. Walpole himself confirmed these payments on 21 April 1727, and subsequently a payment of £1500 was made on 28 April, and then another of £1000 was made on 9 June. When George I died on 11 June 1727, in Osnabrück in Germany, the work covered by these payments had not been completed, even though Bridgeman and Wise had received the money. The final document in this first set is the account for the £831.15s.10d that remained 'in their hands at the time of the late Kings decease'.

Presumably then there was some negotiation and consultation on the fate of the gardens started at Kensington Palace; the work done so far was clearly not entirely to the taste of the new King and Queen, George II and Queen Caroline. They did not, for example, want a menagerie. The second set of documents deals with the renegotiation of the work to finish the Paddock. By now, Wise had retired and Bridgeman was sole Royal Gardener, so the contract is with him alone. The sum agreed for finishing the work at Kensington Gardens was £5000, perhaps somewhere around £500,000 in 2020 (www.nationalarchives.gov.uk/currency-converter). The first document in this collection is from Scrope at the Treasury to Arundell and the other principal officers of the Board of Works. It directs them 'to cause the sum of One Thousand Pounds Ordered by my Letter of this days date to be issued to the Paymaster of the Works at the Exchequer to be paid over to the said Charles Bridgeman ...' as an advance of the £5000; it is accompanied by a copy of Bridgeman's contract. Bridgeman, in his turn, contracts to finish the work by Lady Day 1730. There is no haggling over the price this time. It does not appear that the Board of Works was involved in either an examination of Bridgeman's proposal or the subsequent contract. Whether this reflects a rise in Bridgeman's status, or that of the role of Royal Gardener, or that Bridgeman's operation was on a more business-like footing, is not clear. It may simply be because of the direct involvement of Queen Caroline. The opening paragraph suggests that the work is to be done under her specific direction:

> An agreement for finishing the Royal Paddock pursuant to a Plan thereof as it is now partly put into Execution which Works are to be done in finishing the same; are particularised in the following articles. And also the reforming the Southern parts of the Gardens from the Orangery down to the Road according to Plan thereof drawn by Her Majestys direction for that purpose by Charles Bridgeman. (NA Work 6/114)

Bridgeman's accounts, presented to the Board of Works, and copied in this collection of documents, deal not only with the new work at Kensington Palace, but also with the process of maintaining each section as it is completed so that newly planted trees do not die and turf is watered and cut. This is made more complicated because some of the garden had been landscaped and planted when both Bridgeman and Wise shared the role of Royal Gardener. Consequently, the first of these bills, which is undated but appears to have been presented sometime between October 1728 and March 1729, deals with a payment due retrospectively to both Bridgeman and Wise for 'keeping such part of the New Added Gardens as have been finished & bought into keeping from the beginning of His present Majestys Reign to Ladyday 1728' (Work 6/114, 23). The second and third were submitted by Bridgeman alone in December 1731 as the work was drawing to its conclusion. One lists, by year, each of the new sections as they were 'finished & brought into keeping'. These areas were checked and measured by Henry Flitcroft and Henry Joynes of the Office of Works. Payment was recommended with the stipulation that only when the whole division was complete would the King be liable for the cost of its upkeep:

> NB The several foregoing Quantitys, as particularly set forth from time to time finished are there charged only as brought into keeping when whole of each part was Completed; Although several large Quantitys of each such division had been, for one two, or three months before finished & kept in fine order without being hear charged or made any Expence to the King till the whole of each such part was Compleated. (Work 6/114 28–29)

Another account was presented for the additional expense of tending the saplings planted in the newly wooded areas of the garden until the 'young wood has got above injury of weeds' (NA Work 6/114 30).

These documents represent a record of a closely monitored and documented process. It is impossible to tell whether this was the case in any of Bridgeman's other projects because no other contracts survive, but it seems probable that they followed similar lines. Sarah Churchill makes extensive reference, in her angry and rather rambling letter to Bridgeman's widow on 6 July 1741 generated by Mrs Bridgeman's attempts to recover money she believed she was owed, to something similar. She writes of the 'Four contracts' she had with Bridgeman (Blenheim MSS F1 – 35). Harris, using Sarah Churchill's letters (BL Add MS 61478 9–12, 17–18, 31–34, 43–44 and 47–48) has established that these contracts were almost certainly for Wimbledon where Bridgeman was working (Harris 1985). Sarah Churchill wrote to her daughter on 21 August: 'I was yesterday at Wimbledon from 10 in the morning till eight at night, and I want but very little to make the place complete according to my own taste. Mr Bridgman went with me to take measures to make the way from the common to the house. He says it will be done in a month, and will be a vast addition to the place' (Scott Thompson 1946, 169).The contracts appear to have proposed, as in the contract for Kensington Gardens, a fixed price for which the work on the new garden would be completed: 'to Compleat them all for £2542:3:9 without any further Charge on any Account' and that there would be continued maintenance once they were finished, although, unlike at Kensington Gardens, this appears to have been included in the price: 'When I told you that Mr. Bridgman's agreement with me which I can prove, was, that his Gardiner he employ'd should be paid for keeping the Garden one year, after all the work was finish'd you Answer'd you beleiv'd it; for it was his Way' (Blenheim MSS F1 – 35). Here Sarah Churchill appears to be quoting from previous correspondence with Mrs Bridgeman, in which she seems to suggest that Bridgeman always provided the maintenance of any new work, for a limited time period, within the price he quoted in his proposal. In her letter of 26 July 1741, Sarah Churchill lays out the work to be done in intricate detail:

> He has oblig'd himself to plant all fruit tress, Flowers, and to finish the whole place, and Ground in a handsome Manner, and to make good all trees that dye: and whatever wood he shall use of mine for Stakes and Poles, to tie the Espaliers, he is to deduct for. He is likewise to make all Wood walks clean with Sand, or Gravel, the Terrace-walk handsome, to strip up the Tress in the Vineyard-walk, and the Wood on the outside of the House, to my liking. And in short to Compleat everything without any further Charge to me than the Articles.

She then appears to quote verbatim from her contract with Bridgeman in defence of her position. Beginning with 'Nothing can be more particular than all the Contracts are', The Duchess continues with what appears to be an exact transcript of the contract, since the paragraph finishes with 'And to begin and finish the Road with all possible Expedition. Chas: Bridgman' (Blenheim Palace, Letter Book No.2 fos.24r–25v). This correspondence strongly suggests that Bridgeman's *modus operandi* at Wimbledon was very similar to that at Kensington Gardens. He designed and constructed the garden and then maintained his creation for a period of time. The sums of money referred to in Sarah Churchill's letter are consistent with an operation in which Bridgeman supplied design, labour, plants and maintenance. She asserts that she has paid him a total of £2353, and, in spite of her protests to the contrary, probably owed his estate more, since a further £880.17s.0d was paid to Bridgeman's eldest daughter, in 1748 after the Duchess's death.

Even though they have not survived, there must also have been contracts which were solely for the maintenance of a garden. There were certainly payments. For example, Bridgeman was paid £25 a quarter in the account books of Andrew Marchant, the Duke of Montagu's London Land Steward, for work at Montagu House in Bloomsbury (BH BM17) (Figure 16). As there is no record in the Montagu account books of a substantial payment which might indicate that Bridgeman had designed a garden at Montagu House (a plan of the garden there by Henry Flitcroft suggests it was a very simple, formal garden with a small kitchen garden to one side of the house), it seems likely that this payment was part of a regular maintenance contract (Boughton House archive). It appears that there was also something of the kind in place at Compton Place in Sussex where, between 1728 and 1738, payments to Bridgeman are recorded in Lord Wilmington's Account Book (Willis 2002, 62). Willis suggests that the payments mean that 'Bridgeman was at Compton' between those years, with the implication that Bridgeman was responsible for reshaping the gardens, an interpretation supported by the Inventory from the sale catalogue for Compton Place, which states that the avenue and pleasure grounds were 'Laid out by Mr Bridgman' (Willis 2002, 62 n. 95). It

A COMMERCIAL ENTERPRISE 153

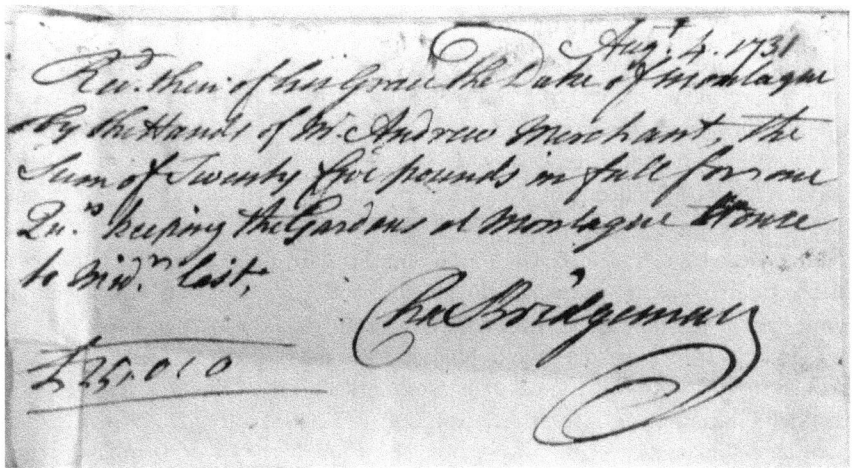

Figure 16. Receipt for £25 signed by Charles Bridgeman. BH BM17. Reproduced by kind permission of the Buccleugh Archives, Boughton House.

may be that Bridgeman also reshaped the landscape at Compton Place, but there appears to be no record of this at the moment.

The realisation of Bridgeman's plans would have needed a significant labour force in an age when all earth moving was done by hand. Pope's line, 'The vast parterres a thousand hands shall make' in *Epistle to Burlington,* may be literary hyperbole, but it does suggest a recognition of the degree to which physical labour was necessary. The source of this labour seems to have been the pool of skilled and unskilled labourers that comprised somewhere between 'two-thirds and three-quarters of the population' in the period 1700–1750 (Malcolmson 1981, 19; Cowell 2009, 145). In the countryside, where most of Bridgeman's commissions were undertaken, they were 'day labourers, a wage proletariat living in the farmer's cottage, and having no land beyond a garden, if as much' (Mingay 1990, 90). Agricultural work provided 'the single most important source of wage-payment', although the income for this was supplemented by other work by all members of the household and supported by domestic self-sufficiency (Malcomson 1981, 24, 35). These labourers were rarely engaged in farm work continuously throughout the year. The normal pattern of their employment might amount to less than 250 days, and was seasonal (Malcolmson 1981, 37). They were hired on a daily or weekly basis by a bailiff, steward or foreman for manual work, usually on a farm 'where they were needed to supplement the labour available from the farmer's household' (Malcolmson 1981, 35). Cowell suggests that the work required of a farm labourer was much the same as that needed to construct or maintain a garden; as she puts it, 'The same skills and strength were required to dig a ha-ha as a field drain; to scythe a lawn as a hayfield; to construct temples as to repair farm buildings' (Cowell 2009, 145). Hassell Smith suggests, in a study of seventeenth-century labourers on the Stiffkey estate in Norfolk, that, in fact, casual labourers grouped themselves into 'specialist "firms" or "companies" of somewhere between two to three and eight men' skilled in exactly the areas that might have been pertinent to the construction of a designed landscape. He makes the point that 'cutting a water-course' was both 'onerous' and 'skilled', and it is easy to see how this skill might transfer itself to the building of canals and cascades in a garden (Hassell Smith 1989, 21). The picture in London was similar. Here there was also a pool of labour for daily or weekly hire, but again, as Longstaffe-Gowan suggests, labourers in London gardens may also have had some specialist knowledge. Although they 'performed the common drudgery of gardening – trenching, digging, hoeing and weeding', these tasks required the acquisition of skills which he suggests came from 'casual observation, and not through instruction' (Longstaffe-Gowan 2001, 157–158).

Bridgeman employed his own labourers, though they were probably from this casual pool. This is certainly the case in his role as Royal Gardener, since the minutes of the Board of Works make it clear that hiring a workforce was the responsibility of the Royal Gardener. An entry in the minutes for 30 September 1723, when Henry Wise held the post of Royal Gardener jointly with Joseph Carpenter, reads: 'Ordered that for the future the Labourering works at Kensington be done by the Office Labourers and not by Mr Wise & Mr Carpenters Men' (NA Work 4/2), suggesting that a distinction was made between men employed by the Royal Gardener and those employed by the Office of Works. Bridgeman was certainly employing his own labourers in 1734, and, again, a clear demarcation existed between them and those employed by the Office of Works:

> 24[th] September ... Order'd that the Clerk of the Works take care, that the Labourers in trust, do daily attend on the spot, to see that the Labourers Employ'd by Mr Bridgman, in making the ground keep to ye Work and that he keep a distinct Acc[oun]t of every mans time & and Business and that Mr Bridgman be acquainted therewith. In case the Labour in trust be absent from his Duty a Sufficient Person shall be Employ'd in his room, and be paid out of the Labourer in trusts Allowance. (Work 4/6)

He also charged explicitly for labour at Kensington Gardens, in accounts submitted in 1731, 'For 2 Gardiners Employed 216 days ea', '490 Single Days of Labourers from June 3 to Dec 25th 1731', '687 single days works of Gardiners from Oct 11th to Novr 15th ... all working tools & utensils being included' (NA Work 6/114). He also seems to have used his own men while working on the landscape at Richmond Park for Queen Caroline, when Royal Gardener. Pope's letter to the Earl of Oxford in 1726 concerning his garden at Twickenham suggests that Bridgeman's men were working at Richmond Park before his appointment as Royal Gardener. Part of his letter reads: '... just turfed a little Bridgemannick Theatre myself. It was done by a detachment of His men' (Pope in Sherburne 1956, 372).

Paying for that labour must have been the most significant part of Bridgeman's costs. It is difficult to find reliable data on labourers' wages for the relevant part of the eighteenth century, but what figures there are suggest some discrepancy between the wages paid in the countryside, and those in London and the surrounding area. Cowell argues that, 'In an age of no statutory minimum wage and little communication among men in different localities at the lowest end of the social scale to compare working conditions, the variation in labouring wages was considerable' (Cowell 2009, 146). Cowell shows that the daily rate of pay for a labourer at Hartwell in Buckinghamshire in that period was 10d a day (Cowell 2009, 146). She and Malcolmson suggest that the wages for an agricultural labourer in the middle of the eighteenth century were similar: somewhere between 10d and 1s 3d a day (Malcolmson 1981, 37; Cowell 2009, 146). These amounts tally with those given by Elizabeth Gilboy. For example, she shows that wages for labourers in Oxfordshire were 1s 2d a day in 1720 (Gilboy 1969, 265), and that labourers' wages in the City of London and its immediate environs were significantly higher. A labourer working in Southwark was paid 1s 10d a day in 1727, while in Dartford the wage in 1722 was 1s 8d (Gilboy 1969, 259). However, in spite of this, some labourers working in gardens were paid significantly less: a 'woman weeder' in 1702 was paid 8d a day, although labourers in the orchard at Westminster were paid 1s 6d a day until 1720 (Gilboy 1969, 13). None of this is consistent with the rates that Bridgeman itemises in his supplementary account for Kensington Gardens, where the rate charged for 'Gardiners' is significantly higher at 2s a day (NA Work 6/114).

Because of these costs, payments made to Bridgeman from estate accounts probably show when he hired and paid his own labourers. Brown has shown, in relation to Nathaniel Richmond's work at Shardeloes in Buckinghamshire in the second half of the eighteenth century, that it is possible to see, in payments made to the landscaper, whether or not he provided the labour, since this was probably the most significant cost in the project. He suggests that Richmond's payments at Shardeloes between 1763 and 1765 probably indicate that he was operating in what Brown terms a 'design and build' role: he was paid £870. However, between 1765 and 1769 he was paid only £190.6s.9d, while John Hencher was paid £1257.8s.7d. Brown argues that this indicates that the two had switched roles. Richmond's contractual agreement had changed to a 'design and inspect role', while Hencher, operating now as Richmond's contractor, was probably responsible for the hiring of labour (Brown 2000, 223). Bridgeman's estimate of £5000 at Kensington Gardens explicitly covers the provision of labour. If we use this as a model, it is likely that the very considerable costs involved at Sacombe (£1128.0s.3d), Briggens (£1773.8s), Wimpole (£2280.6s.6d), Down Hall (290.10s.2d), Wimbledon (£880.17s.0d), Richmond Park Lodge (£6483.4s.7¾d) and St James's Square (£5630) (St James's Square Trustees 1726) probably all show that Bridgeman provided the labour.

It is possible that Bridgeman provided labour only when his clients had no recourse to estate labour of their own. Some of the sites listed above are not part of a landed estate, but instead were bought by those whose wealth had come from trade. These clients' properties were usually significantly smaller than the estates of the nobility, which tended to comprise tenant farms and an agricultural infrastructure, as well as a park. For example, at Sacombe in Hertfordshire, the estate of Edward Rolt, the park extended to 90 acres or 0.36 km^2, and at Purley in Berkshire, the estate of Frances Hawes, it measured 113 acres or 0.46 km^2. The size of the overall land holding seems to have made very little difference to the size or design that Bridgeman created; it simply occupied a significantly larger proportion of the land available. At Sacombe, for example, the design occupied 42 acres (0.17km^2) of the 90 acres (0.36km^2); at Gobions, where the estate at 500 acres was rather bigger, the woodland garden was around 39 acres (0.16 km^2). Because these estates were without a workforce of agricultural labourers habitually employed to work on the land, Bridgeman provided workmen and foremen of his own. This was sometimes the case with members of the nobility, too. The Duchess of Marlborough's house at Wimbledon was probably similar. Although her principal residence was at Blenheim Palace, it was not her property but administered by her as her husband's trustee (Harris 1985, 1). Wimbledon Park, which comprised a house and park, had been bought by her at her own expense in 1733 (Harris 1985, 2).

While it is hard to know whether Bridgeman saw this as a business opportunity in the modern sense, it is certainly an example of the relationship between supply and demand. It was not always necessary for Bridgeman to provide labour. This certainly appears to have been the case at Wolterton. A letter from William Brand, Walpole's Head Gardener, makes it clear in a letter to Horatio Walpole on 23 April 1732 that the workforce landscaping the lawns to the north of the house was employed by the estate:

S[i]r
This last week wee plowed some of ye Lawns next the Church And I have staked each made a Line of Earth from the Stopp to the Lower End soe as it Show were the Earth to be taken off and were to make good ... I have carried sand into the Kitchen Garden and Bowling Green in order to make it better ... Mr Bayfield have ordered tomorrow ffour Labourers and four of our carts to remove Earth in the Lawns ...'. (WH Box 28L 8/14)

It is also clear from a letter from the Chief Land Steward Bayfield to Walpole on 4 June 1731 that William Brand, and presumably – although not explicitly stated – workers employed by the estate, were responsible for laying the roads and walks to Bridgeman's design:

... Will Brand Have gon on very well for this weeke and have Leveled all the ... Road in the Brick Kiln close and Gathered up all the Rubbish of the C ... & which Laid a ...? a very good Road and taken away a Good quantity of earth on the east front Down to the ... pond & levelled the Ground & filled up the Hole before the front of the Stables & made it fit for the pavior ... Will Brand have made one of the Slopes & is doing the other on the Right and Left side of the Stone Slopes on the North Front and Carrying and Leveling the Lawn before ... . (WH Box 29L 8/15)

At Boughton, we can probably assume that any work recorded in the estate accounts after 1728 (when John Booth and the Duke of Montagu corresponded about Bridgeman's visits to Boughton (Boughton House archive)) is part of Bridgeman's plan. Entries in the Boughton Account Books for 1729 and 1730 include payment for a number of activities by estate labourers in the garden: William White was paid for tree planting, once on 3 March, 'Wm. White for Lab[oure]rs in the Warren and planting Chestnuts &c in Mo[nth] of Feb £14.12'; and again on 2 April, 'Wm White ditto – Planting Yews on the Mount for ditto £19.2.3' (NTS Boughton Account Book 43).

Whether the workforce was comprised of labourers employed by Bridgeman or directly by his client, they needed to be supervised and directed, and, given the number of commissions Bridgeman was involved in, some kind of delegation of supervision would have been needed. There is certainly evidence that he struggled to visit all his clients. Indeed, Bridgeman's absence is a theme which is repeated in what little correspondence there is. In an exchange between the Duke of Montagu and John Booth in 1728 about Boughton House, the Duke wrote that he 'Wishes Mr Bridgeman would go down with you to see the ground of the Park in order to [see] the scheme I propose' (Vol. 16), and received the reply on 24 September that 'Mr Bridgman is so closely Engag'd at Windsor that I can't get a sight of him' (NRO Bath X881B). At Stowe in 1721 they seem to be waiting for Bridgeman with regard to the digging of a hog pond: 'My Lord would not have it donn [until] Mr Bridgman Coms' (HEH Box L9F7 Farm and Garden Accounts folder) cited in Willis 2002, 11 n. 19. He fails to appear at Amesbury despite promising to be there: Henrietta Howard complains to John Gay in 1731 that she 'was never so peevish in my life than I have been about this journey of Bridgeman's ... I find, upon strict inquiry, that he did not go so soon as I expected' (Murray 1824, Vol. 2, 20–21).

It seems that employment of a foreman to oversee work in the absence of the landscape designer was customary in the first half of the eighteenth century. There is evidence that in his capacity of Royal Gardener Wise employed the services of a foreman, as is shown by the following entry in the minutes of the Board of Works for 23 November 1715: 'Orderd the Severall Clerks to View & Examine and Report to this Board (what Tubbs & Potts are wanting in his Maj[estys] Gardens at Hampton Court Kensington and Windsor) on Wednesday next; in the performance of this they are to take Mr Wise's fforeman's Assistance' (NA Work 4/1). Cowell suggests that the business model of the landscape improvers of the mid-eighteenth century required the services of a number of foremen. She outlines the importance of this role for Lancelot Brown, who was, she suggests, 'above all a contractor, supplying the plan for improvements, advice, and sporadic supervision of the foreman he established to execute his design' (Cowell 2009, 153). She shows that Woods, too, depended on a number of foremen for the 'successful execution of his designs', in common she suggests with 'most of the other major improvers' (Cowell 2009, 153). She suggests that these foremen, referred to as 'Mr Woods' man' or 'Mr White's man', performed a difficult role, responsible for overseeing the design and for negotiating with the staff already in place at the estates they worked in. There was often resentment of the foreman's role from the head gardener, and the foreman's conduct was reported on by the chief steward. They seem to have been responsible for hiring men: 'Men wanting to be hired would wait every morning in the market place waiting for the bailiff, or steward or foreman to take them on for the following week', and for keeping worksheets recording work done (Cowell 2009, 148). Woods employed some of his own 'companies' of men who moved with him from commission to commission (Cowell 2009, 149).

Bridgeman charged the Office of Works twice for the services of foremen in the 'Bill of Work done beyond the Contract of £5000' at Kensington Gardens, issued to the Office in 1731: 'A foreman's time 18 days in attending and seeing the said Works properly & well executed at 3s 6d per day ... 3.3.0' and 'A Foreman's time 15 days in Setting and Directing and attending the said work at 3s 6d per day ... 2.12.6' (NA Work 6/114). Indeed, Item 48 in the same document makes it clear that Bridgeman employed a foreman to direct the work at Kensington Gardens:

> But upon your Lordships Orders coming to us Wee enquired of the Clerk of Works at Kensington what he knew of the same Who told us that he had no orders to take an Account of the Works yet Mr Bridgemans forman did give him Notice from time to time as the parcells were severaly finished agreeable to Mr Bridgemans Account. (NA Work 6/114)

It is possible that Thomas Bayfield, Walpole's chief steward, was also referring to two of Bridgeman's foremen when he wrote to Horatio Walpole on 2 January 2 1726: 'Will Brand is got to worke to Dig in order to plant out his you[n]g setts according to Mr Kings direction but seeme not well to put them out & say it will not be well done & Mr King have orderd him to goe two spittes Deep'; and on 30 November 1728: 'Mr Parrie the overseer of the worke is very serviceable in giving orders How to Levell the Ground & in Raise the Large furr tree when transplanted ...'. It seems a strong possibility that Mr King was working in some capacity for Bridgeman. However, since the letter of 30 November is concerned, in some detail, with the construction of the house, it might be that 'Mr Parrie' worked for Ripley, the architect, although the work he is concerned with is definitely in the garden (WH 8/5A Box 73L). It is also possible that Horace Walpole, in his *The History of the Modern Taste in Gardening*, is referring to Bridgeman's foreman at Houghton when he writes 'One of the first gardens planted in this simple, though still formal style, was my father's at Houghton. It was laid out by Mr Eyre, an imitator of Bridgman' (Walpole 1995). Brown and Williamson make the point that contemporary accounts often refer to Lancelot Brown's assistants and foremen as 'imitators', and that the word is only used in a pejorative sense at the end of the eighteenth century (Brown and Williamson 2016, 137). Bridgeman's father also may have fulfilled some supervisory role at Down Hall. Adrian Drift, Matthew Prior's private secretary, records a 'Mr Bridgman Sr' going to Down Hall in 1722 to 'clear all debts due' (BL Add MS 70362, 82). A foreman was present at Stowe in 1714, where accounts show a payment to 'Mr Bridgman's man' of £1.2s.6d in 1714 (Willis 2002, 109 n. 14); and at Kedleston there are two payments to 'Mr Bridgman's man'; a guinea on 14 September and £51.11s on 10 November 1722 (Willis 2002, 430). This is the terminology used to refer to both Brown's, and Woods's foremen, so it seems likely that it also refers to Bridgeman's. The considerable disparity between the two sums paid to 'Mr Bridgeman's man' at Kedleston suggests the varied responsibilities of the foreman. It might be that the guinea represents around seven days of supervision, if we use the pay of the foreman at Kensington Gardens as a yardstick, or alternatively it may have been an inspection fee. On the other hand, £51.11s was a considerable amount of money in 1722 and suggests an altogether more substantial role.

In the absence of a foreman, or of Bridgeman himself, the workforce on a landed estate seems to have often been supervised by a fluid combination of stewards and bailiffs, working sometimes in conjunction with head gardeners. Mingay shows that 'The sheer size and complexity of large estates necessitated the employment of full-time officials, men who specialized in estate management' (Mingay 1963, 59). It does seem that the stewards and head gardeners were willing and enthusiastic collaborators in Bridgeman's work. At Wolterton, Bayfield, the land steward, supervised the work, as is shown in a letter to Walpole of 6 May 6 1732: '... wee Have Had a Great deele of Raine so as the Lawn on the North front plow very Well and is plowed up and the Little Carts and some Men I Have Gott too Worke and Levelling it, and Carrying earth up towards the front, up to the Slope up into the House' (WH Box 28L 8/5A)). At Boughton, it was Diston Stanley, the land steward for Boughton House, who appears to have been responsible for the supervision and payment of the labourers (NTS Account Books 33–51). However, Bridgeman was not completely absent from either site. Both stewards, Bayfield and Diston Stanley, entertained Bridgeman, presumably when he came to see the progress of the work. Bridgeman came to Boughton in 1731, and to Wolterton with Ripley in 1737. Both visits seem to have involved eating and drinking. Bayfield's letter to Walpole reads: 'We have some ale brewed which

I believe is very good but very Little wine for what was left by Mr Charters is part drunke when Mr Bridgeman and Mr Ripley have been here' (Box 29L 8/29), while Stanley notes on 27 April in his accounts: 'provisions when Mr Booth & Mr Bridgman were at Boughton in August and December last ... Bill 141 £4.7.5' (NTS Account Book 51).

It seems that Bridgeman also sourced plants and trees for his clients from nurseries. There is certainly evidence that Bridgeman dealt directly with Brompton Park Nursery for both plants and seeds. Willis suggests that Joseph Carpenter, at Brompton Park Nurseries, provided Bridgeman with plants for Kedleston, Briggens, Carshalton, Compton Place, Purley and Stowe (Willis 2002, 33 n. 41). These sites include two where Bridgeman was paid for the provision of plants only. In 1721 Samuel Tufnell paid a Charles Bridgeman for 'Works & plants in ye Gardens' at Langleys in Buckinghamshire, and in the same year, Bridgeman was paid £5.13s for trees at Briggens in Hertfordshire (Skelton pers. comm. 2019). This raises the possibility that one of the areas of Bridgeman's business was acting as a middleman for the provision of plants, but it is much more likely that he was engaged in some way with these estates. He also provided seeds for Down Hall from Brompton Park Nursery. On 13 March 1722, an entry in the accounts for Down Hall reads: 'To Mr Charles Bridgeman Sr Mr Carpenter Bill for seeds for the Gardens at Down Hall £2 16 8d' (BL Add MS 70362).

While there is nothing to link Bridgeman to any other nurseries in London, there is no reason to suppose he did not use them occasionally. There is no evidence to link Bridgeman to nurseries in the provinces, either, although his clients, sourcing plants for themselves, perhaps for Bridgeman's designs, did. At Boughton, a local nurseryman, Thomas Cross, was used to supply both trees and seeds, although here the transaction was handled by the estate rather than by Bridgeman (NRO Boughton Account Book 41). The elms planted at Boughton in 1730 were supplied by him at the cost of £950, which suggests a substantial operation (Account Book 43), and he was also paid for seeds in the same year (Crispin Powell pers. comm. 2015). Elms were also bought from 'Mrs Chamberling' and from Thos. Chamberlayne (presumably a married couple) in 1729, from Cransley, close to Boughton (Account Book 41). On 11 October 11 1721 there was another payment for seeds for Down Hall, this time 'To Mr Walker for Mr Adams who payed John Hogray for seeds for Down Garden' (BL Add MS 70361). This time the order does not seem to have come through Bridgeman. It is difficult to establish whether John Hogray was a seed merchant in London, but it is likely he was.

Bridgeman did not always need to supply plants for his landscapes. Some estates coped with the volume of trees and other plants needed by establishing their own nurseries, possibly specifically to provide plants for the new landscape, and growing trees and other plants from seedlings, although presumably the seedlings, or the seeds from which they were grown, were commercially produced. At Wolterton, a nursery seems to have been established by Joseph

A COMMERCIAL ENTERPRISE

Carpenter in 1722, after Horatio Walpole's purchase of the estate but before the fire which destroyed the house; in fact. before Bridgeman became involved in the planning of the garden (WH Box 73L 8/5A). A fence was erected in 1732 to stop the 'Herdes from comeing in to the bowling Green and Nursery' (WH Box 28L 8/14). At Boughton, a new nursery was also established c.1728. In 1729 two payments were made to labourers which specify work 'in the new Nursery' (Boughton Account Book 39). Perhaps it was used to raise the elm plants supplied by Thomas Cross.

Whether this gardening enterprise of Bridgeman's deliberately set out to make money or not, a great deal of it changed hands. The archives of modern banks hold at least some records from the eighteenth century. It is possible to search a limited archive from Coutts, Goslings, Child and Co., Drummonds and Hoare's Banks and, while the first four revealed no transactions by a Charles Bridgeman, there was evidence of financial activity at Hoare's Bank; an account for 'Charles Bridgman' in November 1716, which was closed in January 1717/18, through which large sums of money were channelled. The total deposited and then drawn in that period was £350.10s, roughly £41,000 today (Customer ledger/folio 19/345). In 1726, in another transaction, a 'Mr Charles Bridgman' deposited £107.19s.3d and withdrew it five days later (Customer ledger/folio 28/83). The accounts in Customer ledger/folio 19/345 show money paid in between November 1716 and September 1717, and the same amount withdrawn by January 1718. Customer ledger/folio no: 28/83 also shows money paid in and then withdrawn on the same day. It was not particularly unusual in the eighteenth century for bank accounts to be opened simply to cash a single note and then closed again (Pamela Hunter pers. comm. 2017). It may also be that Bridgeman had other accounts at Hoare's Bank but that these are unrecorded. Other banks recorded the names of clients who opened accounts but Hoare's did not, probably because they knew their clients well (Pamela Hunter pers. comm. 2017). It is almost impossible to be sure whether these deposits and withdrawals were made by Bridgeman, but, given the dates, it seems likely.[3] The entries between 1716 and 1717 may relate to work at Stowe, since they do not match the payments to Bridgeman from Edward

---

[3] My thanks to Pamela Hunter, Archivist at Hoare's Bank, for these entries. The entries are as follows: 'Credits:12 Nov 1716 By mony rece'd p note £75-5-0; 23 May 1717 By notes 25, 25, 25:5 £75-5-0; 15 June 1717 By note £100; 7 Sept 1717 By note £100 [Total] £350-10-0. Drawings: 23 May 1717 To my note 12 Nov £75-5-0; 19 June 1717 To my note 15 June £100; 9 Sept 1717 To part 100 ye 7 Sept £50; 21 Sept 1717 To clear ditto £50; 16 Jan 1717/8 To part 25 ye 23 May £5; 20 Jan 1717/8 To my notes 23 May 25: 5 and 25 £50-5-0; 29 Jan 1717/8 To clear 25 ye 23 May £20; [Total] £350-10-0 (Customer ledger/ folio 19/345). Bridgman, Charles, Mr Opened 20 May 1726 with deposit (£107-19-3) by note. Closed 25 May 1726 when same withdrawn (Customer ledger/folio no: 28/83). There are also two references to a Charles Bridge, which may be a mis-spelling of Bridgeman's name: Customer ledger 20, folio 6; 15 June 1717, To Charles Bridge £150; 7 Sept 1717, To Mr Bridgman £150 (Customer ledger/folio 19/345).

Rolt's account at the same bank. Two payments of £50 and £30 respectively were made to 'Charles Bridgman' in 1715 (Customer ledger 17, folio 339), one of £60 in 1716 (Customer ledger 18, folio 266) and one of £214.0s.3d in 1718.[4] Willis notes an account at Gosling's Bank from which Sir Joseph Jekyll paid Bridgeman £10 in 1722 (Willis 2002, 428). Child and Co. have a receipt for a payment made by Sarah Bridgeman into the bank of £440 on 18 July 1740. Of course there are also payments to Bridgeman recorded in estate records, many of which have already provided evidence of his work at specific sites. Payments to him in his capacity as Royal Gardener, both for his annual maintenance contract and for work done outside it, are recorded in the Abstract of the Accounts of the Office of Works Work 5/56–5/5.

Records of Bridgeman's financial transactions are sparse and incomplete. However, an overview of what records there are shows a business that was, in any terms, successful. If we add together all the sums we know that he was paid between 1714 and 1738, it comes to a total of £59,270.14s.6½d, roughly £6,981,650 in today's money (https://www.nationalarchives.gov.uk/currency-converter/#currency-result). This figure can only be a partial representation of what Bridgeman earned and so must be treated with some caution. (A table presenting Bridgeman's known earnings by year appears in full in Appendix IV). The incompleteness of the records makes it impossible to see a comprehensive picture of what he earned annually, and so there are enormous discrepancies between years. For example, all available records for 1727 suggest Bridgeman was only paid £100, while the following year, 1728, he was paid £9043.4s.7¾d. We should not assume that because yearly income is so much lower in 1726, Bridgeman was less successful. His earnings are likely to be well in excess of this total since there are many landscapes on which we know he worked but for which no accounts exist. It is also difficult to measure Bridgeman's outgoings, which, especially since they involved the hire of labourers, must have been considerable. It is therefore impossible to calculate what kind of a profit he made.

Incomplete as the figures are, they do suggest some important points about Bridgeman's income. The anomaly between his income in 1726 and 1727 is probably a reflection of the importance to Bridgeman's income of his yearly stipend as Royal Gardener. It is clear from these two years that Bridgeman's work as Royal Gardener and for the Office of Works was very lucrative and formed a substantial part of his income. In addition to his regular quarterly payment of £555 (shown above as a yearly sum of £2220 for convenience) and his contract at Windsor Castle, he seems to have been employed on a more casual basis to execute work which fell outside these contracts. The survival of the meticulous

---

[4] June 1715, To Charles Bridgman [sic] £50 (Customer ledger 17, folio 339); 2 July 1715, To Mr Bridgman £30; 16 June 1716, To Mr Bridgman £60 (Customer ledger 18, folio 266); 4 Aug 1718, To Charles Bridgman £214-0-3 (Customer ledger 20, folio 436).

accounts of the Office of Works in the relevant part of the eighteenth century also makes it simple to quantify this reliable part of Bridgeman's income.

It is also probably clear from the figures that at Sacombe, Wimpole, Down Hall, Richmond Park Lodge, Kensington Gardens, St James's Square and Wimbledon, Bridgeman was acting as a managing contractor, employing labour and contracting work to other artisans. At St James's Square, where, in 1726, he was paid £5630 by the trustees, Longstaffe-Gowan notes that the work was 'subsequently described as "finely paved all over with Heading Stone, and has a large, beautiful oval [round] basin of water, surrounded with a broad Gravel Walk, and Iron Rails, on a Dwarf-wall, forming an Octagon, and at each Outside the railing the square was paved with Purbeck stone"' (Longstaffe-Gowan 2001, 196). Chancellor credits John Mist, Bridgeman's brother-in-law who was a pavior frequently employed by the Office of Works (Work 4/1–4/7) with the paving at St James's Square, and since Bridgeman was paid for the project, this raises the possibility that he contracted the work to Mist (Chancellor 1907, cited in Willis 2002, 32). It may be that this was not the only project where this happened. We can also see that there are fewer payments in 1736, 1737 and 1738. It may be that records of payments in these years have not survived, or it may be that, towards the year of his death, he was less able to work, as discussed in Chapter 1.

But in spite of the large sums of money which Bridgeman was paid, his wife Sarah Bridgeman seems to have been very short of money after his death in July 1738. The abstract of accounts for the Office of Works shows that his payment as Royal Gardener stopped abruptly on the day of his death; for example, his monthly pay for work at Windsor Castle, usually £11.13s.4d, is calculated as £7.3s for the month of July 1738 (Work 5/58). Sarah Bridgeman's proposed sales of plans to the Treasury and the Office of Works are prefaced with a statement about this, and her letters to Sarah Churchill, reported in the latter's own letters, suggest that she had debts she was unable to pay: 'And in some of your Letters to seem to put it upon my Generosity, Mr Bridgman has not left effects to pay his Debts, and it would be the ruin of his Family' (BP MSS F1–35). It is difficult to understand why she was in such straits, given the sums of money mentioned above. It is not at all clear what happened to Bridgeman's money. In the provision he made for his wife and children he seems to have thought there would be ample means to support them (NA PROB 11/692/74). In spite of being cautious about the slowing of payments in the last years of Bridgeman's life, perhaps he did have fewer commissions between c.1734 and 1738, either because the rise of the 'natural' garden made him less popular or because illness made it less easy for him to manage his business. Perhaps the business practices of the early eighteenth century created a liquidity problem. As McKendrick et al. have shown, 'Credit and debt [in the eighteenth century] …were almost universal' (McKendrick, Brewer and Plumb 2007, 207). They suggest that 'A substantial proportion of the assets of nearly all eighteenth-century business enterprises, especially those of merchants, middlemen and retailers, was in the form of short term credit which had been extended to customers and clients' (McKendrick, Brewer and Plumb 2007, 207). Bridgeman's Probate Inventory suggests that this may have been a contributing factor, since it states that Bridgeman was owed 'divers Sumes of Money' ... 'from the Crown and several of the Nobility and Gentry' (NA PROB.3/37/95).

Bridgeman sits between two systems through which a garden designer might operate in the eighteenth century: one is patronage, the system under which most landscape design was undertaken in the generation before Bridgeman, but the other is running a business on proto-modern terms, clearly the case for the generation of landscape improvers working after 1750. The ways Lancelot Brown and his imitators worked typifies the latter approach, and the similarity to Bridgeman's case is immediately obvious.

The business practice of Brown, and his contemporaries and imitators Nathaniel Richmond, Richard Woods and Thomas White, is evidenced in a wealth of correspondence between improver and client, and between client and client, and in accounts, the very survival of which suggests a different approach. Although Brown and Williamson make the point that, of the probable 250 sites Lancelot Brown worked on, his surviving account book contains only 16 names, and his bank accounts mention only 90 commissions, the relative abundance of this documentary material makes it easy to see how these ran their businesses (Brown and Williamson 2016, 9). For example, after an initial visit and assessment by Brown, the surveying, the draughting of plans and the construction were subcontracted to foremen or assistants, who he paid to hire labour and complete the work (Brown and Williamson 2016, 136–137). Foremen were essential to Brown's business model, and the relationship between the 'improver' and his foremen had a flexibility and fluidity to it which meant that the foreman was not contracted solely to the improver but could work for himself and others (Brown 2000, 225). Richmond, himself one of Brown's foremen/contractors, operated in a similar way (Brown and Williamson 2016, 142). Brown has shown that payments to Richmond indicate that he was responsible for fulfilling a contract which he defines as 'arranging the materials supply, labour, and supervision of works on site'. He uses the example of a substantial payment from Sir Clayton Kendrick of £600 between 1759 and 1761 (Brown 2000, 223). Woods charged for his time and expenses, and separately for the plans, and these charges were itemised in the contract and in his bills (Cowell 2009, 159, 160). We have seen above that Richmond's payments at Shardeloes indicate that he was probably responsible for fulfilling the contract there between 1763 and 1765, while payments between 1765 and 1769 suggest that that responsibility had shifted to John Hencher. Brown uses the example of Jonathan Midgley, paid by Lancelot Brown as a 'foreman' between 1760 and 1778 but who was also working independently at Ashburnham in the same years, to suggest that Lancelot Brown also worked in the same way. In both cases, Brown suggests that sometimes labour and materials were supplied by the client, sometimes by the foreman/contractor. By the mid-to-late eighteenth century the role of landscape improver had become, if not a modern business, certainly well on the way to it. Indeed, Brown has suggested that the way Nathaniel Richmond and other 'gentleman improvers', such as Brown and Woods, organised their businesses was affected by the changes in international business organisation in the mid-eighteenth century (Brown 2000, 218).

David Brown may well be right when he suggests that, by 1759, 'the market for landscape improvement had widened and was largely free from individual aristocratic patronage' (Brown 2000, 222), and in Bridgeman's career we may well be seeing the beginning of its end. We might place Bridgeman somewhere on a trajectory towards the commercialisation of gardening. In some regards, as evidence in Chapter 6 suggests, he was running a business, and it was more closely aligned to those of the landscape improvers of the mid-eighteenth century than to Brompton Nurseries. Bridgeman appears to have made initial, and short subsequent, visits to sites. Although, with the exceptions discussed above, contracts appear not to have survived, they clearly did exist, and the work was undertaken as laid out in them. Unlike Brown, Bridgeman seems to have conducted his own surveys, and, as an accomplished draughtsman, probably personally drew a large proportion of the plans which resulted. Subsequent work on the landscape seems to have been either the responsibility of the estate, or, like Brown, he seems to have used foremen to oversee the work, hire the labour, and see it to its completion. On occasion he also supplied plants, although not from his own nursery, and he was a competent engineer with a good working knowledge of hydraulics. Of Lancelot Brown, Brown and Williamson have contended that 'In an entrepreneurial age, Brown was the entrepreneur's entrepreneur. He was an astute businessman with a genius for organizing complex projects, and making them profitable', the 'head of an extensive and complex business organisation' (Brown and Williamson 2016, 136). It would be misleading to suggest that Bridgeman's operation was as organised as that, but, as Brown suggests, Bridgeman 'pursued largely commercial open markets for widely differing clients' and, although financially embarrassed at the end of his life, ran a successful, emergent business, which anticipated those in the generation that followed him (Brown 2000, 221).

CONCLUSION

CHARLES BRIDGEMAN DESERVES greater fame than posterity has granted him. This book has been an attempt to set right that injustice, to remove him from obscurity and place him in the canon of famous gardeners and garden designers of the past and present. The names of Bridgeman's near contemporaries, André Le Nôtre, William Kent, Lancelot Brown and Humphrey Repton, are common currency even amongst those whose knowledge of gardening and landscape history is sketchy, as are the names of Gertrude Jekyll and Vita Sackville West in the modern era. Bridgeman's name should be equally well known.

As we have seen, he was far more famous, popular and highly regarded in his period than his modern reputation suggests: a man of competence, taste and intellect, esteemed by his peers and in great demand amongst his clientele. His popularity may have been because he was a consummate practitioner, probably a better practitioner than several on the list above whose names are better known. In an age when a successful garden designer needed to be competent in a number of disparate disciplines, he was the master of them all. His surveying was accurate and rigorous. He was conversant with techniques of building, planting and hydraulics. He was a skilled draughtsman, producing accurate scale plans, but also an artist, capable of beautiful watercolour versions of his designs, and bird's-eye views in which the landscape was visualised in a three-dimensional form.

He may also have been something of an entrepreneur, and perhaps this was another reason for his popularity. He seems to have created some kind of proto-business infrastructure which allowed him to manage a number of projects simultaneously. As a result, he appears to have been able to deliver as much or as little of the landscape as was required. He could supply any or all of the following: an accurate survey, a viable plan for a landscape, hydraulics that were practical and efficient, sourced plants, labour, and on-going maintenance. In short, the service he presented to his clients was something approaching the complete service offered a generation later by Lancelot Brown though it was perhaps more of an innovation in the early eighteenth century. Although Bridgeman was, for some reason, financially embarrassed at the end of his life, we might see in his operation an emergent business which anticipated those in the generation that followed him. His role in the emergence of the professional gardener is one way we might assess his importance in the history of gardening.

Bridgeman the person, to a large degree, remains slippery. His social position, and his own sense of it, is hard to pin down. He probably came from a relatively humble background to a position of wealth and artistic influence, falling with happy synchronicity, like many of his contemporaries – for example William Kent, Thomas Ripley and James Gibbs – into a space created by changes in society between the demise of patronage and the rise of the professional practitioner; what he made of this is harder to determine. Even in writing this book, it has been difficult to get any sense of his personality. We might hope to find him in his relationships with others, but he remains stubbornly shadowy. His relationships with his landed clients, like the Earl of Oxford, give little away; they are appropriately professional and deferential. There are perhaps more glimpses of his personality in his relationships with those with whom he shared a more equal social standing – for example, with Matthew Prior, Adrian Drift and Thomas Hall – but they are no more than glimpses. There is also little concrete evidence of whether he was a loving father and husband. Perhaps he was far too busy to cultivate close relationships with anyone. The early eighteenth century was probably a place where the transactional was of more consequence than the personal.

Sadly neither Bridgeman's work nor his reputation have survived. His work went out of fashion very quickly in the years that followed his death. It is even arguable that he became unfashionable before his death; his commissions certainly seem to have diminished after 1735. It is undeniable that the rise of the popularity of the natural garden resulted in many of his landscapes being remodelled, often very quickly after their construction, for example by Kent at Rousham and Claremont, by Woods at Brocket Park, and by Brown at Moor Park and Houghton. At Moor Park, Lord Anson brought in Brown to create a small lake and hills to replace Bridgeman's canal and formal garden. (Horace Walpole was not impressed. He described the hills as 'artificial molehills' and complained that it was 'as unnatural as if it was drawn with a rule and compasses'.)

But in the end, beyond Bridgeman the man, beyond his artistic skills, beyond his business innovation, beyond even the survival of his work (although there is enough for us to know it did exist), we come back to the English landscape, and what he did to it. His landscapes were not paintings, nor even simply building projects; they were, and to some extent still are, physical places to be in and to move through, and that was the ultimate purpose of their creation. It is perhaps difficult, from the vantage point of the twenty-first century, to gauge the experience of being in them. There are very few accounts of the experience of being in a Bridgeman landscape that date from the earlier part of the eighteenth century when they were created; as touched on in Chapter 4, the fashion for gushing accounts of the feelings engendered by a designed landscape did not really emerge until around 1740. In any case, the eighteenth-century experience of them would by no means have been fixed. Gardens are organic, and what was planted in Bridgeman's would have grown, died and been replaced even in the lifetime of his clients. They would then, as they do now, have looked different depending on the seasons: low winter light reveals planes and hollows unseen in the summer.

Perhaps our best chance to understand the physical impact of a Bridgeman landscape comes with the few that have survived more or less as Bridgeman intended them. However, even where Bridgeman's gardens have survived or been restored, we cannot assume we experience them as Bridgeman's contemporaries did. What we experience when we walk through a Bridgeman landscape is also mediated by our own world view. It is always dangerous to assume that the people of the past experienced landscape as we do, a problem of phenomenology which assumes an innate link between human beings who live in vastly different cultural and social universes. In fact, although the early eighteenth century was on the cusp of the Enlightenment and a commercial revolution, and characterised itself as a place where reason and knowledge were paramount, it was still a more brutal, polarised society than modern Britain. In terms of experience of landscape, it was arduous to work the land or build structures from it, or in it, and travelling through it, even for short distances, was at best slow and muddy, at worst perilous.

Yet, in spite of all the caveats above, if we are to fully understand the impact of a Bridgeman landscape we have to attempt to experience it physically. Although mostly what we are left with is archaeology and our own imagination to gauge the visual and spatial impact of Bridgeman's work, there are two largely intact landscapes where we can get more of a sense of Bridgeman's design when it was new; at Claremont, in Surrey, and at Lodge Park, in Gloucestershire. Both have been sensitively restored by the National Trust. The first sight of the amphitheatre at Claremont is extraordinary (Figure 14), a hillside cut away to reveal green, monumental terraces, crisply and satisfyingly symmetrical, given scale by the fully grown trees that flank them. It is impossible to mistake it for anything other than man-made. The pool in front of it, once perfectly circular, was designed to mirror its shape. Even in Kent's modified form and no longer a circle, the surface of the water creates light and texture which perfectly complements the earth sculpture. Closer to the base of the terraces, the perfect elliptical curve of the upper rim becomes the horizon. The terraces make the climbing of the hill into which they are cut an easy matter, and, viewed from above, they become soft and mossy undulations, leading the eye back downwards to the – at that time – circular pool. The experience of Lodge Park is different but no less exciting. The landscape stands on a high, wind-blown expanse of limestone plateau. George Lambert's painting of 1747 shows Bridgeman's landscape behind the Lodge, and a visit to the park immediately reveals that the sense of grandeur depicted can still be experienced (https://www.nationaltrustcollections.org.uk/object/562393). Bridgeman's wide avenue flanked by double planted trees still marks the breadth of the Cotswold plain, leading the eye down the gentle slope and across to the horizon, where his woodland planting deliberately narrows the perspective to a focal point. The surprise of the deeply incised valley, invisible until you are upon it, remains.

Moving through a Bridgeman landscape reminds us of what is probably the primal function of all designed landscapes: to mark the land with a human intentionality that is beyond the utilitarian, and is available, for those privileged enough, to be interacted with; if you are not, it can always be viewed with awe and wonder from afar. In a sense the purpose, ritual or aesthetic is irrelevant; it is the marking that matters. Bridgeman is one in a long trajectory of what we might term landscape manipulators who have understood the power of writing meaning on the land through the media that the English countryside does best: grass, trees and water. In this sense, although almost certainly unwittingly, he is the successor to the Neolithic and Bronze Age builders of barrows, and the Iron Age builders of hill forts. He is, also in this sense, the predecessor of Lancelot Brown, another marker of the land with trees, earth and water. Interestingly, we have not fallen out of love with Lancelot Brown's work, or so it seems. Perhaps this is because his landscapes were relatively inexpensive to create in the first place, and, crucially, to maintain. They have therefore endured, becoming, as we have seen, the default model for parkland in England. Perhaps because of their popularity it is harder to find manipulators of the landscape on a grand scale after Brown, but two late twentieth and early twenty-first century landscape architects have begun again to explore the potential of earth, grass and water. Charles Jenks, an American landscape architect who died in 2019, created landscapes of crisp and precise organic, turfed earth sculptures interspersed with water. The gardens 'Cells of Life' at Jupiter Artland near Edinburgh, and the 'Garden of Cosmic Speculation' at his home in Portrack, Dumfries and Galloway, although both created with the explicit purpose of mirroring scientific concepts, could have been by Bridgeman (Anderton 2016, 66–73). Kim Wilkie is another modern designer who works with turfed earth landforms, on a grand scale. At Great Fosters in Surrey, he built a turfed amphitheatre that is the focus at the terminus of an avenue. At Boughton House, between 2007 and 2009, he created 'Orpheus', a seven-metre deep inverted grassed and terraced pyramid with a square pool at the bottom, as a specific echo of the eighteenth-century seven-metre terraced pyramid that stands beside it (kimwilkie.com). Wilkie explicitly references Bridgeman in his work, and acknowledges his own place as the successor to earth sculptors in the British Isles. As he writes: 'Britain is a good place for earthworks' (kimwilkie.com). This is perhaps where Bridgeman most clearly belongs: not simply to the seventeenth- or the eighteenth-century gardening tradition in England or in Europe, or with those who recognised the commercial potential of altering the landscape, but with those who have understood, and still understand, the shape, climate, geology and vegetation of the English landscape and how to make a meaning from it that reflects us and our place in it. This is surely the true meaning of 'Genius loci'.

APPENDIX I: A SUMMARY OF WILLIS'S CATALOGUE FROM *CHARLES BRIDGEMAN AND THE ENGLISH LANDSCAPE GARDEN*

THE FOLLOWING LIST is a summary of Willis's catalogue (Willis 2002, 177–186 and 425–438). Since the dates he gives are largely conjectural, the plans are listed in alphabetical order without dates. The plans for which Willis withdrew attribution in his 2002 addendum have been excluded. All catalogue numbers quoted in the list below are current and not necessarily those given in Willis's text. Each catalogue number (where appropriate) is preceded by its holding institution.

1. Amesbury Abbey, Wiltshire (BoL MSGD a3* fo.33)
2. Audley End, Essex (BoL MSGD a4 fo.60)
3. Audley End, Essex (BoL MSGD a4 fo.67)
4. Blenheim Palace, Oxfordshire (BoL MS Top Oxon a37* fo.2)
5. Blenheim Palace, Oxfordshire (BP)
6. Boughton House, Northamptonshire (bird's-eye view)
7. Boughton House, Northamptonshire (plan)
8. Boughton House, Northamptonshire (plan)
9. Brampton Bryan, Herefordshire (SM Vol. 111/43)
10. Brocket Hall, Hertfordshire (BoL MSGD a3 fo.7)
11. Brocket Hall, Hertfordshire (BoL MSGD a4 fo.40)
12. Buckingham House, Middlesex (SM 111/42)
13. Claremont (BoL MSGD a4 fo.81)
14. Claremont, Surrey (SM 62/1/1)
15. Down Hall, Essex (BL Add MS 70371)

16. Down Hall, Essex (BoL Gough Maps 46 fo.262)
17. Eastbury, Dorset (BoL MSGD a3 fo.10)
18. Eastbury, Dorset (BoL MSGD a3* fo.9)
19. Eastbury, Dorset (BoL MSGD a4 fo.21)
20. Fulham Road (NA MPE 1/482)
21. Greenwich Park, Middlesex (BoL MSGD a4 fo.49)
22. Greenwich Park, Middlesex (CL Art/II)
23. Greenwich Park, Middlesex (CL CMP 30)
24. Greenwich Park, Middlesex (CL MSS Art/6)
25. Gunton Hall, Norfolk (BoL MSGD a4 fo.75)
26. Hackwood, Hampshire (BoL MSGD a3 fo.4)
27. Hackwood, Hampshire (BoL MSGD a4 fo.24)
28. Hackwood, Hampshire (BoL MSGD a4 fo.34)
29. Hampton Court (NA MPD 1/23)
30. Hampton Court, Middlesex (BoL MSGD a4 fo.62)
31. Hampton Court, Middlesex (BL K.XXIX.14u)
32. Hampton Court, Middlesex (BoL MSGD a4 fo.74)
33. Hampton Court, Middlesex (HH drawings fo.39)
34. Hampton Court, Middlesex (NA MPD 1/23)
35. Hampton Court, Middlesex (SM 36/3/1).
36. Houghton, Norfolk (BoL MSGD a4 fo.57)
37. Hyde Park Road (NA MPD 1/164)
38. Kedleston, Derbyshire (SC)
39. Kensington Gardens, Middlesex (BL K.XXVIII.10.d.1)
40. Kensington Gardens, Middlesex (BoL MSGD a3* fo.15)
41. Kensington Gardens, Middlesex (HEH ST MAP 147)
42. Kensington Gardens, Middlesex (NS CC.2753)
43. Ledston, West Yorkshire (BoL MSGD a3 fo.19)
44. Ledston, West Yorkshire (BoL MSGD a4 fo.85)
45. Ledston, West Yorkshire (OT)
46. Lillington Manor (WO CR 556/197)
47. Lodge Park, Gloucestershire (BoL MSGD a4 fo.68)
48. Lumley Castle, County Durham (SH)
49. Marble Hill, Middlesex (NRO MC 184 10/1 and /2)
50. Mereworth, Kent (MSGD a4 fo.52)
51. Moor Park (MSGD fo.58)

APPENDIX I

52. Moor Park, Hertfordshire (BoL MSGDa4 fo.48
53. Purley, West Berkshire (BoL MSGD a4 fo.54)
54. Richmond Gardens, Surrey (MR 1/528)
55. Richmond Gardens, Surrey (MR 1/696)
56. Richmond Gardens, Surrey (NA Work 32/96)
57. Richmond Gardens, Surrey (Work 32/282)
58. Rousham, Oxfordshire (BoL MSGD fo.63)
59. Sacombe, Hertfordshire (BoL MSGD a4 fo.29
60. Sacombe, Hertfordshire (MSGD fo.64)
61. Scampston, North Yorkshire (BoL MSGD a4 fo.27)
62. Scampston, North Yorkshire (BoL MSGD aa3 fo.73)
63. Scampston, North Yorkshire (BoL MSGD fo.66)
64. St James's Park (SM 62/1/1)
65. St James's Park, Middlesex (NA Work 32/70)
66. Stilton (BoL MSGD a3 fo.40r)
67. Stilton (BoL MSGD a3 fo.40v)
68. Stilton (BoL MSGD a4 fo.3)
69. Stilton (BoL MSGD a4 fo.51)
70. Stowe, Buckinghamshire (BoL MSGD a4 fo.46)
71. Trafalgar (formerly Standlynch), Wiltshire (BoL MSGD a3 fo.24)
72. Tring, Hertfordshire (BoL MSGD a4 fo.25)
73. Tring, Hertfordshire (BoL MSGD a4 fo.32)
74. Tring, Hertfordshire (BoL MSGD a4 fo.78)
75. Unidentified (BoL MSGD a4 fo.22)
76. Unidentified (BoL MSGD a4 fo.33)
77. Unidentified (BoL MSGD a4 fo.36)
78. Unidentified (BoL MSGD a4 fo.43)
79. Warwick Priory (WO CR 26.2.1 and 2)
80. Warwick Priory, Warwickshire (WO CR 217)
81. Warwick Priory, Warwickshire (WO CR.56)
82. Wimbledon House (BoL MSGD a4 fo.44)
83. Wimbledon House, Surrey (BoL MSGD a3 fo.31)
84. Wimpole, Cambridgeshire (BL Add MS 36278)
85. Wimpole, Cambridgeshire (BoL MSGD a4 fo.30)
86. Wimpole, Cambridgeshire (BoL MSGD a4 fo.31)
87. Wimpole, Cambridgeshire (BoL MSGD a4 fo.35),

88. Wimpole, Cambridgeshire (BoL MSGD a4 fo.69)
89. Wimpole, Cambridgeshire (Bambridge Collection NT)
90. Wimpole, Cambridgeshire (Bambridge Collection NT)
91. Wimpole, Cambridgeshire (Bambridge Collection NT)
92. Wimpole, Cambridgeshire (Bambridge Collection NT)
93. Windsor Castle, Berkshire (SM 111/45)
94. Windsor Forest (NA MR 1/279)
95. Wolterton (BoL MSGD a3 fo.33).
96. Wolterton, Norfolk (BoL MSGD a4 fo.10)
97. Wolterton, Norfolk (BoL MSGD a4 fo.18)
98. Wolterton, Norfolk (BoL MSGD a4 fo.20)
99. Wolterton, Norfolk (BoL MSGD a4 fo.55)
100. Wolterton, Norfolk (BoL MSGD a4 fo.56)
101. Wolterton, Norfolk (BoL MSGD a4 fo.61)

Willis also suggested, based on documentary evidence, or on other scholarly research, that Bridgeman might have been involved at Badminton in Gloucestershire, at Briggens in Hertfordshire, at Castle Hill in Devon, at Cliveden in Buckinghamshire, at Coopersale in Essex or Welford in Berkshire, at Dallington in Northamptonshire or The Rolls House in London, at Esher in Surrey, at Gobions in Hertfordshire, in the construction of Cavendish Square, Grosvenor Square and St James's Square in London, at Hartwell in Buckinghamshire, at Longford Castle in Wiltshire, at Shardeloes in Buckinghamshire, at Wrest in Bedfordshire and at Wroxhall Manor in Warwickshire.

APPENDIX II: A REVISED CATALOGUE

THE PLANS WHICH make up a revised corpus are listed below. Surveys are shown in italics. Only those which can accurately be dated have dates added.

1. Amesbury Abbey (BoL MSGD a3* fo.32) (1738)
2. Audley End (BoL MSGD a4 fo.60)
3. Audley End (BoL MSGD a4 fo.67)
4. *Blenheim Palace* (held at Blenheim Palace) (1709)
5. Boughton House (held at Boughton House)
6. Boughton House (held at Boughton House)
7. Boughton House, bird's-eye view (held at Boughton House)
8. Brocket Hall (BoL MSGD a3 fo.7)
9. Brocket Hall (BoL MSGD a4 fo.40)
10. Claremont (SM 62/1/2)
11. Down Hall (BL Add MS 70371) (1720)
12. Down Hall (BoL Gough Maps 46 fo.262)
13. Down Hall (BoL MSGD a4 fo.29)
14. Eastbury (BoL MSGD a3* fo.10)
15. Eastbury (BoL MSGD a3* fo.9)
16. Eastbury (BoL NA MSGD a4 fo.21)
17. Fountain Garden (NA Work 32/311)
18. Gobions (BoL Herts Map a1)
19. Great Saxham (BoL MSGD a3 fo.41)
20. *Greenwich Park* (CL CMP/30)
21. Gunton (BoL MSGD a4 fo.75)
22. Hackwood (BoL MSGD a3 fo.4)

23. Hackwood (BoL MSGD a4 fo.24)
24. Hackwood (BoL MSGD a4 fo.34)
25. *Hampton Court* (held at Hovingham Hall)
26. *Hampton Court* (BoL MSGD a4 fo.62)
27. *Hampton Court* (BL K.XXIX.14.u)
28. *Hampton Court* (BoL MSGD a4 fo.74)
29. *Hampton Court* (NA MPD 1/23)
30. Hampton Court (NA Work 32/313A)
31. Hampton Court (NA Work 32/313B)
32. *Hampton Court* (SM 36/3/1)
33. Houghton (BoL MSGD a4 fo.57)
34. Kedleston Hall (SC Object 109274)
35. Kensington Gardens and Hyde Park (BoL MSGD a3* fo.15)
36. Kensington Gardens and Hyde Park (HEH ST Map 147)
37. Kensington Gardens and Hyde Park (NS CC.2753)
38. Ledston (BoL MSGD a4 fo.85)
39. Ledston (held at Otterden Place)
40. *Lillington Manor* (WO CR 556/197) (1711)
41. Lodge Park (BoL MSGD a4 fo.68)
42. Lumley Castle (held at Sandbeck House)
43. Lumley Castle (held at Sandbeck House)
44. Mereworth (BoL MSGD a4 fo.52)
45. Moor Park (BoL MSGD a4 fo.58)
46. Moor Park (BoL MSGD a4 fo.48)
47. Octagon Basin, Windsor (RCIN 929581)
48. Purley (BoL MSGD a4 fo.54)
49. *Richmond Gardens* (NA MR 1/528)
50. *Richmond Gardens* (NA MR 1/696)
51. Richmond Gardens (NA Work 32/282)
52. Rousham (BoL MSGD a4 fo.63)
53. Sacombe (BoL MSGD a4 fo.64)
54. Scampston (BoL MSGD a4 fo.27)
55. Scampston (BoL MSGD a4 fo.66)
56. Scampston (BoL MSGD a4 fo.73)
57. *St James' Park* (NA Work 32/70)
58. *St James's Park* (SM 62/1/1)

APPENDIX II 177

59. St James's Park (RC RCIN 929582)
60. Standlynch (BoL MSGD a3 fo.25)
61. Stowe, bird's-eye view (BoL MSGD a4 fo.46)
62. Tring (BoL MSGD a4 fo.32)
63. Tring (BoL MSGD a4 fo.78)
64. Unidentified (catalogued as Tring by Willis) (BoL MSGD a4 fo.25)
65. Unidentified (BoL MSGD a4 fo.37) (catalogued as Scampston by Willis)
66. Warwick Priory (WO CR 56)
67. *Warwick Town and Priory* (WO CR 217)
68. *Warwick Town and Priory* (WO CR 26.2.2)
69. Wimbledon (BoL MSGD a3 fo.31)
70. Wimbledon (BoL MSGD a4 fo.44)
71. Wimpole (Bambridge Collection)
72. Wimpole (Bambridge Collection)
73. Wimpole (Bambridge Collection)
74. Wimpole (Bambridge Collection)
75. Wimpole (BL Add MS 36278 Ml)
76. Wimpole (BoL MSGD a4 fo.30)
77. Wimpole (BoL MSGD a4 fo.31)
78. Wimpole (BoL MSGD a4 fo.35)
79. Wimpole (BoL MSGD a4 fo.69)
80. Windsor 2 Parks and Forest (RC RCIN 929579)
81. *Windsor Forest* (NA MR 1/279)
82. Windsor Forest (RC RCIN 929578)
83. Windsor Forest (RC RCIN 929579)
84. Wolterton (BoL MSGD a4 fo.56)
85. Wolterton (BoL MSGD a4 fo.10)
86. Wolterton (BoL MSGD a4 fo.55)
87. Wolterton (BoL MSGD a4 fo.61)
88. Wolterton (BoL MSGD a3 fo.18)
89. Wolterton (BoL MSGD a4 fo.20)

APPENDIX III: BRIDGEMAN'S PROJECTS BY YEAR

THE PURPOSE OF the table is to present some indication of Bridgeman's workload by year, albeit partly estimated. In general, the evidence used for this is in estate accounts or bank accounts, although sometimes it is correspondence in which he is mentioned. X is used to show sites where there is dateable evidence. Since only the years for which there is documentary evidence are included, there are often empty cells interposed into what is a long period of documented work at a site. This does not necessarily mean that Bridgeman interrupted his work at the site; it simply means there is no documentary evidence for his presence during this particular year. At the bottom of the table, ✓ indicates probable dates for those significant sites where it is known that he worked but where there is no dateable documentary evidence for his involvement. Gunton and Scampston are omitted completely because there is no possibility of determining a date; so are minor and conjectural sites. *M* indicates sites where there is no evidence of a plan, but there are regular quarterly payments over a long period suggesting a maintenance contract only. I have included Bridgeman's work as Royal Gardener in this category, in addition to his design work at Kensington Gardens.

Year	Warwick Priory	Wroxhall Manor	Sacombe	Stowe	Claremont	Carshalton	Purley	Down Hall	Briggens	Wimpole	Kedleston	Cliveden	Wolterton	King's College	Marble Hill	Lodge Park	Montagu House M	Twickenham	Richmond	Kensington Palace	St James's Palace	Chicheley	Shardeloes
1738																							
1737													×										
1736																							
1735																				×			
1734																							
1733																							
1732																							
1731																		×	×				
1730											×							×		×	×		
1729											×		×			×	×			×	×		
1728													×	×	×		×			×	×		
1727															×		×	×		×	×		
1726				×				×		×							×	×		×	×	×	×
1725				×						×						×	×	×	×				
1724								×		×			×	×	×								
1723				×				×				×											
1722			×					×		×	×												
1721				×			×	×	×	×													
1720			×	×		×		×	×														
1719																							
1718			×		×																		
1717			×	×																			
1716			×	×																			
1715			×	×																			
1714		×		×																			
1713		×		×																			
1712		×		×																			
1711	×	×		×																			

Year	Compton Place M	St James's Park	Boughton	Bower House	Amesbury	Houghton	Wimbledon	Ledston	Standlynch	Badminton	Esher	Brocket	Dallington House	Goldings	Longford	Royal Gardener M	Claremont	Eastbury	Gobions	Hackwood	Moor Park	Purley	Rousham	Tring
1738	X				X											X								
1737	X														X	X								
1736	X															X								
1735	X												X	X		X								
1734	X										X	X				X								
1733	X									X						X								
1732	X						X	X	X							X								
1731	X				X	X	X									X								
1730	X				X											X								
1729	X		X	X												X								
1728	X	X	X													X	✓		✓					
1727																X	✓	✓	✓					
1726	X															X	✓	✓	✓					
1725																	✓	✓	✓	✓	✓		✓	✓
1724																	✓	✓	✓	✓			✓	
1723																	✓	✓	✓			✓	✓	
1722																	✓		✓			✓	✓	
1721																	✓					✓	✓	
1720															✓								✓	
1719																								
1718																								
1717																								
1716																								
1715																								
1714																								
1713																								
1712																								
1711																								

APPENDIX IV: BRIDGEMAN'S INCOME

THE TABLE BELOW shows the data which it has been possible to piece together regarding Bridgeman's income. The information presented comes from a variety of sources: from *Charles Bridgeman and the English Landscape Garden*, from the archive of the Office of Works, Work 6/114 (which deals with the reshaping of Kensington Gardens), from the yearly abstract of the Office of Works (Work 5/57, 5/58 and 5/59 1726–1739) and from Nicky Smith's work on Lodge Park (Smith 2006). I have included all the payments made to Bridgeman from the Office of Works, except those between 1726 and 1728 made to him and Wise jointly, because it is not clear how the payments were divided. I have recorded Bridgeman's payment for the work at Kensington Gardens as a single payment, even though it was paid in instalments during the course of the work (Work 6/114).

Date	Income £.s.d	Bank	Site	Total for year £.s.d
1714	1.2.6		Stowe	1.2.6
1715 13 June	50.0.0	Hoare's Bank	Sacombe	
1715 2 July	30.0.0	Hoare's Bank	Sacombe	80.0.0
1716 16 June	60.0.0	Hoare's Bank	Sacombe	
1716 11 Aug	188.16.0		Stowe	
1716 16 Aug	20.0.0			
1716 12 Nov	75.5.0	Hoare's Bank		344.1.0
1717 23 May	75.5.0	Hoare's Bank		
1717 15 June	100.0.0	Hoare's Bank		
	150.0.0	Hoare's Bank	Sacombe	
1717 7 Sept	100.0.0	Hoare's Bank		575.5.0
	150.0.0	Hoare's Bank	Sacombe	

1718 4 Aug	214.0.3	Hoare's Bank	Sacombe	214.0.3	
1719	156.7.6		Langleys	156.7.6	
1720	122.11.0		Purley		
1720	534.0.0		Sacombe		
1720	22.0.0		Briggens	678.11.0	
1721	221.0.0		Down Hall		
1721	10.0.0		Dallington		
1721	5.13.0 13.0.0 21.0.0		Briggens		
1721	122.11.0		Purley		
1721 March	138.0.0		Briggens		
1721 March	1773.8.0		Carshalton	2304.12.0	
1722	10.0.0	Gosling's Bank	Dallington		
1722	400.0.0		Wimpole		
1722 14 Sept 10 Nov	1.1.0 51.11.0		Kedleston		
1722 15 Aug	69.10.2		Down Hall	532.2.2	
1724	1474.3.3	Williams and Glyn's Bank	Wimpole	1474.3.3	
1725	280.0.0		Wimpole		
1725	50.0.0		Montagu House	330.0.0	
1726 20 May	107.19.3	Hoare's Bank			
1726	126.3.3		Wimpole		
1726	5630.0.0		St James's Square Trustees		
1726	60.0.0		Kedleston		
1726	126.3.3		Wimpole		
1726	100.0.0		Montagu House		
1726	50.0.0		Shardeloes	6200.5.9	
1727	100.0.0		Montagu House	100.0.0	
1728 27 Jan 10 April	40.0.0 120.0.0		Compton Place		
1728	2220.0.0		Royal Gardener		
1728	140.0.0		Windsor Castle		
1728	100.0.0		Montagu House		
1728	6483.4.7¾		Richmond Park Lodge	9103.4.7¾	
1729	2220.0.0		Royal Gardener		
1729	140.0.0		Windsor Castle		

APPENDIX IV

1729	100.0.0	Montagu House	
1729	120.0.0	Compton Place	
1729 22 Dec	70.0.0	Lodge Park	
1729	2.3.4	St James's Park	
1729 June	1.10.0	Hampton Court	
Nov	1.5.0		
1729	140.0.0	Windsor Castle	
June	175.0.0		
1729	120.0.0	Compton Place	
1729	240.2.0	Fulham Road	3330.0.4
1730	2220.0.0	Royal Gardener	
1730	100.0.0	Montagu House	
1730	140.0.0	Windsor Castle	
1730 Feb	4.11.8	Hampton Court	
May	5.0.0	Gardens	
Dec	5.6.8		
1730 March	11.10	Richmond Old Lodge	
May	32.0.0		
Sept	14.6.8		
Nov	36.0.0		
1730	473.2.2	Hyde Park Wall	
1730	841.6.0	Hyde Park Road	
1730	248.16.2¼	Fulham Road	
1730	120.0.0	Compton Place	4251.19.4¼
1731	5000.0.0	Kensington Gardens	
1731	2220.0.0	Royal Gardener	
1731	140.0.0	Windsor Castle	
1731	100.0.0	Montagu House	
1731	120.0.0	Compton Place	
1731 27 March	5.19.6	Ledston	
5 April	21		
23 Oct	7.10.6		
1731 Jan	1.10.0		
March	73.14.8		
March	358.14.2		
May	0.12.8		
June	5.2.11		
	436.15		
Sept	169.12.10		
Dec	0.19.0		
	200.0.0		

Date	Amount	Place	Total
1731	2.10.0	Kensington	
1731 March	4.2.4	Richmond Hermitage	
July	4.1.9		
1731 March	36.5.1	Richmond Old Lodge	
June	24.8.7		
1731 June	2.7.6	Bushy Park	
1731 March	11.9.6	Hampton Court Gardens	
1731	100.0.0	Fulham Road	9046.16.0
1732	2220.0.0	Royal Gardener	
1732	140.0.0	Windsor Castle	
1732	120.0.0	Compton Place	
1732	483.7.0	Kensington Gardens	
1732 March	0.15.10	Kensington Gardens	
	14.7.3		
1732 June	77.14.1¾	Kensington	
Sept	2.1.2		
1732	68.19.7	Richmond Old Lodge	
1732 June	7.9.11	Hampton Court Gardens	3197.6.10¾
Sept	62.12.0		
Dec	11.14.4		
1733	2220.0.0	Royal Gardener	
1733	140.0.0	Windsor Castle	
1733	120.0.0	Compton Place	
1733	235.0.4	Kensington Gardens	
1733	4.8.11	Kensington	
1733	1.14.2	St James's Park	2721.3.5
1734	2220.0.0	Royal Gardener	
1734	140.0.0	Windsor Castle	
1734	120.0.0	Compton Place	
1734	52.10.0	Esher Place	
1734	11.13.4	Kensington	
	11.13.4		
	3.0.0		
1734 March	1.1.0	Kensington Gardens	
Nov	1280.10		
Dec	420.10.0		
	346.11.11		

APPENDIX IV

1734	16.3.9¼		Hampton Court Gardens	
1734	679.16.10		Hyde Park	
1734	20.15.10 10.17.6		St James's Park	5335.3.6¼
1735	2220.0.0		Royal Gardener	
1735	140.0.0		Windsor Castle	
1735	120.0.0		Compton Park	
1735	20.0.0	Goslings Bank	Dallington	
1735 March	97.6.4		Kensington Gardens	
1735 June Sept	2.1.2 31.6.5		Kensington	
1735 Sept	2.18.4		Richmond Old Lodge	
1735 June Dec	7.17.9 6.2.8½		Hampton Court	2647.12.8½
1736	2220.0.0		Royal Gardener	
1736	140.0.0		Windsor Castle	
1736	120.0.0		Compton Place	2480.0.0
1737	2220.0.0		Royal Gardener	
1737	140.0.0		Windsor Castle	
1737	120.0.0		Compton Place	
1737 June Sept	16.3.7 0.7.1		Hampton Court Gardens	
1737	343.10.0		King's Private Road	
1737 Nov	2.17.0		Kensington	
1737 Nov	0.12.8		Kensington Gardens	2843.10.4
1738	1133.14.2½		Royal Gardener	
1738	77.3.0		Windsor Castle	
1738	120.0.0		Compton Place	
1738	3.19.11½		Kensington	
1738	18.6.6½		King's Private Road	
1738	23.14.2½		St James's Park	1376.17.11
1748?	880.17.0		Wimbledon	

GAZETTEER OF BRIDGEMAN SITES

THIS GAZETTEER CONTAINS all the sites on which Bridgeman may have worked. For most, there is an Ordnance Survey grid reference, the principal geology and what has become of the site (accurate in November 2022). The catalogue numbers of all the plans attributed to Bridgeman in this book have been added, including the new additions to the catalogue.

Amesbury Abbey, Wiltshire

- Grid reference: SU 15097 41718
- Principal geology: Park to the east of the Avon, alluvium – clay, sand and gravel; to the west (Vespasian's Camp), chalk.
- Amesbury Abbey is now a private nursing home. The park to the west of the river Avon is owned by Sir Edward and Lady Antrobus.
- BoL MSGD a3* fo.32

Bridgeman's clients at Amesbury Abbey were the Duke and Duchess of Queensberry. Charles Douglas, Duke of Queensberry, married his cousin, Catherine Hyde. He inherited Amesbury Abbey in 1725. The Duke and Duchess were prominent in the court of George I. He remained at court following the accession of George II, but resigned his offices after George II banished his wife Catherine from Court because of her outrage at the refusal of a licence for John Gay's play *Polly*, which satirised Sir Robert Walpole. The Duke and Duchess of Queensberry moved in circles which included Pope, Prior and Swift. John Gay lived with them at Amesbury.

The house which the Duke of Queensberry inherited was designed by John Webb for the Marquess of Hertford in 1660. It was built on the same plot as the current, much larger house, with which it was replaced by Sir Edward Antrobus in 1834. The illustrations of the house drawn by Flitcroft, engraved by Kent and published in 1727 in *The Designs of Inigo Jones*, show a house in the style of Inigo Jones, the front elevation with nine bays and a pedimented portico, with two columns and two angle pillars (Willis 2002, plate 37a, Bold 1989, plates 63 and 64). To this structure, two wings to the east and west were added, to a design attributed to Flitcroft, to whom payments were made by the Duke of Queensberry between 1731 and 1740 (VCH 54). When the Duke of Queensberry inherited the house it was around 60 years old. Although strictly speaking the house was built before the popularity of Palladianism, Bold suggests that it 'is an elaboration of an early Palladio design, the Villa Godi at Lonedo (Bold 1989, 94) and that 'it had already inspired the first house of the neo-Palladian movement and Inigo Jones revival, William Benson's Wilbury'. This may account for the undocumented, but clearly verifiable decision of the Duke of Queensberry to extend the house rather than rebuild it.

Bridgeman's design was preceded by a survey taken in 1726 by Flitcroft which shows the demesne lands in detail (WRO 944/1). Bridgeman's design is held at the Bodleian Library in the Gough Collection catalogued as MSGD a3* fo.32. It is in ink, pencil and watercolour, signed by Bridgeman and dated 1738. The plan depicts, on the east of the river Avon, a double avenue running south to the church, the medieval canal (also shown on the Flitcroft survey), walks following the natural course of the river, asymmetric rectilinear plantations of trees to the south of the house and a kite-shaped kitchen garden. To the west of the river, the Iron Age hill fort, Vespasian's Camp, is incorporated in the design. On a cliff above the river, the plan shows diamond shaped earthworks, Gay's Cave cut into the cliff and above, rising terraces culminating in a circular cabinet at the centre of which is an octagonal building. There is also documentary evidence, through letters between the Duchess of Queensberry and John Gay, and Henrietta Howard, Countess of Suffolk, that Bridgeman was involved at Amesbury (Burgess 1966, 96). Sir Howard Colvin has also suggested that MS Maps, Misc.a.1 may also be a plan for Amesbury. The former park is divided in ownership between the Antrobus family and the private nursing home.

Audley End, Essex

- Grid reference: TL 52464 38167
- Principal geology: Chalk, and clay, silt and sand alluvium.
- The house and grounds are now owned by Historic England.
- BoL MSGD a4 fo.60
- BoL MSGD a4 fo.67

Audley End was built between 1605 and 1614 for Thomas Howard, 1st Earl of Suffolk, Lord Treasurer to James I. In the mid-eighteenth century, when the landscape attributed to Bridgeman was designed, it was owned by Charles Howard, 9th Earl of Suffolk, husband of Henrietta Howard, for whom it is likely that Bridgeman designed a garden at Marble Hill.

The house for which the landscape was designed was the second house to be built precisely on the footprint of the cloister of Walden Abbey (http://list.english-heritage.org.uk). It was built to a U-shaped plan in three storeys, with mullioned windows and parapets to hide the roof line. It was sold to Charles II in 1668, and Sir Christopher Wren did extensive work on the house. It was returned to the Howards in 1701 and Sir John Vanbrugh was commissioned to make improvements, resulting in the demolition of the decaying outer court in 1721. Further demolition was carried out in 1752. It has largely retained its seventeenth-century character although with significant adaptations. A late sixteenth-century stable block of red brick with gabled wings lies 300 m to the north-west of Audley House (Pevsner and Bettley 2007).

Formal gardens were originally laid out c.1615. Development of the park took place in the early and mid-eighteenth century, when both Lancelot Brown and Richard Woods worked on the pleasure grounds. Robert Adam designed ornamental garden buildings, and there is a 52 m vine house. The formal parterre dates from 1831. The site covers approximately 240 hectares and has now been partly returned to agricultural use (http://www.parksandgardens.org).

Two Bridgemanic plans for the landscape exist in the Gough Collection at the Bodleian Library, catalogued as MSGD a4 fo.60 and MSGD a4 fo.67. MSGD a4 fo.67 is in ink and watercolour. MSGD a4 fo.60 is in pencil. Neither is signed by Bridgeman. Willis suggests that the two plans might also be connected to a visit made by Dubois to Charles Howard at Audley End in 1726 (Willis 2002, 64 n. 107). It is not clear what alterations were to be made.

Badminton, Gloucestershire

- Grid reference: ST 80603 82848
- Principal geology: Fuller's Earth formation, limestone.
- The house is privately owned by the Duke of Beaufort.

The title of Duke of Beaufort was held from 1726 to 1745 by Henry Somerset. He was responsible for extensive remodelling of the house and park. He was, like his father, a staunch Tory (http://www.oxforddnb.com).

The house was built between 1664 and 1691 by Henry, 1st Duke of Beaufort, possibly to his own design. It is shown in Kip and Knyff's engraving c.1710. This shows the north front flanked by wings three bays long from which extend low projections northwards (Verey and Brooks 1999, 381). The north range was twice as long as that of the previous house, and, while the east range was largely new, the south range and part of the west range were retained from the earlier house. The 3rd Duke was responsible for extensively remodelling the house, reducing the north front to three storeys, and the rebuilding of the west range. The work was done by Francis Smith of Warwick. Gibbs was also consulted between 1730 and 1735. The 3rd Duke also began the process of deformalising the gardens with the advice of Bridgeman. Kent worked on both house and garden for the 4th Duke, but not until 1745–50, after Bridgeman's death (Verey and Brooks 1999, 380).

The vast formal avenues shown in Kip and Knyff were probably designed by John Mansfield with a formal parterre influenced by Henry Wise around the house (http://list.english-heritage.org.uk). Evidence of Bridgeman's involvement in the landscape comes in four letters written to the 4th Duke when he was Lord Noel Somerset. These letters suggest that Bridgeman had produced a plan for Badminton. A letter from the Duchess on 11 March 1733/34 states that 'The draught Bridgeman sent down for Badminton is one of the Grandest things I have seen, and will I believe answer in execution as well as it does upon paper ...' (Willis 2002, 427) which suggests that, at the very least, Bridgeman provided some kind of design for the landscape, even if he did not personally supervise its execution. Letters from 17 March and 30 March support his involvement at least at the planning stage of the landscape: on 17 March, the 3rd Duke of Beaufort writes 'Pray put Bridgeman in mind yt ye Temple is broader than the Plan of ye House he put into ye Design which he left here', and on 30 March he wrote 'pray send ye Plans of ye Ground Plots of ye Houses from Bridgeman as soon as you can for I want 'em sadly' (Willis 2002, 426).

A drawing and a painting by Wootton show a landscape of Bridgeman-style planting (Willis 2002, plates 86 and 87). Kent was commissioned by the 4th Duke to simplify the landscape, and Thomas Wright designed various garden buildings.

Blenheim Palace, Oxfordshire

- Grid reference: SP 44105 16092
- Principal geology: Hanborough sand and gravel member, limestone.
- The house and estate are privately owned by Duke and Duchess of Marlborough.
- A plan for the landscape hangs in Blenheim Palace.

Blenheim Palace, designed by Sir John Vanbrugh (assisted by Nicholas Hawksmoor), was built between 1705 and 1722 for the Duke of Marlborough as a reward for his services to Queen Anne in defeating the French. The house was designed by Sir John Vanbrugh and Nicholas Hawksmoor and rivals the Baroque Palaces of Europe in size and splendour. Externally it has four corner towers, and the north front has a nine-bay central façade. The interiors were worked on by many prominent artists of the period, including Sir James Thornhill and Grinling Gibbons.

Bridgeman's involvement seems likely solely to have been in drawing the map of Blenheim which is currently held at Blenheim Palace. Henry Wise worked at Blenheim from 1705, and perhaps the drawing was executed for him, or for Vanbrugh himself. 'A Plann of Blenheim' is held at Blenheim Palace, signed '1709/ Bridgman Discript'. Wise worked at Blenheim between 1704 and 1716. Green suggests that Wise was employed not only to lay out the gardens but also to

GAZETTEER OF BRIDGEMAN SITES 193

dig the foundations of the house, using the following quotation as evidence: 'men were instantly set to work under ye Conduct of one Mr Wise to open ye Ground, cut down Trees etc. in order to ye laying the foundation' (Green 1956, 97). The date 1709 is the earliest on any of Bridgeman's work. Although Willis suggests that Sarah Churchill's correspondence dealing with a dispute between her and Bridgeman's widow after Bridgeman's death involved work at Blenheim, it is much more likely that the site discussed is Wimbledon rather than Blenheim (Willis 2002, 46–47).

Boughton House, Northamptonshire

- Grid reference: SP 90127 81539
- Principal geology: Alluvium (in the river valley), Northampton Sand Formation Ironstone and Whitby Mudstone Formation elsewhere.
- The house and estate are privately owned by the Duke of Buccleugh.
- Two plans and a bird's-eye view hang in Boughton House.

John Montagu, 2nd Duke of Montagu (1690–1749), created the gardens at Boughton House. He inherited the title in 1709. He married Mary Churchill, the fourth and youngest daughter of John and Sarah Churchill, the Duke and Duchess of Marlborough, and held many high offices under George I and George II from 1705 until his death. He was a fellow of the Royal Society. His London residence, Montagu House, became the site of the British Museum.

A house has stood on the site of the present house since c.1500. Substantial work done on the north front of the house by the 1st Duke between 1683 and 1709 has largely obscured the original house. Behind the façade there are significant remains of the original house, which had a simple north front, an oblong west court and principal ranges around smaller east courts. At this time a new north front was erected with pavilions to the north-east and north-west. The north façade is, Pevsner suggests, 'the most French looking C17 building in Britain' (Pevsner and Cherry 1973, 112). The Duke had been an ambassador to Paris from 1669 to 1672 and was appointed to the post again in 1678–1679. Service buildings were constructed in the very early part of the eighteenth century and a detached kitchen was added in 1735 (http://www.heritagegateway.org.uk).

Three drawings attributed by Willis to Bridgeman, dated between 1725 and 1731, are held at Boughton House. The gardens, designed by Van De Meulen and Gabriel Delahaye (Willis 2002, 55), were laid out for the 2nd Duke in the seventeenth century, and consist of a formal landscape with waterworks and canal, using the river Ise which flows from north to south across the site. Plans of the original landscape are in the Bodleian Library catalogued MSGD a4 fo.84, MS Maps Northants a1, and in the National Archives MPHH 1/24, all dated 1712. This layout had clearly been modified by 1725, the date of what Willis calls a 'Bridgemanic bird's eye perspective' (Willis 2002, 55). This drawing shows a broad axial avenue leading to a bowling green and flanked by other avenues, and a wilderness with geometric planting. Direct evidence of Bridgeman's involvement exists in the correspondence of Charles Lamotte, the Duke's steward. Bridgeman was expected at Boughton on 15 September 1729. It seems likely that Switzer was also involved. He was paid £5.1s.6d for seeds 16 March 1730.

Bower House, Havering-atte-Bower, Essex

- Grid reference: TQ 51270 92748
- Principal geology: Stanmore Gravel Formation surrounded by Bagshot Formation Sand.
- Bower House is used as a Christian Training Centre.

The Bower House (1729) was the first commission of Henry Flitcroft (www.havering.gov.uk). It was built by John Baynes, Sergeant-at-law. Willis suggests that Thornhill was responsible for the paintings in the stairwell. It would appear, from the plaque over the door, which reads 'H.FLITCROFT. ARCHITECTUS. C.BRIDGEMAN. DESIGNAVIT', that Bridgeman designed the landscape at Bower House. There are no plans or documentary evidence to support this.

Briggens, Hertfordshire

- Grid reference: TL 41404 11235
- Principal geology: Head (clay, silt and gravel) – and glaciofluvial deposits (sand and gravel).
- Briggens is now a hotel run by Hotelmix.

The house was built c.1719 by the Master Mason Christopher Cass (1678–1734) for Sir Robert Chester, who was a director of the South Sea Company. It has been much altered, first c.1770 by the addition of two-bay North and South blocks and a second floor, and then again in 1899 and 1908.

Bridgeman's involvement seems to have been in designing a landscape in the park, although there is no plan. An estate plan dated 1781 (D/eh p14) shows a landscape which contains an amphitheatre, a canal and a round basin, all distinctively Bridgemanic. Estate accounts indicate that Bridgeman was allocated £21 and an additional £13 for trees (Willis 2002, 62 n. 97). Carpenter provided plants for Bridgeman for Briggens (Willis 33 n. 41).

Brocket Hall, Hertfordshire

- Grid reference: TL 21427 13022
- Principal geology: to the south, chalk, to the north of which is an area of clay-with-flints Formation, and further north Kesgrave Catchment sub-group, sand and gravel.
- Brocket Park is owned on a long leasehold by Club Corporation of Asia and is run as a hotel and golfing venue.

GAZETTEER OF BRIDGEMAN SITES

- BoL MSGD a3 fo.7
- BoL MSGD a4 fo.40

Thomas Winnington, who owned the estate in the early to mid-eighteenth century, was born in 1696. He married Love Reade in 1719 and came into the possession of Brocket Hall, Hertfordshire, through her. He was from a Tory family, and at first supported the opposition, but from 1729 he served in Walpole's government. He retained his political appointment after Walpole's fall. After his death, a pamphlet linked him to the Jacobite interest, but this was strenuously denied by his friends (http://www.oxforddnb.com).

There are few details of the house prior to its rebuilding in 1752 by James Paine. In 1700 the Brocket estate was described thus: 'Brocket Hall was the ancient seat of the Brockets situated upon a dry hill in a fair park, well wooded and greatly timber'd enclosed with a brick wall on the west side of the road for the length of a mile and plentifully watered with the River Lea' (Chauncy 1700). A plan of 1752 (HALS) shows that the old Manor House stood to the north of an adjoining walled garden containing serpentine paths. The park and garden were redesigned by Richard Woods c.1760.

Two plans for Brocket Hall, catalogued as MSGD a3 fo.7 and MSGD a4 fo.40, are in the Bodleian Library, and are attributed to Bridgeman. Although in some ways uncharacteristic of Bridgeman's work, MSGD a3 fo.7 has strong similarities with Bridgeman's signed plan for Hampton Court in the depiction of the fields on the edges of the park (SM, Drawer 36.3.1). Interestingly, MSGD a4 fo.40, although clearly based on MSGDa3 fo.7, appears to offer a considerably simplified version of the landscape. There is further evidence in a letter from Lord Hervey to Stephen Fox dated 10 August 1734 which refers to 'the execution of "my friend Winnington's commissions" including "giving the plan to Bridgeman"' (BL Add MS 51345 (Holland House Papers) fos.63r–64v). Forty guineas were also paid to Bridgeman's widow on 14 June 14 1739 (C. Hoare and Co., Bankers Ledger O). It seems unlikely that Winnington implemented the plan in its entirety. He appears to have planted only the blocks of woodland to the east and south sides of the park, a framing vista towards the Lemsford Mill entrance, and the fields to the west which were decorated with circular copses. He also seems to have constructed a kitchen garden to the north-east, an arbour and two square buildings on the corners nearest the river Lea (Gatland 2007, 117). (See Chapter 3 for further discussion of these plans.)

Carshalton House, Surrey

- Grid reference: TQ 27719 64424
- Principal geology: to the north, Hackney Gravel member, to the south, Chalk Formation.
- Now part of St Philomena's Catholic School.

The mansion at Carshalton was built between c.1685 and c.1700 for a tobacco merchant, Edward Carleton, probably incorporating earlier material from a pre-existing building. It was bought by John Fellowes, sub-Governor and a Director of the South Sea Company, in 1716. He made substantial alterations to Carleton's house, including the addition of a third storey to replace the existing attic and dormer windows. The house is built of brown brick and has a hipped slate roof.

Bridgeman had been paid substantial sums of money by Fellowes by March 1721, comparable in amount to that paid to him for work at Sacombe, suggesting substantial involvement (Skelton 2017, 27). However, there is little archaeological evidence of what he designed, and, to date, no plan. There is evidence that, in 1720, Joseph Carpenter supplied trees to Fellowes and that work was also done on the estate by John Mist and George Devall (Skelton 2017, 29).

Claremont, Surrey

- Grid reference: TQ 13486 63482
- Principal geology: Bagshot formation, sand.
- Claremont is now used as a school.
- SM 62/1/2

Bridgeman's client at Claremont was Thomas Pelham-Holles, 1693–1768. Very wealthy from two inheritances in 1711 and 1712, he was a fervent Whig, a member of both the Kit-Kat Club and the Hanover Club, and as such found favour with George I, who raised him to the peerage as Viscount Houghton and the Earl of Clare. In 1715 he was created Duke of Newcastle upon Tyne. He became the third most influential minister in the Whig government after Walpole and Townshend (http://www.oxforddnb.com).

Vanbrugh bought the land upon which the present house stands in 1708 and built a house and walled garden, both of which he crenelated. He sold the estate to the Duke of Newcastle in 1714 and was commissioned to extend the house by adding two wings on arcaded basements, replacing the battlements with a pediment, and to build a Belvedere, in all probability inspired by Elizabethan and Jacobean architecture, on an adjoining knoll (Worsley 1995, 188). A 100-ft, two-storey room was added in 1719–1720. This house was demolished when the estate was sold in 1768 to Lord Clive. Although one fireplace by Vanbrugh survives in the current house, more of Vanbrugh's work survives in the gardens. The Belvedere, which stands on a hillock to the west of the house, was designed by him for Newcastle. It is built of brick with four square towers. The building is of two storeys, the towers three. The White Cottage is also by Vanbrugh (Nairn, Pevsner and Cherry 1971, 161).

Bridgeman's contribution to the landscape was the amphitheatre and the round pond, to the south-west of the house and Belvedere. Two possible designs exist, both attributed to Bridgeman by Willis (Willis 2002, 49 and 427). A4 fo.81

in the Bodleian Library is catalogued as unidentified, but Willis records the suggestion of John Harris that it is a preliminary design for Claremont. It is a drawing in pen and ink, with some watercolour, showing the house and two avenues, both of which start at the house and fan out to make a triangle. The more southerly of the two is axially aligned to the Belvedere. Although showing the bowling greens to the west of the Belvedere, this drawing depicts neither the round pond nor the amphitheatre (see Chapter 3 for discussion of this drawing). The other drawing attributed to Bridgeman, and much more plausibly his, is in the Sir John Soane Museum, 39 Drawer 62/1/2. It shows the amphitheatre and round pond, in pen, ink and wash. A very similar design appears in Switzer's *Introduction to a General System of Hydrostaticks and Hydraulicks* of 1729. Switzer indentifies this design as Bridgeman's, although there are significant differences between the designs (Willis 2002, 49). An engraving by Roque and Benazech of 1754 shows the amphitheatre and the pond, enlarged and embellished with an island by Kent.

Cliveden, Berkshire

- Grid reference: SU 91017 85186
- Principal geology: Gerrards Cross Gravel.
- National Trust.

Documentary evidence suggests that in 1723 Bridgeman was working on a major design for the Earl of Orkney at Cliveden. It is likely that Bridgeman was responsible for the amphitheatre to the north-west of the house on the precipitous slope that borders the Thames. In a letter written on 2 October 1723, the Earl outlines the difficulties the dramatic site at Cliveden was posing: 'I must do the best I can but it is a greater work than I thought but I still think it will be much better than was Intended (but the Amphitheatre is quite struck out) wher[e] to get turfe and trees for la grand [sic] machine, beside ther[e] is great difficulty to get the slope all that side of the hill where the precipsce was, but Bridgeman mackes difficultys of nothing[.] I told him that if I had thought [it] had been the one Half of what I see it will cost, I believe I never had done it, he says the beginning is the worst' (Fraser Collection MS 1033). 'La grand machine' is almost certainly a metaphorical reference to the earthworks required in the construction of the amphitheatre, and not, as Willis suggests, a 'hydraulic machine later abandoned' (Willis 2002, 427). The amphitheatre, shown in a plan c.1723 (National Trust Yearbook 1994, 52), is characteristic of Bridgeman's work, although it is unlikely that the plan is by him. It is more likely that Bridgeman is responsible for the design showing the parterres to the south of the house (National Trust Yearbook 1994, 51).

Compton Place, East Sussex

- Grid reference: TV 60290 98586
- Principal geology: Lewes Nodular Chalk Formation.
- Compton Place is a language school.

Compton Place, near Eastbourne, was acquired by James Burton in 1544. It is likely that he was the builder of the Elizabethan mansion which became incorporated into the building remodelled in 1724 by Colen Campbell for Spencer Compton, the younger son of the Earl of Northampton (historicengland.org.uk/listing).

Bridgeman seems to have worked at Compton Place in Sussex from 1728 for Spencer Compton, 1st Earl of Wilmington. He was paid £120 every year for the following ten years. It is not clear what these payments were for, although their regularity suggests a maintenance contract.

Dallington Hall, Northamptonshire/The Rolls House

- Grid reference for Dallington Hall: SP 73708 61809
- Principle Geology: Northampton Sand Formation.

In 1722 Bridgeman was employed in some capacity by Sir Joseph Jekyll, Master of the Rolls. The work was either at Dallington Hall in Northamptonshire, or The Rolls House in London. He was paid £10 from Jeykll's account with Gosling's Bank on 17 March 1722. There is also another small payment of £20 to Bridgeman, by Sir Joseph Jekyll, from his account at Goslings Bank on 31 May 1735 (Willis 2002, 428).

Dawley, Middlesex

- Grid reference: TQ 08025 77098
- Principal geology: clay and silt.

Dawley was the seat of Henry St John, Viscount Bolingbroke. James Gibbs worked on the house. It was demolished c.1770. The site is very close to the northern perimeter of Heathrow Airport.

There is documentary evidence that Bridgeman worked, in some capacity, at Dawley in 1725. Willis cites a letter from Pope to Bridgeman which suggests that Bridgeman and Bolingbroke were in communication, and that this indicates that Bridgeman was in some way involved at Dawley: 'My Lord Bolingbroke received yours and shall be glad to see you at your earliest conveniency' (Willis 2002, 79). Willis does not, however, give any reference for this letter.

Donington Park, Leicestershire

- Grid reference: SK 42060 26894
- Principal geology: very complicated geologically, but a combination of Helsby sandstone and Helsby mudstone.

GAZETTEER OF BRIDGEMAN SITES 199

Originally a deer park, formally created in 1229, Donington Park was, at the Dissolution, granted to the Grays of Langley who built a Lodge there. On acquiring the park in 1595, Sir George Hasting of Gopsall built a stone hall around which a garden was laid out. Repton carried out work on the pleasure ground in the 1790s (www.heritagegateway.org.uk).

Camilla Beresford has correctly identified MSGD a4 fo.33 and fo.43, from Gough Drawings, as plans for Donington Park (http://www.treeandwoodland.co.uk/unidentified-map-discovery-donington-park). It is likely that Willis includes them in his corpus because they are part of Gough Drawings. Although there are some stylistic resemblances to Bridgeman's work, it is not clear that either plan is his, although the landscape may be.

Down Hall, Essex

- Grid reference: TL 52189 13073
- Principal soils: Head – clay, silt, sand and gravel.
- Down Hall is now a hotel.
- BoL Gough Maps 46 fo.262.
- BL Add MS 70371.
- MSGD a4 fo.29.

Matthew Prior (1664–1721) was the son of a joiner from Dorset. He attended Westminster School for a period before his father died, and then again under the patronage of Charles Sackville, Earl of Dorset. A poet and diplomat, he conducted secret negotiations with the French in 1711 at the behest of Robert Harley, Earl of Oxford. Harley's son, Edward Harley, provided half the purchase price for Down Hall, on the condition that the house would revert to him on Prior's death. Down Hall was bought in 1720. The plan was to demolish the old house and to rebuild it to a design by Gibbs. It appears that, because of Prior's death in 1721, this was not done and the old house was finally demolished and rebuilt in 1871.

There are two plans for Down Hall. The first, Gough Maps 46 fo.262, is in the Bodleian Library. The second, inscribed with the words 'Copy of the first (?) Plan for Down Hall', is in the British Library, BL Loan 29/357. Both show a *patte d'oie* axially aligned to the house, extending from a lawn in front of it. Connecting these three avenues are serpentine paths leading to cabinets containing basins. The central avenue terminates in an octagonal basin. On either side of the house is a formal parterre. The house shown is entirely consistent with the engraving entitled 'Down. Entrance Front. Engraving from Gibbs, *A Book of Architecture* (1728) pl. 55' (Willis 2002, pl. 66a).

There is considerable documentary evidence that Bridgeman was asked by Prior to redesign the landscape. Letters to Edward Harley (HMC 58 Bath III) and to Lord Chesterfield (Willis 2002, 74), dated between September 1720 and Prior's death on 18 September 1721, detail the progress of Bridgeman's work. After Prior's death, Bridgeman continued to be paid for work at Down Hall until August

15 1722, when 'the Balance of his Account No 106 £69.10.2d' was settled (Add MS 70362). In tandem with his work at Down Hall, Bridgeman was also working directly for Edward Harley at Wimpole, his presence there documented in a letter of Prior to Edward Harley in March 1721, and in a poem *Hue and Cry*, reputedly by Thornhill, about the trip taken by Bridgeman, Gibbs, Wootton and Thornhill to Wimpole in 1721. Bridgeman also visited the Library at Wimpole in 1721 and 1725 (Willis 2002, 69). Edward Harley's MS Accounts in Child's Branch of Williams and Glyn's Bank Ltd, London, show substantial payments to Bridgeman in the years after Prior's death: £221 in 1721, £400 in 1722, £470 in 1723, £1474.3s.3d in 1724 and £280 in 1725. These payments may be for Down Hall or for Wimpole; it is not clear which.

Eastbury House, Dorset

- Grid reference: ST 93228 12661
- Principal soils: Seaford chalk formation.
- BoL MSGD a3* fo.9.
- BoL MSGD a3*fo.10.
- BoL MSGD a4 fo.21.

Eastbury House was begun by George Dodington, a highly successful financier and contractor in the service of William III. The house was designed by Vanbrugh in 1718. However, Bridgeman's client for the landscaping of the park was Dodington's nephew, George Bubb Dodington, who inherited Eastbury in 1720. Bubb Dodington entered parliament for his uncle's seat, Winchelsea, in 1715. In the Whig split of 1717, he identified himself with Walpole and Townshend. In 1740, Bubb Dodington finally broke with Walpole.

Vanbrugh's design for the house at Eastbury was initially commissioned by George Dodington. It was, in size, second only to Castle Howard and Blenheim (Willis 2002, 47). Vanbrugh's first design for the house (1716) was published by Campbell in *Vitruvius Britannicus* (1717). In this design Vanbrugh experimented with a free-standing portico (Worsley 1995, 93). The design, which was begun in 1718, had rusticated columns and was in sombre greensand ashlar (Worsley 1995, 100; Newman and Pevsner 1972, 192). Five engravings of the house appear in *Vitruvius Britannicus III* Pl.17 (1725) including engravings of the Temple (pl. 18) and the Bagnio (pl. 19). The house was finished in 1738. Only the stable block of the house and a gateway survive. In 1762 Earl Temple demolished a large part of the house with dynamite.

The Bodleian Library holds three drawings of Eastbury, MSGD a3* fo.9, MSGD a3 fo.10 and MSGD a4 fo.21. In *Vitruvius Britannicus III* Campbell shows, in pl. 15, a layout of the grounds described as 'an exact Plan of the Gardens, designed and finished by the ingenious Mr *Charles Bridgeman*' (Willis 2002, pl. 26). It is unclear whether Bridgeman's client for the design of the landscape was initially

George Dodington or his nephew. Work on the house stopped on the death, in 1720, of George Dodington, and was not restarted until 1724. The date of *Vitruvius Britannicus III* (1725) in which the engraving of the garden appears does not clarify this one way or the other. However, since the majority of the work on the house and landscape was executed for George Bubb Dodington, it is plausible to suggest that he was Bridgeman's client. Two of the three drawings in the Bodleian, MSGDa3* fo.9 and MSGD a3*fo.10, are of very similar design. Both show a series of formal geometric parterres, axially aligned to the house and culminating in an amphitheatre to the east of the house. To the south a mount is shown. Both show the wider park arranged in rectilinear enclosures surrounded by square plantations of trees. MSGD a4 fo.21 shows only the parterres, and offers what appears to be two versions of the same parterre by way of a curious arrangement of a flap of paper that can be lifted. A survey published in RCHME: Dorset, IV (1972) p. 92 shows that the earthworks for the parterres are still visible (Willis 2002, pl. 27).

Esher Place, Surrey

- Grid reference: TQ 13390 64868
- Principal geology: London Clay and Bagshot sand.

Willis suggests that Bridgeman worked at Esher Place for Henry Pelham, brother of Thomas Pelham–Holles, 1st Duke of Newcastle, for whom he had worked at Claremont in the same parish. He was paid £52.10s on 17 March 1735 from Pelham's account at Hoare's Bank (Willis 2002, 428). The house at Esher was remodelled by Kent from 1729. Rocque's survey of 1737 shows the house with its surrounding landscape. There is no obvious indication that this is a Bridgeman design, although the sum paid would be consistent with payment for a design (see Lodge Park). Perhaps the payment was for the supply of plants or labourers.

Gobions, Hertfordshire

- Grid reference: TL25290 03816
- Principal geology: Lambeth group clay, silt and sand, in the valley of the brook; London Clay formation elsewhere.
- The house was demolished in the 1840s.
- BoL Herts Map a1.

Gobions was the property of the More family from c.1390. It was sold in 1693 to Richard Beachcroft, from whom Jeremy Sambrooke bought it. Sambrooke made his fortune in the East India Company, and acceded to a baronetcy on the death of his nephew in 1740. He employed James Gibbs to remodel aspects of the house, and to design buildings for the garden (Friedman 1984, 301). The house was demolished when the Gobions estate was bought by Robert Gaussen, who owned neighbouring Brookmans Park, in 1836.

The garden at Gobions is detached from the house, in the valley of a tributary of Mimshall Brook. It was reached by an avenue running south-east from the house. There is extensive cartographic, documentary, pictorial and earthwork evidence of the landscape at Gobions. Earthworks in the valley, although rather degraded, echo to a very large degree a recently discovered map (Gough Maps Herts a1), which is discussed in great and helpful detail by Anne Rowe and Tom Williamson in 'New Light on Gobions' (Rowe and Williamson 2012) and which can be attributed to Bridgeman. Dury and Andrews's map of Hertfordshire (1766) and plans of the estate from 1815 (HALS 34137), 1833 (HALS 66507) and 1836 (HALS 34188), and the Tithe map from 1844 (DSA4/62/2), also show a very similar landscape, although degrading over time. There are also two written records. George Bickham described it in his appendix to *The Beauties of Stow* (1750) and William Toldervy describes the landscape in great detail in an extended paragraph in *England and Wales described in a series of Letters* (1762). Jean Baptiste Chatelain produced two engravings, one of the Bowling Green, and one of the Canal and Temple, in 1748, and a drawing of the Grotto entitled 'Gubbins Park – In the Woods' (HALS North M.27) was executed in 1814. There are also prints of the house and of the Folly Arch in the Gerish Collection (DE/GR/56/2/9). It is also possible to see the remains of the grotto and the site of the cascade. In addition, LIDAR (2 m resolution: https://www.geomatics-group.co.uk) shows an avenue running south-west from the site of the house, an avenue south to the Folly Arch and a rectangular basin to the north of the wood.

Bridgeman has been widely credited with designing the landscape for Gobions (Willis 2001, 428; Friedman 1984, 301; HALS 34418; www.heritagegateway.org). The evidence for this seems to have its origins in Walpole's representation of Bridgeman's work there as 'the dawn of modern taste', and the Bridgemanic features depicted in a survey of the estate by Thomas Holmes. Willis adds Gobions, or Gubbins, in his catalogue of additional documents, drawings and attributions in the 2002 reprint of *Charles Bridgeman and the English Landscape Garden*, siting the Holmes map and the 1815 map of the estate in the Hertfordshire Archive (HALS 34137) in which the landscape is described as 'done by Bridgeman'.

Goldings, Hertfordshire

- Grid reference: TL 30925 14070
- Principal geology: Clay sand and silt.
- Goldings is currently divided into flats, and with considerable new building in the vicinity of the house.

The estate at Goldings was inherited by Thomas Hall, a London merchant, in 1731. He employed Henry Flitcroft to make extensive alterations, and, although no plan exists, it is clear from letters that Bridgeman was also engaged to remodel the landscape at some point between 1731 and 1738, probably around 1735. The house that Thomas Hall owned was demolished in the nineteenth century and it is unclear how much of the existing landscape is Bridgeman's.

Great Saxham Hall, Suffolk

- Grid reference: TL 79081 62710
- Principal geology: Lowestoft formation – Diamicton.
- Currently privately owned by Colonel Gordon Lennox.
- BoL MSGD a3 fo.41.

The estate at Great Saxham in Suffolk was bought from the estates of Bury St Edmunds Abbey by Sir Richard Long, who sold it to John Eldred (1552–1632), a Levant merchant and traveller. He built a hall which was demolished in 1774, and the current house was originally designed by Mure, and finished, after his bankruptcy, by Joseph Patience (Smith 2011). During the period in which Bridgeman was working, the estate was owned by Sir John Eldred.

A survey of 1729 records the house and garden. It shows an outer court to the north of the house, and a garden to the immediate south, with an orchard enclosed to the south and partially to the west and east by a narrow moat (IRO t4/33/1.24). In the wider landscape, to the south, a *patte d'oie* of avenues extends out through fields. The Tithe map of 1839, which records the slightly altered position and orientation of the hall, shows none of these features, consistent with the suggestion, made in the diary of a subsequent owner, Thomas Mills, that Mure remodelled the landscape, with the involvement of Lancelot Brown (B ST Ed RO MR11B.P15 Ts/1).

Evidence of Bridgeman's involvement is found in a plan in the Gough Collection, MSGD a3 fo.41, which shows the hall and adjacent gardens, clearly recognisable by the moat, with Bridgeman's pencil annotations for what appears to be redesigning the landscape with serpentine paths and cabinets. A note in what appears to be Bridgeman's hand reads: 'For John Eldred Esq[ui]re to be left at The Ram at Newmarket 22 fruit trees to be sent next week as concluded by particulars Bury Carrier at ye Bull Inn Bishops Gate B.' It is not clear whether any of these proposals were ever carried out.

Greenwich Park

- Grid reference (taken from the Queen's House): TQ 38715 77687
- Principal geology: to the south, Harwich formation sand and gravel; on the steep slope in the centre of the park, London group, clay, silt and sand; to the north, a narrow band of London Clay.
- CL CMP/30.

Greenwich Park is a site of considerable importance. It contains many significant buildings including The Queen's House, designed and built by Inigo Jones for

Anne of Denmark, consort of James I, the Royal Observatory, and the Naval Hospital, both designed by Sir Christopher Wren and built between the late seventeenth and early eighteenth centuries. The park was formally laid out, partly, at least, to a design by André Le Nôtre in the later seventeenth century (https://historicengland.org.uk/listing/the-list/list-entry/1000174).

It is unlikely that Bridgeman worked at the site. His only connection with it is three plans attributed to him by Willis, a4 fo.49 in the Gough Collection, and in the Maritime Museum, Greenwich. Of these, only one is likely to be in his hand. (For a fuller discussion of the site and plans see Chapter 3.)

Gunton Hall, Norfolk

- Grid reference: TG 22779 34156
- Principal soils: Briton's Lane sand and gravel member, sand and gravel.
- BoL MSGD a4 fo.75.

Sir William Harbord, 1st Baronet, was the son of John Morden and Judith Cropley. He married Elizabeth Britiffe in 1732 and died in February 1770. In 1742 he inherited Gunton Hall.

The present house at Gunton was designed by Matthew Brettingham c.1742 for Sir William Harbord, and stands on, or near, the site of the earlier house. However, since Bridgeman died in 1738, it is clear that his design for the mount at Gunton cannot have been designed as part of the remodelling of the house and park. A fire at the Hall in the late nineteenth century destroyed many records, so it is difficult to ascertain the nature and location of the earlier house, and the layout of the park and gardens. The earliest surviving map, a survey of 1754, shows the 1742 house and the medieval parish church which was replaced by a chapel in 1766, designed by Robert Adam (Williamson 1998, 237). The park, within which the new house lay, extended to 150 hectares, created by enclosing agricultural land, although, again, it is impossible to say when this occurred. The line of a former road and of relict field boundaries can be seen in lines of timber depicted on the map (Williamson 1998, 237). The remains of an avenue of trees from the road to the south of the Hall, and axially aligned to it, suggests that this was the approach, although, again, it is impossible to say at what point this approach was abandoned for the curving drive from the west by which the Hall is approached today. To the west of the Hall are two essentially non-geometric lakes. The more southerly had a cascade at its southern end (Williamson 1998, 237). The 1754 survey shows a geometric, trapezoidal wilderness to the northwest of the house. This feature seems more conventionally associated with the late seventeenth or early eighteenth centuries and therefore it seems likely that the wilderness is the remains of the garden built for the pre-1742 house. The 1st Edition OS (1886) shows that the avenues are not quite axially aligned on the Hall although the 1754 survey suggests they are (http://digimap.edina.ac.uk/ancientroam/historic).

GAZETTEER OF BRIDGEMAN SITES

On the western edge of the wilderness, the survey depicts a mount surmounted by a summerhouse. This mount still survives. It has a basal diameter of c. 20 m, tapering to around 4 m at the summit, and it is possible to discern paths winding to its summit. It is clear that an attempt has also been made to depict these paths on the survey. The summerhouse on the summit is no longer in existence but its octagonal base, built of good quality white bricks over a base of poorer-quality bricks, can still be discerned (Williamson 1998, 237). A4 fo.75, held in the Bodleian Library, is a design for this mount and has plausibly been attributed by Willis to Bridgeman. The design, which is beautifully executed, shows the mount situated within the allees shown on the survey on the western edge of the wilderness. It appears smaller than it is in actuality, and is without the octagonal summerhouse. From the southerly junction of three allees, terraces rise up the naturally occurring sandy ridge, tapering towards the most southerly point (Williamson 1998, 237). The transverse allée shown on the survey bisects a wide walk leading towards the mount. As far as it is possible to determine, the design fits into the western edge of the geometric wilderness, which may represent an extension of an earlier garden. It is unclear how much of this design was constructed.

Hackwood House, Hampshire

- Grid reference: SU 64729 49639
- Principal soils: Seaford chalk formation.
- Privately owned.
- BoL MSGD a3 fo.4 (pencil annotations only),
- BoL MSGD a4 fo.24,
- BoL MSGD a4 fo.34,

Charles Powlett, 3rd Duke of Bolton (1685–1754), inherited the title from his father in 1722. In 1725, under Walpole, he became a privy councillor and constable of the Tower of London. He voted against the Excise Bill in 1733 and was consequently dismissed from all his positions by Walpole. He returned to government in 1740. It is assumed that the 3rd Duke of Bolton was Bridgeman's client here. However, the inclusion of the design in Switzer's *Ichnographia Rustica* in 1718 calls this into question.

Hackwood House is a former Elizabethan hunting lodge, enlarged in 1687 with further additions in 1759–1765. Pevsner, however, suggests that Hackwood Park was built in 1683–1688 by Charles Powlett. From illustrations, it seems to have been a single pile house of thirteen bays with wings at right angles joined to the main block by quadrant colonnades. It was remodelled in 1761–1763 by John Vardy and again in 1805 by Samuel Wyatt. Wyatt doubled the depth of the main block on its north front and heightened them to two storeys.

The park was first enclosed in 1226 and has expanded over several centuries (Bullen et al. 2010, 308). Three Bridgemanic drawings, MSGD a4 fo.24, MSGD a4 fo.34 and MSGD a3 fo.4, are in the Bodleian Library. MSGD a3 fo.4 shows what appears to be an estate survey onto which have been appended pencil additions which correspond very closely with the plan shown in A4 fo.34. This plan shows an intricate garden of straight and serpentine walks to the east of the house, enclosed within bastions forming a roughly kite-shaped enclosure. The principal axis is the broad Walk aligned east–west. It appears that three canals were intended to run parallel to the western edge bounded by a raised terrace at the edge of the garden. Between the straight walks, the plan shows an amphitheatre and a number of cabinets enclosed by trees and reached by serpentine paths. MSGD a4 fo.24 shows detail of a second amphitheatre axially aligned to the house. Willis suggests that this amphitheatre was not implemented and a French formal garden was constructed on the site instead (Willis 2002, 429). It seems likely that the buildings were designed by James Gibbs as illustrated in his *Book of Architecture* (1728). The remains of the rotunda and his menagerie pavilion survive. The cubs, two small wooden pavilions with seats, may also be by Gibbs (Pevsner 2010, 308). Pevsner suggests that the design is after the manner of Le Nôtre. Aerial photographs, modern cartographic evidence and satellite images show that a considerable proportion of Bridgeman's design was built. Hackwood was included in Switzer's list of 'august designs' in *Ichnographia Rustica* (I, 85). Gibbs designed a portico and garden buildings there.

It is probable that, at some point between 1723 and 1724, Bridgeman began work at Hackwood. Here two plans exist in Gough Drawings (MSGD a4 fos. 21 and 24) which Willis attributes to Bridgeman and although, again, there is currently no documentary evidence of Bridgeman's presence there, earthwork evidence suggests that the design as shown in these plans was constructed (Jenny Milledge pers. comm. 2016). Since an estate map dated 1725 shows earthworks similar to those on the two plans in Gough Drawings, it is likely that the work was begun earlier in the 1720s.

Hampton Court Palace, Surrey

- Grid reference: TQ 15786 68476
- Principal geology: Kempton Park Gravel member, sand and gravel.
- Royal Palace.
- SM 36/3/1.
- BoL MSGD a4 fo.62.
- BoL MSGD a4 fo.74.
- NA MPD 1/23.
- NA Work 32/313A.
- NA Work 32/313B.

GAZETTEER OF BRIDGEMAN SITES 207

- NA Work 32/311 (of the Fountain Garden).
- HH Hampton Court.
- BL K.XXIX.14.u.

Hampton Court Palace was built in 1514 for Cardinal Wolsey by Henry VIII, but passed back to the King when Wolsey fell from favour. It was modernised and extended by William and Mary, and, at the same time, the gardens were altered by William Talman, George London and Henry Wise to include the Great Parterre, the Privy Garden and the Wilderness.

Bridgeman's involvement with the Palace seems to have been in two phases. It is likely that the signed drawing held at the Sir John Soane Museum was done for Henry Wise, during Wise's time as Royal Gardener. As Royal Gardener, Bridgeman had the right to live at Wilderness House at Hampton Court. His Inventory post mortem lists separately possessions there. The gardens at Hampton Court were specifically itemised in Bridgeman's contract as Royal Gardener, so that his involvement there was considerable. Presumably the other surveys attributed to Bridgeman (fo.39 at Hovingham Hall, a4 fo.62, a4 fo.74, BL K.XXIX.14U and MPD 23 (3)) are likely to date from this period. It does not seem that Bridgeman made any significant changes to the gardens.

Houghton Hall, Norfolk

- Grid reference: TF 79171 28838
- Principal geology: Centrally, Lewes nodular chalk formation; to the north, Briton's Lane sand and gravel member; to the south, Sheringham Cliffs formation, clay, silt, sand and gravel.
- Privately owned.
- BoL MSGD a4 fo.57.

Sir Robert Walpole was the most powerful politician of his generation. The Walpole family had lived in north Norfolk since the fourteenth century and had become prominent there before Walpole's rise to political power. Walpole was educated at Eton and King's College, Cambridge, but his education was cut short by the death of his elder brother, Edward, and he returned to Houghton to learn to manage the estate. He inherited the estate at Houghton on the death of his father in 1700 and entered parliament eventually as MP for Castle Rising. At the elections of 1702 he was returned for King's Lynn and remained in parliament continuously, except for a short break in 1712, until his elevation to the Lords in 1742. He became Britain's first Prime Minister in 1714 (http://www.oxforddnb.com).

It appears that Walpole originally intended to drastically alter the Jacobean house he had inherited, but instead, in 1722, the foundations for a new house were laid on a site several metres to the east of the original house. The new house was, depending on viewpoint and political persuasion, either a creation that inspired awe at its magnificence or derision at its extravagance and tastelessness.

The Earl of Oxford, Walpole's political opponent, said of it: 'I think it is neither magnificent nor beautiful; there is very great expense without either judgement or taste' (Williamson 1998, 48). Colen Campbell published a classically Palladian design for Houghton in *Vitruvius Britannicus III*, claiming it as his own. However, it seems likely that the original design may have been by Gibbs, especially since the house that was built was markedly less Palladian than the design published (Worsley 1995, 108). Thomas Ripley was also involved with the construction and William Kent was responsible for the elaborate decoration of the interior and for the design of the furniture. The house was built in Whitby stone ashlar, a powerful statement of extravagance in itself since it had to be transported from Yorkshire. The house is Palladian with some Baroque references. It has a three-storey, nine-bay centre with four advanced angle towers, surmounted by stone domes by Gibbs instead of the pedimented towers of the drawing published by Campbell. There are single-storey colonnaded wings connecting to two-storey, seven-by-seven service wings (http://www.britishlistedbuildings.co.uk/en-221600-houghton-hall-with-courtyard-walls-attac).

The development of both the park and the house at Houghton is relatively well-documented. A park had been established around the house around 1700 and it was extended to cover c.220 hectares in 1720. Around 1722, Bridgeman may also have begun work at Houghton for Sir Robert Walpole. Walpole began to build Houghton in 1722 and Willis suggests that planting of trees in the park had started by 1717 (Willis 2002, 85). However, although a plan for Houghton in Gough Drawings (a4 fo.57) is likely to be by Bridgeman, and is attributed to him by Willis, the level of his involvement and the timing of it is less sure. Horace Walpole attributes the work to 'Kingsmill Eyre', and the only documentary evidence that places Bridgeman at Houghton is from 1731 when Sir Thomas Robinson visited and was shown 'a large design for the plantations, in the country, which is the present undertaking ...' (Willis 2002, 85).

Kedleston, Derbyshire

- Grid reference: SK 31285 40296
- Principal geology: Siltstone.
- National Trust.
- SC Object 109274.

Bridgeman's client was Sir John Curzon 3rd Baronet (1674–1727), Member of Parliament for Derbyshire from 1701 to 1727.

The house for which Bridgeman designed aspects of the park was built in the 1720s for Sir John Curzon, apparently to designs by Francis Smith of Warwick. Willis says that it was 'an unpretentious building, three storeys high, with dormer windows and a walled garden' (Willis 2002, 87). It was demolished in stages, and the current house was built between 1758 and 1765. Originally designed by Matthew Brettingham, the central block was redesigned by James Paine in 1761 and the south front by Robert Adam in 1760. Gibbs was also involved at Kedleston, receiving ten pounds, which, Willis speculates, was for designing the temple which appears in his *Book of Architecture* in 1728. All the existing garden buildings seem to date from the construction of the present hall.

Bridgeman's involvement is suggested by two separate entries in Sir John Curzon's account books. On 14 September 1722 there is an entry 'To Mr Bridgeman's man by order £1-0-0' and on 14 September 1726, 'Paid Mr Bridgeman £63-0-0' (pers. comm. Marilyn Lindley and Ann Jones). An unsigned and undated estate map which predates the construction of the new house shows a distinctly Bridgemanic landscape of tapering grass terraces and a basin and canal (CMS ref. 109518). The basin and canal are clearly those shown in a plan held in the Scarsdale Collection (Object 109274) and attributed to Bridgeman by Willis. The detailed drawing shows a straight-sided canal beginning and terminating in a basin, with weirs at regular intervals. Each of the weirs has the depth of the drop appended, and the drawing also depicts the sight lines from an unspecified viewpoint beyond the edge of the page. The canal is shown in section in the bottom right-hand corner (Willis 2002, pl. 205b). It is likely that this was payment of £63 was for the plan. Bridgeman charges Sir John Dutton a similar amount for a plan for Lodge Park. Gibbs also contributed to the landscape; he writes of his proposal for the park to include two pavilions 'opposite to one another, on each side of a Vista proposed to be cut through a Wood, and to be terminated with an Obelisque upon a Hill fronting the House' (Willis 2002, 87).

Kensington Gardens

- Grid reference (taken from Kensington Palace): TQ 25894 80016
- Principal geology: Lynch Hill gravel member, sand and gravel on London Clay.
- Royal Park.
- BoL MSGD a3 fo.7.
- BoL MSGD a3* fo.15.
- NS CC.2753.
- HEH ST Map 147.

In 1689, Nottingham House was bought from Daniel Finch, Earl of Nottingham, to provide a retreat from London for William III and Queen Mary. The house was enlarged by Sir Christopher Wren and became an important Royal palace. The gardens were remodelled, at the same time, by George London and Henry Wise. After the accession of Queen Anne, Henry Wise had sole responsibility for the gardens and created several wildernesses in 12 hectares of gravel pits to the north of the palace. Forty-one hectares was taken from Hyde Park to form a paddock to house a menagerie (historicengland.org.uk/listing/the-list/list-entry/1000340).

Bridgeman's involvement began when he was appointed joint Royal Gardener in 1726, following the death of Joseph Carpenter. With Henry Wise, he began alterations to Kensington Gardens. After the accession of King George II and Queen Caroline, a new contract for the remodelling of the gardens was drawn up, and Bridgeman continued to work there after the retirement, in 1727, of Henry Wise. The contracts are bound in one volume, held in the National Archives (Work 6/114, Work 16/39/1). He created the Round Pond and the northerly section of the Serpentine, and plantations, vistas and walks, between 1728 and 1731.

King's College, Cambridge

- Grid reference: TL 44690 58327
- Principal geology: Sand and gravel.

On 20 December 1724 the Fellows of King's College asked that 'Mr Provost do send down Mr Bridgman to Lay out the Ground from the West side of the new building to the Road; and to draw two or three Schemes of different designes for our consideration' (King's College Congregation Book, 1722–1778, fo.12, cited in Willis 2002, 84). It is not clear how much of the design was executed at the time (Willis 2002, 84) since, in 1763, it was still under construction: 'all of which designed to be done (when the remaining Part of the great Square is finished) according to the Plan given by the late ingenious Mr Bridgman' (Cantabrigia Depicta, cited in Willis 2002, 84).

Langleys, Essex

- Grid reference: TL 69946 13586
- Principal geology: London Clay.
- Privately owned.

In 1711 Langleys was bought by Sir Samuel Tufnell, who seems to have been the son of a rich London merchant (https://historicengland.org.uk/listing/the-list/list-entry/1000241) and to have had some links to the South Sea Company; he was named, in a list circulating in January 1722, as an MP who had received free stock in the company in return for their votes on the South Sea bill (www.historyofparliamentonline.org). He demolished part of the house and remodelled it to designs by William Tufnell (apparently no relation).

Bridgeman appears to have worked at Langleys, although the precise nature and extent of his work is not clear. Tufnell's estate receipt book records a payment of £156.7s.2d in 1722 for 'Works & plants in ye Gardens' (https://historicengland.org.uk/listing/the-list/list-entry/1000241; Willis 2002, 60). No plan has come to light, and the first evidence of the layout of the garden is in Chapman and Andre's map of 1777 (https://historicengland.org.uk/listing/the-list/list-entry/1000241).

Ledston Hall, West Yorkshire

- Grid reference: SE 43460 28880
- Principal geology: Brotherton formation limestone.
- Now owned by a charitable trust, The Wheler Foundation.
- BoL MSGD a4 fo.85.
- OT. A plan is held at Otterden Place.

Lady Elizabeth Hastings (1682–1739), known as Lady Betty, was the eldest surviving daughter of the Earl of Huntingdon. Ledston Hall, the estate of her maternal grandfather, was bestowed on her by her brother George on the death of her father, on the condition she made no claim on her father's estate. She refused all offers of marriage and remained single, devoting herself to charitable causes and to the upbringing of her half-sisters by her father's second marriage. Her political opinions are unknown, but her father was a Jacobite sympathiser.[1]

Ledston Hall is located on the site of a monastic grange established by the Cluniac Priory of St John Pontefract. A medieval chamber and an undercroft are thought to be part of the medieval buildings, and other medieval masonry forms part of the Hall. Following the dissolution, the Witham family incorporated parts of the grange building into a courtyard house, enlarged first by the 1st Earl of Strafford who, in c.1660, added a south wing; and then by Sir John Lewis, who added an extension to the north range and a new north wing. Lady Betty herself made some stylistic alterations to the main façade. These different phases are clearly visible in the fabric of the building. Pevsner suggests that the front is 'an outstanding example of that transitional phase in English architecture which falls between the Jacobean style (to which the concept of the deep forecourt with wings of the same height as the centre belongs – cf. ... Blickling ...) and the style of Pratt, May, and the young Christopher Wren' (Pevsner and Radcliffe 1967, 304–305). The garden sides of the house are more irregular and show clearly the different stages of development.

Three maps show the development of the park: Saxton's map of 1577, Warburton's 1720 map and Jeffrey's map of 1775. There have been three phases of development of the park. In the first, between 1653 and 1671, Sir John Lewis enclosed the whole deer park and built two lodges. In the second, after inheriting the estate in 1705, Lady Betty was responsible for laying out much of the garden at the Hall. The third phase, in the nineteenth century, destroyed much of the eighteenth-century garden (http://www.heritagegateway.org.uk). Evidence of Bridgeman's involvement is present both in documents and cartographically. Two payments were made by Lady Betty to Bridgeman in 1731 for 'the designe of Mr Bridgemans' and a reference is made to Bridgeman's proposals in an undated letter from T. Coke to Lady Betty. Three drawings attributed to Bridgeman also

---

[1] See online at http://www.oxforddnb.com/view/article/12564

exist for Ledston. MSGD a4 fo.85 is a pen-and-ink drawing held in the Bodleian collection. It shows an outline of the plan which is depicted in ink and watercolour on a plan held at Otterden Place in Kent. A two-page description of the garden, possibly in Bridgeman's handwriting, is also held at Otterden Place. A second drawing, MSGD a3 fo.19, is also held at the Bodleian. This, although showing the outlines of the garden given more detailed treatment in the other two drawings, appears to be considerably less detailed and seems to be a survey of the whole estate. It appears, from crop marks, that a considerable proportion of the garden was constructed (Willis 2002, 61 and plates 48b, 207a and 207b).

Lillington Manor, Warwickshire

- Grid reference: SP 32498 67420
- Principal geology: Mercia Mudstone.
- WO CR 556/197.

Bridgeman's survey of Lillington Manor and its land (1711) is held at Warwickshire Record Office (CR 556/197). It is referred to in the notebook which accompanies a survey undertaken by Bridgeman and James Fish the younger of Warwick Priory (CR 26.2.1). Presumably it was undertaken for Henry Wise when he bought Warwick Priory in 1711. The manor house is located next to the church of St Mary Magdelene.

Lodge Park, Gloucestershire

- Grid reference: SP 14617 12263
- Principal geology: White limestone formation.
- National Trust.
- BoL MSGD a4 fo.68.

Two separate individuals were involved with the creation of Lodge Park, part of the Sherborne Estate in Gloucestershire. The deer park, deer course and its attendant Lodge were created in the seventeenth century by John 'Crump' Dutton (1594–1657). Bridgeman's client was John 'Crump' Dutton's great nephew, Sir John Dutton. He represented Gloucestershire in parliament between 1727 and 1741 as a Whig (http://www.oxforddnb.com). He was cultured and his estate accounts show that he purchased contemporary books on design such as William Kent's *The Designs of Inigo Jones* (Smith 2006, 237).

The Lodge, which stands within the deer park around which Bridgeman's landscape was designed, was built c.1630. It was intended as a grandstand to view deer coursing. Originally constructed with two rooms, a hall on the ground floor and a banqueting chamber on the floor above, deer coursing could be watched from the interior, or from the roof above, which is surrounded by a parapet. Its design has been associated with the architect Balthazar Gerbier (d.1683), a contemporary of Inigo Jones. Sir John Dutton refurbished it from about 1725 onwards and accounts mention work done by Wootton and William Kent, who provided furniture. Post-1725 alterations have been removed recently and the building has been restored to its seventeenth- and eighteenth-century state (http://list.english-heritage.org.uk/resultsingle.aspx?uid=1000770).

The park, originally known as New Park, was originally open fields and common grazing, and was formed between 1624 and 1640 as a deer park for Sherborne House three miles away. Bridgeman's design (MSGD a4 fo.68) was for the deer park to the east of the Lodge. In pen and ink, the drawing shows a landscape aligned from a terrace built out from the eastern side of the Lodge, through a bastion above the river, across the river Leach flooded to form a serpentine lake and up the slope further east to an eye-catcher within tapering terraces planted with trees confined within hedges. The design is not axially aligned to the Lodge, which sits at a 45-degree angle to the terrace. Although the drawing depicts the river Leach as a lake, clearly visible beneath it is the outline of a smaller straight-sided canal, the earthwork of which is still visible today. It is not clear when this canal was created but it seems likely that it is from the early eighteenth century. The relationship between this canal and the lake bears a very strong resemblance to that between the canal and lake at Wolterton Hall, and it is likely both landscapes were created in the early to mid-1720s. Estate accounts show that Bridgeman visited Sherborne House in 1725 and 1729. In 1729 the accounts detail £70 paid to 'Mr Bridgeman for his journeys to Shireborn and making a plan for my New Park'. Trees were bought for the new park on an extravagant scale: 1050 holly sets, for example, in 1729. Between 1724 and 1729, 100 flowering trees, 19,200 ash sets, 7000 elms, 700 wych elms, 50 yew sets and 6000 Scots firs were ordered (Smith 2006, 242). 1st Edition OS 1883 clearly shows that Bridgeman's geometric plantations of trees on the rising ground to the east of the river Leach were not just planted, but survived into the late nineteenth century. The National Trust has been restoring some of Bridgeman's planting on the western side of the river Leach since the 1990s.

Longford Castle, Wiltshire

- Grid reference: SU 17161 26669
- Principal geology: River deposits, sand and gravel.
- Longford Castle is the home of the Earl of Radnor.

Jacob Des Bouverie (bap. 1694, d.1761) was descended from Flemish silk weavers. In 1736 he succeeded his elder brother Sir Edward Des Bouverie as 3rd Baronet and inherited Longford Castle in Wiltshire. He changed his name to Bouverie by Act of Parliament in 1737 and sat as MP for Salisbury from 1741 to 1747. His political sympathies were Tory. He employed Kent and Goodison to work on Longford Castle and remodelled the park around the Castle (http://www.oxforddnb.com).

Longford Castle was built by Thomas Gorges to replace a former mansion house. It is said to have been modelled on the castle at Uraniborg in Sweden at the behest of his new Swedish wife, Helena Snakenburg, and comprises a triangular plan with corner towers (http://www.heritagegateway.org.uk). However, Pevsner points out that Uraniborg in fact has four towers and a more likely model is Gripsholm, built in 1537 (Pevsner and Cherry 1975, 303). When drawn by John Thorpe, a sign of the Holy Trinity was put at the centre of the triangular court. Piles had to be driven into the marshy soil on the flood plain of the river Avon and the cost of the building was very expensive. It was sold by Lord Coleraine to Sir Edward Des Bouverie in 1717. There has been considerable restoration work on the building at various points in its history; in the eighteenth century, between 1802 and 1817, and again in the 1870s. Willis suggests that Roger Morris was employed on the house (Willis 2002, 58).

Bridgeman's involvement with Longford Castle rests on a reference in a letter from Jacob Bouverie to Hitch Younge on 7 November 1737, in which he writes 'I have been a good deal at a loss for want of Bridgeman's Company ...' (Willis 2002, 58). The reference comes from John Cornforth, *Longford and the Bouveries*, and Willis states that it was confirmed by Helen Matilda, Countess of Radnor, and William Barclay Squire (*Catalogue of the Pictures of the Earl of Radnor*, II) (Willis 2002, 432).

Lumley Castle, County Durham

- Grid reference: NZ 28793 51035
- Principal geology: Glaciolacustrine deposits with High Pennine middle coal measures and sandstone in the Lumley Park Burn valley.
- Lumley Castle is now run as a hotel.
- Two plans for Lumley Castle are in the private archive of the Earl of Scarborough.

Lumley Castle is medieval, and stands on high ground with the river Wear to the west and the deeply incised Lumley Park Burn to the east. It is the property of the Earls of Scarborough. The 2nd Earl of Scarborough, Richard, born in 1688, was a Whig Member of Parliament for East Grinstead and later for Arundel, and Lord Lieutenant of Northumberland, and he acceded to the title on his father's death in 1721 (http://www.cracroftspeerage.co.uk/online/content/scarbrough1690.htm).

Lumley Castle was substantially remodelled during the eighteenth century. In 1721, Vanbrugh remodelled the south and west ranges of the Castle, so that the main views from the Castle were to the west over Chester-le-Street. There was also activity in the garden and park. In 1701, George London wrote to Lord Cowper that he was intending to visit Lumley Castle, presumably in order to work on the gardens, and Bridgeman probably worked with Vanbrugh on the gardens. It is likely that Bridgeman's plan dates from the early 1720s. Switzer also stayed at the Castle in 1729, although it is not known whether he had any influence on the gardens. Later in the century, in 1730, estate records show the laying out of walks and plantations, and it is suggested that these might have been the work of Thomas Wright, whose first patron was the Earl of Scarborough. A 1768 plan for the estate by Thomas White also survives (http.//historicengland.org.uk/listing/the-list/list-entry/1001395).

There are two plans for Lumley Castle which have strong stylistic links to Bridgeman's work. Both are held at Sandbeck Park. It is likely, then, that Bridgeman played some part in the design for the garden when Vanbrugh was working there, especially so since the focus of Bridgeman's plan is the vista to the west of the Castle. Bridgeman had probably also collaborated with Vanbrugh at Sacombe and at Hackwood. It is possible that a third plan, undated but stylistically early eighteenth century, also dates from this period.

Marble Hill, Surrey

- Grid reference: TQ 17299 73622
- Principal geology: Langley silt member, clay and silt.
- English Heritage.
- NRO MC 184/10/1.
- NRO MC184/10/2.

Marble Hill was built by Henrietta Howard, Countess of Suffolk (1688–1767). She married Charles Howard in 1706. The marriage proved unhappy. She became the mistress of George II, who provided the funds for her to buy land in Twickenham, and she began Marble Hill in 1724. After her husband's death and the end of her relationship with George II, she retired to Marble Hill and married George Berkeley in 1735.[2]

Marble Hill was built between 1724 and 1729 on the banks of the Thames at Twickenham. The first design of the house may have been by Colen Campbell; Mrs Howard was a subscriber to *Vitruvius Britannicus III*. However, the house that was built was by Roger Morris and Lord Herbert, Earl of Pembroke. The house is Palladian and is composed of three storeys. Its main elevations face north and south and have five bays. Pope complimented Mrs Howard in 1727 on a room modelled on Palladio's interpretation of a Roman atrium (Worsley 1995, 139). The house had been altered externally, but was restored to its original eighteenth-century state in the 1960s. It is under the management of English Heritage.

There is considerable evidence of Bridgeman's involvement in the construction of the park. He wrote to Pope on 28 September 1724 making it clear that he and Pope had visited Marble Hill with Mrs Howard and that he was drawing up plans for the garden (BL ADD MS4809 fo.141V). Two separate plans exist for the

---

[2] See online at http://www.oxforddnb.com/view/article/13904

garden. Both are currently in the Norfolk Records Office. Although it is tempting to assume that these are the plans that Bridgeman was referring to in his letter, the cartouche on both reads 'The Plan of the House, Garden and Inclosures of Marble Hill 10 mile West from London Belonging To the Right Honourable The Countess of Suffolk'. Since Henrietta Howard did not become Countess of Suffolk until 1731, this makes it unlikely that these are the drawings referred to. MC 184/10/2 has on the reverse a map of south-west Scotland and the beginnings of a drawing of the Marble Hill garden. The finished drawing also contains a key to which alterations have been made. MC184/10/1 is a more polished version of the above. Both are probably the work of James, surveyor to the Duke of Argyll, and done in 1752.

Mereworth Castle, Kent

- Grid reference: TQ 66890 53225
- Principal geology: Atherfield clay formation, sandstone and mudstone.
- Privately owned.
- BoL MSGD a4 fo.52.

John Fane, 7th Earl of Westmorland (d.1762), was baptised at Mereworth, Kent in 1686. After a successful military career, he entered parliament in 1708 as a Whig. He fell from favour with the King and Walpole in 1734 for supporting a motion which prevented the dismissal of officers from the army on political grounds. He acceded to the title of Earl of Westmorland in 1736 and sat as a Tory in the House of Lords.[3]

Mereworth Castle was built to replace a castle licensed in 1332. It was designed by Colen Campbell and is a copy of Palladio's Villa Rotunda, with only minor changes of plan and elevation (Worsley 1995, 108). It is a square block with four fronts, each identical except that the east and west lack portico steps. It has a hipped slate roof surmounted by an almost hemispherical dome with a blind lantern surrounded by high half columns. It is aligned roughly north–south and has two free-standing pavilions to the left and right. The building is stuccoed an ochre colour. It was originally moated and parts of the moat can be seen to the north (http://list.english-heritage.org.uk). Pevsner suggests that, since Fane did not inherit his peerage, the Earldom of Westmorland, until 1736, when Mereworth was built he could 'indulge his fancy'. The resulting house was not, as Palladio's villa had been, a belvedere, but a castle, hence the moat (Newman 1969, 403). Horace Walpole said of Mereworth Castle in 1752 that it was 'perfect in Palladian taste' (Worsley 1995, 115).

The park at Mereworth is a landscaped valley behind the house. Evidence of Bridgeman's involvement in the site is a rudimentary plan in the Bodleian Library, catalogued MSGD a4 fo.52 and attributed by Willis to him. It clearly

---

[3] See online at http://www.oxforddnb.com/view/article/9134?docPos=1

shows, in plan, the square block of Mereworth Castle, with porticos and free-standing pavilions. The steps on the north and south fronts are shown, as are the boundaries of the formal gardens around the house. A feature with apsidal ends is also shown to the north of the house. It is, in fact, a very similar shape and position to the pond which currently exists at Mereworth but to the south of the house. The plan, which is undated, has, intriguingly, on the reverse, 'a small plan without name' which is crossed out, 'Lord Westmorelands/but of no use now', and 'Colonell Fanes of Mereworth' (MSGD a4 fo.52).

Montagu House, London

- Grid reference: TQ 30051 81725
- Principal geology: clay, silt and sand.
- The house was sold to the British Museum in 1759 and demolished in the 1840s.

Bridgeman seems to have taken on a contract for £25 a quarter to maintain the gardens of Montagu House in London for the Duke of Montagu. An entry in Andrew Marchant's estate account books, Ledgers VI–VII 1725–1731, records: 'Paid Cha[rles] Bridgman for keeping the Garden ½ Year to Xmas Last £50.00'. The Northamptonshire Record Office also holds a receipt from 22 January 1725 signed by Bridgeman for £50.

Moor Park, Hertfordshire

- Grid reference: TQ 07528 93301
- Principal geology: sand, silt, clay and gravel.
- Moor Park is now a hotel and golfing venue.
- BoL MSGD a4 fo.48.
- BoL MSGD a4 fo.58.

Moor Park was built for Benjamin Styles, who inherited a large fortune from the commercial enterprises of his father. The original Manor of the More, started in 1426 but enlarged and altered, first by Archbishop Neville and then by Cardinal Wolsey, occupied a site close to the river Colne. However, in 1617, the first of three houses was built on a new site on the hill south-west of the original house for the Earl and Countess of Bedford. Two successive houses were built, probably on the same footprint, and using, to a greater or lesser degree, some of the fabric of the preceding house. The second of these was in 1680, for the Duke of Monmouth, and the third, from 1720 onwards, for Benjamin Styles. Styles had also made a fortune of his own in the South Sea Company before it crashed. Under the direction of James Thornhill, the existing red-brick mansion was cased in Portland stone, extended and refurbished, at the cost of £130,000 (Williamson 2000, 28). Styles's house is five by eleven bays. The entrance portico on the south-western side has four columns. The garden side, on the north-eastern side, has an engaged portico. The ground floor has banded rustication. Pavilions were attached to the house by quadrant colonnades added in 1725 but were demolished in 1785. The interior of the house was lavish. It was decorated with paintings by Jacopo Amigioni, who lived in England 1729–1736. In the gallery were grisailles painted by F. Sleter. These replaced paintings by Thornhill, who was dismissed in a lawsuit in 1728.

It is clear that a significant designed landscape predated Bridgeman's design both in the immediate vicinity of the house and in the wider park. The garden that existed at Moor Park is described by Sir William Temple in *Upon the Gardens of Epicurus: or, Of Gardening, in the Year 1685*. It is a description of the garden as he remembered it from 30 years before, when he spent his honeymoon there in 1655. The garden, built by Lucy Harrington, the Countess of Bedford, was built on the side of a gentle hill. There was a gravel terrace along the length of the house from which three sets of steps led down to a large parterre divided into quarters (Temple in Dixon Hunt and Willis 1975, 98). The sides of the parterre were bordered with cloisters, paved with stone at ground level and roofed with lead forming a walkway fenced with balustrades. There was a grotto with 'Figures of shell-rock-work, fountains and waterworks' (Temple in Dixon Hunt and Willis 1975, 98). Bridgeman probably made use of much of the basic structure of this garden in his own design, including the terrace, the cloisters and the piping for the waterworks.

Although it is impossible to be precise about the date upon which Bridgeman began work on the landscape, it is likely to have been around 1720. It was certainly considerably developed by 1724. Visitors also clearly saw some of the new features of Bridgeman's design under construction, and also finished. Edward Southwell Jr in 1724 and Sir John Evelyn in 1726 both comment on aspects of the design shown in the two plans attributed to Bridgeman by Willis, MSGD a4 fo.48 and a4 fo.58 (Jeffery 2014, 15).

Purley Hall, West Berkshire

- Grid reference: SU 64618 75782
- Principal geology: clay, silt, sand and gravel.
- Purley Hall is owned by JJ Media Group.
- BoL MSGD a4 fo.54.

Purley Hall was the property of Francis Hawes, a director of the South Sea Company. When the company collapsed in 1722, Hawes had his assets seized (https://historicengland.org.uk). Purley Hall was confiscated by the government and sold, although he was allowed to remain as a tenant for some years.

Purley Hall is a Jacobean house built by Francis Hyde in 1609, which has been subject to extensive remodelling, undertaken first by Francis Hawes in

1719–1726 and by John Wilder in 1818–1829. The original building was a two-storeyed double-depth house with plain triangular gables to the attics. The remodelled north front has a narrow inset centre and stone quoins from the early eighteenth century. There are *oeil-de-boeuf* windows to the rusticated basement. The steps are almost certainly eighteenth-century. The entrance hall has fielded grisaille paintings after Thornhill (Tyack et al. 2010, 430–431). From MSGD a4 fo.54, held in the Bodleian Library, it appears to have been a Palladian Villa with four pavilions linked by curved arcades to a central block, modelled on the Villa Mocenigo (Willis 2002, 61 and pl. 47b).

The Bridgeman plan is inscribed on the back with 'Francis Haws Esqr.', and presumably predates the failure of the South Sea Company, as do the accounts from March 1721. These record the payment to 'Mr Bridgeman' of 'his bill for laying out the gardens at Purley, £122 11s 0d', and also other substantial payments for trees, plants including fruit trees (Hussey 1970). The plan shows a Palladian villa with a kitchen garden to the side and a sunken bowling green, leading to a formal pond with straight sides and an apsidal end. It appears that some of this was constructed, since a pond with an apsidal ending on its western end, joined to a canal formed from a branch of the river Pang, forms part of the landscape today (OS 1:10 000 June 2013; http://digimap.edina.ac.uk/roam/os). On the eastern side of the canal, opposite the pond, is the Flint Temple (Willis 2002, 61).

Richmond Gardens, Surrey

- Grid reference (from Kew Palace): TQ 18479 77469
- Principal geology: sand and gravel.
- NA MR 1/528.
- NA MR 1/696.
- NA Work 32/282.

Richmond Gardens is not one of the five gardens in Bridgeman's contract as Royal Gardener, and payments to him must have been made separately, as Desmond suggests: '[Bridgeman's] responsibilities for the Royal Gardens excluded Richmond Lodge which was subject to a separate contract' (Desmond 1995, 6). This seems to be supported by Sarah Bridgeman's request to the Treasury, made after Bridgeman's death for payment of debts: 'And for keeping the Royall Gardens at Richmond, by Contract, and Extra Bills there. ye Sum of £1847.8s.5d' (CCXCIX (T.1:299) 10, fos.23–24).

However, Bridgeman was probably responsible for work at Richmond Gardens, including remodelling the gardens for Princess Caroline before her accession to the throne in 1727, and probably before he became Royal Gardener. The quotation from Pope's letter, cited above, suggests that this was the case. He was certainly at Richmond in 1735, when Lady Burlington describes a conversation with him in a letter to her husband: 'There is a new design going forward at Richmond in ye garden ... I took ye liberty to differ with Mr Bridgeman ... he said that 3 slopes made it look bigger; I think one wou'd not only be handsomer, but look (in his style) more grande' (Willis 2002, 103). Willis attributes two plans to him, both held in the National Archives: MR 1/696 and Work 32/282. Of these, MR 1/696 probably relates to the period before 1727, since it refers to the Prince and Princess of Wales, and Work 32/282 probably shows the remodelled landscape for Queen Caroline after her accession.

Rousham Park, Oxfordshire

- Grid reference: SP 47840 24220
- Principal geology: Dyrham formation, siltstone and mudstone, interbedded.
- Privately owned.
- BoL MSGD a4 fo.63.

Colonel Robert Dormer-Cottrell inherited Rousham in 1719 and it was he who commissioned Bridgeman to transform the gardens. At his death in 1737, when the gardens were nearly complete, his younger brother, Lieutenant-General Sir James Dormer (1679–1741), inherited Rousham. There is some suggestion that he had been consulted by his brother on the remodelling of the garden (https://doi.org/10.1093/ref:odnb/7835).

Rousham was built in c.1635 for Sir Robert Dormer. A considerable part of the building is seventeenth-century, although remodelling by William Kent took place between 1738 and 1740, and the house was enlarged again c.1860 by William St Aubyn. It is a three-storey Jacobean House aligned north–south. It has a seven-window range front, a crenelated parapet and a three-storey porch. Alterations made by Kent in the eighteenth century included the addition of an ogee cupola and flanking the house with two two-storey pavilions with canted bay windows and ogee niches containing classical statues by Henry Cheere. The interior was extensively remodelled and decorated by Kent. Although much of the remodelling of the house is of great interest, Bridgeman's landscape must have been for the original, unextended and unremodelled Jacobean house (http://www.britishlistedbuildings.co.uk/en-252860-rousham-house-rousham-oxfordshire).

Bridgeman's plan for Rousham is in the Bodleian Library and is catalogued as MSGD a4 fo.63. It shows the area of the garden which borders the Cherwell and where the remnants of Bridgeman's design, modified by Kent, exist today. It appears to be shown on a 1719 estate map suggesting that it was constructed before this date, or that the survey accommodated what was then a proposal from Bridgeman. The drawing shows that the southern bank of the Cherwell has been straightened to accommodate a broad walk. To the east of the site are two square ponds linked to a small apsidal ended cabinet, from which runs, roughly north–south the elm walk, terminating at the top of a small incline in a statue. In the south of the site an amphitheatre borders on the Cherwell. Smaller cabinets in the wood are linked by narrow serpentine paths. The drawing also has, probably in Bridgeman's handwriting, detailed measurements to do with the way water would be used in the site. Kent's alterations to the garden left most of the basic structure intact, but softened the lines and added significant garden buildings and features. Letters between Clary the gardener, the Steward, Kent and General Dormer offer a description of that process which took place between 1738 and 1742 (Müller 1997).

Sacombe House, Hertfordshire

- Grid reference: TL 33950 18996
- Principal geology: clay, silt, sand and gravel.
- Privately owned.
- BoL MSGD a4 fo.64.

Thomas Rolt purchased the Sacombe estate in 1688 for £22,500. He had made a fortune in the East India Company and as President of Surat and Governor of Bombay. His son Edward Rolt inherited the estate in 1710 on the death of his father (Milledge 2009, 38–39). Well-educated at Merton College, Oxford, then a hot-bed of Tory, Stuart and Royalist supporters, he entered parliament in 1713 and was suspected of Jacobite sympathies (Milledge 2009, 43). He married Anne Bayntun, daughter of Sir Henry Bayntun of Spye Park, whose marriage portion was £5000 (Milledge 2009, 38–39).

The house at Sacombe was medieval. It was described as 'little and old' by Sir Mathew Decker when he visited in 1728 (Milledge 2009, 390). Edward Rolt first commissioned Vanbrugh and then Gibbs to replace it. Gibbs's design of a Palladian house was published in *A Book of Architecture* (pl. 53) in 1728, but was never built (Willis 2002, pl. 46a). However, Vanbrugh did design a walled garden with substantial buttressed walls located within the park and shown on the plan attributed to Bridgeman (Milledge 2009, 41). The house and the walled garden were eventually demolished in 1783.

The park at Sacombe was shown on Seller's county map of 1676 as a deer park, and the park has been shown on all subsequent maps (http://www.heritagegateway.org.uk). Edward Rolt began to improve Sacombe c.1714 when he paid Henry Wise £8.14s.6d, probably for plants from Brompton Park Nursery (Milledge 2009, 40). It would appear from estate accounts that he employed Bridgeman in some capacity from 1715, when a payment of £80 was made to him. Payment continued for another seven years until Edward Rolt died of smallpox in 1722, at which time Bridgeman was named as his principal creditor. There are two plans for Sacombe attributed to Bridgeman by Willis. Both are in the Bodleian Library and are part of the Gough collection. The first, MSGD a4 fo.29, is a pen-and-ink survey with 'Mr Rolt Sacombe' written on the reverse. It shows the main features of a landscape and with a key which identifies by letter its various components. In spite of being identified as Sacombe on the reverse, it seems likely that this sketch map is, in fact, of Down Hall. For further discussion, see Chapter 3. The second plan, MSGD a4 fo.64, is a beautifully coloured design showing an axial walk leading to a canal and rectangular basin and a *patte d'oie*, one branch of which leads to a theatre. Vanbrugh's walled garden is shown. These features are described in some detail both by Decker, visiting in 1728, and by Salmon, visiting in the same year (Decker *Account* WSRO 2057/45/2; Salmon *History of Hertfordshire* p.225. Both cited in Milledge 2009, 42). There is considerable evidence at Sacombe today that a large part of Bridgeman's design was completed (Milledge 2009).

Scampston Hall, North Yorkshire

- Grid reference: SE 86475 75533
- Principal geology: sand and gravel.
- Privately owned.
- BoL MSGD a4 fo.27.
- BoL MSGD a4 fo.66.
- BoL MSGD a4 fo.73.

Because the three Bridgemanic drawings for Scampston are undated, it is difficult to tell which of two Sir William St Quintins was Bridgeman's client. The first is the 3rd baronet (c.1662–1723), who was Whig MP for Hull for 11 successive parliaments between 1695 and 1723. He acquired considerable property in the East Riding of Yorkshire after the death of his grandfather in 1697, including the two manors at Scampston which cost around £10,000 (http://www.oxforddnb.com). On his death in 1723, the estate and title passed to his nephew, the second Sir William St Quintin. He was the son of his uncle's younger brother, Hugh, a merchant. He sat as MP for Thirsk between 1722 and 1724. He appears to have used Lancelot Brown to landscape the grounds at Scampston, but no mention is made of Bridgeman (http://ingilbyhistory.ripleycastle.co.uk).

The Scampston estate was acquired by the St Quintin family at the end of the seventeenth century. It is unclear from available sources whether the house was built by Sir William St Quintin, the 3rd baronet, c.1700, or for Thomas Hustler in the late seventeenth century, presumably before the purchase of the estate by Sir William St Quintin (http://www.scampston.co.uk/hall/history-of-scampston-hall.html). The current house was remodelled to a design by Thomas Leverton in 1795 or 1803, but a painting of the original house exists (http://www.scampston.co.uk/hall/history-of-scampston-hall.html). At the rear of the present house the brickwork of this earlier house can be seen. It was a nine-bay, two-storey building with single-storey wings which was extensively altered in 1759 by the addition of a large two-storey projecting bay on the south front. In 1777–1778 Palladian turrets were added. Pevsner attributes these to Lancelot Brown (Pevsner and Neave 1995, 670). A Palladian Bridge, also attributed to Lancelot Brown and dated by Pevsner as 1773, occupies a site at the northern end of a shallow fish pond (http://www.heritagegateway.org.uk). To the north-west of the Hall is a four-acre walled kitchen garden c.1740 (Pevsner and Neave 1995, 670).

Three plans attributed to Bridgeman form part of the Gough Drawings in the Bodleian Library. They are catalogued as MSGD a4 fo.27, MSGD a4 fo.66 and MSGD a4 fo.73. A fourth drawing, MSGD a4 fo.47, was attributed to Bridgeman but the attribution has been withdrawn. The most complete and detailed is a4 fo.73. It is in ink and watercolour and shows the house with two pavilions flanking a courtyard. Axially aligned to the house is a bowling green and a canal terminating in a basin. A second canal crosses at right-angles, joined to it by a cascade halfway along its length. The bowling green is flanked by two parterres, the canal by planting interwoven with straight and serpentine paths linking small cabinets. It has strong Bridgemanic characteristics. To the east of the house is a kitchen garden, which bears a striking resemblance to the kitchen garden depicted in a4 fo.20, a plan for Wolterton. Both the other drawings depict a similar design but in pen and ink. A4 fo.66 appears to have pencil additions that suggest a process of design underway. Although there is little trace of any of Bridgeman's design now, there is evidence that some landscaping did take place because the main road was diverted away from the house and three interconnected lakes were created (Pevsner and Neave 1995, 670).

Shardeloes, Buckinghamshire

- Grid reference: SU 93806 97860
- Principal geology: Chalk.

The house at Shardeloes was probably built by William Drake, some time after he had acquired the manor in 1632. His descendant, Montague Garrard Drake, had planned to replace it with a building designed by Leoni. He had already attached offices and stables by Francis Smith of Warwick between 1722 and 1726, but died before the new house could be built. The present house was begun in 1758 by another William Drake (Pevsner and Williamson 1994, 617–619).

Evidence for Bridgeman's involvement in this site comes from an engraving in *Vitruvius Britannicus IV* which shows a Bridgemanic style landscape with axial avenues, a basin and canal and an ornamental lake. The engraving, dated 1739, shows a manor house, which was demolished and rebuilt between 1758 and 1766.

Stanmer, East Sussex

- Grid reference: TQ 33635 09461
- Principal geology: Newhaven chalk formation.
- In local authority ownership.

Stanmer was sold in 1713 to Henry Pelham, first cousin of the Duke of Newcastle. He began to build a new house in 1722 on the site of the old manor house, employing Nicholas Dubois, the Office of Works' Master Mason. It is a two-storey brick house faced with cream sandstone, and commands views to the south-east and is surrounded to the south-east and south-west of the house by gardens (https://historicengland.org.uk). Great Wood occupies the slope of a hill to the north-east of the house.

Although there is no surviving plan, and in fact no record of the landscape until an estate survey of 1799 (ESRO ACC3714/4), it is likely that Bridgeman was employed at Stanmer at the same time as Dubois. Willis refers to a letter from Dubois to Pelham dated 6 July 1726 which suggests that Bridgeman was brought in to work on the landscape (BL Add MS 33085, cited in Willis 2002, 64 n. 107).

St James's Park

- Grid reference: TQ 29655 79828
- Principal geology: Alluvium.
- Royal Park.
- NA Work 32/70.
- RCIN 929582.

St James's Park was created as a Royal Park by James I. Charles II had the park redesigned by the French landscape architect, André Mollet, and opened it to the public.

Bridgeman's survey, Work 32/70, resembles Mollet's plan but includes Buckingham House. The cartouche suggests (not in contemporary handwriting) a date between 1710 and 1725. This date precludes the production of the plan as part of Bridgeman's role as Royal Gardener. Since the second plan, RCIN 929582, held in the Royal Collection, is catalogued as by Henry Wise, it is likely that Bridgeman executed them both for Wise, in his capacity as Royal Gardener.

St James's Square, London

- Grid reference: TQ 29508 80348
- Principal geology: clay and silt.

The Minutes of the Trustees of St James's Square record that Bridgeman was paid £5630 for the construction of St James's Square in 1726, undertaken with his brother-in-law, the pavior John Mist. This is a staggering amount of money, and converts to around £484,000 (www.nationalarchives.gov.uk/currency). He was asked to construct a pond 105 ft in diameter surrounded by gravel and iron railings in an octagon, beyond which the square was paved with Purbeck stone, probably, again, by John Mist (Willis 2002, 32).

Stowe, Buckinghamshire

- Grid reference: SP 67498 37459
- Principal geology: sand, gravel and diamicton.
- National Trust.
- BoL MSGD a4 fo.46.

The mansion at Stowe was begun by Sir Richard Temple, the 3rd baronet, in 1677. It was remodelled and extended by his son, Lord Cobham, from 1714 onwards. Sir John Vanbrugh was his architect, and Charles Bridgeman was employed to design the landscape between 1713 and 1734. After 1734, William Kent designed buildings and the Elysian Fields, and James Gibbs worked on the Hawkwell Field. Lancelot Brown was head gardener from 1741 until 1750.

Documentary evidence, a letter from Perceval to Dering (BL Add MS 47030 fos.156–159), shows that Bridgeman began working at Stowe from 1713 onwards. An undated entry from the '1714' packet of the Stowe Accounts 1710–1720, records that 'Mr bridgmans man' was paid £1.2s.6d (HEH Box L9F6, cited in Willis 2002, 109 n. 14). There are two further notes from 1716: one from 11 August 'in which Bridgeman acknowledges payment of £188.16s 0d from William Jacob (then steward at Stowe), and the other from 16 August in which Bridgeman asks Jacob for a further £20.0s.0d' (Willis 2002, 109 n. 14). Although the nature of his work at Stowe in this period is not clear, it seems likely that his role was both to design and then to maintain what had been built. Bridgeman continued to work at Stowe, where he presented a new proposal for the garden probably in 1720 (Willis 2002, 110). Estate records show that work was begun on these new gardens, presumably those shown in the bird's-eye view of Stowe attributed to Bridgeman by Willis (MSGD a4 fo.46), on 'October ye 3d 1720' (HEH Bundle L9F9, cited in Willis 2002, 111 n. 19). Subsequent entries in the same accounts held in the Henry E. Huntington Library show Bridgeman's activity at Stowe between 1720 and 1726. It is possible that his activity there was curtailed by his appointment as Royal Gardener in 1726. Bridgeman's final documented visit to Stowe appears to have been on 21 September 1726, with Gibbs (HEH Stowe Account book 132, cited in Willis 2002, 112 n. 23).

Trafalgar Park, Wiltshire (Standlynch House)

- Grid reference: SU 18582 23764
- Principal geology: chalk.
- Privately owned.
- BoL MSGD a3 fo.25.

Standlynch House was built for Sir Peter Vandeput, whose ancestors had immigrated under Elizabeth I. His sister was married to Roger Morris.

The house at the centre of the present house was designed by Roger Morris. It is built of brick with stone dressings and is seven bays wide and two-and-a-half high. The windows on the east and on the west front and the east door have Gibbs surrounds. The west front has a three-bay pediment. It is aligned east–west. There are two pavilions, three-by-nine bays and two-storeyed, connected to the house by corridors. After the death of Sir Peter Vandeput, it was owned by Henry Dawkins, who added wings and a porch (Pevsner and Cherry 1975, 529–531).

Bridgeman's involvement in Trafalgar Park, known at that time as Standlynch House, rests on three plans in the Bodleian Library attributed to him by Willis in the 1995 edition of *Charles Bridgeman and the English Landscape Garden*. In the revised 2002 edition, Willis withdrew the attribution of two drawings, MSGD a3 fos.25 and 36, leaving only MSGD a3 fo.24. In fact, it is probably only MSGD a3 fo.25 that is in Bridgeman's hand.

Tring Park, Hertfordshire

- Grid reference: SP 92694 11184
- Principal geology: Chalk.
- School for the Performing Arts.
- BoL MSGD a4 fo.32.
- BoL MSGD a4 fo.78.

Tring Park is a mansion house built by Sir Christopher Wren in 1682 for Henry Guy, Secretary to the Treasury under Charles II. It was sold to Sir William Gore in 1705 and passed to his son, also William, on his death in 1708. It was altered in 1786 for Sir Drummond Smith, and again in 1872 for the Rothschild family, although these later alterations retained Wren's original conception and ground plan (https://historicengland.org.uk/listing/the-list/list-entry/1000218?section=official-list-entry). This particularly applies to the great hall and the staircase. It is a three-storey house, brick built with stone dressings and a mansard roof. The two-storey east wing may be by Gibbs.

The park is to the south of the mansion house and was developed by William Gore, Bridgeman's client from 1710 onwards, when Akeman Street, which had separated the house and potential park, was closed. To the south-east the park is bounded by the scarp slope of the Chilterns, criss-crossed by geometric paths through woodland, rising in a geometric design to the King Charles II ride which extends 200 m along the top of the scarp to a rond-point which gives an impressive panorama to the north and north-east. Within the woodland are two buildings, an obelisk and a summer house, both attributed to James Gibbs. The park was bisected by the construction of the A41(M) in 1974.

Willis attributes three plans in Gough Drawings, MSGD a4 fo.25, MSGD a4 fo.78 and MSGD a4 fo.32, to Bridgeman. Of these, a4 fo.25, although likely to be by Bridgeman, is probably not of Tring. The other two appear to be for Tring and are inscribed on the reverse with 'Mr Frs. Gore' and 'Mr Gore of Tring'. The designs suggest a canal extending south from the mansion house towards the edge of the scarp, where the terraces of a theatre rise as it meets the slope. A plan by Colbeck, dated 1719, and an engraving in *Vitruvius Britcnnicus IV* by Badeslade in 1739, show the canal, and terraces surmounted by a pyramid. In spite of this cartographic evidence, it is not clear exactly what parts of Bridgeman's design were constructed. Few surface earthworks remain outside the wooded scarp slope. Recent LIDAR (2019) shows faint traces of the canal to the north of the A41 (M) but nothing to suggest either the terraces or the pyramid.

Twickenham, Pope's garden

- Grid reference: TQ 16077 72780
- Principal geology: clay, silt, sand and gravel.

Bridgeman may have also been involved in Pope's own garden at Twickenham. Pope wrote to the Earl of Oxford in 1725 that he had 'just turfed a little Bridgemannick Theatre myself. It was done by a detachment of His workmen from the Prince's' (G. Sherburn: Correspondence of Alexander Pope, vol. 2 1956, 14 cited in Desmond 1995, 5).

Warwick Priory, Warwickshire

- Grid reference: SP 28289 65284
- Principal geology: Helsby sandstone formation to the south, and sand and gravel river deposits to the north.
- Now owned by Warwickshire County Council, and housing the County Record Office.
- WO CR.56.
- WO CR 217 (Warwick Town and Priory).
- WO CR 26.2.2 (Warwick Town and Priory).

Warwick Priory stands on a sandstone hill just to the north-east of the centre of Warwick. The site slopes steeply down to the north. It was an Augustinian Priory until the Reformation, dedicated originally to St Sepulchre. It was surrendered to the crown in 1536. The Priory was granted to Thomas Hawkins (alias Fisher) who demolished the Priory buildings and built a house on the same footprint. Henry Wise bought it from its then owner, Lady Bowyer, in 1709, but she continued to live in it until her death in 1727. In this year, Wise retired from his role as Royal Gardener and moved into it. The majority of the house was demolished c.1926 and moved in its entirety to Virginia by A.W. Wedell, where it was reassembled. The remaining buildings from part of the Warwickshire Record Office. The park became an amenity owned by Warwickshire Country Council and open to the public in 1953. The more northerly section of the site has been disrupted by the building of the railway which runs east to west through the valley below the Priory.

Bridgeman's involvement with Warwick Priory seems to have been in two stages, both connected with Henry Wise. In 1711, as a draughtsman and surveyor, he 'assisted' in and 'Completed' a survey with James Fish the Younger, a local Warwickshire surveyor, of Wise's newly acquired properties of Warwick Priory and Lillington Manor (CR 26.2.1). It is also likely that Bridgeman was the draughtsman for a plan for a remodelled landscape at Warwick Priory (CR. 56), dating from 1727, the date of Wise's retirement to Warwick Priory. It is unclear whether Bridgeman was responsible for anything more than drawing the plan, and, indeed, whether the landscape it shows was ever built. LIDAR is inconclusive, partly because of the disruption caused by the building of the railway.

Westbury House, West Meon, Hampshire

- Grid reference: SU 65671 23856
- Principal geology: Newhaven chalk formation and alluvium.

The house, although an early twentieth-century replacement for the house Bridgeman may have designed for, is derelict and the subject of a planning application.

Westbury House in West Meon was built in the Palladian style for Admiral Philip Cavendish c.1722 (Willis 2002, 62 n..95). The house burnt down in 1904, but was rebuilt and became first a prep school and then a care home. The care home was closed in 2016 and the building remains empty (www.eastmeonhistory.net/westbury-house).

Evidence in a document held in East Sussex Record Office, 'A Particular of the Estate [of the] Late Adml: Cavendish in Hampshire', suggests that the gardens were laid out by 'Mr Bridgman' (MSS G/Ha/42 and G/Ha/66(2a), cited in Willis 2002, 62 n. 95), although the precise nature of the work and the scale of it are not clear.

Wimbledon Park, Surrey

- Grid reference: TQ 24681 71545
- Principal geology: sand and gravel.
- BoL MSGD a3 fo.31.
- BoL MSGD a4 fo.44.

Wimbledon House was bought by the Duchess of Marlborough in 1722. She demolished the remains of the existing house and commissioned a new house. Although Willis suggests that Lord Pembroke and Roger Morris managed the project jointly (Willis 2002, 59), Roger Morris is given credit for the house in *Vitruvius Britannicus V* (1771, pls. 20–22). Colvin also suggests the involvement of Francis Smith of Warwick (Colvin 1995). The house was separated from its park by housing development and demolished in 1949.

GAZETTEER OF BRIDGEMAN SITES 229

Bridgeman probably began working for the Duchess of Marlborough at some point after 1732, when she began to build a house in Wimbledon Park (Nairn, Pevsner and Cherry 1971, 521). He was certainly working for her there in the summer of 1735, when she wrote to her granddaughter that 'Mr Bridgman's account is a great mistake' (Scott Thompson 1946, 156) and that 'Mr Bridgman went with me to take measures to make the way from the common to the house. He says it will be done in a month, and will be a vast addition to the place' (Scott Thompson 1946, 169). There are two undated plans for Wimbledon, MSGD a3 fo.31 and MSGD a4 fo.44, both inscribed on the back to indicate that they are for the Duchess of Marlborough, which show Bridgeman's plans for the gardens. Willis suggests that both are intended to address the Duchess of Marlborough's need to enter the house at first-floor level (Willis 2002, 59). John Roque's engraving of 1746 shows that the design favoured was MSGD a4 fo.44. It also shows a small wilderness with serpentine paths and two groves, which may also be Bridgeman's work.

Wimpole Hall, Cambridgeshire

- Grid reference: TL 33536 50980
- Principal geology: mudstone and chalk.
- National Trust.
- BoL MSGD a4 fo.30.
- BoL MSGD a4 fo.31.
- BoL MSGD a4 fo.35.
- BoL MSGD a4 fo.69.
- BL Add MS 36278 MI.
- There are also four additional drawings held in the Bambridge Collection at Wimpole Hall.

Edward Harley, second Earl of Oxford (1689–1741) was the son of Robert Harley, the 1st Earl, Chancellor of the Exchequer, Lord Treasurer and leader of the Tories during the reign of Queen Anne (Willis 2002, 69). He married Lady Henrietta Cavendish Holles (1694-1755) in 1713, daughter and heir of John Holles, 1st Duke of Newcastle. Her fortune was reputed to be £500,000, and she also inherited Wimpole Hall. Harley devoted much of his life to collecting manuscripts and books. Unfortunately, he mismanaged his financial affairs significantly and had to sell Wimpole in the late 1730s and move to his London residence in Dover Street. He died in 1741.

Wimpole Hall is largely an eighteenth-century house, but with seventeenth-century origins and some significant alterations and additions in the nineteenth century. It was begun c.1640 for Sir Thomas Chicheley to replace an earlier moated manor house. This building is at the core of the remodelled house.

It is built of red brick and has a double-pile central block with lower flanking wings. The south front is symmetrical comprising seven central bays and wings of five bays each. This front was remodelled by Flitcroft in 1742, although the chapel was designed by Gibbs c.1720. He also added a library wing to the northwest. Flitcroft also remodelled the fourteenth-century church in 1749 (www.parksandgardens.org).

There is documentary evidence that Bridgeman visited Wimpole. His visit in 1721 is recorded in James Thornhill's poem *A Hue and Cry after Four of the King's Liege Subjects, who were lately suppos'd to be seen at Roystone in Hartfordshire*, although there is some suggestion that Bridgeman himself is author of the ballad (Willis 2002, 436). He is also recorded by the antiquarian Humfrey Wanley as having frequently visited Harley's library between February 1721 and April 1725 and looked at 'fine books'. Letters held in The Portland (London) Collection in Nottingham University Library contain references to Bridgeman's involvement at Wimpole (Willis 2002, 437).

Windsor Forest

- Principal geology: a very large area composed of a bedrock geology of clay overlaid with sand, gravel, alluvial and pebble deposits.
- Crown Estate.
- NA MR 1/279.
- RCIN 929578.
- RCIN 929579.
- RCIN 929579.
- RCIN 929581.

Windsor Forest was the area to the south of Windsor Castle, now – in much shrunken form –Windsor Great Park. Originally reserved as a Royal hunting demesne, by the seventeenth and eighteenth centuries parts of it were in the process of being laid out as a designed landscape. Charles II and William III had created the long walk by the end of the seventeenth century.

Bridgeman's plan shows 'A General Plan of Windsor Forest as it was in it's Grandeur and Extent in the Reign of King James ye First'. It is not a contemporary presentation of the Park. The words 'Bridgeman Pinxit' on the cartouche below the 'Scale of Miles' suggest that it is an original work by Bridgeman but perhaps executed for Henry Wise between 1702 and 1714.

Wolterton, Norfolk

- Grid reference: TG 16309 31846
- Principal geology: sand and gravel.
- BoL MSGD a4 fo.10.
- BoL MSGD a4 fo.18.

- BoL MSGD a4 fo.20.
- BoL MSGD a4 fo.55.
- BoL MSGD a4 fo.56.
- BoL MSGD a4 fo.61.

The estate at Wolterton was bought by Horatio Walpole, brother of Sir Robert Walpole, in 1722. He was a diplomat and politician, serving both in negotiations in Europe and in Walpole's government. He sat in the Commons from 1710 to 1756, first for seats in Lostwithiel, Castle Rising and Bere Regis, but latterly for the Norfolk constituencies of Great Yarmouth and Norwich. Between 1721 and 1730, during the period which covers the building of Wolterton Hall, he was employed as Secretary to the Treasury and cofferer to the Royal household.[4]

Walpole had begun to reshape the gardens under the direction of Joseph Carpenter when a fire destroyed the original house. He commissioned Ripley to design and build a new house on a slightly different footprint. The house is in the Palladian style, built of brick and stone under a slate roof. Originally the entrance was on the first floor of the north front, but the steps have been removed and the door is now a window. The house was completed in 1741 (historicengland.org.uk/listing/the-list/list-entry/1001022).

Wolterton was a substantial project for Bridgeman. Seven plans are held in the Bodleian Library (see above). The work is well documented in letters from Britiffe, Walpole's steward, to Walpole, beginning with the summons of 'Mr Ripley & Mr Bridjely' to see Britiffe on 9 December 1724, at which meeting Britiffe was able to 'Impart to them what [Walpole] desired' (Box 73L 8/5A). Although it is impossible to be sure, it seems likely that the 'Mr Bridjely' referred to in this letter is, in fact, Bridgeman. Both Bridgeman and Ripley were involved in the construction of the house and landscape park at Houghton Hall for Sir Robert Walpole between 1722 and 1730 (Williamson 1998, 49–50) and it is completely plausible that this letter indicates that he was involved in the creation of the landscape at Wolterton from 1724. Bridgeman seems to have been involved at least until 1737, when the steward wrote to Walpole '… we have some ale Brewd w[hi]ch I … is very good but very little wine for what was left by Mr Charters in part dranke when Mr Bridgman and Mr Ripley Have been Heere (w[hi]was but very little) …' (Wolterton archive 8/20 Box 29L).

Wroxall Manor, Warwickshire

- Grid reference: SP 21475 70791
- Glaciofluvial deposits.

Bridgeman may also have been employed in 1714 to produce a survey of Wroxall Manor in Warwickshire. Willis notes that William Ryland's *Records of Wroxall*

---

[4] See online at https://www.oxforddnb.com/display/10.1093/ref:odnb/9780198614128.001.0001/odnb-9780198614128-e-1004518?rskey=h5FN1j&result=3

Abbey and Manor, Warwickshire contains an illustration, the caption of which reads 'This plan and survey of the Manor of Wroxhall was made by Mr Bridgman in the year of our Lord one thousand seven hundred and fourteen: I have known this plan and survey for upwards of sixty-two years when in the possession of my grand-father Christopher Wren, Esqr. Wroxhall February the eighteenth 1831 Chris Wren'. (Willis 2002, 437). Willis reproduces part of this plan (Willis 2002, 240a and b) dated 1714.

Unidentified plans

- MSGD a4 fo.25 (catalogued as Tring by Peter Willis).
- MSGD a4 fo.37 (catalogued as Scampston by Peter Willis).

GLOSSARY

Allée A straight, wide, often tree-lined avenue with a function as both as a promenade and an extension to the view, either to a terminal feature such as a temple or an obelisk or to the horizon.

Axis An imaginary line connecting two or more points in a garden, one of which is often the mansion house.

Bastion A term derived from military architecture where it means a high projecting wall of a fortification. Bastion gardens were built between retaining walls, often in star formations mimicking forts of the seventeenth and eighteenth centuries.

Bosquet, Grove, Wilderness The term 'bosquet' is French and is usually translated as 'grove'. Bridgeman uses the terms 'grove' and 'wilderness' interchangeably. These terms are all used to refer small wooded areas in a garden, often planted formally and usually bisected by allées or straight and serpentine paths.

Cabinet A small enclosure within a grove, usually surrounded by clipped hedges and often containing something of interest, a seat, perhaps, or sculpture.

Exedra A semi circular recess or platform with a solid back.

Haha A deep ditch with a brick or stone wall dropping vertically from the level of the lawn on the garden side. On the opposite side the ditch rises steeply to join the parkland again at ground level. The purpose is to create a stock defence without interrupting the view.

Menagerie A small collection of animals kept in captivity.

Oeil-de-boeuf **window** A small, round or elliptical window.

Patte d'oie A French term meaning goose's foot, used to describe three, four or five paths radiating from a central point.

Quincunx Five objects arranged within a rectangle with one object in each corner and one in the centre. In a geometric garden, trees are often planted in this pattern.

Rond-point A circular feature where several allées or paths meet.

Ziggurat A temple in ancient Mesopotamia constructed in successively receding steps. Bridgeman's designs often employed the silhouette of one in the planting of woodland.

BIBLIOGRAPHY

PRIMARY SOURCES (ALPHABETICALLY BY REPOSITORY)

Bodleian Library
MSS Maps Herts a1
From the Gough Collection:
The Gough Drawings (MSGD): a3* fo.32, a4 fo.60, a4 fo.67, a3 fo.7, a4 fo.40, a3*fo.10, a3* fo.9, a4 fo.21, a4 fo.75, a4 fo.24, a4 fo.34.a3 fo.4, a4. fo.62, a4 fo.74, a4 fo.57, a3* fo.15, a4 fo.4 f.85, a4 fo.68, a4 fo.52, a4 fo.58, a4 fo.63, a4 fo.64, a4 fo.66, a4 fo.27, a4 fo.73, a3 fo.25, a4 fo.46, a4 fo.36, a4 fo.78a4 fo.25, a4 fo.37, a3 fo.31, a4 fo.44, a4 fo.30, a4 fo.31, a4 fo.35, a4 fo.69, a4 fo.56, a4 fo.10, a4 fo.55, a4 fo.61, a3 fo.18, a4 fo.20, a3 fo.41, a3 fo.40 r and v, a4 fɔ3, a4 fo.51, a4 fo.29, a4 fo.49, a4 fo.81, a4 fo.33, a4 fo.43, a4 fo.22, a3 fo.19, a4 fo.37, a3 fo.24, a3 fo.36, a3 fo.33, a3 fos.82–86, a3 fos.21,22,23, a3 fo.20, a3 fo.35, a4 fo.47
Gough Maps 46 fo.262
Gough Maps 29 fo.21

Blenheim Palace
Plan, MSS F1-35, Letter Book No. 2 fos.24r–25v

Boughton House archive
Two plans for garden of Boughton House attrib. Bridgeman
Bird's-eye view of Boughton House and gardens attrib. Bridgeman
Surveys of gardens: John Booth (1714) and 1746
Boughton House Archive Box 54

British Library
Add MS 70371, Add MS 36278, K.XXIX.14.u, Add MS 70362, K.Top XXVIII 10 d.2, KTopXXVIII 1 c., Add MS 4809 fo.141v, Add MS 51345 (Holland House Papers) fos.63r–64v, Add MS 2235 fo.94, MSS Portland fo.307, Add MS 70362/82, Add MS 70370/160, Add MS 4809, fo.141v, MSS Portland fo.307, Loan 29/20, Add

MS 29/316 and 317, Add MS 70361, Add MS 70362, Add MS 18240, Add MS 39167, HMC 29

Cambridgeshire Archives
For Wimpole Hall: R77/1, R93/62 266/1, R93/62

Essex Record Office
D/DTu 276, Q/SR53/92, Q/SR 51/12, T/A 418/196/5, T/A574/5, D/P4/28/4, D/DU 81/17,TS/M 71, D/DB F1, D/DU 363/3

Hatfield Hall
Map of Gobions
Holmes map

Henry E. Huntington Library
HEH ST map 147, HEH Box L9F7 (Farm and Accounts Folder)

Hertfordshire Archives and Local Studies
For Brocket Hall: DEAS/2180, 34137, D/eh p14, D/EOf/3/312, DE/P/P9, DE/P/P15, D/EC1/Z10/342, D/EP/E189/3/1, D/EGR/36, 79958

For Moor Park: D/EOf/5/385, DEX135z12, DE/GH/477, DE/GH/469, D/EBN/(ADD) B177, D/EC1/27/86, D/EX55/Z2/82, DE/GH/489A and B, D2119/2/194A, DE/GH 461-476, DE/GH/415, D/2119/2/194E

For Gobions: Gerish 56, 41151, 34188, 34137, 66507, 34417, 71202, 3/11/04, D/EX5522/49, D/EX886/30/1-2, Acc4571/6/201

For Briggens: D/EHP14

Hovingham Hall
Plan of the Wilderness Garden at Hampton Court

Kedleston Hall Archive
Scarsdale Collection Object 109274

Longleat House Archive
HMC 58:Bath III, Bath X881B

Millenium Library Norwich
Charles Bridgeman 1725 *A Report of the Present State of the Great Level of the Fens called Bedford-Level and of the Port of Lynn, and of the Rivers Ouse and Nean, the two great Sewers of the Country.*

National Archives
Work 1/1, Work 4/1–4/7, Work 6/114, Work 6/115, Work 6/15, Work 5/56 -5/58, Work 5/59, Work 16/39/1, MPD 1/23, MPD 1/164, MR 1/528, MR 1/696, MR

1/279, Work 32/282, Work 32/70, Work 32/313A, Work 32/313B, Work 32/311, Work 32/312, C 11/852/79, PROB 11/516/290, PROB.3/37/95, PROB. II.692, PROB. II.731,CCXCIX (T.1:299) 10 fos.23 -24), C11/1596/8, C11/1842/23, PROB.31/244/57, PROB.3/43/10, PROB.11/789/217, PROB.11/763/370

National Library of Scotland
Acc.11104 (Map.Rol.a.42)

Nationalmuseum, Stockholm
CC.2753

National Maritime Museum, The Caird Library
CMP/30, Art/2

National Monuments Rcord Office
US 7PH GP LOC122 24-12-43 F 6" (Vertical 1943)
SU144/8 (Oblique 1923)

National Trust
Four plans for Wimpole Hall in the Bambridge Collection

Norfolk Record Office
MC 184/10/1, MC 184/10/2

Northamptonshire Archives
Montagu Accounts books 31–51, Account book Elias Walter 26–27, Andrew Marchant Account Book 103, X881B Box 85, M(B) 2/3/1/1-222
Boughton House Archive Vol. 16

Otterden Place, Kent
Plan for Ledston Hall

Oxfordshire History Centre
PAR226/17/M1/1

Royal Collection
RCIN 929578, RCIN 929579, RCIN 929581, RCIN 929582

Sandbeck Park
Two plans for Lumley Castle
1748 plan of coal measures
Thomas White's landscape design

Sir John Soane Museum
SM 62/1/1, SM 62/1/2, SM 36/3/1

Suffolk Archives (Ipswich branch and Bury St Edmunds branch)
T4/33/1.24, HD11/475, HD 115/2/6, HD 1750/117, HD 1186/11/6

V & A
E.433-1951, E.434 -1951

Warwickshire County Record Office
CR 56, CR 217, CR 26.2.2, CR 556/197, CR 136/m/11, CR1841/7

Wiltshire and Swindon History Centre
1552/1/2/13, 944/1 and /2, 1552/1/2/13, 283/6, 283/6/2, 283/92, 283/168A, 283/202, 283/219, 944/3

Wolterton Hall Archive
8/12 box 3lx, Box 73L 8/5A, Box 3LX 8/12, Box 28L 8/5A, Box 28L 8/14, Box 29L 8/20, Box73L8/5a, 8/20 Box 29L, Box 8/13, Box 3LX 8/12, Box 18L8/14, Box 29L 8/15, 10/99, 10/100, 10/101, 10/120LB (Corbridge Survey)

PRINT SOURCES

Addison, J. 1710–1712 Papers from *The Tatler* and *The Spectator*

Anderton, S. 2016 *Lives of the Great Gardeners* London

Appleby, J. A 1996 New Perspective on John Rowley, Virtuoso Master of Mechanics and Hydraulic Engineer, *Annals of Science* 53, pp. 1–27

Ayres, P. 1997 *Classical Culture and the Idea of Rome in Eighteenth Century England* Cambridge

Barnes, G. and Williamson, T. 2011 *Ancient Trees in the Landscape* Oxford

Barnes, T. and Duncan, J. 1992 *Writing worlds: Discourse, Text and Metaphor in the Representation of Landscape* London

Batey, M. 2005 The Pleasure of the Imagination: Joseph Addison's Influence on Early Landscape Gardens', *Garden History* Vol. 33, No. 2 (Autumn), pp. 189–209

Bendall, A.S. 2009 *Maps, Land and Society A history, with a carto-bibliography of Cambridgeshire estate maps c. 1600 – 1836* Cambridge

Bending, S. 1994 'Horace Walpole and Eighteenth-Century Garden History', *Journal of the Warburg and Courtauld Institutes* Vol. 57, pp. 209–226

Bickham, G. 1750 *The Beauties of Stow, a description of the pleasant seat, and noble gardens of the Right Honourable Lord Viscount Cobham* London (ebook)

Binnie, G.M. 1987 *Early Dam Builders in Britain* London

Bold, J. 1989 *John Webb: Architectural Theory and Practice in the Seventeenth Century* Oxford

Bold, J. 2000 *Greenwich: an architectural history of the Royal Hospital for Seamen and the Queen's House* London

Bond, J. and Tiller, K. (eds) 1987 *Blenheim: Landscape for a Palace* Gloucester

Bouchenot-Déchin, P. and Farhat, G. (eds) 2013 *André Le Nôtre in Perspective* Versailles

Bowden, M. 2016 Stonehenge Southern WHS Project: Vespasian's Camp, Amesbury, Wiltshire. Research Report Series no. 49/2016

Bradley, R. 1725 *A Survey of The Ancient Husbandry and Gardening* London

Bridgeman, C. 1924 'The two great Sewers of the Country With Considerations on the Scheme propos'd by the Corporation of Lynn for Draining the said Fens, and Reinstating that Harbour', NRO EA 386.32, Norfolk Record Office

Brogden, W.A. 1973 'Stephen Switzer and Garden Design in Britain in the early eighteenth century' PhD thesis, University of Edinburgh

Brown, D.A. 2000 'Nathaniel Richmond (1724 – 1784), "Gentleman Improver"' PhD thesis, University of East Anglia

Brown, D.A. and Williamson, T. 2016 *Lancelot Brown and the Capability Men* London

Bullen, M., Crook, J., Hubbock, R. and Pevsner, N. 2010 *The Buildings of England: Winchester and the North* New Haven

Burgess, C.F. (ed.) 1966 *The letters of John Gay* Oxford

Campbell, C. 1715 *Vitruvius Britannicus I*

Campbell, C. 1717 *Vitruvius Britannicus II and III*

Campbell, C. 1725 *Vitruvius Britannicus IV*

Castell, R. 1728 *The Villas of the Ancients Illustrated* available online at https://archive.org/details/villasofancients0000cast

CgMs Ltd 2009 Analysis of setting: Listed Buildings, Conservation Areas and Registered Parkland in and near Boughton Park, Kettering JE/KS 6154

Chambers, D. 1993 *The Planters of the English Landscape Garden: Botany, Trees and the Georgics* New Haven and London

Chauncy, Sir H. 1700 *The Historical Antiquities of Hertfordshire* London

Colley, L. 1992 *Britons Forging the Nation* London

Colvin, H. (ed) 1976 *The History of the King's Works Volume V 1660 – 1782* London

Colvin, H. 1995 *A Biographical Dictionary of British Architects* London

Cosgrove, D. and Daniels, S. 1988 *The Iconography of Landscape* Cambridge

Coulton R. 2005 'Curiosity, Commerce, and Conversation in the Writing of London Horticulturalists in the Early-Eighteenth Century' PhD thesis, Queen Mary College, London

Cowell, F. 2009 *Richard Woods (1715 – 1793): Master of the Pleasure Garden* Woodbridge

Crook, J.M., Downes K. and Newman, J. 1976 *The History of the King's Works Vol. 6:1782 – 1851* (H.M. Colvin, General Ed.) London

Dalton, C. 2012 *Sir John Vanbrugh and the Vitruvian Landscape* London

Daniels, S. and Seymour, S. 1990 'Landscape Design and the Idea of Improvement 1730 – 1900' in R.A. Dodgshon and R.A. Butlin (eds) *An Historical Geography of England and Wales* London, pp. 487–520

Daniels, S. and Watkins, C. 1991 'Picturesque Landscaping and Estate Management: Uvedale Price at Foxley, 1770 – 1829', *Rural History* 2, 2, pp. 141–169

Darby, H.C. 1983 *Changing Fenland* Cambridge

Davis, H. (ed.) 1967 *Pope: Poetical Works* London

Decker, M. 1728 'An Account of a Journey to Hartfordshire, Cambridgeshire, Suffolk, Norfolk and Essex' (unpublished manuscript) Wiltshire Records Office 2057/F5/2

De Jong, E. 2000 *Nature and Art: Dutch Garden and Landscape Architecture 1650 -1740* Philadelphia

Desmond, R. 1995 *The History the Royal Botanic Gardens Kew* Kew

Dézailler D'Argenville, A.J. 1709 *La Théorie et la Practique du Jardinage* Paris

Dickinson, H.T. (ed.) 2002 *A companion to Eighteenth Century Britain* Oxford

Dixon Hunt, J. 1986 *Garden and Grove* London

Dixon Hunt, J. 1987 *William Kent: Landscape Garden Designer: An Assessment and Catalogue of His Designs* London

Dixon Hunt, J. and Willis, P. 1975 *The Genius of the Place* Massachusetts

Dodgshon, R.A. and Butlin, R.A. 1990 *An Historical Geography of England and Wales* London

Eburne, A. 2003 'Charles Bridgeman and the Gardens of the Robinocracy', *Garden History* Vol. 31, No. 2 (Winter), pp. 193–208

Eden, P. (ed.) 1975 *Dictionary of land surveyors and local cartographers of Great Britain and Ireland 1550 -1850, Vols I – III* Folkestone

Elizabeth Banks Associates (n.d.) 'Scampston Park: Landscape Restoration Plan Volume 1.'

Evelyn, J. and Hunter A. 1786 *Silva or A Discourse of Forest-trees* London

Fletcher, A. 2007 'Charles Bridgeman at Tring Park: a reassessment' in A. Rowe (ed.) *Hertfordshire Garden History: A Miscellany* Hatfield: University of Hertfordshire Press, pp. 43–47

Fretwell, K. 1995 'Gloucestershire: A Rare Surviving Deer Course and Bridgeman layout', *Garden History* 23 (2), pp. 133–144

Friedman, T. 1984 *James Gibb* New Haven and London

Garnham, T. 2013 *Architecture re-assembled; The use (and abuse) of History* Abingdon

Gatland, E. 2007 'Richard Woods in Hertfordshire' in A. Rowe (ed.) *Hertfordshire Garden History: A Miscellany* Hatfield: University of Hertfordshire Press, pp. 106–133

Gerbino, A. and Johnston, S. 2009 *Compass and Rule: Architecture as Mathematical Practice in England* New Haven and London

Gilboy, E.W. 1969 *Wages in eighteenth century England* New York

Gill, C. 1961 *Merchants and Mariners of the Eighteenth Century* London

Gillespie, W. 1855 *A Treatise on Landsurveying*
Green, D. 1956 *Gardener to Queen Anne: Henry Wise (1653 – 1738)* London
Halpern, L.C. 2002 'Wrest Park 1686 – 1730s: Exploring Dutch Influence', *Garden History* Vol. 30, No. 2, 'Dutch Influences' (Winter), pp. 131–152
Harley, J.B. 2001 *The New Nature of Maps* Baltimore and London
Harris, F. 1985 'Charles Bridgeman at Blenheim', *Garden History* Vol. 13, No. 1 (Spring), pp. 1–3
Harvey, J. 1974a 'The Stocks Held by Early Nurseries', *The Agricultural History Review* Vol. 22, No.1, pp. 1–35
Harvey, J. 1974b *Early Nurserymen* London
Harwood, K. 2007 'Some Hertfordshire nabobs' in Rowe, A. (ed.) *Hertfordshire Garden History: A Miscellany* Hatfield: University of Hertfordshire Press, pp. 49–77
Hassell Smith, A. 1989 'Labourers in Late Sixteenth-Century England: A Case Study from North Norfolk [Part I]', *Continuity and Change* 4 (1), pp. 11–52
Haynes, S. 2012 'The reinterpretation of a prehistoric landscape in the eighteenth century. How far did the presence of prehistoric earthworks at Amesbury Abbey, and in the surrounding landscape, influence the 1738 design of Charles Bridgeman?' MA dissertation, University of East Anglia
Haynes, S. 2013 'Constructing Eighteenth-century Meaning in a Prehistoric Landscape: Charles Bridgeman's Design for Amesbury Abbey', *Landscapes* Vol. 14, No. 2 (November), pp. 155–173
Heward, J. and Taylor, R. 1996 *The country houses of Northamptonshire* Royal Commission on the Historical Monuments of England (RCHME)
Howard Adams, W. 1979 *The French Garden 1500 – 1800* London
Hussey, A. 1970 'Purley Hall Berkshire', *Country Life* CXLVII, 5 February, pp. 310–313.
Inglis, F. 2010 *A Short History of Celebrity* (e-book) Princeton, NJ
Jacques, D. 1983 *Georgian Gardens: The Reign of Nature* Frome
Jacques, D. 2002 'Who knows what a Dutch Garden is?', *Garden History* Vol. 30, No. 2 (Winter), pp. 114–130
Jacques, D. 2014 'Our Late Pious Queen Whose Love to Gard'ning Was Not a Little', *Journal for Eighteenth-Century Studies* available online at https://onlinelibrary.wiley.com/doi/abs/10.1111/1754-0208.12157
Jacques, D. and van der Horst, A.J. 1988 *The Gardens of William and Mary* London
Jay, E. 2014 'Court Patronage Reconsidered: The English Literature in Queen Caroline's Library' *Library & Information* History, Vol. 30, Issue 2 (May), available online at https://www.tandfonline.com/doi/abs/10.1179/1758348914Z.00000000056
Jeffrey, S. 1985 'John James and George London at Herriard: Architectural Drawings in the Jervoise of Herriard Collection', *Architectural History* Vol. 28, pp. 40–70

Jeffrey, S. 2014 'The Formal Gardens at Moor Park in the seventeenth and early eighteenth centuries', *Garden History* 42 (2), pp.157–177

Jeffrey, S. 2018 'Hawksmoor's Vision of Wray Wood, Castle Howard', *Architectural History* Vol. 61, pp. 37–72

Johnson, M. 1996 *An Archaeology of Capitalism* Oxford

Klausmeier, A. 1999 *Thomas Ripley, Architekt* Frankfurt am Main

Laird, M. 1992 *The Formal Garden* London

Laird, M. 1999 *The Flowering of the Landscape Garden* Pennsylvania

Langford, P. 1989 *A Polite and Commercial People England 1727 – 1783* Oxford

Langford, P. 1991 *Public Life and the Propertied Englishman 1689 – 1798* Oxford

Langley, B. 1728 *New Principles of Gardening*

Lefebvre, H. 1991 *The Production of Space* Oxford

Leybourn, W. 1653 *The Compleat Surveyor: Containing the Whole Art of Surveying of Land*

Lilti, A. and Jeffress, L. 2005 *The Invention of Celebrity* Cambridge

Little, B. 1955 *The Life and work of James Gibbs, 1682 – 1754* London

Liu, Y. 2010 'Castell's Pliny: Rewriting the Past for the Present', *Eighteenth-Century Studies* Vol. 43, No. 2 (Winter), pp. 243–257

Longstaffe-Gowan, T. 2001 *The London Town Garden 1700 – 1840* Singapore

Malcolmson, R.W. 1981 *Life and Labour 1700 – 1780* London

Martin, P. 1984 *Pursuing Innocent Pleasures: The Gardening World of Alexander Pope* Hamden, CT

McKendrick, N., Brewer, J. and Plumb, J.H. 1983 *The Birth of a Consumer Society* Bloomington, IN

McKendrick, N., Brewer, J. and Plumb, J.H. 2007 *The Birth of Consumer Society: The Commercialization of Eighteenth-century England* Bristol.

Milledge, J. 2009 'Sacombe Park, Hertfordshire: an early Bridgeman Landscape', *Garden History* Vol. 37, No. 1 (Summer), pp. 38–55

Mingay, G.E. 1963 *English Landed Society in the Eighteenth Century* London

Mingay, G.E. 1990 *A Social History of the English Countryside* London

Mowl, T. 1999 *An Insular Rococco* London

Mowl, T. 2000 *Gentlemen and Players: Gardeners of the English landscape* Stroud

Mowl, T. 2006 *William Kent: Architect, Designer, Opportunist* London

Müller, U. 1997 'Rousham: a transcription of the Steward's Letters 1738 – 42', *Garden History* Vol. 25, No. 2 (Winter), pp. 178–188

Murdoch, T. (ed.) 1992 *Boughton House: The English Versailles* London

Murray, J. (ed.) 1824 *Letters to and from Henrietta Countess of Suffolk* Vols 1 and 2, London

Myers, K. 2010 'Shaftesbury, Pope and Original Sacred Nature', *Garden History* Vol. 38, No. 1 (Summer), pp. 3–19

Myers, K. 2013 'Ways of seeing: Joseph Addison, Enchantment and the Early Landscape Garden', *Garden History* Vol. 41, No. 1 (Summer), pp. 3–20

Nairn, I., Pevsner, N. and Cherry, B. 1971 *The Buildings of England: Surrey* Harmondsworth

National Trust Yearbook 1994 *Cliveden* Swindon

Newman, J. 1969 *The Buildings of England: West Kent and the Weald* Harmondsworth

Newman, J. and Pevsner, N. 1972 *The Buildings of England: Dorset* Harmondsworth

Pannett, D. 1985 'The manuscript maps of Warwickshire 1597-1880', *Warwickshire History* 6:3

Paulson, R. 1975 *Emblem and Expression: Meaning in English Art of the Eighteenth Century* Cambridge, MA

Pedley, M.S. 2005 *The commerce of cartography: making and marketing maps in eighteenth-century France and England* Chicago

Peitzman, S. 2007 *Dropsy, Dialysis, Transplant: A short history of failing kidneys* Baltimore, MD

Peters, B. 1991 'A country house and its landscape 1722 – 1858' MA dissertation, University of East Anglia

Peters Corbett, D. and Arnold, D. 2013 *A Companion to British Art, 1600 to the Present* Chichester

Pevsner, N. and Bettley, J. 2007 *The Buildings of England: Essex* London

Pevsner, N. and Cherry, B. 1973 *The Buildings of England: Northamptonshire* Harmondsworth

Pevsner, N. and Cherry, B. 1975 *The Buildings of England: Wiltshire* Harmondsworth

Pevsner, N. and Neave, D. 1995 *The Buildings of England: Yorkshire and the East Riding* London

Pevsner, N. and Radcliffe, E. 1967 *The Buildings of England: Yorkshire: the West Riding* Harmondsworth

Pevsner, N. and Williamson, E. 1994 *The Buildings of England: Buckinghamshire* Harmondsworth

Phibbs, J. 2006 'Projective Geometry', *Garden History* Vol. 34, No. 1 (Summer), pp. 1–21

Postle, M. (ed.) 2005 *Joshua Reynolds: the creation of celebrity* New York

Rackham, O. 2004 'Pre-existing Trees and Woods in Country-House Parks', *Landscapes* (2), pp. 1–16

RCHME 1979 *An Inventory of the Historical Monuments in the County of Northampton* Vol II: Archaeological Site in Central Northamptonshire, HMSO London

Richeson, A.W. 1966 *English Land Measuring to 1800* Cambridge, MA

Ridgeway, C. and Williams, R. (eds) 2000 *Sir John Vanbrugh and Landscape Architecture in Baroque England 1690 – 1730* Swindon

Roberts, J. 2001 '"Well Temper'd Clay": Constructing Water Features in the Landscape Park. Lancelot Brown (1716 – 83) and the Landscape Park' *Garden History* Vol. 29, No. 1 (Summer), pp. 12–28

Rowe, A. and Williamson, T. 2012 'New Light on Gobions', *Garden History* 40, pp. 82–97

Rumble, L.E. 2001 '"Of Good Use or Serious Pleasure": Vitruvius Britannicus and Early Eighteenth Century Architectural Discourse' PhD thesis, University of Leeds

Salmon, N. 1728 *The History of Hertfordshire* London

Scott Thompson, G. (ed.) 1946 *Letters of a Grandmother* London

Sherburn, G. (ed.) 1956 *Correspondence of Alexander Pope* Vol. 2, Oxford

Skelton, A. 1994 'The Development of the Briggens Estate, Hunsdon, since 1720', *Hertfordshire Archaeology* 12, pp. 111–128

Skelton, A. 2017 *'Tall Hedges and Artificial Slopes' The development of the Carshalton House landscape between c.1680 and 1815* Sutton

Skempton, A.W. 2002 *A Biographical Dictionary of Civil Engineers* Vol. 1, 1500 to 1830, available via https://books.google.co.uk/books

Smith, N. 2006 'Lodge Park and Charles Bridgeman, Master of Incomprehensible Vastness', *Garden History* Vol. 34, No. 2 (Winter), pp. 236–248

Smith, P. 2011 'Great Saxham Hall, The Saxhams, Suffolk: The 'Umbrello', Recording & Analysis', *Research Department Report Series* 73–2011

Steane, J.M. 1977 'The Development of Tudor and Stuart Garden Design in Northamptonshire', *Northamptonshire Past and Present* Vol. 5, Issue 5, pp. 383–405

Stobart, J. and Rothery, M. 2016 *Consumption and the Country House* Oxford Scholarship Online

Stroud, D. 1975a *Capability Brown* London

Stroud, D. 1975b 'The Gardens at Claremont' *The National Trust Yearbook 1975 – 1976* London, pp. 35–37

Summerson, J. 1969 *Architecture in Britain 1530 - 1850* Harmondsworth

Switzer, S. 1715 *The Nobleman, Gentleman, and Gardening: Or, An Introduction to Gardening, Planting, Agriculture, and the other Business and Pleasures of a Country Life.* London

Switzer, S. 1718 *Ichnographia Rustica: Or The Nobleman, Gentleman, and Gardeners's Recreation. Being Directions for the general Distribution of a Country Seat, into Rural and Extensive Gardens, Parks and Paddocks, &c.* London

Switzer, S. 1729 *An Introduction to a General System of Hydrostaticks and Hydraulicks*

Switzer, S. 1742 *Ichnographia Rustica: Or The Nobleman, Gentleman and Gardener's Recreation. Containing Directions for the Surveying and Distributing of a Country-Seat into Rural and Extensive Gardens, by the Ornamenting and Decoration of distant Prospects, Farms, Parks, Paddocks, &c.* London

Thick, M. 1990 'Garden Seeds in England before the Late Eighteenth Century: 1. Seed Growing', *The Agricultural History Review,* Vol. 38, No.1, pp. 58–71

Thomson, J. 1730 *The Seasons*

Thurley, S. 2003 *Hampton Court Palace* Oxford

Tilley, C. 2004 *The Materiality of Stone* Oxford

Toldervy, W. 1762 *England and Wales Described in a series of letters* London (ebook)

Tyack, G., Bradley, S. and Pevsner, N. 2010 *The Buildings of England: Berkshire* New Haven and London

Verey, D. and Brooks, A. 1999 *The Buildings of England: Gloucestershire Vol. 1: The Cotswolds* London
Walpole, H. 1995 (1780) *The History of the Modern Taste in* Gardening, introduction John Dixon Wright, New York
Weatherill, L. 1988 *Consumer Behaviour and Material Culture 1660 – 1760* London
Whatley, T. 1770 *Observations on Modern Gardening, illustrated by descriptions* London
Williamson, T. 1995 *Polite Landscapes: Gardens and Society in Eighteenth-Century England* Stroud
Williamson, T. 1998 *The Archaeology of the Landscape Park* Oxford
Williamson, T. 2000 *Suffolk's Garden and Parks: Designed Landscapes for the Tudors to the Victorians* Macclesfield
Williamson, T., Barnes, G. and Pillatt, T. 2017 *Trees in England: Management and Disease since 1600* Hatfield
Williamson, T. and Spooner, S. 2016 'Gardens and the Larger Landscape' in S. Bending (ed.) *A Cultural History of Gardens in the Age of the Enlightenment* London, pp. 193–218
Willis, P. 2002 *Charles Bridgeman and the English Landscape Garden* Newcastle
Worsley, G. 1995 *Classical Architecture in Britain The Heroic Age* Singapore
Woudstra, J. 2009 'The re-instatement of the Greenhouse Quarter at Hampton Court Palace', *Garden History* Vol. 37, no. 1 (Summer), pp. 80–100

WEBSITES

www.ancestry.co.uk
https://archive.org/details/theorypracticeg00DeYz/page/4
http//www.bl.uk/rehelp
http://collections.soane.org
http://discovery.nationalarchives.gov.uk
https://digimap.edina.ac.uk
http://find.galegroup.com/bncn/start.do?prodId=BBCN&userGroupName=univea&finalAuth=true
http://www.geo.hunter.cuny.edu/terrain/ter_hist.html
www.geomatics-group.co.u
https://historicengland.org.uk
jupiterartland.org.
kimwilkie.com
http://mapapps.bgs.ac.uk/geologyofbritain/home.html
https://www.oxforddnb.com/
https://www.royalparks.org.uk/__data/assets/pdf_file/0006/41766/kensington-gardens-management-plan.pdf
www.theislandwiki.org/index.php

INDEX

Addison, Joseph   81, 82, 84–85
Amesbury Abbey (Wiltshire)   ix, 3, 18, 20, 26, 33,36, **41**, 43, 58, 63, 66, 67, 90, 102–104, **105**, 111, 125 135, 157, 171, 175, 189–190
Ancient Rome   6, 87–90, 96
Anne, Queen   2, 27, 192
Armstrong, John   6
Audley End (Essex)   18, 59,67, 72, 171, 175, 190–191

Badeslade, Thomas   16, 113, 227
Badminton (Gloucestershire)   18, 58, 191–192
Bank of England, The   3, 4, 143
Baroque   5, 90, 91, 208
Bayfield, Thomas   116, 120, 156, 158, 159
Beaufort, 3rd Duke of (*see under* Henry Somerset)
Beauties of Stow, The (Bickham)   106, 202
Bell Inn, The, Stilton   19, 26, 46, 173
Bickham, George   45, 106, 124, 139, 202
Blenheim Palace (Oxfordshire)   ix, 10, 26, 28, 37, **39**, 90, 97, 99, 156, 171, 175, 192–193, 200
Board of Works   14, 19, 30, 117, 149, 150, 154, 157

Bolingbroke, 1st Viscount (*see under* St John, Henry)
Bolton, 3rd Duke of (*see under* Powlett, Charles)
Book of Architecture, A (Gibbs)   117, 199, 206, 209, 221
Booth, John   62, 157
Boughton House (Northamptonshire)   26, 27, 33, 43, 62, 63, 92, 111, 123, 124, 125, 126, 134, 157, 159, 160, 161, 171, 175, 193–194
Bouverie, Sir Jacob   58, 213
Bower House (Essex)   18, 59, 194
Boyle, Richard   59, 140, 141
Brampton Bryan   46
Brand, William   120, 125, 156–157, 158
Brettingham, Matthew   204, 209
Bridgeman, Charles
  birth and early life before 1719   10–17
  character   21–23
  death   2, 19–20
  draughtsman   2, 16, 26, 36–42, 47, 61
  early career 1719–1726   2, 17–18
  hydraulics engineer   14, 16, 126–128, 133, 135–136
  income   9, 18, 19, 20, 42–43, 52, 59, 117, 118, 123, 131, 138,

247

148–151, 152, 161–164, 183–187, 194, 195, 198, 200, 201, 209, 210, 213, 217, 219, 221, 224, 225
  later career 1726–1738   18–20
  Royal Gardener   1, 2, 8,13, 14, 18, 19, 29, 68, 80, 118, 122, 136, 147–151, 154, 162, 163, 179, 184, 185, 186, 187, 207, 209, 219, 224, 225
  surveyor   14, 15–16, 114–115
  will   20–21
Bridgeman, Charles Jnr   13, 13n.2
Bridgeman, Charles Snr   11, 159
Bridgeman, Charles, Mayor of Hertford   11, 21, 141
Bridgeman, Elizabeth (see under Elizabeth Price)
Bridgeman, Sarah   10,13, 20–21, 30, 33–35, 52, 147, 151, 160, 162, 163, 219
Bridgeman, Sarah Jnr   13n.2, 21, 34
Bridgeman, Stephen   124
Bridgeman's landscape plans   25
  catalogues
    revised catalogue   175–177
    Willis's catalogue   25–27, 171–174
  sources of
    Bambridge Collection   27, 229
    Boughton House   27
    British Library   27
    Caird Library   28
    Cronstedt Collection   31–32
    Gough Collection   32–36, 68
    Henry E. Huntington Library   3, 31–32, 225
    King's Collection   31
    National Archives   29–32
    Office of Works   29–32
    Otterden Place   27
    Sandbeck House   27
    Scarsdale Collection   27

Sir John Soane's Museum   31, 36, 46
Waller collection   27–29, 56
Briggens (Hertfordshire)   4, 58, 155, 160, 184, 194
Britannia Illustrata (Kip and Knyff)   97, 98
Britiffe, William   116, 231
Broad Street   14, 20, 35, 115
Brocket Hall (Hertfordshire)   3,18, 43, 52, 67, 168, 171, 175, 194–195
Brompton Park Nursery   6, 9, 14, 16, 141, 145, 146, 160, 165, 221
Brown, Lancelot   1, 6, 8, 45, 56, 60, 80, 111, 130, 155, 157, 159, 164, 165, 167, 168, 170, 191, 203, 222, 225
Bubb-Dodington, George   3, 17, 200–201
Buckingham House   46
Burlington, Lord (see under Boyle, Richard)

Campbell, Colen   80, 90, 97, 208, 215
Caroline, Queen   2, 81, 138, 139, 141, 149, 150, 154, 219–220
Carpenter, Joseph   14, 17, 47, 147, 154, 160, 161, 194, 196, 210, 231
Carshalton House (Surrey)   4, 160, 184, 195–196
Cass, Christopher   80, 116, 194
Cassiobury   58
Castell, Robert   89
Castle Howard   59, 64, 200
Catalogus Plantarum   145
Cavendish, Sir Philip   17, 228
Charles Bridgeman and the English Landscape Garden (Willis)   5, 10, 23, 25, 55, 81, 183, 202, 226
Chatelain, Jean-Baptiste   106
Chester, Robert   4, 17, 194
Child and Co. Bank   161
Choisy, Chateau de   96, 97

INDEX

Churchill, Sarah 18, 19, 21, 43, 147, 151–152, 156, 163, 192, 193, 228–229
Claremont (Surrey) ix, 1–2, 3, 36, 43, 48, 58, 59, 65, 90, 91, 96, 121, **122**, 140, 168, 169, 171, 175, 196–197, 201
Clinton, Henry 16, 126
Cliveden (Berkshire) 17, 58, 121, 197
Cobham, 1st Viscount Cobham (*see under* Temple, Richard)
Commerce 142–143
Compleat Gard'ner, The (London and Wise) 146
Compton Place (East Sussex) 19, 147, 152–153, 160, 184, 185, 186, 187, 198
Consumerism 137
Cooper, Anthony Ashley 81, 82, 83
Coopersale 11
Coutts Bank 161

D'Argenville Dèzailler, Antoine-Joseph 92, 99, 100
Dahl, Michael 22
Dallington Hall (Northamptonshire) 58, 184, 187, 198–199
Dawley (Middlesex) 198
Dean Street 14
Devall, George 13, 20, 29, 196
Donington Park (Leicestershire) 48, 198
Dormer-Cottrell, Colonel Robert 17, 220
Dormer, Sir James 220–221
Douglas-Hamilton, George 17, 58, 121–122, 140, 197
Douglas, Catherine 4, 138, 141, 189, 190
Douglas, Charles 3, 103, 144, 189, 190

Down Hall (Essex) ix, 3, 17, 27, 36, 42, 51, **53**, **54**, 56, 90, 97, 99, 118, 124, 134, 135, 140, 155, 160, 163, 171, 175, 184, 199–200
Drake, Montagu Garrad 59
Drift, Adrian 22, 51–52, 159, 168
Drummonds Bank 161
Dubois, Nicholas 18, 149
Dutch gardens 6, 91, 92, 93–94, 101
Dutton, Sir John 43, 125, 212–213

East India Company 4, 9, 105, 142, 143, 201
Eastbury House (Dorset) 3, 17, 33, 43, 48, 66, 67, 97, 98, 111, 125, 172, 175, 200–201
Eldred, Sir John 55
England and Wales described in Letters (Toldervy) 106
Englishness in garden design 92–94
Esher Place (Surrey) 3, 19, 59, 140, 186, 201

Fane, John 216
Fellowes, Sir John 4, 17, 195, 196
Fish, James the younger 10, 16, 17, 63, 228
Fish, James the elder 16
Flitcroft, Henry 80, 90, 103, 135, 144, 151, 189, 190, 194, 202, 230
Foremen 157–159
Fox, Stephen 43, 52, 195
French gardens 6, 81, 91, 92, 93, 94

Gay, John 22, 138, 140, 157, 189, 190
Geometric gardening 6, 95, 101–110
George I, King 2, 27, 149, 189, 196
George II, King 2, 27, 37, 149, 150, 189, 215
Gibbs, James 4, 22, 79, 90, 91, 95, 105, 117, 140, 141, 168, 191, 198, 199, 200, 206, 208, 209, 221, 225, 226, 230

Gobions (Hertfordshire)   ix, 4, 6, 17, 55, 61,62, 72, 98, 103, 104–109, **107**, 110, 111, 117, 124, 139, 156, 175, 201–202
Goldings (Hertfordshire)   4, 19, 20, 115, 143, 202–203
Gore, Sir William   3, 17, 139, 143, 226
Goslings Bank   161, 184, 187, 198
Gough Collection (including Gough Drawings)   9, 32–36, 60, 63, 67, 96, 118, 199, 204, 206
Gough, Richard   32, 35, 36
Grand Tour   32, 87, 90
Gray's Inn Chapel   13
Great Saxham Hall (Suffolk)   ix, 55–56, **57**, 62, 125, 175, 203
Greenwich Park   28–29, 46, 47, 91, 96, 172, 175, 203–204
Gunton Hall (Norfolk)   3, 5, 67, 172, 175, 179, 204–205

Hackwood House (Hampshire)   3, 17, 36, 55, 68–70, 74, 100, 110, 117, 172, 175–176, 205–206, 215
Hall, Thomas   4, 19, 21, 115, 143, 168, 202
Hamilton, Gawen   79
Hampton Court Palace and gardens (Surrey)   ix, 15, 17,19–20, 26, 30, 31, 37, **40**, 42, 56, 58, 63, 66, 74, 140, 148, 157, 172, 176, 185, 186, 187, 195, 206–207
   Fountain Garden   37, 58, 175
   Lower Wilderness Garden   17
Harbord, Sir William   204
Harley, Edward   11, 12, 17, 21, 22, 47, 51, 96, 139–140, 141, 154, 168, 199, 200, 208, 227, 229
Hastings, Lady Betty   3, 18, 43, 211
Hawes, Francis   4, 17, 139, 156, 218
Hawksmoor, Nicholas   17, 29, 46, 90, 98, 99, 192
Henrietta Street   14, 20

Herbert, Henry   4, 48, 90, 215, 228
History of the Modern Taste in Gardening, The (Walpole)   6, 55, 80
Hoare's Bank   59, 161, 183, 184
Holkham Hall (Norfolk)   5, 65
Houghton Hall (Norfolk)   3, 4, 5,17, 36, 43, 68, 71, 91, 100, 110, 124, 159, 172, 176, 207–208
Howard, Henrietta   3, 37, 43, 48, 141, 157, 190, 215–216
Hydraulics   16
   cisterns   135
   drainage of the Fens   ix, 16,18,126–128, **129**
   lakes and ponds   128–133
   piping   134–135
   rivers and canals   9, 133, 134–136

I Quattro libri dell'architettura (Palladio)   4
Ichnographia Rustica I and II (Switzer)   59, 86, 88, 89, 101, 122, 206
Instructions pour les Jardins Fruitiers et Potagers (de la Quintinie)   146
Introduction to a General System of Hydrostaticks and Hydraulics, An (Switzer)   43, 86, 133–134, 197
Italian gardens   87, 91, 92, 93

James, John   98, 99
Jekyll, Sir Joseph   58, 162
Jenks, Charles   170
Jones, Inigo   90, 189, 204, 213
Joynes, Henry   46, 151

Kedleston Hall (Derbyshire)   18, 27, 42, 159, 160, 172, 176, 184, 208–209
Kensington Gardens   2, 19, 31–32, 33, 45, 117–118, 123, 124, 126, 128, 149–151
   Round Pond   2, 128–131

Serpentine   131–132, 148, 149–151, 154, 155, 157, 159, 163, 172, 176, 179, 185, 186, 209–210
Kent, William   7–8, 59, 64, 66, 73, 79, 80, 95, 123, 136, 140, 141, 142, 149, 167, 168, 189, 191, 192, 197, 201, 208, 212–213, 220–221, 225
King's College, Cambridge   18, 210
Kip, Jan and Knyff, Leonard   59, 191, 192

Labour   153–157
Land Tax 1691   144
Langley, Batty   85, 93, 123, 126, 136
Langleys (Essex)   17, 59, 160, 184, 210
Le Nôtre, André   37, 64, 65, 66, 73, 87, 91, 96, 97, 98, 102, 115, 167, 204
Ledston Hall (West Yorkshire)   5, 18, 43, 47, 63, 66, 172, 176, 185, 211–212
Lemprière, Clement   33–35
LIDAR   1n.1, 51, 105, 118, 135, 201, 227, 228
Lillington Manor (Warwickshire)   28, 172, 176, 212, 228
Lincoln, 7th Earl of (*see under* Clinton, Henry)
Lodge Park (Gloucestershire)   ix, 2, 6, 18, 43, 52, 68–71, **69**, 100, 102, 123, 125, 126, 128, 135, 169, 172, 176, 185, 209, 212–213
London, George   6, 8, 16, 59, 64, 65–66, 91, 95, 145, 207, 209, 214
Longford Castle (Wiltshire)   19, 212–213
Lumley Castle (County Durham)   27, 66, 67, 91, 117, 172, 176, 214–215
Lumley, Richard   214

Marble Hill (Surrey)   3, 4, 18, 37, 48, 67, 115, 172, 215–216

Marchant, Andrew   19, 152, 217
Marlborough, Duchess of (*see under* Churchill, Sarah)
Mereworth Castle (Kent)   36, 55, 172, 176, 216–217
Mist, John   13, 18, 163, 196, 224
Mist, Sarah (*see under* Sarah Bridgeman)
Montagu House   19, 26, 147, 152, **153**, 184, 185, 193, 217
Montagu, 1st Duke of (*see under* Montagu, Ralph)
Montagu, 2nd Duke of (*see under* Montagu, John)
Montagu, John   19, 43, 62, 152, 157, 193, 217
Montagu, Ralph   99–92, 134, 193
Moor Park (Hertfordshire)   4, 5, 7, 17, 36, 56, 68, 71, 72, 87, 91, 109, 134, 135–35, 168, 172, 176, 217–218
Morris, Roger   48, 80, 90, 214, 215, 225–226, 228

Natural gardening   6–8, 80–8, 86–87, 95, 110
Nature, concept of in gardening   8, 81–86
New Principles of Gardening (Langley)   93, 123
Newcastle, Duke of (*see under* Pelham-Holles, Thomas)
Nobleman, Gentleman and Gardener's Recreation, The (Switzer)   59
Nurseries   145–146

Observations on Modern Gardening (Whately)   88
Office of Works   5, 13, 18, 29–32, 43, 80, 115, 138, 149, 158, 162, 163, 183
Orkney, Earl of (*see under* Douglas-Hamilton, George)
Otterden Place   27, 212

Oxford, 2nd Earl of (*see under* Harley, Edward)

Palladianism   4–5, 90, 91, 190, 208, 219, 221, 222, 228, 231
Palladio   96, 215, 216
Pelham-Holles, Thomas   3, 196, 201
Pelham, Henry   19, 59, 140, 201
Pembroke, Earl of (*see under* Herbert, Henry)
Pope, Alexander   21, 22, 37, 46, 48, 79, 81, 82, 83–84, 86, 115, 138, 140, 153, 154, 189, 198, 215, 219, 227
Powlett, Charles   3, 17, 205
Price, Elizabeth (née Bridgeman)   13n.2, 21, 35
Prior, Matthew   3, 12, 17, 21, 22, 27, 51, 89, 90, 139, 140, 141, 159, 168, 189, 199, 200
Purley Hall (West Berkshire)   4, 68, 71, 123, 125, 139, 156, 160, 173, 176, 184, 218–219

Queensberry, Duchess of (*see under* Douglas, Catherine)
Queensberry, Duke of (*see under* Douglas, Charles)

Repton, Humphrey   65, 66, 167, 199
Richmond Palace, park and gardens (Surrey)   18, 30, 31, 43, 45, 63, 64–65, 138, 149, 154, 155, 163, 173, 176, 184, 185, 186, 187, 219–220
Richmond, Nathaniel   155, 164, 165
Rigaud, Jacques   35
Ripley, Thomas   4, 74, 75, 80, 90, 116, 124, 149, 159, 168, 208, 231
Robinson, Sir Thomas   43, 65, 90, 208
Rokeby Park   90, 135
Rolls House   58
Rolt, Edward   4, 9, 161–162, 221

Rolt, Thomas   9, 221
Rousham Park   ix, 17, **49**, **50**, 51, 58, 59, 68, 110, 123, 124, 128, 133, 135, 168, 173, 176, 220–221
Rysbrack, John Michael   79, 138

Sacombe House (Hertfordshire)   9, 14, 66, 67, 97, 102, 109, 111, 118, 125, 133, 155, 156, 163, 173, 176, 183, 196, 215, 221–222
Sambrooke, Jeremy   4, 17, 103, 104, 201
Sandbeck House   27, 215
Scampston Hall (North Yorkshire)   3, 74, 123, 124, 173, 176, 179, 222–223
Scarborough, 2nd Earl of (*see under* Lumley, Richard)
Seasons, The (Thomson)   140
Shaftesbury, 3rd Earl of (*see under* Cooper, Anthony Ashley)
Shardeloes (Buckinghamshire)   59, 155, 184, 223
Sir John Soane   36
Sir John Soane Museum   31, 66, 197, 207
Somerset, Charles   3, 18, 191
South Sea Bubble   3
South Sea Company   3, 4, 139, 142, 143, 196, 210, 217, 218–219
St James Park   31, 56, 91, 148, 155, 173, 176, 184, 185, 186, 187, 224
St James Square   18, 163, 224
St John, Henry   198
St Quintin, William   3, 222
Standlynch (*see under* Trafalgar Park)
Stanley, Diston   43, 159
Stanmer Park (East Sussex)   18, 223–224
Stowe   10, 17, 26, 42, 147, 157, 159, 160, 173, 177, 183, 225
Stukeley, William   104
Styles, Benjamin   4, 17, 36, 87, 217

INDEX 253

Suffolk, Countess of (*see under* Henrietta Howard)
Surveying   113–115
Switzer, Stephen   6, 8, 36, 59, 63, 64, 65, 85, 86, 95, 99, 101, 122, 126, 134, 136, 146, 194, 197, 206, 214

Talman, William   90
Temple, Richard   3, 10, 141, 225
Thèorie et la Pratique du Jardinage, La (Dezaillier d'Argenville)   92, 98
Thomson, James   140
Thornhill, Sir James   22, 79, 80, 97, 141, 192, 200, 217–218, 219, 230
Toldervy, William   106, 108, 124, 139, 202
Tories   2–3, 88, 213, 229
Townshend, Charles   141, 200
Trafalgar Park (Wiltshire)   20, 58, 173, 177, 225–226
Tring Park (Hertfordshire)   3, 4, 17, 48, 51, 68–70, 90, 123, 124, 125, 139, 143, 173, 177, 226–227
Tufnell, Samuel   17, 59, 210
Twickenham   59, 140
Twickenham, Pope's garden   18, 154, 227

Unidentified landscape MSGD a4 fo.25   ix, 48, 68, 70, **119**, 120–121, 173, 177

Vanbrugh, Sir John   5, 9, 17, 46, 48, 59, 63, 80, 90, 91, 97, 98, 117, 192, 196, 200, 214, 221–222, 225
Vandeput, Sir Peter   58, 225–226
Versailles   64, 87, 91, 94, 96, 97, 98, 102
Vertue, George   79
Vespasian's Camp   20, 90, 103, 104, 118, 189, 190

Villas of the Ancients Illustrated, The (Castell)   89
Virtuosi of St Luke   18, 79, 141
Vitruvius Britannicus I, II, III and IV (Campbell et al.)   4, 43, 59, 80, 97, 122, 200, 208, 215, 227, 228

Wales, Prince of (*see under* George II, King)
Wales, Princess of (*see under* Caroline, Queen)
Walpole, Horace   6–7, 55, 80, 81, 92, 100, 139, 168, 216
Walpole, Horatio   3, 18, 21, 100, 116, 120, 156, 160, 230–231
Walpole, Sir Robert   2, 3, 18, 32, 36, 80, 100, 113, 138, 189, 200, 205, 207, 216, 231
Warwick Priory (Warwickshire)   10, 16, 17, 18, 26, 67, 125, 173, 177, 212, 227–228
Warwick Town (Warwickshire)   10, 16, 63, 177
Webb, John   103, 189
Westbury House (Hampshire)   17, 228
Westmorland, 7th Earl of (*see under* Fane, John)
Whigs   2–3, 4, 52, 88, 196, 216, 221
White, Thomas   158, 164, 215
White, William   157
Wilkie, Kim   170
Williams and Glyn's Bank   184, 200
Wimbledon Park (Surrey)   18, 43, 72, 155, 156, 163, 173, 187, 193, 228
Wimpole Hall (Cambridgeshire)   11, 17, 27, 42, 68, 71, 72, 140, 155, 163, 173, 177, 184, 200, 229–230
Windsor Castle   46, 56, 148, 157, 173
   Maestricht Garden   46, 96
   Octagon Basin   176, 184, 185, 186, 187
Windsor Forest   ix, 25, 37, **38**, 42, 56, 173, 177, 230

Winnington, Thomas   3, 18, 43, 52, 195
Wise, Henry   2, 6, 8, 9, 10, 14, 16–17, 18, 27, 28–29, 36, 46, 47, 56, 59, 63, 64, 65–66, 95, 117, 145, 147, 148, 150, 154, 157, 192, 192, 207, 209, 212, 221, 224, 227–228, 230–231
Wolterton (Norfolk)   ix, 3, 4, 5, 18, 26, 42, 47, 58, 60, 63, 67, 72–73, 74–77, **76**, 80, 91, 98, 100, 116–117, 120, 123, 124, 125, 128
   Construction of the lake   132–133, 147, 156, 159, 173, 177, 223, 230–231
Woods, Richard   52, 60, 157, 159, 164, 165, 168, 191, 195
Wootton, John   22, 79, 95, 138, 140, 141, 192, 200
Wray Wood   99
Wren, Christopher   73, 90, 191, 204, 211, 226, 232
Wrest Park   94
Wroxhall Manor (Warwickshire)   231–232

Zincke, Christian Friedrick   79

Garden and Landscape History

Previously Published

1. *Designs Upon the Land: Elite Landscapes of the Middle Ages*
Oliver H. Creighton

2. *Richard Woods (1715–1793): Master of the Pleasure Garden*
Fiona Cowell

3. *Uvedale Price (1747–1829): Decoding the Picturesque*
Charles Watkins and Ben Cowell

4. *Common Land in English Painting, 1700–1850*
Ian Waites

5. *Observations on Modern Gardening, by Thomas Whately:
An Eighteenth-Century Study of the English Landscape Garden*
Michael Symes

6. *The Landscape Studies of Hayman Rooke (1723–1806):
Antiquarianism, Archaeology and Natural History in the Eighteenth Century*
Emily Sloan

7. *Transhumance and the Making of Ireland's Uplands, 1550–1900*
Eugene Costello

8. *The Foldcourse and East Anglian Agriculture and Landscape, 1100–1900*
John Belcher

9. *Erasmus Darwin's Gardens: Medicine, Agriculture and the Sciences in the Eighteenth Century*
Paul A. Elliott

10. *Rediscovering Lost Landscapes: Topographical Art in north-west Italy, 1800–1920*
Pietro Piana, Charles Watkins and Ross Balzaretti

11. *Cottage Gardens and Gardeners in the East of Scotland, 1750–1914*
Catherine Rice

12. *Territoriality and the Early Medieval Landscape:
The Countryside of the East Saxon Kingdom*
Stephen Rippon

13. *"Turbulent Foresters": A Landscape Biography of Ashdown Forest*
Brian Short

14. *Common Land in Britain: A History from the Middle Ages to the Present Day*
Angus J.L. Winchester

www.ingramcontent.com/pod-product-compliance
Lightning Source LLC
Chambersburg PA
CBHW051607230426
43668CB00013B/2012